Creating the Computer

KENNETH FLAMM

Creating the Computer

Government, Industry, and High Technology

THE BROOKINGS INSTITUTION
Washington, D.C.

Copyright © 1988

THE BROOKINGS INSTITUTION

1775 Massachusetts Avenue, N.W., Washington, D.C. 20036

Library of Congress Cataloging-in-Publication data:

Flamm, Kenneth
  Creating the Computer.

  Includes index.
  1. Computer industry. 2. Electronic data processing
—Economic aspects. 2. Electronic data processing—
Social aspects. I. Title.
HD9696.C62F55 1988 338.4′7004 87-32644
ISBN 0-8157-2850-6
ISBN 0-8157-2849-2 (pbk.)

9 8 7 6 5 4 3 2 1

THE BROOKINGS INSTITUTION is an independent organization devoted to nonpartisan research, education, and publication in economics, government, foreign policy, and the social sciences generally. Its principal purposes are to aid in the development of sound public policies and to promote public understanding of issues of national importance.

The Institution was founded on December 8, 1927, to merge the activities of the Institute for Government Research, founded in 1916, the Institute of Economics, founded in 1922, and the Robert Brookings Graduate School of Economics and Government, founded in 1924.

The Board of Trustees is responsible for the general administration of the Institution, while the immediate direction of the policies, program, and staff is vested in the President, assisted by an advisory committee of the officers and staff. The by-laws of the Institution state: "It is the function of the Trustees to make possible the conduct of scientific research, and publication, under the most favorable conditions, and to safeguard the independence of the research staff in the pursuit of their studies and in the publication of the results of such studies. It is not a part of their function to determine, control, or influence the conduct of particular investigations or the conclusions reached."

The President bears final responsibility for the decision to publish a manuscript as a Brookings book. In reaching his judgment on the competence, accuracy, and objectivity of each study, the President is advised by the director of the appropriate research program and weighs the views of a panel of expert outside readers who report to him in confidence on the quality of the work. Publication of a work signifies that it is deemed a competent treatment worthy of public consideration but does not imply endorsement of conclusions or recommendations.

The Institution maintains its position of neutrality on issues of public policy in order to safeguard the intellectual freedom of the staff. Hence interpretations or conclusions in Brookings publications should be understood to be solely those of the authors and should not be attributed to the Institution, to its trustees, officers, or other staff members, or to the organizations that support its research.

For Daniel and David

Foreword

MANY modern high-technology industries trace their origins to the period in the 1940s when the first electronic digital computer was developed. At that time, massive government investment in research and development was spurred by wartime necessity. Since then, a complex interaction of forces has shaped the dramatic growth of the computer industry.

In this book, a companion volume to *Targeting the Computer: Government Support and International Competition,* Kenneth Flamm identifies the technologies important to the creation of the computer and the specific programs and research groups responsible for major advances. He shows how innovations have affected industrial competition and how firms have experimented with new and evolving competitive strategies. He documents the role of government support for technology and describes the critical technological and economic links between national and international markets. His analysis of how these market strategies, technological trends, and national policies interact and how they continue to influence developments in the computer industry yields valuable lessons for policymakers.

Kenneth Flamm is a senior fellow in the Brookings Foreign Policy Studies program. He is grateful to John A. Alic, Nestor E. Terleckyj, and Larry Westphal for providing many useful comments on a long first draft of the manuscript. He also received helpful suggestions on some or all parts of the manuscript from Ramon Barquin, Charles Bashe, Robert Costrell, Bob O. Evans, Peter Evans, Joseph Fennell, Sidney Fernbach, Harry G. Hedges, Robert Z. Lawrence, Richard R. Nelson, Almarin Phillips, William B. Quandt, F. M. Scherer, John D. Steinbruner, Shigeru Takahashi, Richard Thomas, Akio Tojo, Jack E. Triplett, Victor Vyssotsky, and Clifford M. Winston.

In addition, the author would like to thank Saul Amarel, Glen Bacon, Eric Bloch, Howard Campaigne, Arnold Cohen, Fernando Corbato, Kent Curtis, Michael Dertouzos, Robert M. Fano, Daniel L. Flamm, David S. Flamm, Craig Fields, A. G. Fraser, Kazuhiro Fuchi, Katsuya Hakozaki, Robert E. Kahn, J. C. R. Licklider, Robert Lucky, John McCarthy, William C. Norris, Jack Osborne, Emerson W. Pugh, Sidney Rubens, Tsuneo Saito, Paul B. Schneck, Robert Spinrad, Kenneth G. Stevens, Jr., Louis D. Stevens, James Thornton, Cliff A. Warren, Gordon Welchman, Terry Winograd, and Lowell Wood for giving generously of their time in personal interviews and conversations that contributed much to this volume. He is also grateful to William Asprey of the Charles Babbage Institute and Uta Merzbach of the Smithsonian Institution for giving him access to selected interview transcripts from their institutions' invaluable collections.

Daniel A. Lindley III provided research assistance. Theresa B. Walker edited the manuscript, and Mark R. Thibault and Daniel A. Lindley III verified its factual content. Donna Dodenhoff prepared the index. Ann M. Ziegler and Virginia Riddell provided secretarial support.

Funding for this study was provided in part by grants from the Ford Foundation, the German Marshall Fund of the United States, and the John D. and Catherine T. MacArthur Foundation. The author and Brookings are most grateful for that support.

The views expressed in this book are those of the author and should not be ascribed to those persons or organizations whose assistance is acknowledged or to the trustees, officers, or other staff members of the Brookings Institution.

BRUCE K. MACLAURY
President

December 1987
Washington, D.C.

Contents

1. Introduction   1
   A Technology-Intensive Product *1*
   The Computer at the Center of a Policy Revolution *2*
   Origins of Key Technologies *3*
   The Nature of Commercial Competition *3*
   International Ties *5*
   Summary *6*

2. The Technological Landscape   8
   The Structure of a Computer System *9*
   The Technology Base and the Role of Government *12*
   Special Cases *23*
   Conclusion *28*

3. Military Roots   29
   Origins of the Computer *29*
   Military Influence *34*
   An Emerging National Science and Technology Policy *41*
   The Origins of a Commercial Industry *46*
   Summary *75*

4. IBM and Its Competitors   80
   The Origins of U.S. Computer Firms *81*
   IBM's U.S. Competitors *102*
   Reactions Abroad *132*

5. Competition in Europe   134
   Britain *136*
   British Computers in the 1950s *142*
   France *150*

Germany *159*
Other European Developments *165*
Summary *166*

6. Computers in Japan   172
First Steps *173*
An Evolving Industry *175*
Turmoil in the 1970s *192*
Summary *200*

7. How Computer Firms Compete   203
The Pace of Technological Progress *204*
Economies of Scale and Scope *210*
Reaping the Benefits of Research Investment *217*
Technological Differentiation and Competition *226*
Japan's Challenge *232*

8. The Changing Face of Competition   235
The Computer Industry Today *235*
The Role of Government *251*
Government and Computer Innovation *253*
Implications for High-Technology Industries *255*

Appendix   259

Index   271

Tables

2-1.	Progress in Machine Computation Speeds	9
3-1.	Early U.S. Support for Computers	76
4-1.	Chief Producers of Digital Computers, 1954	82
4-2.	Importance of Foreign Markets to American Computer Firms	101
4-3.	Data Processing Revenues, U.S. Computer Firms	102
5-1.	International Use of Computers	135
5-2.	Distribution of National Firms in International Markets	135
5-3.	Percentage of U.S. Computers in the British Market	149
5-4.	Top European Computer Producers, 1986	169
6-1.	The Growth of National Computer Production in Japan	178
6-2.	Market Share in Japan, General Purpose Computers	185
6-3.	Top Japanese Computer Producers, 1986	202
A-1.	Principal Developments in Computer Technology	260
A-2.	Key Developments in Memory Technology	262
A-3.	Important Technological Advances in Computer Hardware	264
A-4.	Important Technological Advances in Computer Software	266

Figures

2-1. Basic Elements of a Computer   10
4-1. IBM's Research and Development as a Percent of Net Income,
      1942–85   86
4-2. The IBM System 360 and 370 Architecture   100
4-3. Important Computers according to Performance-Oriented
      Criteria, 1950–75   104
5-1. Relative Shares of the Top Computer Companies in the
      European Market   168
6-1. Japan's Imports of Computing Machinery   180
6-2. Relative Shares of the Top Computer Companies in the
      Japanese Market, 1986   201
6-3. Top Japanese Computer Producers, 1986   202
7-1. Distribution of Value of Installed U.S. Computer Base,
      by Monthly Rental Class   230
8-1. U.S. Domestic Computer Consumption   238
8-2. Revenues for Computers Shipped to the U.S. Market   239
8-3. Shifts in the Allocation of Development Resources at IBM,
      1950–80   241

CHAPTER ONE

Introduction

THE COMPUTER is arguably the most economically important technological innovation of this century. At a minimum, computer prices have fallen at a steady rate that eclipses any sustained price decline in recorded economic history. In real terms this price has fallen, on average, more than 20 percent each year over the last three decades and may even have exceeded 25 percent (that is, relative to some average price for all goods and services produced in the economy). This decline is almost an order of magnitude (power of ten) greater than equivalent magnitudes measured during the first great Industrial Revolution, when a rapid improvement in technologies for applying mechanical energy to producing goods and services occurred in the Western economies of the early part of the eighteenth century.[1] Furthermore, this enormous decline in the price of computing power shows signs of sparking an economic and social transformation that may ultimately prove as profound as that set off by that first industrial revolution.

Unfortunately, aggregate statistics on production, trade, and research in technology-intensive industries—like the computer industry—yield few clues to the internal dynamics of the processes that have stimulated and supported important innovations. To discern these inner workings, this book scrutinizes the economic history of a technological advance.

A Technology-Intensive Product

Computers exemplify what can be called a "high-tech" good. This product is one in which research and development (R&D) costs, or other

1. See Kenneth Flamm, *Targeting the Computer: Government Support and International Competition* (Brookings, 1987), chaps. 1 and 2, for a brief survey of some evidence on these points.

1

measures of science and engineering inputs, are a far greater part of the value added or shipped than is generally true for industry. In the United States, a narrow definition of high-technology industries would include pharmaceuticals, computers, communications equipment, electronic components, and aerospace products. If one excludes aircraft and missiles as industries dominated by military demand, computers top the list of those industries with a heavy R&D content that are oriented mainly to commercial markets. Rapid technological advance, constant and unceasing change, marks life in the computer business to an extent unequaled even in other high-technology industries, and this characteristic may bring into sharper focus issues that are less obviously important in other technology-intensive industries.

Furthermore, computers are becoming increasingly integrated with communications equipment, instrumentation, and electronic components into a single industrial complex. Even the more parochial insights gained from studying the computer industry have increasing relevance far beyond the nominal boundaries of this sector.

The Computer at the Center of a Policy Revolution

The birth and early development of the computer coincided with a revolution in national policy that was instrumental in the creation of a new type of industry, from which the computer and other high-technology products would emerge. The catalyst for this change was World War II. The resulting, unprecedented scientific mobilization of the United States, which continued during the years of the cold war that followed, had profound economic implications for the country. High-technology industries, based on competition through continuous innovation and fueled by the steady reinvestment of profit in research and development, blossomed forth.

These new, and at the time, exotic developments were nurtured by government markets and generous public financial support for investments in technology. As technology matured, the fledgling computer industry ventured into the rigors of the commercial marketplace.

National science and technology policy was, of course, crucial to the development of the modern computer industry, and when necessary, I have drawn attention in this book to the connections between national policy and the course of development of individual technologies, products, and companies.[2] The primary focus of this book, however, is not national policy but the computer industry itself—as a unique industrial entity.

Origins of Key Technologies

It is possible to document in a straightforward fashion that governments around the globe have poured vast sums into the development of computer technology. It is much more difficult to assess how productive these investments were, given that their nature and volume changed greatly over time, and that the private sector undertook similarly impressive investments in new technology. One purpose of this study is to analyze technological advance in order to understand the links between government-sponsored research programs, private development efforts, and the concrete beginnings of important new technologies.

This analysis focuses on people and their movement among research projects and product development efforts in different organizations. People are clearly the medium in which computer technology has been stored and transmitted. The history of the computer industry is the history of trained individuals acquiring knowledge—formal and informal—then applying that knowledge, often in a new organizational or institutional setting.

Much early work on radically new concepts—as opposed to refinements, improvements, and incremental advances built on current practice—has often been financed with government help. By tracking the origins and history of key pieces of technology, a simple but important point can be established: at certain, crucial moments in history, private commercial interests, in the absence of government support, would not have become as intensely involved in certain long-term basic research and radical new concepts.

The Nature of Commercial Competition

Industries built around continuous heavy investment in innovation are a fairly recent phenomenon, and during the first several decades of

2. These themes are the subject of a companion volume. See Flamm, *Targeting*.

postwar economic history, firms in the computer industry were groping with the unknown, struggling to define competition in such products. A central argument made in this book is that technological differentiation—defining new market niches and selling to them—has been the fundamental strategy for competing in computers.

As technological advance continuously lowered the costs of information processing, successful entrants to the industry have pioneered new markets and applications, with new products tailored to those markets. In existing markets and applications, it has been difficult to counter the advantages enjoyed by an alert and competent market leader.

The advantages of the market leader, it will be argued, revolve around economies of scale and scope. Because the costs of developing a new product are for the most part independent of the scale on which that product is later produced, volume of sales and size of market can be crucial in determining the average cost of producing a technology-intensive product. Given a particular new product, the largest producer may have the lowest costs.

Economies of scope occur when producing several different products within a single firm is cheaper than producing the same output of each product in different firms. These economies may prove important if the same fixed investment in new technology can be used in a range of different products. When drawing on the same basic technologies, a firm can define standards for product design and component use and interconnection and adhere to them to further reduce the costs of developing a whole family of products.

The static advantages of size, however, are far from permanent. New technology leaks out over time to competitors, who may then produce without incurring the costly initial investments in developing the technology. The correct view of competition, then, may be to think of continuous investments in technology creating a sequence of temporary monopolies on new products, with rents earned on current products financing the investments required by the next round of innovation.

But the advantages of size do not necessarily lead a successful innovator to pioneer the next round of innovation. If new products compete in existing markets for technology-intensive products, then a new firm with no existing product lines at stake may well have a greater incentive to hasten the development of the next round of advanced products than the current market leader.

Users of computers also make large, relatively fixed, product-specific investments in programming and using computers. Maintaining standards within a company's entire product line can greatly reduce a user's cost in moving to a new computer system, as well as encourage the user to purchase computers manufactured by the same company. Today, standards are a central issue shaping competition in the computer industry, and support for industrywide international standards by coalitions of firms and nations promises to further recast the rules of the game.

Thus a realistic model of competition in this industry must include continuous investments in creating a superior, closely held technology; advanced, differentiated products over which an innovator holds a monopoly (though temporarily); and significant monopoly rents received by an innovator, which justify and finance continued investment in research and development. This book will show how the fundamentals of competitive strategies in today's computer industry have evolved over three decades of pitched battle in the marketplace.

Technological differentiation emerged as the most important element of competition in the 1950s, while the internal company standard—the concept of compatibility within a firm's entire product line—was the winning formula of the 1960s. In the 1970s, industry standards that extended beyond the boundary of any single company became important, and today's industrial combatants fight a multidimensional battle, wielding not only the traditional weapons of price and performance but also standards, and prowess in specialized applications.

International Ties

With its economy mostly untouched by the devastation of war, the United States bore much of the burden of postwar investments in military capability among the Western allies. The first substantial investments in computer technology were motivated mainly by military objectives.

By the early 1960s, though, the economic implications of the new technology were becoming clear. Britain, France, Germany, and Japan realized that they were far behind in an area of enormous economic importance. Crash programs to assist national producers in acquiring leading-edge technological capability were started, and serious effort was expended in designing policies to close the "technology gap." Competition for international markets based on technological advantage led to an increasing American presence in foreign markets, and nowhere was "the American challenge" so evident as in computers.

Even before their global reach had become so prominent, American computer makers had moved decisively into international markets. The economics of investments in technology—relatively fixed sums spent on research and development, largely independent of the volume of sales—argued for reaching out to the largest possible market. Unit costs would decline with market size, and the greatest possible return on fixed R&D investments would then be harvested.

Furthermore, the technology of computing was truly international in origin. The first modern electronic computers, by any definition, were built in Britain. The first magnetic disks and drums were based on technology developed in Germany during World War II. The United States had added its own ingredients to this mix and become the unchallenged technological leader after less than a decade of heavy investments. Acquiring access to new technology developed in the United States then became critical in the efforts of other countries to catch up.

Thus the computer was part of a global industry right at its birth and would stay international in scope as it developed. Much of this account is about interactions across national boundaries as firms reached out for new technology and new markets.

Summary

In analyzing the origins and growth of the computer industry, this book develops three basic themes: private firms and their commercial technologies have been closely linked to public investment in computer technology, the ever-present climate of radical technological change has shaped the evolution of the varied strategies used by firms in the computer industry, and the economic imperatives of a high-technology industry have pushed the industry into a single, global marketplace.

The origins of key technologies and companies involved in the computer business and how firms have interacted with one another and the government in the marketplace are investigated. The first steps taken around the globe to commercialize the industry, the emergence of competition from the mid-1950s to the mid-1970s, the national policies that affected the growth of the computer industry, and the emergence of international competition are analyzed. Concluding chapters focus on the evolution of competitive strategies among computer companies, survey current changes in the economics of the industry, and interpret the current state of the industry in light of its distinctive history.

CHAPTER TWO

The Technological
Landscape

THE IDEA of constructing machinery or automata capable of performing mathematical calculation has ancient roots. Mechanical aids to assist in performing calculations also have a long history, and the electromechanical relay calculators and differential analyzers constructed in the late 1930s were the culmination of a more or less continuous, incremental history of advance.

The electronic digital computer, however, represented an enormous technological leap. Introducing electronics into computing machinery cut drastically the time required to perform a calculation. (Table 2-1 lists the addition and multiplication times of some early large-scale calculators and computers.) In 1945 the time needed to do a multiplication on Howard Aiken's electromechanical Mark I calculating machine was a full 6.0 seconds, compared with 2.8 milliseconds on its electronic contemporary, the Electronic Numerical Integrator and Calculator (ENIAC)—roughly a two-thousandfold decrease. It took another fifteen years of accelerated technological development to achieve another one-thousandfold decrease.[1] Even more remarkably, the Mark I and the ENIAC cost roughly the same amount to build, so that corresponding declines in price for a given computing performance were also achieved.

Technological improvements in computers in subsequent years followed a much more incremental, though somewhat irregular, pattern. In the early 1950s the introduction of more complex circuitry brought another order of magnitude of gain in arithmetical operation speed.[2] In the late 1950s perhaps another order of magnitude improvement was

---

1. This gain was achieved by the IBM Stretch computer.
2. These computers processed multiple bits of data in parallel (a bit-parallel design) rather than serially. A bit is a binary digit, that is, taking on only the values 0 or 1.

Table 2-1. *Progress in Machine Computation Speeds*

Computer	Year opera- tional	Addition	Multiplication	Technology
		Arithmetic speed in milliseconds		
		Including memory access time		
Harvard Mark I	1944	300.0	6000.0	Electromechanical
ENIAC	1945	0.2	2.8	Special purpose electronics
IBM SSEC	1948	<1	20.0	Mixed electromechanical and electronic
Manchester Univ. Enhanced Mark I	1949	1.8	10.0	True electronic computer
Cambridge Univ. EDSAC	1949	1.5	6.0	⎫
Pilot Ace	1950	0.54	2.0	⎪
SEAC	1950	1.5 max	3.7 max	⎬ Bit serial designs
UNIVAC I	1951	0.5	2.15	⎪
EDVAC	1952	0.2–1.5	2.2–3.6	⎭
Harvard Mark III	1951	5.0	13.0	Mixed serial/parallel design
ERA 1101	1950	0.1	0.35	⎫
MIT Whirlwind I	1951	0.022	0.375	⎬ Bit parallel designs
IAS computer	1952	0.062	0.72	⎪
SWAC	1952	0.064	0.37	⎭
		Excluding memory access time		
IBM NORC	1955	0.015	0.031	⎫
Philco 1000	1956	0.0055	0.13	⎪
Philco 2000	1957	0.0017	0.0403	⎬ Early supercomputers
UNIVAC LARC	1960	0.004	0.008	⎪
IBM Stretch	1961	0.0014	0.0025	⎭

Sources: W. A. Atherton, *From Compass to Computer: A History of Electrical and Electronics Engineering* (San Francisco Press, 1984), pp. 274–75, 279, 285, 294; Martin H. Weik, "A Third Survey of Domestic Electronic Digital Computing Systems," Report 1115 (Aberdeen Proving Ground, Md.: Ballistic Research Laboratories, 1961), pp. 1051–58, 1083–84; John Varick Wells, "The Origins of the Computer Industry: A Case Study in Radical Technological Change" (Ph. D. dissertation, Yale University, 1978), pp. 266–68; Anthony Ralston and Edwin D. Reilly, Jr., eds., *Encyclopedia of Computer Science and Engineering*, 2d ed. (Van Nostrand Reinhold, 1983), pp. 538–39; Nancy Stern, *From ENIAC to UNIVAC: An Appraisal of the Eckert-Mauchly Computers* (Digital Press, 1981), p. 63; and Simon Lavington, *Early British Computers: The Story of Vintage Computers and the People Who Built Them* (Digital Press, 1980), p. 125. See also table 3-1. Author added the final column.

produced by using better components and designs. These advances in computer technology were the outcome of a close relationship between government and industry. The development of the electronic digital computer was the product of a partnership between private interests and public purposes that continues today.

The Structure of a Computer System

Essentially, a computer system consists of a central processor, memory, and input-output peripheral equipment (figure 2-1). The sys-

Figure 2-1. *Basic Elements of a Computer*

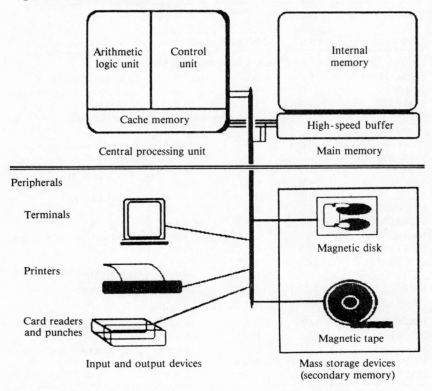

tem's function is to manipulate data. The input-output subsystem connects the machine to the real world, which feeds it data (punched cards, human keystrokes from a terminal, digitized images, frequency samples from sound signals, electrical voltage levels from an industrial control sensor) and to which data are eventually returned. The central processor performs various operations on the data. The memory permits the machine to be programmed, that is, instructed to perform a sequence of operations, and to remember the results of those operations. One of the remarkable cornerstones of theoretical computer science is that with only a small vocabulary of logical operations, the simplest processor, along with the simplest memory, can accomplish virtually any symbolic or arithmetic task that can be precisely defined.

The basic computer design first devised in the 1940s called for data to be read into the processor, where it would be operated on by the processor, then written out. This was the serial design, so-called because a single processor would execute programmed instructions one after another, sequentially, over time, in a sequence determined by the program.[3]

In the first computers, a single processor did everything: instructed the input-output system on what it needed, supervised the retrieval of information from memory, performed simple checks on itself to ensure correct functioning, and looked for signs that the outside world wanted the computer to interrupt what it was doing. Much time was chewed up in performing routine supervisory activity. Worse, the effective speed of the slowest component in the system could drag the speed of the entire system down if the processor had to wait for the slow component to complete its assigned task.

Most of the progress in computer design since then has come from inserting more intelligence into the system to free the processor from these tasks. Specialized processors called channels were developed to handle the routine parts of dispatching input and output data on their own. The channels could even fetch data and have it ready in memory when needed by the central processor. Other intelligent controllers were invented to handle memory access.

Soon a hierarchy of memory came into being. A small amount of very expensive, very fast storage, known as registers, available within the processor, was later supplemented by larger amounts of high-speed cache memory, accessible at speeds comparable to that of the processor. The cache memory, in turn, served as a depository for data called up in advance by the memory controller from slower memory stores. In the late 1950s lookahead was invented: the auxiliary processors would examine programming steps not yet processed, predict which new instructions, or data, would be demanded by the processor, and load them into fast memory to be readily accessible. Eventually, pipelining was developed: a single operation was broken down into even finer, more rudimentary tasks, the ability to perform operations was duplicated in subunits within the processor, and the subunits, operating in assembly-line fashion, could then process many instructions, in varying stages of completion, at any moment in time.

After these advances, the remaining bottleneck was the sequential,

3. It is also known as the von Neumann design after the scientist who first described it in detail. The von Neumann design is now commonly referred to as a single instruction stream, single data stream (SISD) computer. It executes an order taken from a single sequence of instructions (a program). The operation performed by the processor acts on an operand selected from a single sequence of data items. See Michael J. Flynn, "Very High-Speed Computing Systems," *Proceedings of the Institute of Electrical and Electronics Engineers* (IEEE), vol. 54 (December 1966), pp. 1901–09.

one-at-a-time way in which instructions were processed. The effective physical limits to the speed at which electronic components can operate are fast being approached. The only credible strategy for steady improvement in the effective rate at which electronic computers can process data would seem to be to harness many processors, in parallel, to work on different sets of instructions, from the same problem, at the same time.[4]

The challenge—to devise an effective way to use multiple processors to simultaneously attack different parts of a large problem—has so far been successfully met only in special applications. Currently, only problems with a very regular structure—performing arithmetic on vectors and matrices, or processing the bits of data that make up a satellite or television image—are usefully run on such machines.[5] Pioneers on the frontiers of research on computers currently are exploring ways to solve the difficult communication and coordination problems so that parallel computer architectures can handle more general problems.

Thus the essential structural components of a computer system are its central processor, the hierarchy of storage areas that make up its memory, and mechanisms for moving data to and from the external world. The great improvement in computer hardware that has occurred, however, comes from two sources: improvements in how the parts of the system are designed, connected, and controlled—the computer's architecture—and advance in the basic physical components with which the system is built. It has been argued that of a roughly five order of magnitude (10^5) improvement in computer processing speeds since the 1950s, three orders of magnitude are due to better components, two due to improvements in architecture.[6]

The Technology Base and the Role of Government

By the mid-1950s the basic design of a modern computer, the so-called von Neumann architecture, had been set out in reasonably

4. This machine would be a multiple instruction, single or multiple data stream (MISD or MIMD) computer.

5. Vector or array processors perform a single instruction on multiple data elements and can be classified as SIMD computers.

6. R. W. Hockney and C. R. Jesshope, *Parallel Computers: Architecture, Programming, and Algorithms* (Bristol, U.K.: Adam Hilger, 1981), p. 3.

complete form. Many possible modifications to this design—having a single central processor control an array of storage and peripheral devices of varying speeds, carrying out computations or manipulating data in a serial, sequential fashion—had already been suggested to improve the performance of the system. Some had been implemented in real systems, but in other cases technology was not sufficiently developed to implement these improvements successfully, and better components were needed before practical use of these ideas could be made.

The key ideas used in mainstream computers of the standard, von Neumann, serial architecture had largely been put forward by the mid-1960s. Most of these "great ideas in computer design" were first explored with considerable government support. When the real explosion in commercial computer use took place in the early 1960s, advances based on purely commercial developments became more common.

Major developments in component technology followed a course similar to that of computer architecture. Four principal areas of innovation must be noted: rotating magnetic storage, use of transistors, development of the magnetic core memory, and use of integrated circuits. All were introduced by the mid-1960s, and all benefited from significant government-funded research support. (Table A-1, p. 260, contains a detailed description of innovative ideas in computer design and technology.)

In both architecture and components, of course, considerable progress was made after the early 1960s, and continued declines in price relative to performance have reflected refinement of these areas. Significantly, the initial demonstration of radically new devices and architectural concepts was pioneered in an environment in which government shared risks and costs. Development and refinement of the advances largely occurred in a commercial setting, as industry applied these ideas to more business-oriented applications.

Electronic Components

While architectural improvements might result in some gains, the key to vastly better performance clearly lay in much faster components. The critical bottlenecks were in speed and reliability of the basic logic circuits making up the processor and in the access time for a fast and reliable memory technology.

The first computers used war-vintage solutions to these problems.

Vacuum tube logic and mercury delay line memories, both adapted from wartime radar work, were employed. Miniaturized vacuum tubes, while reasonably fast, were fragile, prone to failure, and required great amounts of power, which also meant that they produced a lot of heat that had to be dissipated. Nonetheless, the tubes performed acceptably in early machines.

The mercury delay lines were another matter. They worked by converting electrical pulses into sound waves, which traveled through a tank full of mercury and were then converted back into electrical pulses and routed back to the front of the tank for recycling. Because sound waves were orders of magnitude slower than electrical pulses, data could be stored in this manner. Accessing any particular piece of information could require cycling through all the data in storage, however, in a serial fashion, so such a memory was inherently slow. The mercury tanks were also affected by external shock and temperature, and their delicate mechanism made them prone to frequent breakdown.[7]

As an alternative, the cathode ray tube (CRT) looked attractive for a time. Because the phosphor on the inside of such a tube (the ancestor of a modern television picture tube) retained an electrical charge for a short while, it could be used as a store for data. It had the advantage of making stored information available randomly, that is, without having to move through all preceding locations in memory to reach a desired storage location as was the case with acoustic delay lines. Producing a tube with a sufficiently homogeneous and uniform coating of phosphor material, however, was extremely difficult and the constant bombardment of electrons produced considerable nonuniform wear and tear on the coating. Thus the CRT, like the acoustic delay line, suffered from unreliability.

Attention then turned to magnetic storage. Magnetic drums developed after the war could be made to work reasonably reliably, but because of the mechanical motions required to access data on the drum, they were

7. The average access time for a word of memory was about 200 microseconds for the mercury delay lines in the first Standards Eastern Automatic Computer (SEAC) and Universal Automatic Computer (UNIVAC I) compared with 12 microseconds for the cathode ray tube (CRT) memory of the IBM 701. See N. Nisenoff, "Hardware for Information Processing Systems: Today and in the Future," *Proceedings of the IEEE,* vol. 54 (December 1966), p. 1821. UNIVAC I was unavailable for use nearly 40 percent of the time, half of that because of unscheduled maintenance. See Montgomery Phister, Jr., ed., *Data Processing Technology and Economics,* 2d ed. (Santa Monica Publishing Company and Digital Press, 1979), p. 439.

inherently slow. Vacuum tubes could also be used for memory. Two tubes were needed to represent a single bit of information, though, which meant that enormous numbers of expensive, power-hungry, and relatively unreliable tubes were needed to build even small memories.

The solution to this memory problem came in the early 1950s, when magnetic core memories were perfected and built for Project Whirlwind at MIT. These memories used rings (or cores) of ferromagnetic material with fine wires threaded through them. A binary digit was stored by setting the direction of magnetic flux in the ring. Steady improvements in core memories kept them a competitive technology for primary computer memory until the early 1970s, when they were gradually replaced by integrated circuits.[8]

Improving the reliability, speed, and power requirements of computer logic circuits proved more difficult. The solution had appeared in 1947, when the transistor was invented at the Bell Telephone Laboratories. The transistor was a semiconductor device, that is, a piece of normally nonconductive crystalline material into whose crystal structure had been inserted controlled amounts of impurities that permitted the flow of an electric current under certain conditions. The transistor operated both as an electronic switch and as a semiconductor amplifier—one voltage applied to the transistor regulated the flow of another voltage through the device. This same electronic principle was used by many of the vacuum tubes in conventional computer designs of the time.

The transistor had obvious promise for computer design. It was small, solid, and fairly impervious to shock, and it consumed little power. Diodes made from semiconductor material had already been developed, and these, along with transistors, could be used to replace the temperamental hot glass tubes that had plagued computer designers.

The first computer to use solid state (semiconductor) logic was the National Bureau of Standards' Standards Eastern Automatic Computer (SEAC). Although tubes were still used in the computer's power supply, its logic was designed using only germanium diodes. Successful operation proved that solid state computers were feasible using existing technology. Commercial computers built in the 1950s frequently used this combination of solid state logic and vacuum tube amplification.

Germanium diodes were fairly expensive, however, it was not until transistors and diodes were manufactured from silicon, a cheaper and

8. To this day, magnetic cores are used in some military systems where ruggedness, immunity to power failure, and radiation resistance are important.

more abundant material, that solid state computers would come into their own. Early transistors also suffered from serious problems with reliability and quality and were extremely expensive. The development of methods for making reliable, consistent, and cheap transistors was clearly necessary before transistor computers could become an economic alternative to vacuum tube machines.

It is important to observe that the early development of the U.S. semiconductor industry was driven by government funding, particularly by the military services. The original invention of the transistor at the civilian Bell labs built in part on the foundations laid by a large government research program in semiconductor materials, used in detectors for radar, carried out during the war. About 25 percent of the Bell labs semiconductor research budget over the period 1949–58 was funded by defense contracts, and all of the early production of Western Electric, the Bell system's manufacturing affiliate, went to military shipments.[9] Direct grants and premium prices received from the Department of Defense paid for much of the industry's research, and funds were paid out to refine production methods and build up capacity far beyond prevailing levels of demand. As late as 1959, a congressional committee estimated that 85 percent of U.S. electronics R&D was paid for by the federal government.[10]

Many of the first development efforts financed by the military, at Bell labs and elsewhere, were aimed at improving the speed and reliability of early transistors and diodes. Computer applications were among the earliest defense systems into which these components were inserted,[11] and companies that pioneered transistor development—including Bell

9. See C. A. Warren and others, "Military Systems Engineering and Research," in M. D. Fagen, ed., *A History of Engineering and Science in the Bell System: National Service in War and Peace (1925–1975)* (Murray Hill, N.J.: Bell Telephone Laboratories, 1978), p. 621; and Richard C. Levin, "The Semiconductor Industry," in Richard R. Nelson, ed., *Government and Technical Progress: A Cross-Industry Analysis* (Pergamon, 1982), p. 26.

10. *Coordination of Information on Current Federal Research and Development Projects in the Field of Electronics,* Committee Print, prepared for the Senate Committee on Government Operations, Subcommittee on Reorganization and International Organizations), 87 Cong. 1 sess. (Government Printing Office, 1961), p. 138.

11. Perhaps the first use of transistors in a computer-like digital circuit was in a gating matrix built at Bell labs in 1949 as part of a "simulated warfare" computer. See W. S. Brown and others, "Computer Science," in S. Millman, ed., *A History of Engineering and Science in the Bell System: Communications Science (1925–1980)* (Indianapolis: AT & T Bell Telephone Laboratories, 1984), p. 366.

labs, and later, Philco—received military contracts to build computers using the components they had developed.

Before its fall from political grace in the early 1950s, the National Bureau of Standards (NBS) had shared the responsibility for running the defense computer and electronics research program—some of the later successes of the U.S. semiconductor industry, for example, built on early work done for the U.S. Army under NBS supervision. The basic photolithographic techniques used to etch integrated circuits were derived from technology used to print discrete electronic circuit components on ceramic substrates, developed at Centralab in the early 1950s on an NBS-administered Army contract.[12] Similarly, printed circuit boards and wave-soldering techniques, which were to reduce greatly manufacturing cost for commercial electronic equipment, were developed in a research program run by NBS and the Army.[13]

Other technological candidates for memory and logic circuitry were also pursued in the 1950s, including magnetic amplifiers of various types, magnetic thin films, plated wires, tunnel diodes, superconducting films, and the parametron. These technologies were particularly important abroad, where the costs of transistors and magnetic cores were significantly higher, because of slower development and less production experience than in the United States.

In 1959 component technology took another leap forward with the invention of the integrated circuit (multiple interconnected circuit components constructed on the surface of a single silicon chip). All three armed services had started programs aimed at producing a new generation of components with functional characteristics similar to those of the integrated circuits. After the integrated circuit (IC) was announced, military orders poured in. Though the firms that developed the concept purposefully avoided military funding for their research so that the basic technology was privately owned, the motivation for developing the device was the announced intention of the armed forces to provide a substantial market for devices with the appropriate characteristics.[14]

12. Jack S. Kilby, a coinventor of the integrated circuit, had worked on this technology at Centralab before moving on to Texas Instruments. See Jack S. Kilby, "Invention of the Integrated Circuit," *IEEE Transactions on Electron Devices*, vol. ED-23 (July 1976), pp. 648–49.

13. S. F. Danko, "Printed Circuits and Microelectronics," *Proceedings of the Institute of Radio Engineers*, vol. 50 (May 1962), pp. 937–38, 941. As late as 1961, half of the value of U.S. shipments of printed circuit boards went to military users.

14. See Norman J. Asher and Leland D. Strom, "The Role of the Department of

Close to a decade passed before the integrated circuit was cheap enough to become widely used in commercial electronics. During these crucial years the U.S. military again played the key role in funding development of technology and providing a large market for these premium-priced components. Industry sources estimate that defense customers ended up paying for nearly half of all semiconductor research and development from the late 1950s to the early 1970s.[15]

Defense users also pioneered the use of integrated circuits in computers. In 1960, just one year after the integrated circuit had been invented, the Air Force awarded Texas Instruments a contract to build the first computer using ICs, and in 1961 the first such military computer was produced. The Air Force's decision to use ICs in the Minuteman II missile was particularly important: in 1965 these purchases alone accounted for about one-fifth of sales in the industry.[16] ICs did not appear in commercial computers in the United States until 1965.

U.S. producers again had a substantial lead in the technology because of the government-funded effort to accelerate development of the components. In the late 1960s, ICs gradually came to be the dominant technology used in the circuitry of computer processors. In the early 1970s ICs also began to replace magnetic cores in computer memories, and by the late 1970s, had displaced cores as a primary memory technology in all but very specialized computers.

So the success of U.S. computer firms was built on a technology base in electronic components that, in its infancy, benefited greatly from a healthy diet of government support. As the technology matured, however, and new types of components moved into the commercial mainstream, direct support from government became much less important in a booming commercial market.

Yet even in the 1980s, government support for the most advanced, leading edge in components technology plays an important role. The Defense Department continues to be the largest funder of research on semiconductors made of advanced, exotic (nonsilicon) materials like gallium arsenide, and research supported at American universities has

Defense in the Development of Integrated Circuits," IDA Paper P-1271 (Arlington, Va.: Institute for Defense Analyses, 1977), pp. 1–7.

15. John G. Linvill and C. Lester Hogan, "Intellectual and Economic Fuel for the Electronics Revolution," *Science*, March 18, 1977, p. 1108. See also U.S. Department of Commerce, Industry and Trade Administration Office of Producer Goods, *A Report on the U.S. Semiconductor Industry* (GPO, 1979), p. 8.

16. Asher and Strom, "The Role of the Department of Defense," p. 21.

led to significant new innovations in software for circuit design and modeling—and even to influential new types of computer architectures.[17]

Magnetic Storage

Initial developments in magnetic mass storage technologies drew heavily on government-sponsored work. (Table A-2, p. 262, lists the chief developments in memory technology.) As shall be seen, technology developed by Engineering Research Associates (ERA) for the U.S. intelligence community was the basis for the first magnetic drums used for storage in commercial American computers. ERA transferred this technology to IBM in the early 1950s. Government users also influenced the early development of magnetic tape.[18]

The next stride in large-scale magnetic memory was the development in the mid-1950s of the first disk storage systems. By using a stack of flat magnetic platters with an array of read-write heads inserted between them, a much greater volume of information could be packed in a small volume and accessed quickly. The prototype of a magnetic disk storage system, using a single platter, was demonstrated by Jacob Rabinow, of the National Bureau of Standards (NBS), in 1951.[19] The recording head

17. On circuit design, see Flamm, *Targeting*, pp. 69–72; Arthur Richard Newton and Alberto L. Sangiovanni-Vincentelli, "Relaxation-Based Electrical Simulation," *IEEE Transactions on Electron Devices,* vol. ED-30 (September 1983), p. 1184. Very recent influential innovations in circuit design drawing heavily on military-funded research include microprocessors making use of reduced instruction set computer (RISC) architectures, which are now showing up in great numbers in commercial computers and advanced simulation software for silicon device fabrication. The simulation software is used widely throughout the U.S. semiconductor industry and is based on the SUPREM process modeling software developed at Stanford University. On RISC see C. Gordon Bell, "RISC: Back to the Future?" *Datamation,* vol. 32 (June 1, 1986), pp. 96–108; "A RISC System That Likes Floating Point," *Electronics,* vol. 58 (July 15, 1985), pp. 54–56; Tom Manuel, "The Frantic Search for More Speed," ibid., vol. 60 (September 3, 1987), pp. 59–62. Note that an IBM research project of the early 1970s was the forefather of the later government-funded university work on RISC microprocessors. The genesis of SUPREM is described in Charles P. Ho and others, "VLSI Process Modeling— SUPREM III," *IEEE Transactions on Electron Devices,* vol. ED-30 (November 1983), p. 1438. Simulation of optical lithography to etch semiconductors was pioneered at the University of California, Berkeley, in the 1970s with NSF funding. See W. G. Oldham and others, "A General Simulator for VLSI Lithography and Etching Processes: Part II: Application to Deposition and Etching," ibid., vol. ED-27 (August 1980), p. 1455.

18. See table A-2 in this volume; and Kenneth Flamm, *Targeting the Computer: Government Support and International Competition* (Brookings, 1987), pp. 118–19.

19. Charles S. Bashe and others, *IBM's Early Computers* (MIT Press, 1986), p. 280.

was in contact with the surface of the disk, however, and wear on the head and storage media was a serious problem.

IBM developed the first commercial computer system using disk storage as an internal project, and announced it in 1956. Even here, however, significant influences came from government-sponsored research projects. Rabinow's work at NBS directly inspired the idea of using magnetic disks, and the key engineers developing the system at IBM's newly opened San Jose research lab had been recruited from the University of California, Berkeley, where they had learned the basics of magnetic recording technology by working on the CALDIC magnetic drum computer funded by the U.S. Office of Naval Research.[20] Finally, the initial stimulus to IBM's disk efforts was an Air Force request for proposals to design and build a mass storage device for information used in an air base supply system (though IBM's bid lost).

This product, the IBM Type 350 magnetic disk system, was released as a peripheral for the RAMAC 305 (random access method of accounting and control) business computer. It used compressed air forced through the read-write heads to keep them from making physical contact with the magnetic media. The system was imperfect, though, requiring bulky and expensive air compressors, prone to mechanical breakdown, and the pressurized air tended to introduce destructive dirt particles into this so-called hydrostatic air bearing. Through the late 1950s, however, the Type 350 was the only reliable magnetic disk system available commercially.

Technically superior systems were developed at about the same time for military users, however. In 1956 the Autonetics computer division of North American Aviation delivered the RECOMP military computer, which used a magnetic disk drive with a hydrodynamic (self-acting) air bearing. With this bearing mechanism, the surface friction of the rotating magnetic media generally pulled along a wedge of air, which supported a "flying," airfoil-like head assembly floating just above the disk.[21] Similar principles were used in other companies. In that same year, Sperry Rand revealed details of a magnetic drum with a flying head,

20. Ibid.; and interview with Louis D. Stevens, October 6, 1986. The CALDIC graduates included Stevens, Roy Houg, Joe Helland, and later Albert S. Hoagland. Other engineers involved, including John Haanstra, had worked on another Berkeley computing project, a numerical sieve to compute prime numbers.

21. In the Autonetics disk, a stationary head was separated from a rotating flexible magnetic disk. The same principle was applied in the "Bernoulli" disk drives widely used with personal computers in the 1980s.

developed for the UNIVAC LARC supercomputer being built for the Atomic Energy Commission.[22] Other magnetic storage systems with hydrodynamic heads were built for military users in the late 1950s.[23]

IBM's first magnetic storage product with a hydrodynamic head was also built for a military customer (a magnetic drum for the SAGE air defense computer, in 1957). The first commercial IBM disk drive system with the more advanced flying heads, the 1301 disk drive, was shipped in 1962, and it too had first been developed for defense users (the Stretch IBM 7030 supercomputer, built for the Atomic Energy Commission and National Security Agency). Similar systems had already been delivered by much smaller competitors, but IBM, by then the market leader, was to carry the day commercially.[24]

From the mid-1960s on, however, on the strength of internally funded research initiatives, IBM was to excel in the development of innovative improvements to magnetic storage systems. Superior head designs, better magnetic materials, data encoding algorithms, precision motor mechanisms, and perhaps most important, advanced manufacturing technology, were to protect that leading position.

Computer Architectures

From the earliest days of computing, it was clear that a hierarchy of memories, of different speeds and costs, could be organized to give the user the illusion of access to a much larger amount of memory than was

22. H. F. Welsh and V. J. Porter, "A Large-Capacity Drum-File Memory System," *1956 Proceedings of the Eastern Joint Computer Conference* (New York: American Institute of Electrical Engineers, 1957), pp. 136–39. A descendant of this system was shipped as the UNIVAC Randex Storage System in 1960. See J. W. Schnockel, "A Quarter Billion Digits Stored in New Drum System," *Computers and Automation,* vol. 9 (December 2, 1960), p. 1B.

23. R. T. Pearson, "The Development of the Flexible-Disk Magnetic Recorder," *Proceedings of the Institute of Radio Engineers,* vol. 49 (January 1961), pp. 164–74; and S. K. Chao, "System Organization of MOBIDIC B," *1959 Proceedings of the Eastern Joint Computer Conference* (New York: Eastern Joint Computer Conference, 1959), pp. 105–06.

24. Telex announced a flying head disk drive in 1960. See "New Random-Access Disc-Memory with Flying Heads," *Computers and Automation,* vol. 9 (September 1960), p. 3B. Bryant Computer Products announced its system in early 1961. See Joseph S. Smith, "New Magnetic Memory Disc File Delivered," *Computers and Automation,* vol. 10 (March 1961), pp. 2B–3B. In an internal IBM evaluation, the Bryant system, based on a product delivered to military customers, was rated as good or better than the IBM 1301. See Bashe and others, *IBM's Early Computers,* p. 650.

directly accessible by a program. The first step down this road was the index register, which allowed the programmer to access a storage location by specifying only its relative displacement from some base location.

Further development of this concept permitted the burden of keeping track of the absolute locations of data in memory to be shifted from the programmer to the computer, and the control program, that is, the operating system, which supervised its routine housekeeping chores. Later developments included much larger chunks of memory, pages or segments, which could be moved in or out of primary memory from slower and cheaper secondary memory devices automatically, by the computer. The programmer could use much larger amounts of storage in programs than were immediately available without worrying about explicitly directing the required "swapping" of memory. This line of advance culminated in the development of virtual memory, which permitted the use by programs of vast amounts of memory, far exceeding the physical primary memory installed in a machine. Through the design of hardware and software mechanisms that automatically transferred data back and forth from secondary to primary memory in a manner completely hidden from the programmer, programs addressing large amounts of storage could be run on machines with fairly small amounts of actual primary memory.

Another key area of innovation included strategies to contain the damaging effects of errors, which inevitably occurred as individual components in a large and complex system failed. Protection mechanisms were added to hardware to control the access of a program to areas of the system that a program had no legitimate reason for entering. Tags were added to data to restrict the manner in which they could be used to a particular intended function. Error correction codes were added to allow the detection of faulty memory and the reconstruction of its correct contents. Redundancy, extra subsystems, were added to computers to make recovery from hardware failure possible.

Much effort, as noted earlier, went into adding satellite processors to relieve the central processor of routine system management tasks. The input-output channel was invented for this purpose, and other specialized secondary processing elements were later added to speed the operation of the central processing unit. Additional functional processing capacity took the form of pipelining, mentioned earlier, multiple arithmetic units, and even multiple central processors.

The flexibility of the computer system was increased by micropro-gramming its instruction set, that is, defining the operations performed by the computer in terms of a much more rudimentary set of logical operations at the level of the electrical pulses passing through the circuits making up the central processor. By changing the electronic connections defining how the instructions sent to the processor were decoded into more basic manipulations of electrical pulses, the entire instruction set of the computer could be redefined. Switching to alternative circuitry, containing a different microprogram, could be used to change the computer's instruction set, perhaps to emulate the operation of an entirely different computer. Another design alternative providing greater system flexibility was the pushdown stack, which replaced specialized intermediate storage areas within the central processor with a set of general purpose storage locations, accessed in a first-in, last-out fashion, rather like the spring-loaded dispensers for serving trays found in many cafeterias.

In sum, architectural innovations in computer hardware fall into four main areas: memory organization, processor parallelism, processor function, and processor structure. (Table A-3, p. 264, provides a detailed list of important technological advances in computer hardware.) As was true of advances in component technology, the first steps in architectural innovations were linked to government support for computer develop-ment in the 1950s and early 1960s. Use of the innovations in commercial products were refined and extended by private efforts in later years.

But even today, government retains a powerful influence at the most radical leading edge of architectural innovation in computers. Research on novel types of parallel architectures and the financial backing for the first working models of these new concepts rely heavily on federal funding. And development of the largest and most powerful computers of the day—even those with more conventional designs—continues to rely heavily on demand by government agencies.[25]

Special Cases

In some cases, government-supported projects influenced, but did not dominate, the early commercial development of computers. The

25. See Flamm, *Targeting,* pp. 65–68, 81–82, 108–10.

development of computer graphics techniques is an example. The forerunner of modern graphics was the display console attached to the MIT Whirlwind computer, built with Navy and Air Force funding in the early 1950s. The SAGE air defense system, the large-scale follow-up to that early experiment, further developed display technology and gave birth to the light pen, which allowed an operator to "draw" electronically on a display tube. These concepts were extended with the development of the first digital drawing tablets, the Rand tablet, developed with support from the Advanced Research Projects Agency (DARPA) in the early 1960s;[26] the invention of the mouse, a digital marker whose motion is matched on a graphics display, at the Stanford Research Institute (again with DARPA support) in the mid-1960s; and the refinement of the idea of interacting with a computer through the manipulation of images on a graphics display, icons, at the Xerox Palo Alto Research Center in the 1970s. Commercial products embodying these traditions were introduced by Xerox with its Star workstations in the late 1970s, and Apple, with its Macintosh personal computer, in the early 1980s.

The first commercial graphics terminals came from two sources. General Motors (GM) embarked on its ambitious DAC-I computer design project in the late 1950s, and the terminal built by IBM to GM's specifications later evolved into the IBM 2250 display system.[27] Specialized graphics hardware developed at MIT with Air Force and DARPA support, at about the same time, was used by Digital Equipment Company (DEC) in its first commercial display terminal, the DEC 340.[28]

Perhaps the best example of an important innovation with no clearly detectable roots in government-funded research efforts was the microprocessor, first designed by the Intel Corporation in 1971 for use in an electronic calculator. Advanced commercial silicon IC technology was used to put the entire central processor unit of a computer on a single chip. Because the level of miniaturization possible with the semiconductor technology of the time was fairly limited, only the simplest of computers could be put on a chip—it could handle only four bits (that is,

26. "Defense" was appended to the agency's name in 1972.

27. Gerald S. Devere, Barrett Hargreaves, and Dennis M. Walker, "The DAC-I System," *Datamation,* vol. 12 (June 1966), pp. 37–39; A. Van Dam, "Computer Graphics," in Anthony Ralston, ed., *Encyclopedia of Computer Science and Engineering,* 2d ed. (Van Nostrand Reinhold, 1983), p. 322; and M. David Prince, *Interactive Graphics for Computer-Aided Design* (Addison-Wesley, 1971), pp. 5–11.

28. Karl C. Wildes and Nilo A. Lindgren, *A Century of Electrical Engineering and Computer Science at MIT, 1882–1982* (MIT Press, 1985), p. 350.

a piece of information with only $2^4 = 16$ possible values) at a time. This capacity was still sufficient for a simple calculator—the application for which the chip was designed.

Clearly, however, a computer with such little power would not have been of much interest to the military at the time. In fact, as Robert N. Noyce and Marcian E. Hoff, Jr., of Intel have noted, the military was then developing more powerful processors to be implemented with a set of several integrated circuits.[29] Thus the microprocessor, in many ways, was the application of existing leading-edge technology to a new commercial market made possible by the improving price performance of semiconductor devices.

Software

Federally supported innovation in computer hardware created a significant technology base for later development and application to commercial needs. But commercial software, with some exceptions, has largely been developed by private firms that are in close contact with the needs of commercial markets.

Consider batch (noninteractive) operating systems.[30] The first operating systems were developed for machines that were employed mostly on government-sponsored projects. As computer use expanded into more commercial applications, however, improvements in systems software were often undertaken by computer users and computer manufacturers. By the late 1950s, when business computing started to dominate the market, the development of operating systems began shifting toward the commercial marketplace.

In computer languages, government support has also been less important than in hardware. A panel of computer scientists in the late 1970s made a list of the thirteen most important languages:[31] Algol, APL, APT, Basic, Cobol, Fortran, GPSS, JOSS, Jovial, Lisp, PL/I, Simula,

29 Robert N. Noyce and Marcian E. Hoff, Jr., "A History of Microprocessor Development at Intel," *IEEE Micro,* vol. 1 (February 1981), pp. 8–21.

30. A batch operating system schedules jobs in a sequential, one-after-another queue and offers little or no interaction between users and the computer while the job is running.

31. In 1977 a major language was defined as one that had been created and in use by 1967, remained in use by 1977, and had considerable influence on the field of computing. See R. L. Wexelblat, ed., *History of Programming Languages* (Academic Press, 1981).

and Snobol. Of these languages, only four—APT, JOSS, Jovial, and Lisp—were heavily dependent on government support in their development. APT, the first applications-oriented language, was designed in 1956 to ease the programming burden for computerized numerical control of machine tools for Air Force applications; JOSS was developed at the Rand Corporation to assist in mathematical computation; Jovial was invented at the Systems Development Corporation for use on real-time command and control applications; and the development of Lisp, invented in the universities in the late 1960s, benefited from large-scale government support as part of the funding of artificial intelligence by DARPA from the early 1960s on. Another language, Cobol, though largely implemented by private interests, benefited from a government-sponsored definition, and its designation as a military standard for "business" types of applications in an era when military computer demand remained a relatively large fraction of the computer market. Institutional support by the National Science Foundation for the Dartmouth computer facility also paid for some of the development costs for Basic.

Although in general the government role has been less significant in the development of software than in hardware innovation, some major exceptions have occurred. (See table A-4, p. 266, for a systematic listing of the principal developments in the evolution of computer software.) In the development of time-sharing (interactive) operating systems, the early interest of DARPA played a crucial role. Of the first twelve systems that can loosely be described as having a general purpose time-sharing orientation, six, including the most sophisticated and advanced systems, were developed with DARPA sponsorship.[32] IBM entered the field relatively late, after it became clear that serious efforts elsewhere were yielding their first fruits. What ultimately became IBM's chief time-sharing system drew heavily on concepts from government-sponsored work at MIT.[33]

Since the late 1960s computer networks have also developed under the considerable patronage of DARPA. Firms from the United States

32. T. James Glauthier, "Computer Time Sharing: Its Origins and Development," *Computers and Automation,* vol. 16 (October 1967), p. 25.

33. Ibid., pp. 25–26; and R. J. Creasy, "The Origin of the VM 370/Time-Sharing System," *IBM Journal of Research and Development,* vol. 25 (September 1981), pp. 484–87. Time-sharing operating systems were already being marketed for such commercial computers as the Digital Equipment Corporation's PDP-1 and PDP-6 by 1965, when IBM's large time-sharing system project was begun.

are currently the world leaders in networking technology, and this lead has a direct link to government-supported research projects. The most widely used protocol for transporting data among computers over commercial networks, for example, is taken directly from the ARPANET system.[34]

Another key area of software in which government support proved crucial was artificial intelligence (AI), that is, a diverse collection of techniques that make machines act "smarter" in ways that mimic humans. Since the late 1950s, the U.S. government, particularly the Department of Defense, has invested heavily in expert systems, studies of language, learning and vision, and manipulation and reasoning about objects. The problems were difficult and the progress was slow—many commercial firms like IBM reacted by phasing out their efforts in these areas in the late 1960s. Federal support continued, however, and in the early 1980s, this effort began to pay off with the first commercial products making use of these techniques. The links from today's commercial AI to a quarter century of government backing are direct and concrete.[35]

In managing large data bases, work done on the Air Force's SAGE system in the early 1950s pioneered techniques for describing records logically and physically. Report-generating packages seem to have been first written at the Atomic Energy Commission's nuclear facility at Hanford, Washington, operated by General Electric in the mid-1950s.[36] Formatted file systems developed for government customers by IBM were the basis for advances in data query languages.[37] Commercial methodologies for programming large, complex applications also drew much from the experience of private contractors on large government projects.[38] Finally, much software for scientific applications, solving equation systems, simulating electronic circuits, finite-element analysis,

34. See William E. Seifert, "Choosing a Transport Protocol," *Systems and Software,* vol. 4 (June 1985), pp. 87–90. The other commonly used protocol, devised for the Xerox ETHERNET network, also has many elements drawn from work on the ARPANET.

35. See Flamm, *Targeting,* pp. 61–65, especially note 44 and pp. 185–86.

36. See J. E. Sammet, "Software History," in Anthony Ralston, ed., *Encyclopedia of Computer Science and Engineering,* 2d ed. (Van Nostrand Reinhold, 1983), p. 1357.

37. See W. C. McGee, "Data Base Technology," *IBM Journal of Research and Development,* vol. 25 (September 1981), p. 514. The first operational relational data base system appears to have been the MacAIMS system, developed at MIT's DARPA-funded Project MAC.

38. See, for example, S. E. James, "Evolution of Real-Time Computer Systems for Manned Spaceflight," *IBM Journal of Research and Development,* vol. 25 (September 1981), p. 424.

and so forth was developed in government laboratories and in federally supported university research projects. In general, though, software innovations that lead to applications of great commercial value have been relatively few (except for space- and defense-related scientific and engineering applications directly relevant to government needs).[39]

Conclusion

The key concepts in the standard, serial computer architecture, which is the backbone of today's commercial industry, were often pioneered in projects that enjoyed government support. Most advances had been introduced by the mid-1960s, and development and refinement of machines based on these architectural concepts proceeded incrementally during the following decades, largely through privately funded efforts. In software, because applications tend to be more differentiated and specialized than basic hardware concepts, government-sponsored projects, although important in some areas, were often less critical to progress. Important exceptions were specialized scientific and engineering applications, time-sharing, networks, and the large collection of themes that is grouped together as artificial intelligence.

39. See Flamm, *Targeting,* pp. 121–23.

CHAPTER THREE

Military Roots

WHEN historians examine the origins of the electronic digital computer, they usually give top billing to the pioneering efforts of the American scientists J. Presper Eckert and John W. Mauchly, who built their Electronic Numerical Integrator and Computer (ENIAC) during World War II. Eckert and Mauchly are justly and widely honored as the men whose efforts and risks led to the first machines recognizable as modern computers. They also founded the first private computer systems company. But historians now also recognize a lesser known history of the computer, one whose roots run deep into the most sensitive and secret corners of a modern military establishment.

It was no accident that the military services largely financed the postwar development of the computer in the 1950s, for computing technology had played a pivotal role in the Allied war effort. The military indirectly bankrolled even the Eckert and Mauchly computer projects, and these relatively open projects were only the tip of a much larger, and sometimes hidden, technological iceberg.

The military computer projects, as well as Eckert and Mauchly's daring bet on an as-yet nonexistent commercial market, led to the first stirrings of interest in computers in the 1950s by business and industry. Indeed the first commercial computers were direct copies or adaptations of machines developed for military users.

After the war, the commercial potential of government-sponsored research became more apparent. The first great political clashes over technology policy in the United States occurred.

Origins of the Computer

By the time war broke out in 1939, engineering and science had already made important advances in several seemingly unrelated areas. Although

29

the war was the catalyst that drew together these advances and produced the electronic digital computer, its origins stemmed from four scientific and engineering traditions. A centuries-old history of the development of mechanical calculating machines formed the first line of activity. The construction of special purpose machines (differential analyzers) designed to approximate the mathematical solution of differential equations used in modeling various physical processes was the second and more recent type of effort. The third stream of developments resulted from rapid progress in developing new generations of electronic components during the war. Finally, a new theoretical perspective on the abstract mathematical conception of information and information processing preceded further breakthroughs in technology.

By the 1930s applied mathematicians had incorporated recent advances in electrical technology into mechanical calculators. Mechanical levers and gears were being replaced with faster and more reliable electrical relays and wheels. In the United States, George R. Stibitz at the Bell Telephone Laboratories constructed a series of electromechanical calculators in the late 1930s that stored and manipulated numbers internally in binary form.[1] The machines were constructed from ordinary telephone relays, wired together in standard telephone equipment racks. They relied on teletype input and output. Larger and more powerful versions of these early relay computers were built for wartime use and continued in service well into the 1950s.

Closely related to this equipment were sophisticated punched card business machines that used electromechanical technology to tabulate, sort, add, and compare data punched into paper cards. Herman Hollerith invented such machinery, and it was first used in the U.S. Census of 1890. Although there were significant competitors, in particular, National Cash Register (NCR) and Remington Rand, International Business Machines (IBM) dominated the U.S. market for commercial punched card machines in the 1930s. IBM had good relations with the government: the establishment of the U.S. social security system and the ensuing demand for punched card machinery to process the massive numbers of

1. See W. H. C. Higgins and others, "Electrical Computers for Fire Control," in M. D. Fagen, ed., *A History of Engineering and Science in the Bell System: National Service in War and Peace (1925–1975)* (Murray Hill, N.J.: Bell Telephone Laboratories, 1978), pp. 166–67; and George R. Stibitz, "Early Computers," in N. Metropolis, J. Howlett, and Gian-Carlo Rota, eds., *A History of Computing in the Twentieth Century: A Collection of Essays* (Academic Press, 1980), pp. 479–83.

cards needed to keep the system's records was significant in helping IBM to weather the depression years.[2]

Technologically, both calculators and punched card equipment relied on electromechanical relays, counters, adders, comparators, and sensors. Wiring together the more sophisticated mathematical capability of the calculator with the data processing capacity of punched card equipment was a logical extension of the art. Columbia University researchers put together this type of installation with support from IBM in the late 1920s and used it for complex scientific calculations.[3] By the later 1930s individual researchers had begun to experiment with circuitry using vacuum tube flip-flop switches and specialized counters, and other electronic circuits, to perform numerical computations.

Numerous efforts were under way in the United States. Inspired by the work of British physicist C. E. Wynn-Williams, who had built pioneering high-speed nuclear particle counters using thyratron tubes (a type of gas-filled electronic valve) in the early 1930s, Joseph Desch and Robert Mumma of NCR had begun working on the application of electronics to arithmetic calculations in 1938 and 1939.[4] Installed in a new research lab established at NCR's Dayton, Ohio, plant, Desch and Mumma had by 1940 built a prototype electronic calculator. At MIT, NCR sponsored a parallel research effort to build a Rapid Arithmetical Machine, conceived by Vannevar Bush and supervised by his associate Samuel Caldwell. Although exotic experimental electronic circuitry was built and tested, MIT never produced a complete machine.[5] At Iowa State University, in 1940, John Vincent Atanasoff built a functional prototype electronic adder. In 1941 he demonstrated it to a visitor, John W. Mauchly.[6] IBM also had a small research effort under way before

2. See Bob O. Evans, "IBM System/360," *Computer Museum Report,* no. 9 (Summer 1984), p. 9; and William Rodgers, *Think* (Stein and Day, 1969), p. 108.

3. See Rodgers, *Think,* pp. 133–48; and Charles J. Bashe and others, *IBM's Early Computers* (MIT Press, 1986), pp. 22–24.

4. See B. Randell, "The Colossus," in Metropolis and others, *A History of Computing,* p. 51. The work of Joseph Desch and Robert Mumma is described briefly in Bryon E. Phelps, "Early Electronic Computer Developments at IBM," *Annals of the History of Computing,* vol. 2 (July 1980), pp. 251–55. Unpublished interviews with Joseph Desch and Robert Mumma conducted by Henry Tropp, January 17 and 18, 1973, available in the Smithsonian Institution, Washington, D.C.

5. Tropp interview with Desch and Mumma, January 17 and 18, 1973. Randell, "Colossus," pp. 80–81; Karl L. Wildes and Nilo A. Lindgren, *A Century of Electrical Engineering and Computer Science at MIT, 1882–1982* (MIT Press, 1985), pp. 228–35.

6. This episode ultimately led to the overthrow in 1973 of patents on the computer

the war, investigating the replacement of mechanical relays with electronic circuits.[7]

Even at this early stage, a key concept had already emerged. Both Stibitz and Atanasoff were using circuitry that processed numbers in digital form, as sequences of binary, on-off electrical pulses that were stored in switches and counted in adders.

The numerous "differential analyzers" built in the United States in the 1930s contributed greatly to the emerging form of the modern digital computer.[8] Vannevar Bush directed most of this work, undertaken at MIT. The differential analyzer was a special purpose machine that could solve certain types of differential equations. It also used the prevailing electromechanical technology and worked by measuring physical phenomena whose behavior could be associated with an equation under study. Electrical and mechanical values were altered to mimic the effects of parameters in the equation to be solved. The U.S. War Department funded much of this work. In fact a differential analyzer was installed by the Army at its Aberdeen Proving Grounds in Maryland, where it was put to work calculating artillery firing tables. Bush's interest in achieving greater computational speeds by replacing mechanical components with electronic circuitry was one of the motivations leading MIT to work jointly with NCR on high-speed electronics.[9]

A new generation of superior electronic componentry was another ingredient in the technological ferment leading to the modern computer. The progress in electronic components built on new and superior vacuum tube devices developed in the 1920s and 1930s by radio engineers and on designs for new high-performance circuits dependent on these improved

---

filed by J. Presper Eckert and John W. Mauchly, on the basis of their work on the ENIAC machine and its successors. See Nancy Stern, *From ENIAC to UNIVAC: An Appraisal of the Eckert-Mauchly Computers* (Digital Press, 1981), pp. 33–36; and Herman H. Goldstine, *The Computer: From Pascal to von Neumann* (Princeton University Press, 1980), pp. 125–26.

7. Phelps, "Early Electronic Computer," pp. 253–58; Charles J. Bashe, "The SSEC in Historical Perspective," *Annals of the History of Computing*, vol. 4 (October 1982), pp. 298–301; and Bashe and others, *IBM's Early Computers*, pp. 36–42.

8. See Vannevar Bush, *Pieces of the Action* (William Morrow, 1970), pp. 181–85.

9. In the late 1930s it also became clear that the principles involved in the differential analyzer could be coupled with a feedback mechanism to the mechanical movement of a gunsight and used to control the fire of a weapon. See Higgins and others, "Electrical Computers," pp. 133–63. See also Jan Rajchman, "Early Research on Computers at RCA," in Metropolis and others, *A History of Computing*, pp. 465–66; and Wildes and Lindgren, *A Century of Electrical Engineering*, p. 92. The analog computers were much faster, though less accurate, than digital machines in solving these problems.

components. The biggest contribution of the new, all-electronic switching and counting circuits was the potential for orders of magnitude improvement in speed.

The research effort put into radar in the 1930s, under government sponsorship in some of the big industrial economies (the United States, Britain, Germany, and France), was crucial to the development of the electronic components used to modulate high-speed, high-frequency electrical pulses. Radar apparatus using the higher frequencies of the electromagnetic spectrum was found to have superior range and diffusion characteristics, and much effort was expended in developing parts capable of handling high pulse rates. Happily, since digital computers rely on electrical pulses, devices capable of responding to high-frequency pulses allow very fast computing. Much of the later rapid progress in computers drew heavily on the fruits of accelerated development of high-frequency electronics for radar.[10]

The final scientific tradition from which computers emerged was mathematical logic. In a famous and original 1936 paper, the young British mathematician Alan Turing tackled a difficult theoretical problem and in the process invented the abstract concept of a general purpose computer.[11] In extending work by Czech mathematician Kurt Gödel, Turing showed that there was no mechanical process by which all provable assertions could be proven.[12] To do so, he invented what is now known as a Turing machine, an abstract theoretical automaton that could recognize and process symbols, including arithmetic, according to a "table of behavior" with which it was programmed. Turing's proof applied this theoretical automaton to the task of computing numbers.

Significantly, Turing's abstract conception of a machine was that it

10. J. Presper Eckert, for example, has commented that experience with electronics used in radar operatus gave him crucial experience in building high-speed circuits. See J. Presper Eckert, "ENIAC," *Computer Museum Report*, vol. 16 (Summer 1986), p. 3. Maurice Wilkes, builder of the Electronic Delay Storage Automatic Calculator (EDSAC), is also emphatic on this point. Maurice V. Wilkes, *Memoirs of a Computer Pioneer* (MIT Press, 1985), pp. 107–08. *IBM's Early Computers* points out that Ralph L. Palmer's electronics group at IBM was largely composed of engineers with wartime electronics experience in radar. See Bashe and others, *IBM's Early Computers*, pp. 60–61, 118.

11. Alan M. Turing, "On Computable Numbers, with an Application to the Entscheidungsproblem," *Proceedings of the London Mathematical Society*, vol. 42 (London, 1936), pp. 230–65.

12. See Andrew Hodges, *Alan Turing: The Enigma* (Simon and Schuster, 1983), pp. 92–110.

be universal and capable in principle of doing any logical operation that could be automated or mechanized. Furthermore, the machine should process symbols, not just numbers. Thus Turing extended the horizons of computing machinery to information processing and the manipulation and interpretation of symbolic concepts.

Turing's ideas crossed the Atlantic with him, when he accepted fellowships for the 1936–37 academic years at the Institute for Advanced Study (IAS), near Princeton University. While there, he met many prominent mathematicians, including John von Neumann, who was later to figure prominently in the development of the computer in the United States. Turing turned down a position as a research assistant to von Neumann and returned to England in the summer of 1938.

While at Princeton, however, Turing became interested in applying logical techniques to codes and ciphers. He envisioned representing letters as binary numbers and multiplying them by other long numbers to encrypt messages. He went as far as building a functioning prototype of an electrical multiplier that processed binary numbers. After returning to England, Turing immediately became associated with the British Foreign Office's Government Code and Cypher School (GC & CS), which was decrypting the message traffic of foreign powers and maintaining the security of British communications.

Military Influence

Progress in computer technology exploded during and after the Second World War. Several military organizations, and organizations funded by the military, promoted the development of computer technology in the United States in the 1940s.

The U.S. Navy

The Navy's interest in the development of advanced technology on a large scale dates back to World War I. Important advances in naval warfare, including the use of mechanical directors and computers for fire control, the use of radio for communication across great distances, and the development of the attack submarine posed new technical problems for strategists. The Navy soon took the lead in applying new technology to military problems. The secretary of the Navy set up a naval consulting board, chaired by Thomas A. Edison, in 1915. Though the board largely confined its work to screening the proposals of outside inventors, it set up a laboratory facility to work on problems of antisubmarine warfare. Another of its initiatives led to the establishment of the Naval Research Laboratory in 1923. The only other significant force in American wartime research during the First World War was the civilian-controlled National Research Council, associated with the private National Academy of Sciences, which had a small budget and largely served as liaison between the scientific community and research needs defined by the military.

The Navy's postwar research efforts included support for the development of radar, radio communications, and the interception and cryptanalysis of foreign communications traffic. Naval interest in these areas reflected the difficulties of communication and reconnaissance over the vast expanses of ocean on which ships operated; telephony and telegraphy, the mainstay of land-based military communications, were not an option. Because signals transmitted by radio could be intercepted much more easily than communications over land lines, cryptanalysis became an economic means of acquiring intelligence about the intentions of foreign, especially naval, military forces.

In 1921 the U.S. Navy began to build a large cryptological unit, which came to dominate the military's codebreaking activities. During the next two decades, the Navy budgeted three to five dollars for every dollar expended for cryptological activities by the U.S. Army and by 1939 was the most significant force in U.S military communications intelligence. In 1935 the Navy's Communications Security Group, known by its designation as OP-20-G, was established to manage the security of U.S. naval communications and to attack foreign codes.[13] This highly secret organization engaged in important, early American work on the digital computer.

In the early 1930s the Navy began to mechanize its cryptanalytical activities. It installed IBM punched card machinery to process code traffic.[14] During that transition, naval intelligence officers approached

13. See William F. Friedman, "A Brief History of the Signal Intelligence Service," SRH-029, June 29, 1942, declassified National Security Agency report released to the National Archives. Friedman was the top cryptanalyst in the U.S. Army's Signal Intelligence Service (SIS) and led the team that broke the Japanese "Purple" diplomatic code in 1940. See also "The Birthday of the Naval Security Group," SRH-150, declassified National Security Agency report released to the National Archives.

14. David Kahn, *The Codebreakers: The Story of Secret Writing* (London:

Vannevar Bush, then vice-president and dean of engineering at MIT, an acknowledged expert on machine analysis because of his leadership of the differential analyzer group at MIT.[15] Bush studied the Navy's plans and concluded that punched card machinery was too slow. He wanted special machinery that was orders of magnitude faster. A small, secret research group was formed at MIT and developed a machine, which, along with those who built it, entered the Navy.[16] By the end of the war, at least seven copies of this particular machine had been built and were instrumental in breaking Japanese codes.[17]

The U.S. Navy also funded considerable work on servomechanisms, which use feedback to control movement, at MIT in the 1930s. Navy officers enrolled as graduate students in MIT's Servomechanisms Laboratory.[18] This work led to another set of routes to the digital computer, the analog computers developed and applied to fire control at MIT, RCA, and the Bell Telephone Laboratories during the war.

Thus two principal lines of advance toward the digital computer—rapid analytical machinery for cryptanalytical applications and analog computers for guidance and fire control—benefited from a steady prewar diet of research support from the U.S. Navy. A third application, computers to calculate ballistics tables for projectiles fired from weapons, was to emerge from the Army funding sources that had originally supported the development of differential analyzers in the 1930s for this purpose.

A Colossus Is Built

Cryptological applications first justified large government expenditures on electronic computing machines. Through rather complex and

Weidenfield and Nicolson, 1967), p. 563, says that the Navy's first IBM machines were installed in 1932.

15. Bush describes the episode in his memoirs. See Bush, *Pieces of the Action*, pp. 192–94.

16. Bush reports that only four people at the Massachusetts Institute of Technology (MIT) knew about the project: Karl T. Compton, then president of the institute, the two young researchers who worked with Bush, and Bush himself. Ibid., p. 193; Randell, "Colossus," pp. 80–81.

17. Bush, *Pieces of the Action*, p. 194. The unnamed machine developed in the late 1930s at MIT for the Navy was comparable in concept (though not, perhaps, in technology or performance, since it used photoelectric sensing circuitry linked to standard punched card machines) to the Heath Robinson machines built later by the British. See Randell, "Colossus," pp. 80–81.

18. See Wildes and Lindgren, *A Century of Electrical Engineering*, pp. 213–17. One of the theses, produced before the United States entered the war, remained classified until 1972.

circuitous events, the British secret service had obtained considerable information and a working model of the encryption machinery (the so-called Enigma) used, in one variant or another, by both the Germans and Japanese for their most secret communications traffic. Turing, along with Gordon W. Welchman and others working at Bletchley Park, wartime headquarters of the GC & CS, had developed statistical and mathematical techniques and constructed an electromechanical machine, the so-called bombe, that enabled them to break the Enigma system of the German Navy during the early part of the war.[19] The mechanization of cryptanalysis on these machines allowed vast quantities of German intercepts to be translated, and articulation of the concept of "information processing" was a logical next step.

In early 1942, however, the German Navy modified its Enigmas to effectively multiply the possible keys used to encode messages by a factor of twenty-six. This essentially halted codebreaking successes against German U-boat communications in the Atlantic, since what took a day using the old methods now took a month. It also created a willingness to invest resources in experiments with novel methods. The British began to explore speeding up the machinery by using newly developed electronic technology to replace portions of the (order of magnitude slower) electromechanical relay machinery. Experts were brought in from the radar research laboratory, the Telecommunications Research Establishment (TRE), and the Post Office Research Station (the British equivalent of the Bell Telephone labs). Initial efforts met with frustrating technical problems, and by the end of 1942, a successful electronic solution had not been found.[20]

The U.S. armed forces had established contacts with the British cryptanalysts well before the United States came into the war formally, and a regular program of missions exchanging technical information and coordinating codebreaking efforts was begun.[21] By mid-1942, OP-20-G

19. See Hodges, *Alan Turing*, p. 181, for an inside view of the wartime breakthroughs at Bletchley Park. That the "bombe" used electromechanical punched card machinery technology is illustrated by the fact that it was constructed on the premises of British Tabulating Machinery, the punched card machinery company that was the British licensee of IBM.

20. In the end, the boarding of a U-boat by the U.S. Navy in October 1942, and the capture of its code books, coupled with unsound German cryptographic procedures, allowed the Allies to resume breaking U-boat communications by using "bombe" technology in late 1942.

21. For the story of these early contacts see Ronald Lewin, *The American Magic: Codes, Ciphers, and the Defeat of Japan* (Farrar, Strauss Giroux, 1982), pp. 46–47.

had developed its own, more advanced version of the British bombe and was well under way on its own attack on German naval ciphers.[22]

In mid-1942, at roughly the same time that U-boat signal traffic decryption was disrupted by changes in the German naval Enigma, the British began to intercept a new type of encrypted teleprinter message, produced by a cryptographic machine, code-named Fish. With others at Bletchley Park, Turing developed a general method for attacking the large number of possible keys used by this device to encrypt high-grade German Army messages.[23] A group under the direction of Max M. A. Newman, a Cambridge mathematician, set out to mechanize the processing of this traffic. Very high speeds were required to break this traffic within a reasonable time, and the same group of engineers from TRE and the Post Office Research Station that had been frustrated in applying electronics to the bombe set about developing the technology to break Fish automatically.

The machine they produced was nicknamed the Heath Robinson, and it was a hybrid of electromechanical and electronic technology.[24] Paper

---

See also "Collection of Memoranda on Operations of SIS Intercept Activities and Dissemination, 1942–1945," SRH-145, declassified National Security Agency report released to the National Archives. Several known cryptanalytical technical exchange missions are described in the following documents: "History of the Special Branch, MIS, War Department, 1942–44," SRH-035, declassified National Security Agency report released to the National Archives; Hodges, *Alan Turing*, pp. 242–55; Lewin, *American Magic*, pp. 136–37; and Gordon Welchman, *The Hut Six Story: Breaking the Enigma Codes* (McGraw-Hill, 1982), pp. 170–79. See also Howard Campaigne, "Forward," in "The Design of Colossus," *Annals of the History of Computing*, vol. 5 (July 1983), pp. 239–40; and Joseph Blum, Robert L. Kirby, and Jack Minker, "Eloge: Walter W. Jacobs, 1914–1982," *Annals of the History of Computing*, vol. 6 (April 1984), p. 100.

22. Hodges, *Alan Turing*, pp. 235–36. The U.S. Navy proposed to attack the new complexities in the U-boat codes by building 360 copies of its bombe and wiring them together in parallel. This plan constituted a massive frontal attack on the problem—the British at that time had only 30 machines, with another 20 under construction. Ultimately, a compromise with GC & CS was reached, with the U.S. Navy building only 100 copies of the machine. Bletchley Park became responsible for coordinating U.S.-British efforts. F. H. Hinsley and others, *British Intelligence in the Second World War: Its Influence on Strategy and Operations*, vol. 2 (New York: Cambridge University Press, 1981), pp. 55–56.

23. Hodges, *Alan Turing*, pp. 228–31; and I. J. Good, "A Report on T. H. Flower's Lecture on Colossus," *Annals of the History of Computing*, vol. 4 (January 1982), p. 55.

24. American engineers at OP-20-G built an improved version of this machine called "Goldberg." (Rube Goldberg, the American cartoonist, drew fantastic contraptions similar to those of the British cartoonist Heath Robinson). Telephone interview with Howard Campaigne, August 1, 1985.

tapes containing encrypted messages and keys were synchronized and used to generate electronic pulses, and logical comparisons were made. The mechanical parts of the operation were prone to breakdown, however, and difficult to synchronize.

To overcome these difficulties, many of the mechanical parts of the machine, including the key tape, were replaced by electronics, and thyratron ring counter circuits were substituted for mechanical wheels. This machine, which went into operation in 1943, had 1,500 vacuum tubes and was named Colossus. A later version, the Mark II Colossus, had 2,400 vacuum tubes and 800 electromechanical relays. By the end of the war, ten of the Mark II machines were functioning in England.[25]

Though much smaller, Colossus was technologically and functionally comparable to the ENIAC, the American machine that was operating two years later and is often called the first modern electronic digital computer. Details of its existence were not revealed until the mid-1970s, however. Although special purpose in nature, Colossus could theoretically be programmed to carry out conventional mathematical calculations. Because of a complete two-way exchange of technological information between the United States and British groups at the time, details of its construction and operation crossed the Atlantic in short order and influenced the engineers working on rapid analytical machinery within OP-20-G. Apparently, moreover, American engineers built relatively faithful copies of Colossus technology.[26]

This technology used at Bletchley Park and in U.S. naval intelligence would greatly affect the postwar development of computers. In the United States, OP-20-G's most important technology-related groups were its Washington cryptological unit, known as Communications Supplementary Activities Washington (CSAW), and its engineering facilities, the Naval Computing Machinery Laboratory (NCML), located on the facilities of the National Cash Register plant in Dayton, Ohio.

In late 1942, after the U.S. Navy had decided to build many rapid analytical machines, Joseph Desch and Robert Mumma and their electronics lab at NCR had been pulled from Army war projects and put to work on these secret Navy tasks. This lab, transformed into NCML, grew from 20 to 1,100 people at its peak. About 1,200 codebreaking

25. Good, "A Report on T. H. Flower's Lecture," p. 57.
26. B. Randell quotes American engineer Arnold I. Dumey as saying that "the only early improvement on Colossus was in a more compact way of holding and running the tapes." See Randell, "Colossus," p. 82.

machines, of about 140 different types, are reported to have been built at the NCR Dayton plant during the war.[27]

The Navy's takeover of the NCR electronics effort may even have indirectly led to the Army's decision to build the ENIAC. For by the end of 1942, the civilian electronics research at MIT and NCR had been abandoned under the pressure of more pressing wartime requirements. The MIT researchers went to work in the U.S. nuclear program.[28] The NCR group had been shifted to an Army calculator project. Desch and Mumma had even produced functional electronic calculator circuits demonstrated to the Army at Aberdeen, Maryland, site of its Ballistics Research Laboratory.[29]

At roughly the same time as the loss of decrypted German naval traffic (because of changes in the German Enigma early in the year) pushed up Allied shipping losses in the North Atlantic to horrendous levels, OP-20-G apparently generated enough pressure to take over Desch and Mumma's lab at NCR, over the protests of the Army.[30] Thus the Army had to look elsewhere for its calculator and, in the end, decided to support a previously ignored proposal submitted by J. Presper Eckert and John W. Mauchly at the University of Pennsylvania.

Engineers with prewar experience in electronic circuitry, from around the country, were sent to NCR to work on cryptanalytical machinery. In particular, a few engineers from IBM, some of whom had been experimenting with the substitution of electronic circuits for slower electromechanical components in IBM punched card machines before the war, joined the staff of NCML.[31] One of these IBM engineers, Ralph L. Palmer, a technical executive officer arriving at NCML in 1943, later steered IBM's transition to electronic technology.[32]

27. See B. Randell, "An Annotated Bibliography on the Origins of Computers," *Annals of the History of Computing*, vol. 1 (October 1979), pp. 116–17, abstracting from an unpublished interview with H. Campaigne.

28. Wildes and Lindgren, *A Century of Electrical Engineering*, p. 231.

29. Tropp interview with Desch and Mumma, January 17 and 18, 1973.

30. Ibid.

31. Desch notes in the Tropp interview that he had quite a few IBM men in uniform working for him during the war. They had been sent to Dayton because of their background, but they did not get access to work at the NCR labs outside of their area. Ibid.

32. See Emerson W. Pugh, *Memories That Shaped an Industry: Decisions Leading to IBM System/360* (MIT Press, 1984), pp. 23–25; Charles J. Bashe, "The SSEC in Historical Perspective," *Annals of the History of Computing*, vol. 4 (October 1982), pp. 301–02.

Other U.S. firms, including IBM and Eastman Kodak, were also building rapid analytical machinery for the Navy, while the Army worked with the Bell Telephone Laboratories to build electrical encryption machinery for voice and teletype data and a large special purpose relay computer for cryptanalytical work.[33] Both Army and Navy intelligence agencies used great batteries of conventional IBM punched card machines. IBM also built special purpose attachments to punched card machines for cryptological applications.[34]

The Navy also worked on two significant external digital computer projects during the war. The Mark I relay computer project at Harvard was designed by Howard Aiken and developed and engineered by IBM. Begun under the financial sponsorship of IBM before the war, the Mark I was taken over by the Navy after hostilities were under way. The Navy also supported the Airplane Stability and Control Analyzer (ASCA), a general purpose aircraft simulator proposed for use as a flight trainer for pilots and a flight characteristics simulator for aircraft designers. Jay W. Forrester and the MIT Servomechanisms Laboratory signed a contract with the Special Devices Division of the Navy's Bureau of Aeronautics in mid-1944 to develop the apparatus, which, though never built, evolved into the Whirlwind computer project.[35] Both the Mark I and the Whirlwind development groups helped pave the way for the technical development of the U.S. computer industry.

An Emerging National Science and Technology Policy

A vigorous debate over postwar science and technology policy began to shape up even before the war had ended.[36] The massive wartime influx

33. Samuel S. Snyder, "Influence of U.S. Cryptologic Organizations on the Digital Computer Industry," SRH-003, declassified National Security Agency report released to the National Archives, p. 4. See also M. D. Fagen, *A History of Engineering and Science*, pp. 291–317; telephone interview with Howard Campaigne, August 1, 1985; Randell, "Colossus," p. 80; and James Bamford, *The Puzzle Palace* (Penguin, 1983), p. 134.

34. Thomas Graham Belden and Mona Robins Belden, *The Lengthening Shadow: The Life of Thomas J. Watson* (Little, Brown, 1962), p. 218; Kahn reports that the Army cryptologists' use of IBM equipment, which dated to 1936, included 13 machines at Pearl Harbor, 407 by the spring of 1945. Kahn, *Codebreakers*, pp. 563, 576. See also Snyder, "Influence of U.S. Cryptologic Organizations," p. 4.

35. See Kent C. Redmond and Thomas S. Smith, *Project Whirlwind: The History of a Pioneer Computer* (Digital Press, 1980), pp. 12–13.

36. James L. Pennick, Jr., and others, *The Politics of American Science: 1939 to*

of resources into research and development, leading to the prospect of further technological breakthroughs, left a permanent commitment to increased public support for research.[37] Though policymakers eventually cut back government support from wartime levels, they were eager to confront new issues like the scale of dollars to be allocated to science and technology, the control of research budgets and priorities, and the types of research to support.

But there were those with a different vision of continued federal support for technology, and a political stalemate developed. In 1947 Congress passed an act establishing a National Science Foundation (NSF) organized along the lines outlined by Vannevar Bush in his 1945 report, only to have it vetoed by President Harry S. Truman over issues of accountability and control. Continued political struggles buried the prospects for action until Congress finally established the foundation in 1950.

The U.S. Navy, with congressional approval, did establish an Office of Naval Research (ONR) in 1946. It was the first U.S. government agency established specifically to oversee the task of research management, and Congress placed it in nominal control of all Navy-supported research, both intramural, as in Navy laboratories, and extramural, in external research institutions, universities, and outside defense contractors. Many supporters of the ONR, including Bush, conditioned their help on "the full understanding on the part of everyone that it was to a considerable extent a temporary program,"[38] to be funded until the establishment of a National Science Foundation.

By the end of 1948, the ONR employed one thousand in-house scientists, funded about 40 percent of basic research in the United States, and was working on research contracts amounting to $43 million ($20 million of its own money, $9 million from other federal agencies, and

---

the Present (MIT Press, 1972); Michael S. Sherry, *Preparing for the Next War: American Plans for Postwar Defense* (Yale University Press, 1977), pp. 120–58; and David F. Noble, *Forces of Production: A Social History of Industrial Automation* (Alfred A. Knopf, 1984), pp. 10–20.

37. Secretary of the Navy James V. Forrestal, in a February 1945 memo to President Roosevelt, wrote: "The problem which began to emerge during the 1944 fiscal year is how to establish channels through which scientists can [contribute to the nation's security by carrying on research] in peace as successfully as they have during the war." Quoted in Mina Rees, "The Computing Program of the Office of Naval Research, 1946–1953," *Annals of the History of Computing*, vol. 4 (April 1982), p. 103.

38. Bush is quoted in Redmond and Smith, *Project Whirlwind*, p. 106.

$14 million of university money).[39] Until the early 1950s, the only other government agency that exerted a role over the external technological development of computers even remotely approaching that of ONR was the National Bureau of Standards, and its involvement had a considerably different orientation.

During the years 1946–50, as different research groups struggled to develop a workable general purpose, stored-program, electronic digital computer, ONR funded a great number and variety of computer projects. These projects included MIT's Whirlwind, Raytheon's Hurricane computer (later renamed RAYDAC), the CALDIC computer at the University of California, Berkeley, and the Harvard Mark III. Opposition from the ONR's mathematics branch, entrusted with supervision of computer research, also created difficulties for computer projects.[40]

Engineering Research Associates

In mid-1945, as it became clear that the war would soon be over, technical personnel working on OP-20-G's codebreaking efforts began to plan a return to civilian life.[41] The Navy, anxious to keep its technical resources intact, offered peacetime civil service appointments to its valued personnel, but they refused to accept. The Navy then tried to interest the National Cash Register Corporation in continuing to supply high-speed analytical machinery for Navy applications. It, too, refused, eager to return to its profitable prewar business in office equipment.

Finally, two senior reserve naval officers in Washington's cryptological unit (CSAW)[42] approached the Navy with the idea of starting a

39. Ibid., p. 105.
40. These included Eckert and Mauchly's fledgling UNIVAC I and the MIT Whirlwind. Harry D. Huskey, "The National Bureau of Standards Western Automatic Computer (SWAC)," *Annals of the History of Computing*, vol. 2 (April 1980), pp. 111–12.
41. This account of the beginnings of ERA draws on Erwin Tomash, "The Start of an ERA: Engineering Research Associates," in Metropolis and others, *A History of Computing*, pp. 485–95; and Arnold A. Cohen and Erwin Tomash, "The Birth of an ERA, Engineering Research Associates, Inc.," *Annals of the History of Computing*, vol. 1 (October 1979), pp. 83–100.
42. Howard T. Engstrom, who had been a professor of mathematics at Yale before the war, and research director for Communications Supplementary Activities Washington (CSAW) during the war, later left Remington Rand, which had purchased Engineering Research Associates (ERA), to become deputy director of the National Security Agency (NSA). Ralph Palmer credited Engstrom with championing the use of high technology

private business to service the computing needs of CSAW and the Navy. Top officials in the Navy encouraged Harold Engstrom and William Norris, and they were soon joined in their efforts by the wartime head of the Naval Computing Machinery Laboratory, Ralph I. Meader. Seventeen different companies and various individuals were contacted, but all declined to invest in a project with highly uncertain economic prospects. Finally, a financial backer with political and Navy connections was found and the newly born Engineering Research Associates, as well as the Navy's NCML, moved onto the premises of an established firm that the backer owned. Although ERA was legally ineligible to obtain large government contracts, the Navy bent the rules and issued noncompetitive contracts to ERA and the established sister firm, which shared the same facility and management in St. Paul, Minnesota. As soon as ERA had qualified as a contractor, the sister firm was dissolved.[43]

ERA's research and development efforts in the late 1940s focused on developing special purpose machines for cryptological applications. The company used the technology under development in the large digital computer projects then under way in the United States and Britain.[44] ERA's expertise was in magnetic drum memory technology, which it developed and incorporated into many of these specialized cryptological

---

in naval intelligence applications. (See Pugh, *Memories*, p. 268). William Norris later became head of Remington Rand's ERA subsidiary, the UNIVAC division of Sperry Rand, and the Control Data Corporation. Rear Admiral Joseph Wenger, who as a captain had headed CSAW during the war, was the first vice-director of the NSA, having held the same position in its predecessor organization, the AFSA. Of the fifty-one members of ERA's founding technical group, forty came from CSAW, five from the Naval Computing Machinery Laboratory, three from the Naval Ordnance Laboratory, and three from research units that were predecessors to the Office of Naval Research. See Arnold A. Cohen, "Biographical Notes," in *High-speed Computing Devices* (Los Angeles: Tomash Publishers, 1983), p. xxxiii; and Bamford, *Puzzle Palace*, p. 119.

43. A proposal for a joint enterprise by Norris and his colleagues was turned down by J. Presper Eckert. The civilians who established ERA explicitly intended to market commercial products based on the technology developed for government applications. See William Norris, "Entreprenueurism—the Past, Present, and Future of Computing in the USA," *Computer Museum Report,* vol. 19 (Spring 1987), p. 12. It was not unknown for patented technology developed for defense to become the property of the developer. Nevertheless, at the time the Navy was sensitive about the circumstances of its noncompetitive contracts with a group of ex-officers. See Tomash and Cohen, "Birth of an ERA," pp. 86–87, 90–91.

44. Samuel S. Snyder, "Computer Advances Pioneered by Cryptologic Organizations," *Annals of the History of Computing*, vol. 2 (January 1980), pp. 61–62; Snyder, "Influence of U.S. Cryptologic Organizations," pp. 5–7; and Tomash and Cohen, "Birth of an ERA," pp. 89–93.

machines, and later used in general purpose computers. Its research on magnetic drums built on captured technology developed in Germany during the war.[45] The company also invented a special magnetic spray coating to improve the performance of the drum memories.[46]

In 1947 U.S. naval intelligence issued an order to ERA to design and construct a general purpose digital computer. The hope was that a general purpose computer could be programmed to do many of the tasks for which ERA had been building special, one-of-a-kind machines and therefore reduce the cost of code cracking. This machine, code-named Atlas, was Task 13, the thirteenth job given to ERA by the Navy, and was operating by the end of 1950.

The Atlas computer development effort drew heavily on the work of others—logical designs produced by von Neumann's computer group at IAS and engineering designs from MIT's Whirlwind computer group. Because of the priority given to the project by military sponsors, the Navy gave ERA engineers access to reports on computer work on other government projects.[47] Technology flowed both ways however—another early task assigned ERA was to produce a survey of computing technology based on its investigations, and this book, published in 1950, became a standard handbook for the industry.[48]

The Atlas, delivered to the Navy at the beginning of December 1950, became fully operational in a week. It was the second electronic stored-program computer to go into regular use in the United States.[49] One year

45. Emmett Quady, who joined ERA in 1947, recalls, "I remember the very first day I went to work they had a captured German magnetic drum of some sort. They'd captured it, you know, in occupation and brought it over." Unpublished interview with Emmett Quady conducted by Robina Mapstone, May 15, 1973, available in the Smithsonian Institution, Washington, D.C. Emerson Pugh describes a special type of magnetic tape material brought over from Germany and used at ERA. Pugh, *Memories*, p. 20, citing an interview with S. M. Rubens, May 30, 1980.

46. Snyder, "Computer Advances," p. 62; and Mapstone interview with Emmett Quady on May 18, 1973. Interview with James Cass by Robina Mapstone, December 18, 1972, available in the Smithsonian Institution, Washington, D.C. In 1949 ERA entered into a design project with IBM to develop a magnetic drum computer, which, though never built, led to a technology transfer and cross-licensing arrangement with IBM that gave IBM access to ERA's extensive patents on magnetic drums. Tomash and Cohen, "Birth of an ERA," p. 91. For an IBM perspective, see Bashe and others, *IBM's Early Computers*, pp. 81–83.

47. Snyder, "Computer Advances," p. 62; and Tomash and Cohen, "Birth of an ERA," p. 89.

48. As Cohen, *High-speed Computing Devices*, p. xix, explains, a Russian translation published in 1952 seems to have been important in the development of Soviet ideas.

49. The first was the National Bureau of Standards' SEAC machine, which was

after delivery to the Navy, ERA received permission to market a commercial version of the Atlas as the ERA 1101.[50] Though only one was built, a more advanced successor, the ERA 1103, also developed originally as a Navy project (the Atlas II) became the first ERA computer to go into large-scale serial production (twenty machines were built). ERA, producing an estimated 80 percent of the dollar value of computers sold in the United States through 1952, became the dominant computer company of its day.[51]

Because of the nature of its market, engineering considerations dominated ERA's business orientation. The company designed and built machines to a user's specifications, then handed the hardware over to the purchaser.[52] In sharp contrast with the experience of firms seeking a commercial market, ERA experienced little feedback from users and little direct contact with what remained a relatively unknown market. The emphasis on technical sophistication over marketing, it may be argued, persisted in the computer companies that the engineers brought up in ERA went on to found.

The Origins of a Commercial Industry

At the war's end, it was far from obvious that the newly developed electronic computers were going to have much practical impact on business. According to prevailing wisdom, the government might need several large electronic computers, but they would have no broader appeal. Nonetheless, as military intelligence organizations began building electronic computers during the war to assist in their cryptological work, parallel developments in computing machinery occurred in more open environments. The idea of applying electronic computers to com-

---

turning out mathematical work regularly in May 1950. The MIT Whirlwind's central machine was working about 1951. See Ralph J. Slutz. "Memories of the Bureau of Standards' SEAC," in Metropolis and others, *A History of Computing*, p. 476; and Robert R. Everett, "Whirlwind," in Metropolis and others, *A History of Computing*, p. 372.

50. The figure 1101 is the binary representation of the decimal number 13.

51. Pugh, *Memories,* p. 19; and Franklin M. Fisher, James W. McKie, and Richard B. Mancke, *IBM and the U.S. Data Processing Industry: An Economic History* (Praeger, 1983), p. 10.

52. The ERA 1101 was offered for sale with no documentation, no operating system, and virtually no input-output other than paper tape. Tomash and Cohen, "Birth of an ERA," p. 90.

mercial and business problems gradually became the driving force behind the spectacular rise of a computer industry.

J. Presper Eckert and John W. Mauchly were foremost among those with the visionary idea of applying computers to everyday industrial and administrative tasks. Mauchly, as a teacher of physics at Ursinus College, near Philadelphia, had begun experimenting with high-speed vacuum tube counting circuits in the late 1930s.[53] Mauchly attended a training course in electronics given at the Moore School at the University of Pennsylvania in 1941 and was then invited to teach there. He soon became associated with Eckert, a graduate student and the top electronic engineer at the school. The Moore School had built a differential analyzer for the Army's Ballistic Research Laboratory (BRL) in 1939, adapted from the design of Bush's MIT machine, and was collaborating with BRL in training computing personnel for the Army. In August 1942 Mauchly submitted a proposal to the Moore School and the BRL to build a high-speed vacuum tube calculator for ballistics calculations. Both recipients ignored the proposal.

In the spring of 1943, at the initiative of BRL's representative at the Moore School, Herman H. Goldstine, Mauchly resubmitted the proposal. Unexpectedly, the Army promptly pursued it, and a contract was signed six weeks later. In retrospect, the dates suggest that the takeover by the Navy at the end of 1942 of the Desch and Mumma group at NCR, which had been working on an electronic calculator for BRL, must have influenced the Army to fund the work at the Moore School.[54]

The design of the machine, the ENIAC, was frozen a year later, in June 1944, and in November 1945, after the war had ended, it was ready for testing. It had most of the elements of a modern digital computer but lacked an internal program store, which allows a computer to treat its own program as data and modify the instructions it follows as they are executed. The ENIAC is often identified as the first electronic digital computer, but the Colossus, completed in great secrecy two years earlier in England, contained circuitry functionally equivalent to that found in ENIAC, though on a considerably smaller scale.

53. The description of J. Presper Eckert and John W. Mauchly draws heavily from Stern, *From ENIAC to UNIVAC*.

54. This point has not been made in the literature on Eckert and Mauchly, perhaps because there is essentially no published information on the work of Desch and Mumma for the Army's Ballistic Research Laboratory at National Cash Register Corporation; the dates given in their unpublished interview with Tropp on September 17 and 18, 1972, do support this inference, however.

The ENIAC was a massive machine, occupying 1,800 square feet. It contained almost 18,000 tubes and consumed 174 kilowatts of power. The system cost almost $800,000 to build.

The decision to build the ENIAC resulted from the Army's pressing wartime needs. The established scientific computing community within the government's Office of Scientific Research and Development, headed by Vannevar Bush, fiercely opposed the Eckert-Mauchly project. At issue were both the digital design of their proposal (an advanced analog differential analyzer was being built at MIT at the time) and their proposed use of electronic circuit elements. Samuel H. Caldwell, Bush's MIT colleague, wrote, "The reliability of electronic equipment required great improvement before it could be used with confidence for computation purposes."[55] Stibitz, at the Bell labs, expressed similar sentiments and suggested using electromechanical relay technology.

After the war, when Eckert and Mauchly turned to more advanced designs, opposition from established figures in computing continued. Howard Aiken, who had struggled at Harvard before the war to seek support for constructing a large electromechanical calculator, opposed their projects, suggesting, "There will never be enough problems, enough work, for more than one or two of these computers. . . ."[56] Thus the Army's willingness to gamble on a radically new approach, and Eckert and Mauchly's stubborn defiance of the scientific establishment led to the birth of the first all-electronic computers. Their achievement in engineering a reliable system composed of eighteen thousand inherently unreliable components must not be understated.

Well before ENIAC was finished, Eckert and Mauchly's group began thinking about a new and improved machine. Two principal shortcomings of the original ENIAC—limited memory available for use in calculation and a complex and difficult procedure for programming calculations using manual switches—were becoming increasingly obvious. Ideas for improving ENIAC revolved around these problems. In August 1944 the concept of an improved machine was broached to the Ballistics Research Laboratory, and by October, a contract had been issued to the Moore School.

By then, an important addition to the Moore School team had been made. The famous mathematician John von Neumann had learned of the existence of the project and had immediately begun regular visits.

55. This letter is cited in Stern, *From ENIAC to UNIVAC*, p. 20.
56. Stern, quoting Edward Cannon of the NBS. Ibid., p. 111.

Von Neumann, a superb mathematician, had become a powerful voice in the scientific establishment that ran the U.S. war effort's research and development program. His most important project at the time was his work on the development of nuclear weapons at Los Alamos National Laboratory, a task requiring tedious and time-consuming numerical calculations. He had also had personal contact with Turing at Princeton before the war and was familiar with Turing's abstract formalization of a computing machine.[57]

Von Neumann's presence stimulated a more formal and rigorous approach to the design of the successor machine, dubbed the Electronic Discrete Variable Automatic Computer (EDVAC). Over the ensuing months of discussion, ideas like the need for more memory and the concept of the stored program gained impetus. In April 1945 von Neumann composed a working draft based on these discussions, and the resulting "First Draft of a Report on the EDVAC" circulated widely among the scientific community.[58] The ideas on the logical design of a computer contained in that document were the basis for machine design well into the 1950s, and the essential architecture for a computer system set out in that report, the so-called von Neumann architecture, is today the basic design of all but experimental or special purpose computers.

Even before the EDVAC report was written, von Neumann had been working on setting up his own computer project at IAS. The nascent conflict over credit for the EDVAC ideas, as well as an overture to RCA to support the construction of an IAS computer, and a failed attempt to lure Eckert to the Princeton project, led to worsening relations with Eckert and Mauchly.

The publication of the EDVAC report, and the public dedication of the ENIAC machine in February 1946, had put the United States at the forefront of computing technology. Even before ENIAC had been completed, streams of visitors were pouring through the Moore School,

57. Hodges, *Alan Turing*, p. 145.
58. Only von Neumann's name was on the report, though it contained many ideas worked out by the entire Eckert-Mauchly group at the Moore School. This has led to an acrimonious historical debate about whether or not von Neumann was primarily responsible for the concept of the stored program, the key dividing line between special purpose digital electronic computing machines like ENIAC or Colossus, and the general purpose electronic digital computer. See Stern, *From ENIAC to UNIVAC*, pp. 74–78; and James E. Tomayko, "The Stored-Program Concept: National Computer Conference, Houston, Texas, June 9, 1982," *Technology and Culture*, vol. 24 (October 1983), pp. 660–63.

eager to hear how the newly developed electronics technology applied to problems of numerical calculation. In contrast to the Navy's ultrasecret work on cryptological machines, information on the ENIAC and EDVAC was widely accessible.

In early 1946 Eckert and Mauchly were pressured to sign a patent release giving the Moore School rights to the technology developed on the EDVAC project, just getting under way. After resisting similar pressures, they had retained rights to patents filed for the ENIAC technology and were clearly interested in commercial applications. In the spring of 1946, they resigned and set up their own firm, intending to manufacture an electronic computer for commercial use. After further wrangling over patent rights on the EDVAC (to which von Neumann also made a claim based on his authorship of the EDVAC report), the Army's patent lawyers ruled that because of the time elapsed since publication of the EDVAC report, the concepts related to EDVAC-type machines were in the public domain. Other groups would use these ideas in designing their computers over the next few years.

Many from the Moore School computer project left after Eckert and Mauchly's departure. Some engineers joined the new commercial venture, and others joined von Neumann's project at the IAS in Princeton. The Moore School's research director left shortly thereafter to start a computer division at Burroughs. Though a prototype was put into fitful operation, the EDVAC project was never fully completed.

Improvement of computer technology owed a great deal to the EDVAC. Its widely circulated design was used in many other computers, and lectures by the Moore School staff were critically important in getting other computer groups started. The presentations given by the Eckert-Mauchly group at a conference held at MIT in 1945 were important in steering the Whirlwind project at MIT toward digital computer technology.[59] A six-week course at the Moore School in the summer of 1946 got the Navy's cryptological establishment interested in general purpose digital computers.[60] This course greatly influenced others, including Maurice Wilkes, who began the Electronic Delay

59. See Redmond and Smith, *Project Whirlwind*, p. 33; and Stern, *From ENIAC to UNIVAC*, p. 55.
60. Snyder, "Influence of U.S. Cryptologic Organizations," p. 7, credits James T. Pendergrass of the Navy's Communications Supplementary Activities Washington, who attended this conference, with promoting Navy interest in general purpose digital computers.

Storage Automatic Calculator (EDSAC) project in England. The EDSAC was explicitly modeled on the EDVAC design and was probably the first full-scale stored-program digital computer to begin operation. Thus, even as the EDVAC project withered on the vine, its seeds were scattered widely.

Eckert and Mauchly, now having ruptured their ties to the academic world, faced serious difficulties. The scientific community was generally negative about their computer project; funding and customers were scarce. Before they had left the Moore School, Eckert and Mauchly had interested the Census Bureau in funding the development of an electronic computer for computation work through the Commerce Department's National Bureau of Standards, and only the NBS continued to actively support them.

Even the NBS could give only minimal backing in the short run, and Eckert and Mauchly were forced to scramble for funding. The Northrop Aircraft Company, in California, approached them about constructing a digital computer to be used for guidance of the Snark missile, then under development for the Air Force. Desperate for cash, Eckert and Mauchly agreed to an arrangement with 80 percent of the contract prepaid, and used this small computer, the Binary Automatic Computer (BINAC), as a development vehicle for the larger commercial machine they sought to market.

The BINAC passed performance trials at Eckert and Mauchly's Philadelphia lab in 1949, the first stored-program computer to function successfully in the United States. It was not well constructed, however, and never performed adequately when moved to California. Development costs, which amounted to $278,000, exceeded the fixed $100,000 fee negotiated with Northrop,[61] and the financial condition of the Eckert-Mauchly operation worsened. Finally, in early 1950, in desperate financial straits, Eckert and Mauchly sold out to Remington Rand.

In 1951 the first Universal Automatic Calculator (UNIVAC) built by Eckert and Mauchly was delivered to the Census Bureau. The UNIVAC became a great commercial success and propelled Remington Rand to market leadership in the early 1950s. By the end of 1952, three had been delivered to the government, and ultimately, forty-six UNIVAC Is were built.[62]

61. Stern, *From ENIAC to UNIVAC*, pp. 122–24.
62. Jean E. Sammett, "Answers to Self-Study Questions," *Annals of the History of Computing*, vol. 6 (October 1984), pp. 406–07.

The Institute for Advanced Study

Von Neumann started his computer project in 1945, securing funding from the Army and Navy ordnance departments and the IAS. RCA entered a joint contract with the IAS to develop a tube-based memory device called the Selectron for the IAS computer system. Beginning in 1946, the logical design of the IAS machine was published in a series of papers by von Neumann and his associates. Although financial support came from the military, and later, the Atomic Energy Commission, there were few security complications, and the reports were widely circulated. Unlike other military projects, working drawings and preliminary designs for the IAS computer were to be distributed to five other development centers, at the University of Illinois, the Oak Ridge National Laboratory, the Los Alamos National Laboratory, the Argonne National Laboratory, and the Rand Corporation, where copies of the machine were to be built.[63]

The influence of the IAS project in the early years of U.S. computer technology was therefore extensive, even before its completion in 1951. As the published design circulated widely, joint projects with other research institutions on subsystems for the Princeton computer were undertaken (with RCA on the Selectron tube storage system, with the Washington laboratories of NBS for controllers for serial-type input-output devices). Other collaborating institutions built copies of the basic design.

These copies included those built at the five laboratories officially designated in the funding contracts for the IAS system—the ILLIAC I built for the Army at the University of Illinois, ORDVAC at Aberdeen Proving Grounds in Maryland, MANIAC I at Los Alamos, the AVIDAC at Argonne, the Oak Ridge ORACLE, and the JOHNNIAC at Rand. Many unofficial "bootleg" copies were also built—the BESK and SMIL machines in Sweden, the BESM in Moscow, the WEIZAC in Israel, the Australian SILLIAC and CSIRAC computers, and the MSUDC at Michigan State.[64] Many pioneers of the computer industry cut their teeth on these projects.

The IAS computer also greatly influenced the logical design of IBM's

63. Julian Bigelow, "Computer Development at the Institute for Advanced Study," in Metropolis and others, A History of Computing, p. 292.

64. Goldstine, Computer, pp. 306–07; and C. Gordon Bell and Allen Newell, Computer Structures: Readings and Examples (McGraw-Hill, 1971), p. 89.

early 700 and 7000 series scientific computers, which evolved from the IAS architecture. Von Neumann started consulting for IBM on a thirty-days-per-year basis in 1951, and key IAS computer group members joined IBM in the late 1950s, when the Princeton computer group disbanded.[65]

MIT and the Whirlwind

Another important influence on the nascent computer industry in the late 1940s was MIT's Whirlwind computer. Like the IAS computer, Whirlwind was built by a university-based group of engineers who carefully documented the machine's development and distributed widely read progress reports on its construction. Whirlwind also had the distinction of being by far the most costly of the early U.S. computer projects. Bitter fights over Whirlwind funding characterized the debates over U.S. research policy affecting computer development in the late 1940s and early 1950s.[66]

Whirlwind had started life as the MIT ASCA project in 1944, intended to supply the Navy with a general purpose flight simulator, provide inexpensive training for pilots of a broad range of aircraft, and supply data on pilot-airplane interaction useful in aircraft design. The project, headed by Jay W. Forrester, an electrical engineering graduate student in MIT's Servomechanisms Laboratory, was largely staffed with young MIT graduate students.

In 1944 the Navy approved a preliminary design study for the ASCA, for $75,000. A full-scale eighteen-month development project, to cost $875,000 was initiated. Originally the project was to use an analog computer, employing the electromechanical differential analyzer technology pioneered at MIT, to control the machine. By the fall of 1945, the war had ended, and Forrester and his colleagues had run into serious design problems in their attempts to build an analog computer sufficiently fast and flexible to handle the real-time control of an aircraft simulator.

At that point, in October 1945, the Archibald conference, an early and important conference on advanced computation techniques, was held at MIT, and the MIT ASCA group learned of the electronic digital

---

65. Goldstine, *Computer*, p. 346; and Cuthbert C. Hurd, "Computer Development at IBM," in Metropolis and others, *A History of Computing*, pp. 401–02.

66. Unless otherwise noted, this section draws on Redmond and Smith, *Project Whirlwind*.

computers, the ENIAC and EDVAC, being built at the Moore School. After further research, the MIT group quickly decided to switch to a digital electronic computer to control its simulator. By the spring of 1946, the MIT group had submitted a revised proposal calling for the construction of a digital computer, the Whirlwind, and a simulator using that computer, to be built by 1950 at a total cost of about $2.4 million. The Navy accepted the proposal and funded it at $1.2 million through mid-1948.[67]

Whirlwind had been funded by the Special Devices Division of the Navy, however, and at the end of 1948, conflicts over funding of the project began to surface. For one thing, the newly born Office of Naval Research had begun to exert authority over all Navy research projects, and the Whirlwind project had been transferred to the mathematics branch of ONR in 1948. For another thing, costs on the Whirlwind computer continued to climb—by early 1948, another $600,000 had been authorized by the Navy, which also extended the original contract another year. When MIT requested another $1.8 million from ONR to cover the fifteen months from June 1948 to September 1949, the matter blew up into a major flap over research policy.

To put it most baldly, MIT's funding requests for Whirlwind for fiscal 1949, now almost $1.5 million, amounted to roughly 80 percent of the 1949 ONR budget for mathematics research, and about 10 percent of the entire ONR budget for contract research.[68]

At that time, the mathematics branch of ONR funded most of the computer projects under way in the United States, and Whirlwind's total funding requests were now running almost five times greater than the projected costs of another of ONR's most ambitious projects, the IAS computer, projected in 1950 to cost a total of about $650,000. MIT mobilized to defend the project, and as part of that defense, Forrester and his associates outlined a sweeping vision of military applications of computers to command and control tasks, including air traffic control, fire and combat control, and missile guidance, as well as to scientific calculations and logistics. The estimated cost of this program was put at $2 billion, over fifteen years.[69] The original justification for the computer, as the controller for a flight simulator, was rapidly replaced by the

---

67. Ibid., p. 43.
68. Ibid., pp. 110–11.
69. Ibid., p. 166.

broader concept of a computerized real-time command and control system.

MIT's conflict with ONR touched on various sensitive issues. One unstated issue must certainly have been the large fraction of public research funds for computers going to MIT. During World War II, MIT had expanded enormously, as research projects funded by the OSRD, largely run by professionals with MIT connections, had poured into the institute. MIT was the largest single recipient of wartime research contracts; its $56.0 million in contracts with the OSRD ran about 20 percent of the nearly $0.25 billion in wartime research conducted by educational institutions and was a significant fraction of the $1.0 billion going to industrial firms.[70] It must have been especially galling to established members of academic mathematical circles to be in a close competition for research dollars with a group of young, largely unknown MIT engineers, with no real finished product to show for their efforts yet.

Top MIT scientists and administrators lobbied for the Whirlwind project with the Navy, but, finally, ONR restrained the funding. The final appropriation for fiscal 1949 was $1.2 million, and the fiscal 1950 budget was trimmed back to $750,000. By this time, MIT had turned to the Air Force with its vision of an air traffic control system, and the Whirlwind project had been given a smaller $122,000 study grant in 1949. A special ad hoc panel reviewed the MIT project and concluded in 1950 that the Whirlwind computer, its original flight simulator objective all but forgotten, lacked a suitable mission.

The Russian thermonuclear test of 1949 had occurred by this time, however, and the Air Force was alarmed about the possibility of a Soviet bomber attack on the United States. The outbreak of the Korean War in 1950 had made the perceived need for an air defense system even more urgent, and the Air Force stepped in to support the Whirlwind project just as the Navy phased out its funding. Of the fiscal 1951 expenditures of more than $900,000, about $600,000 came from the Air Force, the remainder from the Navy. From this time forward, the Air Force's air defense needs dominated computer development at MIT.[71]

---

70. Penick and others, *Politics of American Science*, p. 100.

71. The Navy continued promoting the development of computer science at MIT well into the 1950s, though. MIT had established a Center for Machine Computation, directed by Professor Philip M. Morse, to supervise the use of computing machines at MIT, which included Whirlwind, when it was not being used for air defense studies.

In the atmosphere of crisis prevailing in 1951, the Air Force commissioned Project Charles, a study at MIT of the feasibility of a continental air defense system against long-range bombers. The report issued in the fall of 1950 supported the concept, and MIT set up Project Lincoln, or the Lincoln Laboratories, as a semiautonomous[72] large-scale research and development facility, dedicated to the development of an air defense system. The Whirlwind computer development team was absorbed into this lab and moved away from the MIT campus shortly thereafter, though the original Whirlwind remained on campus. The computer work became a component of the Semi-Automated Ground Environment air defense system (SAGE) developed during the 1950s, and the Lincoln/MIT/IBM SAGE computers contributed greatly to the technological development of the infant U.S. computer industry.

Subsystems of Whirlwind gradually began coming to life in 1949, and by 1951 the entire central machine was functioning.[73] The Whirlwind machine pushed computer technology forward in several, important areas. The development of high-speed electronic logic made the Whirlwind much faster than other machines of its day and a big influence on other computer projects. Its developers devised techniques for checking the integrity of vacuum tube circuit components that vastly increased the reliability of systems using tubes. Graphic display technology was pioneered in devices employing cathode ray tubes (CRTs) that tracked the aircraft position data pouring in and out of the machine. New types of digital switches, including the supercooled cryotron, were developed as a by-product of the research effort.[74]

The center received $650,000 from ONR in 1951, $250,000 in 1952, and $285,000 in 1953. Later allocations were much smaller, although the National Science Foundation began to fund computer facilities and research at MIT after these grants were phased out. See Redmond and Smith, *Project Whirlwind*, pp. 156–58.

MIT had also begun another computer project funded by the Rockefeller Foundation after the war, apparently to draw Norbert Wiener, who refused to work on military research after the war, into computer development. When Wiener showed little interest, MIT returned the funds and concentrated on the Whirlwind project. Karl L. Wildes, "Electrical Engineering at the Massachusetts Institute of Technology," unpublished manuscript, chap. 5, pp. 127–31.

72. Located in Lincoln, Massachusetts, the laboratories were far from MIT's home base in Cambridge.

73. See Everett, "Whirlwind," p. 372.

74. The cryotron, invented by Dudley Buck while working on Project Whirlwind, was the direct forerunner of work on supercooled circuit elements that led to the invention and development of the Josephson Junction. See Redmond and Smith, *Project*

Perhaps the most important development emerging from Whirlwind was the ferrite core memory. A fast and reliable technology for storing data to be accessed frequently by the main processing unit of a computer, so-called primary memory, was a principal goal of early technology development efforts. Eckert and Mauchly and others building "EDVAC-type" serial computers used mercury acoustic delay lines for primary memory, but these were slow and prone to breakdown.[75] Attention then turned to using some form of cathode ray tube for storage, which would have the advantage of making stored data accessible randomly, that is, without having to move through successive locations in memory to reach a desired storage location, as was the case with acoustic delay lines.[76]

As part of its collaboration with Princeton on the IAS computer, RCA developed a special cathode ray tube to be used as a random access memory. Though the project was closely related to RCA's principal postwar research focus, color television, the work was difficult and progress slow; RCA's Selectron memory tube was not produced in quantity until 1951.[77] F. C. Williams, at Manchester University, however, devised a technique for using an ordinary CRT as a storage device in 1947, and variants on the "Williams tube" soon showed up in designs for computer memories, and finally, in the IAS computer. Forrester's group at MIT had devised its own rather complex variant on a CRT memory, but it, like Williams' design, suffered from problems with reliability.

Whirlwind, p. 216; Pugh, *Memories*, p. 216; and Snyder, "Influence of U.S. Cryptologic Organizations," pp. 25–27. The NSA funded a $25 million electronics research effort in the late 1950s known as Project Lightning, which included continued work on supercooled switching devices. Later research at IBM on the Josephson Junction was also partially funded by NSA. See Snyder, "Computer Advances," pp. 67–69.

75. William Shockley, who later developed the transistor and shared in the Nobel Prize awarded for its invention, invented the acoustic delay line during the war. The line was used as a temporary storage device for radar data being displayed on a CRT. Eckert and Mauchly were introduced to the concept of a delay line through Eckert's work on a Moore School subcontract from MIT's Radiation Laboratories, which supervised wartime radar work in the United States. See Stern, *From ENIAC to UNIVAC*, p. 60; Hodges, *Alan Turing*, p. 315; and Arthur W. Burks, "From ENIAC to the Stored-Program Computer: Two Revolutions in Computers," in Metropolis and others, *A History of Computing*, p. 336.

76. A random access memory (RAM) is now commonly and cheaply implemented in semiconductor integrated circuits.

77. See Jan Rajchman, "Early Research on Computers at RCA," in Metropolis and others, *A History of Computing*, p. 468; see also Hodges, *Alan Turing*, p. 321; and Pugh, *Memories*, pp. 35–37.

In 1949 Forrester had begun to work on alternatives to CRT memories, in particular, on a memory device using rings (or cores) of ferromagnetic material, where a binary digit would be stored by setting the magnetic flux of the ring.[78] Forrester was not the only one investigating this idea; An Wang, working on Howard Aiken's computer project at Harvard, had set out a description of a storage device using this principle in late 1949, and Jan A. Rajchman had explored similar concepts at RCA that same year.[79] Forrester's concept was technically superior to the others, however, and was developed and improved as the memory for Whirlwind's successors, the SAGE air defense computers.[80]

Core memories were the technology of choice for fast primary memory for a long time—from the mid-1950s through the early 1970s, when semiconductor integrated circuits began to be used on a large scale. To this day, they continue to be used in extreme environments or when power supplies are liable to be interrupted, as in defense systems. This great advance in computer technology was perhaps the most important legacy of Whirlwind.

Howard Aiken and the Harvard Computers

MIT was not the only influence on computer technology with headquarters in Cambridge, Massachusetts. Harvard University had been involved since 1939. A young instructor of physics, Howard Aiken, had worked with IBM on a project to build an electromechanical programmable calculator, which came to be known as the Harvard Mark I. Aiken was responsible for the overall architecture of the machine, while IBM developed its components and did the systems engineering; the machine was to be donated to Harvard by IBM.

78. The material used in the ferrite cores, called Deltamax, was developed in Germany during the war and brought back to the United States by the military along with the machinery and tooling used to produce it. See Pugh, *Memories*, pp. 39–40. As was true for the magnetic drum memory, German technology contributed to U.S. advances in ferromagnetics in the late 1940s. See Jan Rajchman, "Recollections of Memories from RCA in the Fifties," *Computer Museum Report*, vol. 13 (Summer 1985), pp. 11–13.

79. Pugh, *Memories*, pp. 39, 81–89; and Rajchman, "Early Research," p. 465–69.

80. Pugh, *Memories*, pp. 34–57, describes how early core memories were developed and improved upon in many places, including IBM, in the early 1950s. Eventually, MIT and IBM jointly produced core memories on the SAGE project. Ibid., pp. 93–128.

Construction dragged on well beyond the estimated two years and $100,000 originally budgeted. After the war started, Aiken was inducted into the Navy and put to work on the Navy's computational needs. IBM delivered the machine to Harvard in 1944, where it was taken over by Aiken and the Navy. But relations between Aiken and IBM's president, Thomas J. Watson, Sr., had deteriorated over issues of credit and public claims to the invention of the machine, and IBM and Aiken parted company in a cloud of acrimony.

Aiken went on to design more programmable calculators and computers in his Harvard laboratory after the war. From 1945 to 1947 he built the Mark II for the Navy; it was installed at the Naval Proving Ground in Dahlgren, Virginia, and used in ballistics research. In 1949 the Mark III was finished and again installed in the Navy's Dahlgren research facility. In 1952 the last of this series of machines was finished, though the Mark IV was paid for by and delivered to the U.S. Air Force.[81]

The Harvard Mark series of machines had a fairly small impact on contemporary computer technology. Aiken, conservative in his designs, stressed reliability and the use of proven technologies. Thus both the Mark I and II were electromechanical machines, using relays and rotating counters. The Mark III used a magnetic drum and introduced some electronic circuitry. The Mark IV made use of ferrite core memories, electronic tubes and diodes, as well as relays. Because of the technological conservatism, though, all these machines were slow, even by the standards of the day.

Aiken had a larger impact on computer design and use, however, because of the great number of his graduate students and associates who went on from Harvard to other computer activities. With ONR support, Aiken offered a graduate training course in computing machinery in 1947 and 1948, held symposia, and produced books on scientific computing.[82]

The students and associates of Aiken had a particularly important effect. An Wang, who had worked on ferrite core memories in Aiken's lab at Harvard, after receiving his Ph.D. in 1948, left to start Wang Laboratories in 1951, now a significant force in the U.S. computer

81. M. R. Williams, "Howard Aiken and the Harvard Computation Laboratory," *Annals of the History of Computing*, vol. 6 (April 1984), pp. 157–61.

82. See Mina Rees, "The Computing Program of the Office of Naval Research, 1946–1953," *Annals of the History of Computing*, vol. 4 (April 1982), pp. 105–06.

industry.[83] Richard M. Bloch and a group of veterans of the Harvard Computation Laboratory joined Raytheon and helped make Raytheon one of the important computer companies of the late 1940s and early 1950s.[84]

Other graduate students were influential elsewhere. Grace Hopper, who had learned to program the Mark I with Aiken at Harvard during the war, developed important software for Eckert and Mauchly's UNIVAC I and pioneered language standards and the Cobol programming language later in the 1950s. Kenneth E. Iverson and Frederick P. Brooks, Jr., after studying under Aiken, later developed important software at IBM.[85]

Computers at Bell Labs

The Bell Telephone Laboratories, where George R. Stibitz had pioneered relay computers in the United States in the late 1930s, were an important focus for computer development during and after the war. Stibitz's Model I, completed by S. B. Williams in 1939, was actually a programmable relay calculator and was the first machine known to offer access to remote users, by way of teletype stations. Models 2 through 4 were built during the war; Model 3 was a big step forward in power and programmability and came much closer to the modern conception of a digital computer.[86] These machines read in their program on paper tape

83. W. David Gardner, "An Wang's Early Work in Core Memories," *Datamation*, vol. 22 (March 1976), pp. 161–64; and Pugh, *Memories*, p. 88.

84. Raytheon's Hurricane computer (later renamed the RAYDAC), one of the large computer projects pushing toward completion in the late 1940s, suffered serious delays. It was to be used for guidance in a missile-based coastal defense network manned by the Navy, but only one was built. Saul Rosen, "Electronic Computers: A Historical Survey," *Computing Surveys*, vol. 1 (March 1969), p. 15. Stephen Christian Lutze, "The Formation of the International Computer Industry, 1945–60" (M.A. dissertation, University of California, Santa Barbara, June 1979), pp 28–29. Richard M. Bloch, with Murray Ellis and Robert Campbell, had worked on Howard Aiken's relay computers at Harvard before joining the Raytheon project. See Williams, "Howard Aiken," pp. 158–59.

85. See Williams, "Howard Aiken," p. 159.

86. See George R. Stibitz, "Early Computers," pp. 479–83; W. A. Atherton, *From Compass to Computer* (San Francisco Press, 1984), p. 278; and M. D. Fagen, ed., *A History of Science and Technology in the Bell Laboratories*, vol. 2: *National Service in War and Peace* (Murray Hill, N.J.: Bell Telephone Laboratories, 1978), pp. 163–71.

and were remarkably reliable, but orders of magnitude slower than the electronic machines under development elsewhere.

Bell had also worked on cryptanalytical machinery during the war. A large electromechanical machine named Madam X, built for the Army Signal Corps, performed many of the functions of the Navy bombe, but in a more flexible fashion. Up to 144 units were hooked together in a network of sorts.[87]

After the war, Bell labs built two true general purpose, digital relay computers, the Models 5 and 6. These machines set new standards in durability and reliability and were notable for implementing floating-point arithmetic, useful in scientific computation, in their hardware to speed up scientific calculations. They were far slower than the electronic computers of the early 1950s, though. Bell labs directed its research resources out of computers and into other areas, notably solid state electronics, in the late 1940s and early 1950s. After the transistor was invented within its ranks, however, Bell once again turned to the development of computer hardware and developed transistor computers in the mid-1950s.

IBM in the Late 1940s

In the late 1940s, IBM, along with major competitors in the business machine industry, saw little reason to concentrate resources in a new and speculative activity like electronic computers. Sales personnel in the field were frantically pressing for new and improved models of the current punched card equipment line.

Ironically, IBM's first large-scale venture into the computer area was inspired more by the dispute with Aiken over credit for the Mark I than by any vision of the computer as a long-range business opportunity. Thomas J. Watson, Sr., rankled by Aiken's plans to build successors to the Mark I independently of IBM, started constructing a machine to be known as the Selective Sequence Electronic Calculator (SSEC) soon after the Harvard Mark I was completed.[88] IBM had built relay calcula-

87. Telephone interview with Howard Campaigne, August 1, 1985.

88. See Pugh, *Memories*, pp. 6–11; and Bashe, "The SSEC," p. 304. The feeling was apparently mutual. Aiken vowed not to use any IBM peripherals on his machines and instead installed Western Union teletype printers, paper-tape readers, and punches on the Harvard Mark II. See Ralph A. Niemann, *Dahlgren's Participation in the Development of Computer Technology* (Dahlgren, Va.: Naval Surface Weapons Center, 1982), p. 9.

tors for the Aberdeen and Dahlgren ballistics laboratories during and after the war that were faster than the Mark I, but smaller in capacity.[89] The SSEC was designed to be both bigger and faster than the Mark I— IBM press releases pointed out that arithmetic operations on the SSEC were at least 250 times faster than on the Mark I.[90]

A former assistant of Aiken's, Rex R. Seeber, heavily influenced the SSEC's architecture. Seeber had left the Mark I project after a dispute with Aiken over Seeber's proposal that future models from the Harvard labs be designed to modify their own programming while running, which Aiken had thought unnecessary. Seeber joined IBM and successfully promoted the idea, so the SSEC consequently became the first calculating machine with a dynamically modifiable program.[91] Although the arithmetic unit of the SSEC did incorporate some of the new ideas about electronic circuits, in order to gain computational speed, the bulk of the machine used the older electromechanical wheels and relays technology. The SSEC was more in the tradition of the Mark I than an electronic digital computer as conceived by Eckert, Mauchly, and von Neumann. Inaugurated in 1948, newer technologies soon eclipsed the SSEC and it was dismantled in 1952 to make room for the Model 701, IBM's first true electronic digital computer.

IBM's 701 grew out of a different set of circumstances. After the war, Ralph L. Palmer had returned to IBM from NCML, where he had worked in engineering electronic cryptological machinery for the Navy and had been exposed to the same state-of-the-art electronics technology that had inspired the founders of ERA to go into the computer business.[92]

89. Hurd, "Computer Development at IBM," p. 397; and Bashe, "The SSEC," p. 302. See Niemann, *Dahlgren's Participation*, pp. 3–4.

90. Pugh, *Memories*, p. 7; and Hurd, "Computer Development at IBM," p. 397.

91. R. Moreau, *The Computer Comes of Age: The People, the Hardware, and the Software* (MIT Press, 1984), pp. 39–41, and Bashe, "The SSEC," pp. 310–11, argue that the SSEC was the first computing machine with an internally stored program. Hurd is less generous in his analysis. Hurd, "Computer Development at IBM," p. 397. See also Pugh, *Memories*, pp. 7–11. Since the SSEC generally read in its programming from paper tape, it could punch out tapes and then read in as a program what it had just punched. This is not quite what most analysts have in mind when they refer to an internally stored program. Its electronic and relay memory was limited, and though instructions stored internally were modifiable (and therefore can be considered an internally stored program), the machine operated principally from its externally stored (on paper tape or cards) program.

92. Another key IBM engineer, Stephen W. Dunwell, had worked for OP-20-G's counterpart in the Army Signal Corps. Dunwell also was a leader in IBM's efforts in electronics, and later he directed the development of IBM's Stretch supercomputer in

During the war, IBM had started a small laboratory and factory in Poughkeepsie, New York, to build equipment for "a government need."[93] In this small lab, and not in IBM's main research facility in Endicott, Palmer began to build an electronics group for IBM after he was mustered out of the service. While the engineers in IBM's main Endicott facility, who were well versed in the older electromechanical technology, worked at building the newer relay computers, including the SSEC, and improving IBM's traditional line of accounting machinery, Palmer's development group in Poughkeepsie worked on perfecting electronic circuitry and introducing it into traditional business machines. A series of electronic calculating machines introduced by IBM in the late 1940s resulted from this effort.[94]

In 1948 Palmer's Poughkeepsie lab began aggressive recruiting; the crop of young engineers who joined IBM over the next several years were the technical leadership that propelled IBM into its place as a computing power in the 1950s and 1960s. Palmer's electronics group more than doubled in size in 1949 alone.[95]

IBM's entry into computer production was delayed, however. The company viewed its natural area of concentration as electric accounting machines, which were quite profitable. Managers saw no commercial market for computers. Top engineering management, when evaluating

---

the late 1950s. See Bashe and others, *IBM's Early Computers*, pp. 60, 61, 174. Other prominent IBM engineers exposed to wartime advances in military cryptology included Max Femmer, David Crawford, and Philip Fox. See Erich Bloch, "Remarks," presented at the Computer Museum, Boston, June 15, 1986, p. 36; and Pugh, *Memories*, p. 35.

93. Hurd, "Computer Development at IBM," p. 402.

94. The first electronic calculator produced by IBM, the IBM 603, was the fruit of the small electronics research effort that had been started before the war. It was produced in limited quantities, then replaced by the IBM 604, designed at Poughkeepsie. The plug-programmable 604 was introduced in 1948. The electronic calculator line reached a new level of functionality with the introduction of the Card-Programmed Calculator (CPC), in 1949, which consisted of a 604 tied to an IBM 405 accounting machine. The CPC, in effect a card-programmable version of the 604, was engineered by IBM at Endicott in response to a request from the Northrop Aircraft Company. The CPC was a success; about 250 were installed during the 1949–52 period. See ibid., p. 400; Phelps, "Early Electronic Computer," pp. 258–64; and Bashe and others, "IBM's Early Computers," pp. 34, 44–72.

95. Among the young recruits joining IBM over this period were Charles J. Bashe, who headed the engineering team on the IBM 702 computer, Nathaniel Rochester, who came to IBM from the MIT Whirlwind project and was a key figure in the 701 design, Gene Amdahl, chief designer of the System 360, Erich Bloch, who headed the Stretch design team, and Bob O. Evans, head of the 360 project and later IBM's chief engineer. See Bashe and others, *IBM's Early Computers*, p. 118.

the possibility of constructing electronic computers for the NBS computer program, urged management not to enter the activity, on the grounds that it might endanger IBM's patent position. Instead, they counseled the head of the company, Thomas J. Watson, Sr., to maintain enough of a development effort to recognize significant external innovations when they occurred and to adopt them quickly in IBM products.[96]

Within the company, though, Watson, Sr.'s heir apparent, Thomas Watson, Jr., pushed for IBM's entry into electronic computers. IBM produced the 603 calculator, its first postwar electronic machine, as a direct result of the younger Watson's persistent advocacy of electronics. Watson, Jr., and the young engineers Palmer had brought into the company had struggled to gain approval for a high-speed computer project, using magnetic tape for input and output and electronic memory. This experimental project, called the Tape Processing Machine (TPM), became IBM's first computer project at the end of 1949.[97]

In 1950, when the Korean War began, Watson, Sr., pledged the company's resources to support the war effort. After IBM personnel had surveyed the government's computing needs, Watson, Jr., convinced his father that enough government demand existed to support the production of twenty special purpose computing machines for the war effort. Engineers were then pulled from the TPM project and assigned to what came to be known as the IBM Defense Calculator, later renamed the 701. The 701, funded by IBM in anticipation of a healthy volume of government sales, was completed in under a year and a half and was demonstrated in the spring of 1952.

The 701 used important parts of the TPM technology and was modeled on the logical structure of the IAS computer. Other important influences came from the MIT Whirlwind project and the English computer groups.[98] Nineteen 701s were built by 1954. They were rented for $20,000 a month, when the monthly rate for other IBM machines was $300 or so.[99] The first 701s came out after Eckert and Mauchly's UNIVAC computers were already attracting commercial interest. Racing to catch up, IBM under Watson, Jr., poured resources into the development of its computer business.

96. Pugh, *Memories*, p. 26.

97. Ibid., pp. 27–29; and Phelps, "Early Electronic Computer," pp. 264–65.

98. Phelps, "Early Electronic Computer," pp. 265–66; and C. J. Bashe and others, "The Architecture of IBM's Early Computers," *IBM Journal of Research and Development*, vol. 25 (September 1981), p. 363.

99. Evans, "IBM System/360," p. 10.

The TPM became the IBM 702, IBM's first business-oriented machine, delivered in 1954, and heavily influenced by the IAS computer. Its overall performance was generally considered inferior to that of the UNIVAC, and an improved model, the 705, was announced that same year. An improved version of the scientifically oriented 701 also entered the commercial market as the 704 in 1954. Both these lines of development came from the Poughkeepsie lab. The Endicott lab meanwhile developed a design for a small business-oriented machine, the IBM 650, announced in 1953. The 650 was the first mass-produced computer—more than a thousand were sold. Even for the 650, the most purely "commercial" of the first generation of computers, projected governmental demand played a crucial role in the decision to produce the machine.[100] The Endicott laboratory continued to lead in designing small, cheap computers, including the IBM 1401, "the Model T of the computer industry," of which more than twelve thousand were eventually shipped after 1958.[101]

The West Coast Computer Industry

The aerospace firms of Southern California were the last major group in industry significant in the early development of computers.[102] Aircraft design had, and has, enormous computational requirements, which make it a prime customer for leading-edge scientific computers. The new computing technology was also applied to command and control applications—aircraft and missile guidance and interception, in particular. In the late 1940s these activities centered on Northrop Aircraft, which needed a guidance computer for its Snark missile, and Raytheon, which was testing a control computer at the Navy's facilities at Point Mugu, California.

100. Hurd, "Computer Development at IBM," p. 408, notes that a pledge by IBM's Washington office to sell fifty machines to government users greatly helped to launch the product.

101. Evans, "IBM System/360," pp. 11–12. The 650 was a magnetic drum computer and relied on the magnetic drum concepts developed at ERA and licensed to IBM as part of the technology interchange discussed earlier.

102. This discussion draws heavily on Richard E. Sprague, "A Western View of Computer History," *Communications of the Association for Computing Machinery*, vol. 15 (July 1972), pp. 686–94; Fred J. Gruenberger, "A Short History of Digital Computing in Southern California," *Annals of the History of Computing*, vol. 2 (July 1980), pp. 246–50; and Lutze, "Formation," pp. 79–81. Unpublished interviews with John Alrich, James Cass, Stanley Frankel, Jerry Mendelson, and Emmett Quady by Robina Mapstone in 1972 and 1973, found in the Smithsonian Institution, were also consulted.

The design group was located on the premises at Northrop, which had contracted outside with Eckert and Mauchly for the ill-starred BINAC computer. The computer group within Northrop designed a series of digital differential analyzers to solve the equations required for missile guidance and contracted with a small California firm named Hewlett-Packard to build the devices. In 1950 a large group of these engineers, after unsuccessfully attempting to get Northrop to set up a computer division, left the company and formed the Computer Research Corporation (CRC). With aerospace company and Air Force funding, this group designed and built general purpose magnetic drum computers in the early 1950s.

Like many of the small technology-based companies just described, CRC eventually ran into financial difficulties. In 1953 it was sold to NCR, which after initial hesitation, had become interested in producing computers for the business market. By 1955 most of the original founders of CRC had left to work in other small high-tech start-ups.

Northrop eventually sold its remaining computer operations to Bendix Aviation, which produced the popular, small G-15 computer. Bendix benefited not only from acquisition of Northrop's computer operations, but also from association with a computer research group at UCLA headed by Harry Huskey, who had worked on both the ENIAC and a British computer project and designed the G-15. After a short time, many of the original Northrop personnel left to start their own computer firm, Logistics Research Corporation, which designed and built its ALWAC line of small magnetic drum computers. Logistics Research, in turn, was sold to El-Tronics. Another group left Bendix to form Packard-Bell computers in the mid-1950s, and from these roots, in turn, came Scientific Data Systems, one of the main developers of the minicomputer.[103]

Yet another group of computer designers in close contact with the Northrop group worked at Caltech in the late 1940s, under partial ONR sponsorship. A Caltech researcher designed the MINAC, a design renamed the LGP-30 and built by the Librascope division of General Precision in 1956.[104] Like the Bendix G-15, the LGP-30 was one of the

103. Lutze, "Formation," pp. 129–30; Reminiscences of Jerry Mendelson for Henry Tropp, December 18, 1972, available in the Smithsonian Institution, Washington, D.C.; interview with Mendelson by Robina Mapstone, September 6, 1972, available in the Smithsonian Institution, Washington, D.C.

104. The designer of the MINAC/LGP-30 was Stanley Frankel. Interview with James Cass by Robina Mapstone, December 18, 1972, available in the Smithsonian Institution, Washington, D.C. Librascope's involvement in computing began when it devised a

early small computers in quantity production whose success inspired the minicomputer—more than five hundred of the LGP-30s were built.[105] Control Data acquired both Bendix and Librascope in the early 1960s, and these products were important in Control Data's minicomputer line.

Another firm in California, the Consolidated Electrodynamics Corporation (CEC) formed a computer division in the early 1950s. Drawing on the services of a Norwegian researcher at Caltech who had worked on computer projects, at IAS and in England, CEC designed and built a significant series of computers in the middle of the 1950s.[106] CEC's Electrodata computer division was bought out by Burroughs in 1956, and a computer designed at CEC, the Datatron 205, became the Burroughs 205, the first solid commercial success to make Burroughs influential in the computer business.[107]

Several other companies on the West Coast participated in important computer developments. Hughes Aircraft built military computers before quitting the business in the mid-1950s, and the Rand Corporation built a version of the IAS computer, the JOHNNIAC (named in honor of von Neumann). North American Aviation's Autonetics division, United Aircraft's computer division, and TRW were also participants. The key element in these efforts was the fluid movement of talented engineers from one aerospace patron to another and into start-ups that often survived only long enough to be acquired by a larger firm. In the

---

replacement for the electromechanical computing equipment used in the Norden bombsight.

105. Interview with Cass by Robina Mapstone, December 18, 1972. One major use for these machines was in early process control applications. See Alvin J. Harman, *The International Computer Industry: Innovation and Comparative Advantage* (Harvard University Press, 1971), p. 11.

106. The first CEC Datatron was a fairly advanced computer. The Datatron had index registers, floating-point arithmetic, and magnetic tape input and output. See Moreau, *Computer*, p. 62. IBM thought the Datatron significant competition for its model 650 when it first came on the market. Hurd, "Computer Development at IBM," pp. 407–08. The designer of the original CEC Datatron computer was Norwegian scientist Ernst Selmer, who did the work while on a guest lectureship at Caltech. Selmer apparently was inspired to put index registers in his design through a conversation with Harry Huskey. Interview with John Alrich by Robina Mapstone, February 9, 1973, available in the Smithsonian Institution, Washington, D.C.; and interview with Stanley Frankel by Robina Mapstone, October 5, 1972, available in the Smithsonian Institution, Washington, D.C.

107. See Moreau, *Computer*, p. 62; Fisher and others, *IBM and the U.S. Data Processing Industry*, pp. 79–81; and Barbara Goody Katz and Almarin Philips, "The Computer Industry," in Richard R. Nelson, ed., *Government and Technical Progress: A Cross-Industry Analysis* (Pergamon Press, 1982), pp. 162–232.

longer run, the activities of these aerospace-based firms led to the development of the minicomputer.

The aerospace companies, and the military services that procured their products, were the key customers for the early commercial computer manufacturers building large-scale mainframe computers. A request from the computer group at Northrop, for example, led IBM to build the Card-Programmed Calculator (CPC) in 1948.[108] These engineers also made advances in software that were a critical part of the general advance in computing technology in the 1950s. Aerospace industry users of the IBM 701 formed the predecessor to the SHARE IBM users organization and contributed much to the development of a useful software base for scientific and engineering applications.

Battling over National Policy: The National Bureau of Standards

Conflict over a new and emerging American concern—organizing and managing investments in the development of science and technology—appeared on many fronts in the late 1940s. Key players in the military first tried to convince established businesses and investment bankers that a new and potentially profitable business opportunity was presenting itself. They did not succeed, and, consequently, the Defense Department committed itself to financing an enormously expensive development program for new technologies—like the electronic computer—in which the military had a special interest.

Another skirmish was fought by those who dwelled on the connection between public investment in technology and private profit. During the wartime scientific mobilization, Senator Harley Kilgore of West Virginia had begun arguing in Congress that federal research funds should be distributed more evenly among researchers. He also believed that the entire nation "owned" research paid for by federal funds. Many supporters of the New Deal embraced a corollary to Kilgore's "populist" position by arguing that the results of federal research programs should be made available widely and quickly, particularly to smaller businesses.

Within the executive branch, the populist vision of American science policy found a home in the Commerce Department and its new secretary, Henry A. Wallace, during the last days of the war. Within the Commerce Department, the National Bureau of Standards (NBS) attempted to

108. See Phelps, "Early Electronic Computer Developments at IBM," p. 264.

transform its role from a traditional position as arbiter of weights, measures, and other standards to a new position as manager of a broad industrial research program designed to assist American industry in exploiting wartime advances in science and technology. Eventually, NBS would become directly involved in the birth of the computer.

Like most of the American scientific community, the NBS laboratories were drafted into weapons development during the war.[109] After the war, NBS, using funds transferred to it by the Defense Department, continued to do a great deal of weapons-related research. Its involvement in computers initially began at the instigation of the Navy.[110] Under the sponsorship of the Army Ordnance Department, NBS had also started a program to develop improved components for digital computers.[111] In 1946 NBS had assisted the newly formed U.S. Office of Naval Research in contracting with Raytheon to build a machine for Navy use. The NBS laboratories also began development of input-output equipment for the IAS project during this period.[112]

The fledgling NBS computer development effort was institutionalized in 1947 with the establishment of the National Applied Mathematics Laboratory (NAML) within its ranks. The first chief of the NAML, John Curtiss, rapidly involved the lab in diverse activities supporting the drive to build electronic computers.

In 1948 one of the first official tasks of the NAML was to evaluate Eckert and Mauchly's proposal to build a computer for the Census Bureau. NBS was given the responsibilities for selecting a supplier for the Census machine and supervising its development. NBS approved the purchase from Eckert and Mauchly, as well as the acquisition of two more UNIVACs, one for the Air Force's Air Materiel Command, and one for the NAML's own facilities. When the Eckert-Mauchly Corporation failed a security clearance in 1948,[113] and the Air Materiel Com-

109. See Rexmond C. Cochrane, *Measures for Progress: A History of the National Bureau of Standards*, U.S. Department of Commerce, National Bureau of Standards (GPO, 1966), p. 431.

110. See Harry D. Huskey, "The SWAC: The National Bureau of Standards Western Automatic Computer," in Metropolis and others, *A History of Computing*, p. 419; and Huskey, "The National Bureau of Standards," pp. 111–12.

111. S. N. Alexander, "Introduction," in *Computer Development (SEAC and DYSEAC) at the National Bureau of Standards*, NBS Circular 551 (GPO, 1955), pp. 1–3.

112. Slutz, "Memories of the Bureau," p. 472.

113. Huskey, "The National Bureau of Standards," p. 112. Stern, *From ENIAC to*

mand declined to support the Eckert-Mauchly purchase, NBS began negotiations with Raytheon to supply a version of the computer Raytheon was building for the Navy in its place. In the late 1940s NBS also assisted the Army Security Agency in designing and constructing ABNER, a cryptological computer, and in negotiating UNIVAC purchases for the Air Comptroller's Office and the Army Map Service.[114]

Around 1948 it became clear that the continual delays in the various computer projects going at that time, which included the machines being developed by Eckert and Mauchly, the EDVAC at the Moore School, the MIT Whirlwind, the IAS computer at Princeton, Raytheon's project, and the machines that ERA was known to be working on, were making them fall further and further behind schedule, with no completion date in sight. At that point, at the urging of George Dantzig, who was developing applications of linear programming to economic problems for the Air Force, the Office of the Air Comptroller decided to fund the development of an interim computer as a stopgap measure.[115] Thus was born the NBS Interim Computer, renamed the Standards Eastern Automatic Computer (SEAC) when it became the first operational electronic digital stored-program computer in regular operation in the United States in the spring of 1950.[116]

Shortly thereafter, another decision was made to build a second NBS computer, using odd scraps of leftover funding, at the Institute of Numerical Analysis at the University of California, Los Angeles, which was being set up as one of the four divisions of the NAML. An explicit objective was to test completely different design concepts in this second

UNIVAC, pp. 112–14. Eckert and Mauchly were cleared, but only after losing the chance to land several important government contracts.

114. Snyder, "Influence of U.S. Cryptologic Organizations," p. 10. It is worth noting the apparent difference in internal technological capability between the U.S. Navy codebreakers, who had invested heavily in internal development of new technology during the war, and the U.S. Army cryptologists, who had largely relied on off-the-shelf punched card machinery and special devices built by IBM and the Bell labs. When the emerging role of computers in cryptology became clear at the end of the war, the Army had to rely on outside consultants in developing its most secret apparatus. See Stern, *From ENIAC to UNIVAC*, p. 113; and Huskey, "The National Bureau of Standards," p. 112.

115. Alexander, *Computer Development (SEAC and DYSEAC)*, p. 1; and Slutz, "Memories of the Bureau," p. 473.

116. This claim ignores the Eckert-Mauchly BINAC, which passed initial factory tests in 1949 but never functioned in a satisfactory manner at its final installation site. Stern, *From ENIAC to UNIVAC*, p. 129.

computer, which came to be known as the Standards Western Automatic Computer (SWAC).

After SEAC was built, new additions to the machine were constantly being devised and attached to the existing structures. The NBS used the SEAC program as a vehicle for designing and testing a whole series of experimental computers and peripherals, including the first magnetic disk drive.[117] Ambitious plans were in the works when the NBS was forced to halt its rapid expansion in 1953.

The NBS computing program was caught up in the political debate over postwar science policy, and seemingly minor incidents used to demolish its ambitious industrial research agenda. Troubles had begun in 1947, when the head of the NBS, Dr. Edward V. Condon, who had been active in the Manhattan project and the MIT Radiation Laboratories during the war, had come under attack from individuals on the House Committee on Un-American Activities for associating with alleged Soviet espionage agents.[118] Condon resigned in 1951 and joined the private sector as director of research at Corning Glass. John Curtiss, head of the NAML, also came under attack during this period and was forced out in 1953.[119]

The incident that finally destroyed the NBS computer program, ironically, had nothing to do with computers or any other technical issue. The NBS had been aggressively expanding its functions in testing the claims of products to be used by government agencies. In this tradition, the bureau from time to time would issue circulars summarizing the results of its efforts and making them available to the taxpayer. In 1949, after testing battery additives (which it found worthless), an official of the NBS identified one additive, "AD-X2," by name in a letter to the

117. Designed by Jacob Rabinow, the NBS magnetic disk assembly inspired the later development of the first commercial disk storage system at IBM's San Jose laboratories. See Bashe and others, *IBM's Early Computers*, pp. 279–80. Other notable examples included the input-output systems built for the IAS computer, the DYSEAC process-control computer, which was fitted into two mobile vans and pioneered the use of external interrupts; the AMOS IV weather forecasting computer; the unfinished multiple processor "Pilot" computer, and the FOSDIC optical character scanning machine. See A. L. Leiner, S. N. Alexander, and R. P. Witt, "DYSEAC," in Alexander, *Computer Development (SEAC and DYSEAC)*, pp. 39–40; and Martin H. Weik, Jr., *A Third Survey of Domestic Electronic Digital Computing Systems*, BRL Report 1115 (Aberdeen, Md.: Aberdeen Proving Grounds, 1961), pp. 28, 234, 258.

118. Cochrane, *Measures for Progress*, pp. 485, 491–92.

119. John Todd, "John Hamilton Curtiss, 1909–1977," *Annals of the History of Computing*, vol. 2 (April 1980), pp. 107–08. See also Rees, "The Computing Program of the Office of Naval Research," pp. 100–03.

Better Business Bureau of Oakland, California.[120] The outraged manufacturer mounted a major political campaign in Congress and commissioned a study at MIT that appeared to support the claims made.[121]

The incoming Eisenhower administration temporarily suspended the acting director of the NBS and hastily ordered two advisory reports from the National Academy of Sciences—one on the merits of AD-X2, the other on the nature, organization, and funding of the bureau's expanded activities.

The latter report was issued first, in October 1953, and recommended the removal of all DOD-funded programs from the bureau and a reorientation of the bureau away from applied and developmental work, to basic research on physical constants and testing procedures. The secretary of commerce, Sinclair Weeks, immediately ordered the transfer of four major divisions of the bureau, including important electronics laboratories, to the ordnance laboratories of the armed forces. In subsequent months many other programs, including support for the NBS-supported computer group at the Institute for Numerical Analysis at UCLA, were ended.[122]

Since most of the computer work had been supported by funds transferred to NBS by the military services, and these were abruptly ended, computer development at the bureau suffered a traumatic blow from which it never recovered. In fiscal 1954, the NBS budget had been roughly halved and its staff cut from 4,600 to 2,800, the approximate level at which it was held through the remainder of the decade.[123]

The report on AD-X2, which was released in November of 1953, vindicated the bureau's work and concluded that the MIT tests were deficient in their design.[124] By this time, however, the reorganization of the NBS was well under way.

In retrospect the fundamental issue at stake in these proceedings had little to do with either the merits of battery additives or the acquaintance

120. The bureau later informed Congress that it had identified AD-X2 by name because its producers had claimed that previous statements by NBS did not apply to their product.

121. Cochrane, *Measures for Progress*, pp. 483–87.

122. Ibid., p. 497.

123. Ibid., p. 497, app. F. By 1959 the full-time staff had recovered only slightly, to 2,960. See National Research Council of the National Academy of Sciences, *The Role of the Department of Commerce in Science and Technology*, report to the secretary of commerce by a special advisory committee of the National Academy of Sciences (National Academy of Sciences, 1960), p. 83.

124. Cochrane, *Measures for Progress,* pp. 486–87.

of top NBS scientists with Russian and left-leaning American colleagues. The bureau had vastly expanded its research activities, explicitly intending to produce technological information to be used by small business and to stimulate the formation of new enterprises by popularizing the technical advances made during the war. In the computer contracts it had supervised for the government, the NBS had promoted the small and innovative start-ups dedicated to producing leading-edge technological products, particularly ERA and Eckert-Mauchly, over the slower-moving established industrial firms.[125]

From the viewpoint of Commerce Secretary Weeks, and the incoming administration, these activities meant too much meddling with the normal outcome of free market forces.[126] When Weeks had suspended the director of the NBS in the spring of 1953, he was quoted as saying, "The National Bureau of Standards has not been sufficiently objective because they discount entirely the play of the marketplace."[127]

Perhaps more important, at the time of these events, the first commercial computers (Eckert and Mauchly's UNIVAC, the ERA 1103, the IBM 701) were finally beginning to be offered in the marketplace. Pressures from the military services for a technical czar to push the development of the new machines for the use of the military establishment had subsided somewhat. Computer research at the NBS, decimated by these changes, struggled on with a meager budgetary diet. It was not until the late 1970s that the NBS began once more to build a significant computer research division, this time with a more explicit standardization agenda.[128]

Before losing the political fight, though, the NBS computer program

125. In a 1946 letter to the head of the A. C. Nielsen Company, which was interested in automating tabulation activities, John Curtiss had suggested that Nielsen "could send [his] men directly to two concerns whom I consider now the best ones to bet on among the small electronics outfits with brains (and I think such outfits may win the race). The Electronic Control Corp. (Eckert and Mauchly's firm) and Engineering Research Associates, Inc., St. Paul, Minn." Stern, *From ENIAC to UNIVAC*, pp. 142–43.

126. Weeks, a Massachusetts industrialist, had appointed the president of the Scheaffer Pen Company, Craig R. Scheaffer, as assistant secretary for domestic affairs. Scheaffer had reason for personal concern over the activities of the bureau. Relying on NBS tests, the Federal Trade Commission forced his firm to stop claiming that a Scheaffer pen lasted a lifetime. Cochrane, *Measures for Progress*, p. 485.

127. Ibid.

128. The fiscal 1979 budget for the NBS Institute for Computer Science and Technology (ICST) more than doubled the $4.5 million 1978 budget. But it has remained flat, at the $10 million, through the mid-1980s, and NBS continues to fight chronic attempts to trim back the ICST budget.

made some notable contributions to the state of the art. The SEAC built heavily on the components research that had been ongoing at the NBS in the previous few years. The objective was to get a simple, easily constructed machine with minimal complications in place as quickly as possible. It was based on the simple, serial EDVAC design, used mercury delay line memory—then the most reliable and tested memory technology—and adopted the general logical structure being used on the EDVAC project. Key engineers with experience on other projects were hired.[129] However, the circuit and logic design, and componentry, were entirely the product of the NBS.

The SEAC, besides being the first operational von Neumann-type stored-program computer in the United States, pioneered important technology concepts. All of the logic was implemented with newly developed germanium diodes (10,000 were used); the vacuum tubes within (750) were only for providing power and electrical pulse-shaping circuitry.[130] The computer also used standardized, replaceable circuit modules, an innovation soon adopted throughout the industry. Thus the first computer to use solid state logic was also the first modern computer to be completed in the United States.[131]

The SWAC, built under the direction of Harry Huskey was a higher-performance parallel computer with a Williams tube memory.[132] SWAC ran into trouble with its delicate and finicky CRT memory. It was switched to a magnetic drum unit as it was completed and was not fully operational until the middle of 1953.

Both SEAC and SWAC were built on budgetary shoestrings. SEAC was built in only two years, at an estimated cost of $188,000, while SWAC was budgeted at $170,000.[133] The other major computer projects described costs from three to ten times these magnitudes.

SEAC technology and design ideas influenced the construction of

129. Ralph J. Slutz was brought in from the IAS project, and Samuel Lubkin came from the EDVAC group. See Slutz, "Memories of the Bureau," pp. 427–73; and Huskey, "The National Bureau of Standards," pp. 419—31.

130. Slutz, "Memories of the Bureau," p. 473.

131. SEAC also seems to have been far more reliant on solid state circuitry than the more complex machines that followed. Martin H. Weik, *A Third Survey*, pp. 1072–75.

132. For a more complete account of the origins of the SWAC, see Huskey, "The SWAC," pp. 419–32; and Huskey, "The National Bureau of Standards," pp. 112–17.

133. These were the 1950 cost estimates reported by an ad hoc panel of the Defense Department's Research and Development Board, cited in Redmond and Smith, *Project Whirlwind*, p. 166.

other larger computers. These machines included the FLAC computer, built at the Air Force Missile Test Center in Florida, and the MIDAC computer at the Willow Run Research Center of the University of Michigan.[134] Computer designers in Europe and Japan also made use of the SEAC logic designs and architecture.

Both SEAC and SWAC had some influence on the development of the commercial computer industry, notably in the development of smaller scientific computers. Research projects organized around these two computers planted the first seeds of other important technologies—magnetic disk memories, parallel multiprocessor computer designs, optical character recognition, and the application of computers to practical, industrial mathematics. One group of NBS personnel left the SEAC project to develop a medium-sized computer that became the basis for the Underwood business machine firm's computers.[135] Harry Huskey, chief architect of the SWAC, designed the Bendix G-15, the first small scientific computer produced in reasonable volume and a precursor of the minicomputer.[136] Other veterans of the SEAC project joined IBM.[137]

Summary

During and after the war, for the sake of national security, the government made unprecedented investments in computer technology developed by civilians and private companies (table 3-1). Through the early 1950s the continued reluctance of commercial firms, like IBM and NCR, to invest large sums in risky research and development projects with uncertain markets, forced the government to continue sponsoring the new technology. The cold war, with its ensuing technological military competition, heightened government interest.

134. Alexander, *Computer Development*, p. 3.
135. See Lutze, "Formation," p. 45; and Arthur D. Little, Inc., with the White, Weld & Co. research department, *The Electronic Data Processing Industry: Present Equipment, Technological Trends, Potential Markets* (New York: White, Weld, & Co., 1956), pp. 80–81. The Electronic Computer Corporation (Elecom), founded by Samuel Lubkin and Murray Pfefferman of the SEAC design team, eventually became a division of Underwood and built a few scientific computers in the mid-1950s.
136. Lutze, "Formation," p. 45. The Bendix G-15A computer, priced at $45,000, was a small magnetic drum machine that first became operational in 1956. More than 300 were sold. See Martin H. Weik, Jr., *A Fourth Survey of Domestic Electronic Digital Computing Systems*, BRL Report 1227 (Aberdeen, Md.: Aberdeen Proving Ground, 1964), p. 316; and Arthur D. Little, Inc., *Electronic Data Processing Industry*, p. 53.
137. Interview with Richard B. Thomas, Washington, D.C., August 1, 1984.

Table 3-1. *Early U.S. Support for Computers*

First generation of U.S. computer projects	Estimated cost of each machine (thousands of dollars)	Source of funding	Initial operation
ENIAC	750	Army	1945
Harvard Mark II (partly electromechanical)	840	Navy	1947
Eckert-Mauchly BINAC	278	Air Force (Northrop)	1949
Harvard Mark III (partly electromechanical)	1,160	Navy	1949
NBS Interim computer (SEAC)	188[a]	Air Force	1950
ERA 1101 (Atlas I)	500	Navy/NSA[b]	1950
Eckert-Mauchly UNIVAC	400–500[a]	Army via Census; Air Force	1951
MIT Whirlwind	4,000–5,000	Navy; Air Force	1951
Princeton IAS computer	650[a]	Army; Navy; RCA; AEC	1951
Univ. of Cal. CALDIC	95[a]	Navy	1951
Harvard Mark IV	n.a.	Air Force	1951
EDVAC	467	Army	1952
Raytheon Hurricane (RAYDAC)	460[a]	Navy	1952
ORDVAC	600	Army	1952
NBS/UCLA Zephyr computer (SWAC)	400	Navy; Air Force	1952
ERA Logistics computer	350–650	Navy	1953
ERA 1102 (3 built)	1,400[c]	Air Force	1953
ERA 1103 (Atlas II, 20 built)	895	Navy/NSA	1953
IBM Naval Ordnance Research Computer (NORC)	2,500	Navy	1955
Subtotal	15,933–17,333		
Other machines			
ASA Abner	n.a.	NSA	1952
Air Research OARAC (built by GE)	185	Air Force	1953
IBM 701 Defense Calculator (19 built)	425[d]	IBM, with letters of intent from 18 DOD customers	1953
Technitrol 180	500	NSA	1955
Naval Research NAREC	1,500	Navy	1956
NBS DYSEAC	n.a.	Army	1954

	Copies		
of IAS			
Los Alamos MANIAC I	250–298	AEC	1952
Oak Ridge ORACLE	250	AEC	1953
Rand JOHNNIAC	n.a.	Air Force (Rand)	1954
Argonne AVIDAC	n.a.	AEC	n.a.
Argonne GEORGE	500	AEC	1957
of ORDVAC			
Univ. of Ill. ILLIAC	300–500	Army	1952
Mich. State MISTIC	n.a.	n.a.	n.a.
Iowa State Cyclone	n.a.	n.a.	1959
of SEAC			
Univ. of Mich. (Willow Run) MIDAC (MIDSAC)	n.a.	Air Force	1953(1954)
FLAC	n.a.	Air Force	1953

Sources: Herman H. Goldstine, *The Computer from Pascal to von Neumann* (Princeton University Press, 1972), pp. 242–45, 316–18, 326, 328; Arthur D. Little, Inc., with the White, Weld & Co. research department, *The Electronic Data Processing Industry: Present Equipment, Technological Trends, Potential Markets* (New York: White, Weld & Co., 1956), p. 82; Martin H. Weik, "A Third Survey of Domestic Electronic Digital Computing Systems," Report 1115 (Aberdeen Proving Ground, Md.: Ballistic Research Laboratories, 1961), pp. 213, 236, 282, 393, 567, 635, 639, 676–77, 732, 848, 900, 1016, 1081–83; Martin H. Weik, "A Fourth Survey of Domestic Electronic Digital Computing Systems," Report 1227 (Aberdeen Proving Ground, Md.: Ballistic Research Laboratories, 1964), p. 373; Nancy Stern, *From ENIAC to UNIVAC: An Appraisal of the Eckert-Mauchly Computers* (Digital Press, 1981), pp. 37, 51, 62, 105, 113, 117, 122–23, 132; Kent C. Redmond and Thomas M. Smith, *Project Whirlwind: The History of a Pioneer Computer* (Digital Press, 1980), pp. 107, 110, 127–28, 156–58, 166; Ralph A. Niemann, *Dahlgren's Participation in the Development of Computer Technology* (Dahlgren, Va.: Naval Surface Weapons Center, 1982), pp. 4, 5, 11, 16; Samuel S. Snyder, "Influence of U.S. Cryptologic Organizations on the Digital Computer Industry," SRH 003, declassified National Security Agency report released to the National Archives, p. 7; Samuel S. Snyder, "Computer Advances Pioneered by Cryptologic Organizations," *Annals of the History of Computing*, vol. 2 (January 1980), pp. 60–63. M. R. Williams, "Howard Aiken and the Harvard Computation Laboratory," *Annals of the History of Computing*, vol. 6 (April 1984), p. 160; ONR, *Digital Computer Newsletter*, various issues, 1949–56; S. N. Alexander, "Introduction," in U.S. Department of Commerce, National Bureau of Standards, *Computer Development (SEAC and DYSEAC) at the National Bureau of Standards, Washington, D.C.*, NBS circular 551 (Government Printing Office, 1955), p. 3; H. D. Huskey, "The National Bureau of Standards Western Automatic Computer (SWAC)," *Annals of the History of Computing*, vol. 2 (April 1980), pp. 111–21; John W. Carr III, "Instruction Logic of the MIDAC," in C. Gordon Bell and Allen Newell, eds., *Computer Structures: Readings and Examples* (McGraw-Hill, 1971), p. 209; John Varick Wells, "The Origins of the Computer Industry: A Case Study in Radical Technological Change" (Ph.D. dissertation, Yale University, 1978), p. 268.and the following citations in N. Metropolis, J. Howlett, and Gian-Carlo Rota, eds., *A History of Computing in the Twentieth Century: A Collection of Essays* (Academic Press, 1980): J. C. Chu, "Computer Development at Argonne National Laboratory," p. 346; James E. Robertson, "The ORDVAC and the ILLIAC," pp. 346–47; Harry D. Huskey, "The SWAC: The National Bureau of Standards Western Automatic Computer," pp. 421, 428, 430; N. Metropolis, "The MANIAC," p. 462; and Erwin Tomash, "The Start of an ERA: Engineering Research Associates, Inc., 1946–1955," p. 491.

n.a. Not available.

a. Estimated cost in 1950, in "Report on Electronic Digital Computers by the Consultants to the Chairman of the Research and Development Board," June 15, 1950, app. 4, cited by Kent C. Redmond and Thomas M. Smith, *Project Whirlwind: The History of a Pioneer Computer* (Digital Press, 1980), p. 166.

b. The National Security Agency (NSA) includes Army and Navy predecessor agencies.

c. Cost for three machines.

d. Includes processor, card reader and punch, printer, magnetic tape unit, and power supply.

Eventually, the commercial applications of the research sponsored by the government became clearer. Some industry leaders, like IBM's Thomas Watson, Jr., managed to lead their companies into new ventures in computer technology, buoyed by healthy doses of government support.

This pattern of government-funded research leading to private commercial benefit became more prominent, and the debate over federal technology policy grew. Indeed the debate had begun even before the war was over. Those who opposed any government intervention in the marketplace clashed with those who favored public support for the development of industrial technology.

By the mid-1950s participants in the conflict had devised a uniquely American formula for technology policy. Basic research in universities would be accepted as a legitimate public good to be undertaken by economically disinterested professors in academia. Government support for applied research and development would be acceptable only if aimed at a noneconomic objective, like national security or health. Congress explicitly established the National Science Foundation to support basic research efforts. But because computer science did not mature as a separate academic discipline until the mid-1960s, the foundation largely excluded computer research from support in the first decades after the birth of the computer. Fortunately for the U.S. computer industry, however, the military establishment guaranteed support to the industry for the sake of national security.

The United States military sponsored by far the largest and broadest program for developing computer technology found anywhere in the world during the first decades of the digital computer. Even a partial list of computer projects funded during the late 1940s and early 1950s is impressive for the number, diversity, and cost of projects included (table 3-1). By 1950 the United States was directly funding computer R&D at roughly $15 million to $20 million (current) a year.[138]

Perhaps more important, the many start-up computer firms entering

138. In the late 1940s and early 1950, MIT's Whirlwind project was budgeted at $1.5 million to $2.0 million a year. See Redmond and Smith, *Project Whirlwind,* pp. 118, 120, 126–28, 191. ERA was estimated to be operating with three times the budget and staff of Project Whirlwind. (Jay Forrester is quoted to this effect, ibid., p. 154.) A conservative estimate might be that these two projects accounted for half of all military funding of computer research, an upper limit would be perhaps a third of the total, yielding an estimate of funding in the range of $14 million to $21 million.

the U.S. industry in the early and middle 1950s were chasing after a reasonably large market, dominated by military demand. For almost all of these producers, the military was the first, and generally, the best customer. About eighty different organizations, including numerous small start-ups that later merged with larger producers or disappeared, produced computers in the United States during the 1950s.[139] The U.S. military, or defense contractors, paid for or purchased the first machines made by most of these groups.[140] In later years, military users of the technology continued to take a broad view of activities considered relevant to defense.

139. A 1960 survey of U.S. computers lists sixty-five U.S. manufacturers; this list does not include several well-known computer groups and omits manufacturers who had dropped out of the market. Weik, *A Third Survey*, pp. 1038–42.

140. A quick review of the installations data cited in Weik, *A Third Survey*, supports this contention, as does the detailed analysis of U.S. computers installed before 1956 in John Varick Wells, "The Origins of the Computer Industry: A Case Study in Radical Technological Change" (Ph.D. dissertation, Yale University, 1978), pp. 266–78.

CHAPTER FOUR

IBM and Its Competitors

DESPITE IBM's initial postwar reluctance to go into the business of computer development, by the mid-1950s it had managed to carve out by far the largest share of the market. Indeed IBM's position was to fundamentally constrain the technological strategies open to competitors. By consolidating the economic benefits of size and scope, important in the introduction of the pathbreaking System 360 line in 1964, IBM checked the relative ease with which new players had been entering the fray. Other computer producers now had to grope for a technological strategy to compete. How they found a place in the market, despite IBM's ability to exploit economies of scale and scope in research and development, marketing and maintenance, and software development, emerges as a principal theme in the economic history of computers.

Most successful strategies for competing with the market leader IBM were evident by the late 1960s, including targeting market niches not well served by IBM's general purpose line, pursuing various degrees of software and hardware compatibility with IBM's products, and aiming above or below the range of price and performance spanned by the IBM line. For both IBM and its competitors, the development of computer technology meant investing resources in the innovative activities of an existing stock of trained engineers. People were clearly the medium of technological development and flow, and the evolution of a firm's product line can often be traced to the origins and experience of valued technical personnel. Finally, a successful computer depends not just on the quality of design, but also on the components used in its implementation. Using outdated component technology in a clever design has consistently spelled ruin; conversely, ingenious use of the latest component technology to reduce costs, particularly in more inexpensive machines, has often spawned success.[1]

1. This outcome supports a generalization made earlier: the essential design of a

The Origins of U.S. Computer Firms

In 1956, one of the first studies of the commercial electronic data processing (EDP) industry listed twelve major U.S. producers of digital computers.[2] By 1965 only six of these firms would remain significant producers. By 1975 only five of the original firms would be major forces in the business; by 1986 only four remained.[3] Yet new producers entered the industry even as old ones exited, and the technical roots of many of these firms, old and new, can be traced to experience accumulated in the pioneer days of computing in the 1940s and 1950s.

International Business Machines

Table 4-1 lists the twelve principal computer producers in the United States in 1955, with their overall size and the markets in which they were

---

modern business computer had been worked out by the mid-1960s. Further improvements were based on marginal enhancements to the design, coupled with major advances in component technology. This is not to minimize the importance of the radically new kinds of computer architecture being tested in current vintages of so-called parallel computers. These machines—whose development was largely funded by the U.S. government in the late 1970s and early 1980s—are just now being introduced into the commercial marketplace.

2. See Arthur D. Little, Inc., with the White, Weld, & Co. research department, *The Electronic Data Processing Market* (New York: White, Weld, and Co., 1956). Besides the twelve "major producers" listed, the study mentions three "other producers": Hogan Laboratories, Inc., Logistics Research, Inc., and Technitrol Engineering Company. None survived in the computer business beyond the early 1960s. All three built their first machines on government contracts. Hogan built its Circle computers for the Atomic Energy Commission and the Army in 1953; Logistics Research delivered its first Axel Wenner-Gren Automatic Computer (ALWAC) to a Navy research lab in 1953 as well. See John Varick Wells, "The Origins of the Computer Industry: A Case Study in Radical Technological Change" (Ph.D. dissertation, Yale University, 1978), pp. 269, 271. Technitrol began by building mercury delay line memories for the Army Security Agency (later merged into the National Security Agency [NSA]), and eventually built an entire computer—an improved version of NSA's internally built ABNER computer— for NSA, delivered in 1955. See Samuel S. Snyder, "Computer Advances Pioneered by Cryptologic Organizations," *Annals of the History of Computing*, vol. 2 (January 1980), p. 63. Technitrol seems to refer to this installation as the Technitrol 180 and to give its cost as $500,000. See A. D. Little, Inc., *Electronic Data Processing*, p. 82.

3. The six survivors were Burroughs, IBM, Honeywell, National Cash Register (NCR), Radio Corporation of America (RCA), and Sperry Rand. In 1971 RCA had also dropped out of the general purpose computer business. In 1986 Honeywell sold its commercial computer operations (though it retained a minority equity stake), and Burroughs and Sperry's computer operations were merged into UNISYS.

Table 4-1. *Chief Producers of Digital Computers, 1954*

Firm	Total sales of all products (millions of dollars)	Markets
Bendix Aviation	608	Scientific
Burroughs	169	Business and scientific
Electrodata	1	Business and scientific
IBM	461	Business and scientific
Marchant Calculators[a]	21	Business
Minneapolis-Honeywell	229	Business and scientific
Monroe Calculating Machine	30	Business
NCR	259	Business and scientific
RCA	941	Business
Raytheon Manufacturing	182	Business and scientific
Sperry Rand	696	Business and scientific
Underwood	76	Business

Source: Arthur D. Little, Inc., with the White, Weld & Co. research department, *The Electronic Data Processing Industry: Present Equipment, Technological Trends, Potential Market* (New York: White, Weld & Co., 1956).
a. Sales figure shown is for 1953.

selling machines. Only a year later, the early lead that J. Presper Eckert and John W. Mauchly had carved out for their UNIVAC I disappeared, and IBM seized market leadership (in excess of 70 percent of the value of systems in use worldwide) in computers.[4]

IBM achieved rapid success in computers for two reasons. First, it targeted its product to a specific market niche. A substantial defense market existed for its first computer, which it designed with the scientific computational demands of military systems designers in mind. In contrast, Remington Rand's UNIVAC system was optimized for business applications. Second, UNIVAC's producers neglected to invest the R&D resources required for new products and continued technological leadership. Before they realized what had happened, their static technological lead had vanished.

The 701 Defense Calculator, designed and built for defense users and first delivered in 1953, spurred IBM's initial rapid ascent to market leadership. By the end of 1953, IBM had installed four 701s. Other

4. Montgomery Phister, Jr., ed., *Data Processing Technology and Economics*, 2d ed. (Digital Press and Santa Monica Publishing, 1979), p. 38, table I.31.10. Although they were among the principal producers in 1955, Underwood, Marchant, and Monroe did not last long in the computer industry. Underwood had taken over ELECOM, the Electrical Computer Company, in 1952, and dropped out of computers after the recession of 1957–58. Marchant Calculators sold out to Smith-Corona, and Monroe was sold to Litton Industries in the late 1950s.

computer producers rose to the challenge. During the same period, Rand was delivering six machines to customers, and Engineering Research Associates (ERA) was delivering at least thirteen computer systems.[5] By 1954 the score evened somewhat—IBM delivered fifteen more 701s, Remington Rand produced thirteen more UNIVACs, and ERA delivered eight more 1103s and an 1104. However, in that same year, IBM also produced the first twenty models of its low-cost IBM 650 computer ($3,250 a month rental, versus $15,000 for the 701). By the end of 1955, after shipping even more new models, IBM clearly took the industry lead.

But success was by no means ensured for IBM. Competition included many firms of about its size, and industrial giant RCA was roughly double the size of IBM. These firms had the technological and financial resources to challenge IBM. Other large firms, including General Electric (GE), active in the military computer market, were hovering in the wings, poised to enter the commercial industry.

IBM built on its position as the dominant manufacturer of punched card business equipment. Its traditional skills and experience in manufacturing electromechanical machinery were the base on which an outstanding record of research and development in high-speed peripherals—input-output devices—was built. The card readers and punches used with early computers, even those not built by IBM, were often IBM products. An ambitious development program for printers, magnetic tape drives, and magnetic drums and disks added new strengths to traditional expertise. The availability of quality peripheral equipment for IBM computers was crucial to its phenomenal growth.[6]

IBM thoroughly reorganized itself in the mid-1950s. Over the longer

5. These numbers are based on Wells, "Origins of the Computer Industry," pp. 266–71; for IBM and UNIVAC. Erwin Tomash and Arnold A. Cohen, "The Birth of an ERA: Engineering Research Associates, Inc. 1946–1955," *Annals of the History of Computing*, vol. 1 (October 1979), pp. 91–93. The ERA count includes two 1101s delivered to NSA and one used internally; four 1103s, including one to NSA; three 1102s (a special version of the 1101); three special purpose systems delivered to the John Plain Company, the Civil Aeronautics Administration, and the Office of Naval Research. See also Samuel S. Snyder, "Influence of the U.S. Cryptologic Organizations on the Digital Computer Industry," SRH 003, 1977, declassified National Security Agency report released to the National Archives, p. 8.

6. In 1953, for example, a group of government users picked the IBM 701 over the ERA 1101 because of the superiority of the input-output equipment available for the 701. See Franklin M. Fisher, James W. McKie, and Richard B. Mancke, *IBM and the U.S. Data Processing Industry: An Economic History* (Praeger, 1983), p. 16.

run, it built success on its continuing transformation into a true high-technology business, organized around maintaining a flow of new technology into its products. Thomas J. Watson, Jr., took over the leadership of IBM in the mid-1950s and put in place a systematic approach to R&D. His father, company founder Thomas J. Watson, Sr., had not made research a company priority. He had supported goodwill projects in scientific computing to show off the company's technical capacity but rarely acknowledged any distinction between sales and market research and technical research.

The creation of the IBM 704 computer exemplified the new emphasis on research and development, leading to improved technology, as the key to market leadership. The 704 also showed IBM's new strength in developing the electronic components used in computers. A major computer and in its day the fastest and largest general purpose computer sold commercially, the 704 was designed by a team led by Gene M. Amdahl who took charge of a small development group that was working on a scientific computer to replace the 701 Defense Calculator. The machine finally produced, a major achievement in computer design by a young and talented engineering team, was one of the first commercial computers to incorporate hardware floating-point arithmetic.[7] It also featured advances such as index registers and magnetic core memories.

In 1956 Watson, Jr., continued the organizational shifts aimed at changing IBM into a more research-oriented company. He hired Emanuel R. Piore, formerly chief scientist at the Office of Naval Research and one of the architects of the ONR computer and electronics programs, as director of research. Under Piore's direction, IBM began a program to develop advanced electronic components in the late 1950s, an effort that would bear fruit in the advanced electronics used in later generations of IBM computers.[8]

Some knowledgeable observers date IBM's shift to a business strategy

7. As a graduate student at the University of Wisconsin, Gene M. Amdahl built an experimental computer that could do floating-point arithmetic by using special hardware. Richard A. McLaughlin, "The IBM 704: 36-Bit Floating-Point Money-Maker," *Datamation*, vol. 16 (August 1975), pp. 46–50. Numbers used in scientific calculations are usually expressed as a decimal number multiplied by ten to some power. The algorithms used to handle the numbers are known as floating-point arithmetic, and special hardware to carry out the manipulations greatly speeds scientific calculations. Gene Amdahl's computer was known as the WISC.

8. Emerson W. Pugh, *Memories That Shaped an Industry: Decisions Leading to IBM System/360* (MIT Press, 1984), pp. 193, 214–15.

explicitly based on a continuous investment in research, incorporated into a steady stream of new, technology-intensive products that were more advanced than those offered by its competitors, to the transition between the Watsons in the mid-1950s.[9] The *IBM Journal of Research and Development*, a symbol of the transition, began publication in 1957. IBM was one of the first companies to analyze correctly the nature of a high-technology, research-intensive business in an area of continuous rapid technological progress. IBM's strengthened research organization was an important first step toward dominance of the computer industry.[10]

Statistics on IBM's research activities seem to support this picture. As figure 4-1 makes clear, IBM had been spending about 12 percent to 15 percent of net income on company-funded R&D (except for the years 1944 and 1945, when the share reached one-quarter at the peak of the U.S. war effort). When Watson, Jr., succeeded in steering IBM into computers in 1951, internally financed R&D jumped to 30 percent to 35 percent of earnings and stayed at that level through the mid-1950s.[11] Figures from the early 1960s show IBM's research commitments again jumping to just under half of net earnings and staying at that level until the present day. Clearly, IBM had made a transition to a much more research-intensive business strategy by the late 1950s.

But IBM has not always led the way on technological innovations. In fact, IBM sometimes lagged in the introduction of new technology into its product line: time-sharing systems, the use of integrated circuits, large-scale supercomputers, small-scale minicomputers and microcomputers, and software making use of artificial intelligence concepts are areas in which IBM trailed more aggressive competition.

These episodes are not necessarily errors of judgment or failures, however. Delaying large expenditures on new product development, until faced with the threat of competitors displacing older products, may be more profitable for a firm with control of most of the market. The

9. See for example H. R. J. Grosch, "The Way It Was 1957: A Vintage Year," *Datamation*, vol. 18 (September 1977), pp. 77–78.

10. Competing explanations might focus on the excellence of its marketing, sales, and service organizations, or on scale economies in these areas (IBM became the largest business equipment producer in the U.S. well before the Second World War). For an analysis of the U.S. industry concentrating on scale economies, see Gerald W. Brock, *The U.S. Computer Industry: A Study of Market Power* (Ballinger, 1975), pp. 27–41.

11. As Watson, Jr., tells it, "We were spending only 3 percent of our revenues on research and development, and we doubled that figure very rapidly." Thomas J. Watson, Jr., "The Greatest Capitalist in History," *Fortune*, August 31, 1987, p. 27.

Figure 4-1. *IBM's Research and Development as a Percentage of Net Income, 1942–85*

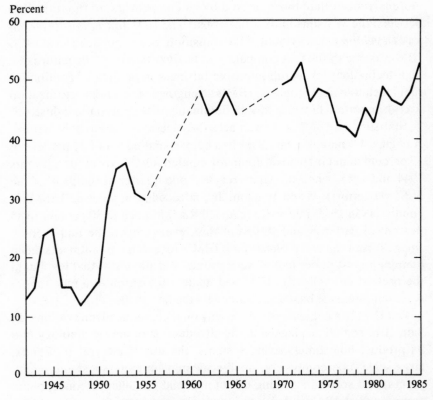

Sources: Alvin J. Harman, *The International Computer Industry: Innovation and Comparative Advantage* (Harvard University Press, 1971), pp. 106–08; Montgomery Phister, Jr., *Data Processing Technology and Economics*, 2d ed. (Digital Press and Santa Monica Publishing, 1979), pp. 310–11; and Standard and Poor's Compustat data base.

function of internal R&D, viewed from this perspective, is defensive as well as offensive. A company with a broad and current technology base can respond to all potential technology-based attacks on its market share, as well as supply the innovations that will be most profitable in more secure markets.

IBM and the U.S. Government

A healthy infusion of research resources from the federal government during the 1950s greatly helped IBM's shift to a technology-intensive business strategy. The U.S. government's role in IBM's early development of computer technology is often overlooked. In fact, IBM's original entry into electronic computers, the IBM 701 Defense Calculator, was only undertaken after government users had expressed interest in supporting the program through their purchases.[12] Furthermore, large-scale federal support for IBM research and development continued well after the first business-oriented models began to role out the doors in the mid-1950s.

More than half of IBM's total revenues from domestic electronic data processing (EDP) activities in the 1950s came from two large government programs: the analog "Bomb-Nav" guidance computer installed in the B-52 bomber and contracts for computers used in the SAGE air defense system.[13] Although the Bomb-Nav computer was important to IBM mainly as a source of revenues and apparently had little impact on IBM's digital computer technology, the computers built for SAGE had a profound technological impact on IBM.[14]

The SAGE project was a descendant of the MIT Whirlwind effort, which had successfully found support from the Air Force after the Navy abandoned the original Whirlwind objectives. Designed as a complete command and control system to defend against a possible Soviet bomber

12. Actually, the 701 was not the first government computer project IBM had undertaken. In 1950 IBM started work on a large, experimental research computer for the Naval Ordnance Laboratories in Dahlgren, Virginia. This machine, the Naval Ordnance Research Calculator (NORC) pioneered key elements of the electronic circuitry used in the 701. The NORC was finished in 1954 and accepted in 1955, after the 701. It was the largest and fastest computer of the day. Though urged by customers to build it for commercial sale, IBM resisted and instead completed development of the 704. IBM then embarked on the more ambitious research effort that culminated in the Stretch computer. Cuthbert C. Hurd, "Computer Development at IBM," in N. Metropolis, J. Howlett, and Gian-Carlo Rota, eds., *A History of Computing in the Twentieth Century* (Academic Press, 1980), pp. 393, 403, 415; Martin H. Weik, "A Third Survey of Domestic Electronic Digital Computing Systems," Report 1115 (Aberdeen, Md.: Aberdeen Proving Grounds, 1961), pp. 390, 716–18; and Saul Rosen, "Electronic Computers: A Historical Survey," *Computing Surveys*, vol. 1 (March 1969), p. 25.

13. Fisher and others, *IBM*, p. 30, citing IBM documents submitted in defense against litigation instituted by the U.S. Justice Department.

14. The AN/ASQ-38 "Bomb-Nav" system for the B-52 was an analog computer. Interview with Emerson Pugh, IBM, Yorktown Heights, New York, June 8, 1984; P. F. Olsen and R. J. Orrange, "Real-Time Systems for Federal Applications: A Review of Significant Technological Developments," *IBM Journal of Research and Development*, vol. 25 (September 1981), p. 405. IBM's first use of silicon transistors, however, was in circuits designed for military bomb-nav systems. See Charles J. Bashe and others, *IBM's Early Computers* (MIT Press, 1986), p. 414.

attack, the SAGE system was one of the largest and costliest military systems projects of the 1950s. Estimates for the entire effort (in dollars of the day) range from $4 billion to $12 billion; $8 billion is probably a reasonable ballpark estimate.[15]

In 1952 IBM was selected by MIT's Lincoln Laboratory as the subcontractor responsible for building fifty-six large computers, costing about $30 million each.[16] SAGE ultimately brought in half a billion dollars of income to IBM in the 1950s.[17] Other contractors included AT&T's Bell Telephone Laboratories and Western Electric units, which designed, engineered, and produced data communications and transmission systems and served as overall coordinators; Burroughs, which built data acquisition and reduction computers; Radio Corporation of American (RCA), Bendix, and General Electric (GE), builders of the SAGE radar systems; and the Systems Development Corporation, which wrote the code required for the SAGE computers' operating system.[18]

Significant benefits to IBM from SAGE work included the access to technical information on computer development at MIT that it obtained, the revenues earned, and perhaps most important, the engineering and production know-how required to mass-produce magnetic core memories.[19] Massive resources were pumped into developing methods of manufacturing cheap and reliable core memory systems in large numbers. IBM's ability to produce inexpensive and dependable core memory systems figured importantly in the competitiveness of the commercial computer systems it delivered in the late 1950s and 1960s.

The SAGE experience has also been credited by Watson, Jr., with teaching IBM how to mass-produce printed circuit boards. An innovative magnetic drum developed for a later version of the SAGE computer was IBM's first magnetic storage device to use a hydrodynamic (self-acting) slider head, the mechanism still used in most magnetic disk systems. At

15. Claude Baum, *The System Builders* (Santa Monica, Calif.: Systems Development Corporation, 1981), pp. 12–13.

16. Pugh, *Memories,* p. 126.

17. Baum, *System Builders,* p. 13. However, as Bob Evans has pointed out to me, IBM's profits or these activities were lower than on other lines of business. Interview with Bob Evans, IBM, Purchase, New York, June 12, 1984.

18. IBM was offered the job and turned it down. Bob Evans, in a key post at IBM at this time, writes that "senior management from the electric accounting machine era worried that IBM would be 'too close to the operational aspects of war time' and therefore declined the undertaking. . . . I believe IBM missed a handsome opportunity." Unpublished communication from Bob Evans to author, July 16, 1986.

19. Pugh, *Memories,* pp. 93–128; and Fisher and others, *IBM,* pp. 28–30.

its peak, 7,000 to 8,000 IBM employees were working on SAGE, compared with a total IBM domestic employment of 39,000 in 1955.[20]

Other key pieces of technology developed for SAGE had important impacts on IBM and the other contractors in the project. SAGE was essentially the first wide-area computer network, the first extensive digital data communications system, the first real-time transaction processing system. Concepts developed for its operation formed the base on which time-sharing and computer networks were later developed. Many of these concepts were consciously transported into the business world just a few years later when IBM announced its Semiautomatic Business-Research Environment (SABRE) airline reservation system.[21] SABRE, fully operational in 1964, was the first commercial real-time transaction processing system. The systems are now commonly used for industrial process control, hotel and airline reservations, and financial transactions at automated teller stations. To better handle equipment failure, the computer centers built for SAGE used pairs of computers wired together, with a redundant machine designed to take over the workload if its twin failed in use. The SAGE system was therefore one of the first operational fault-tolerant computer systems as well.

The benefits from the SAGE investments, while especially important to IBM, were widely diffused throughout the U.S. industry. IBM had honed its memory technology, learned about the architecture of real-time transaction processing systems, earned considerable revenue, and gained thousands of skilled personnel as a result of the effort. AT&T developed the technology of digital data communications and took a commanding lead in high-speed communications networks and modem technology. Burroughs' small SAGE data reduction computer pushed it into the transistor age, with what was probably the first transistor computer to go into mass production. Graphic display consoles developed for SAGE were the first such devices designed by IBM for a

20. See Watson, Jr., "The Greatest Capitalist in History," p. 27; and L. D. Stevens, "The Evolution of Magnetic Storage," *IBM Journal of Research and Development,* vol. 25 (September 1981), p. 667. See Fisher and others, *IBM,* p. 27, for the SAGE employment figure; and Phister, Jr., *Data Processing,* p. 311, for the IBM figure.

21. The system was built in the same federal systems division that had built SAGE. See the discussion in David R. Jarema and Edward H. Sussenguth, "IBM Data Communications: A Quarter Century of Evolution and Progress," *IBM Journal of Research and Development,* vol. 25 (September 1981), p. 395; and Olsen and Orrange, "Real-Time Systems," p. 405.

production computer system and later led to the first computer graphics systems built at MIT in the early 1960s. Commercial time-sharing and networks owe SAGE an equal debt. Some IBM insiders believe that the decision to participate in SAGE may have been the most important management decision of the period.[22]

Ironically, SAGE's main military objective—protecting the United States against a Soviet bomber attack—was irrelevant by the time the system was completed. In the early 1960s the USSR was deploying its first intercontinental ballistic missiles, and the bomber threat became a second-order concern.

Another project important to IBM's computer technology was also undertaken in the late 1950s. This later effort, known as Project Stretch, grew out of IBM's early responses to needs for high-performance computers among government users, particularly the Atomic Energy Commission (AEC) and the National Security Agency (NSA).[23]

Though NSA historically had a close relationship with IBM's competitor, Engineering Research Associates (whose original staff was largely drawn from technical personnel with wartime experience in the Navy's OP-20-G communications intelligence organization), IBM had also built special purpose punched card equipment for intelligence applications during the war. Shortly after its entry into the computer business, IBM began to deliver special purpose computer devices to the NSA. The IBM 703, never sold commercially, was a special purpose high-speed sorting machine, using magnetic tapes. It was delivered to NSA. Later, in October 1957, the first large transistorized computing machine made by IBM was delivered to NSA.[24]

Project Stretch bridged the needs of these two different government

---

22. Pugh, *Memories*, p. 262.

23. Both agencies had been important customers in IBM's early computer markets. The first of IBM's 701 Defense Calculators had gone to the Atomic Energy Commission (AEC) laboratories, as had two more of the remaining seventeen built. The first customer machine had gone to Los Alamos, as had a later one. The fifth machine went to the AEC labs run by the University of California at Livermore. The National Security Agency also took delivery on one of the 701s. The first 704 and 709 also went to the AEC lab at Livermore. See Hurd, "Computer Development at IBM," pp. 405–06; Wells, "Origins of the Computer Industry," p. 274, 276; and Weik, "A Third Survey," p. 522.

24. Hurd, "Computer Development at IBM," p. 411. Interviews by author with Bob Evans, IBM, June 12, 1984, and September 4, 1986. This very large (comparable in size to the later IBM 7090, but much faster) very high performance, and highly classified machine was known as SLED2. IBM's first commercial transistor machine, the small IBM 608 calculator, was not shipped until December 1957. Bashe and others, *IBM's Early Computers*, p. 386.

customers and laid the technological foundations for IBM's System 360. The Stretch computer began as an internal IBM proposal to build a high-performance computer. IBM approached government customers in an effort to secure funding, and the AEC's Livermore lab responded by soliciting an IBM bid on a state-of-the-art machine for its use. After submitting a proposal and completing a design using new "surface barrier" transistors developed by Philco, however, engineering management at IBM decided to withdraw its bid, much to the consternation of Livermore researchers. IBM management had chosen to develop its components internally rather than purchase them from competitors.[25]

Instead, the IBM designers went back to the drawing board and produced a proposal for a computer that would truly "stretch" existing technology, with performance levels multiplying those of the IBM 704 one hundredfold. In 1955 NSA was approached and indicated that it would support the development of the machine. An effort tagged Project Silo was begun with NSA funding to produce high-speed memories for this effort. In late 1955, the AEC's Los Alamos National Laboratory also expressed interest in a computer with these highly ambitious performance targets, and by 1956, both NSA and Los Alamos had agreed to support the project.[26]

Significantly, NSA and AEC had very different computer needs. The Atomic Energy Commission needed the ability to do numerical computations at very high speeds, while NSA's requirements involved processing and manipulating large volumes of character data quickly.[27] The Atomic Energy Commission was essentially the most advanced "scientific" user of the day, while NSA's needs were similar to those of a very demanding "business" customer. Thus the Stretch computer had to be designed with an architecture sufficiently flexible to handle both high-precision scientific calculations and character-oriented applications well—the essence of the revolution IBM was to launch in the commercial world with its System 360 in 1964.

For NSA, the Stretch processor was to be part of a proposal for an elaborate modular data processing complex named Farmer. IBM was to

25. See Pugh, *Memories,* pp. 60–66; Hurd, "Computer Development at IBM," pp. 414–15; Bashe and others, *IBM'S Early Computers,* pp. 416–58.
26. This account follows Pugh, chap. 6. Since the development effort was budgeted at roughly $9 million over the amount of government funding sought, IBM arranged to have free use or ownership of all patents produced by the project, which it would then be free to use in its commercial products. See Pugh, *Memories,* pp. 164–66.
27. See Snyder, "Computer Advances," p. 66.

build the computer within this system, known as Harvest. It included not only the central Stretch computer but also a special purpose statistical and logical coprocessor for character data and a high-speed automated magnetic tape system known as Tractor.[28] When delivered in 1962, the Harvest complex at NSA was the most powerful computer system in existence; Stretch remained in operation for fourteen years.[29]

Component and manufacturing technologies developed on the Stretch project included high-speed core memories, IBM's high-performance micro alloy diffused transistors (MADTs) and associated logic circuitry, a standardized printed circuit card assembly technology known as Standard Modular Systems (SMS), automated design and manufacture of SMS cards, automated component insertion, and automated wire-wrapping machinery to interconnect cards on back panels.[30] These manufacturing technologies were used in producing IBM's second generation of commercial transistorized computers well before the first Stretch had even been delivered.

The basic logic circuit used in high-performance computers, known as emitter-coupled logic (ECL) or current made logic (CML) was invented for the Stretch computer and still dominates the design of fast computers.[31] The architecture of the Stretch computer pioneered signif-

28. The Harvest coprocessor unit, which processed streams of character data in parallel, influenced the development of ideas about specialized processors to manipulate vectors and arrays of data. The technical manuals for IBM's model 7950 Harvest coprocessor were a hot item among computer architects at the time. Interview by author with Victor Vysottsky, Bell Telephone Laboratories, April 30, 1984; and Snyder, "Computer Advances," pp. 66–67.

29. It is worth noting that the decommissioning of Stretch, in about 1976, coincided with the installation of the first Cray 1 supercomputers at NSA. Bashe and others, *IBM's Early Computers*, p. 456.

30. Microalloy diffused transistors (MADTs) were a type of fast germanium switching transistor developed at IBM. See the descriptions of other IBM systems using MADT transistors in Weik, "A Third Survey," pp. 314–56. A description of how this Stretch circuitry led other computer makers to explore similar directions is in C. Gordon Bell, J. Craig Mudge, and John E. McNamara, *Computer Engineering: A DEC View of Hardware Systems Design* (Digital Press, 1978), pp. 109–10.

Bell labs developed wire-wrapping of connector pins as a method of interconnecting circuit components in 1953. IBM's automated wire-wrapping machinery apparently was one of the earliest such applications. By the mid-1960s, automatic wire-wrap machines were available on the open commercial market; Bell and others, *Computer Engineering,* p. 151, describe how the circuitry of the DEC PDP-7 (Programmed Data Processor) was designed to use a fully automated wire-wrapping machine sold by the Gardner-Denver company. IBM in fact had worked with Gardner-Denver to develop the automated wire-wrapping machines used on Stretch. Bashe and others, *IBM's Early Computers*, p. 411.

31. See E. J. Rymaszewski, J. L. Walsh, and G. W. Leehan, "Semiconductor Logic

icant innovations, including the concepts of pipelining and instruction look-ahead, which even now are central to the design of high-performance computers.[32] Most important, key features of the IBM System 360 architecture were first devised for Stretch to allow it to meet the varied demands of business and scientific computing: the eight-bit chunk of data known as a byte, manipulation of data in words of fixed or variable length built up from eight-bit bytes, and a simple system for handling extended sets of alphabetic characters.[33]

Experimental operating systems run on Stretch provided experience with concepts refined and developed in the operating systems shipped with the System 360. On the hardware side, common interface standards for peripherals (another concept introduced commercially in System 360) and new advances in high-speed magnetic tape storage were introduced.[34]

Stretch component technology was also employed in commercial IBM products well before Stretch was finished. IBM had been planning to bring out a transistorized version of its 709 scientific computer, to be known as the 7090, and won a subcontract in 1958 to supply this machine for use in the Ballistic Missile Early Warning System (BMEWS). The

Technology in IBM," *IBM Journal of Research and Development,* vol. 25 (September 1981), pp. 607–08. ECL is sometimes called current mode logic (CML). See R. A. Henle and L. O. Hill, "Integrated Computer Circuits—Past, Present, and Future," *Proceedings of the Institute of Electrical and Electronic Engineers,* vol. 54 (December 1966), pp. 1852–53; and R. W. Hockney and C. R. Jesshope, *Parallel Computers: Architecture, Programming, and Algorithm* (Bristol, U.K.: Adam Hilger Ltd., 1981), p. 357.

32. Pipelining is a technique of hardware design in which multiple subprocessors in a central processing unit are used to decode different segments of a complex instruction simultaneously.

With look ahead, the central processing unit of a computer is designed so that the next instruction to be executed is fetched while the current instruction is still being decoded by other elements of the processor. This also introduces simultaneity into the execution of different instructions.

33. The byte is the standard unit for storing a single character of alphabetic data, made up of a string of binary bits of memory. See Fisher and others, *IBM,* p. 50.

34. The Stretch Experiment in Multiprogramming (STEM) prototype system provided IBM systems developers with early, rudimentary experience with a batch-job, multiprogramming, job-scheduling operating system. These concepts were improved and refined in the System 360 operating systems. See L. A. Belady, R. P. Parmalee, and C. A. Scalzi, "The IBM History of Memory Management Technology," *IBM Journal of Research and Development,* vol. 25 (September 1981), pp. 494–95. See Pugh, *Memories,* pp. 160–86, and Bashe and others, *IBM's Early Computers,* pp. 370–71, for descriptions of advances in technology associated with Stretch. For use of Stretch architectural concepts in System 360, see also A. Padegs, "System/360 and Beyond," *IBM Journal of Research and Development,* vol. 25 (September 1981), p. 378.

BMEWS contract was used to define the engineering requirements for the 7090, and it was decided to wed the 709 architecture to the semiconductor circuits and fast core memory systems being developed for Stretch. Schedules on the BMEWS project were tight, and the Stretch project was delayed because the first core memories developed for Stretch were instead used in the 7090.

IBM's large 7080 business computer used the transistor circuits and core memories developed for Stretch when it was first delivered in 1960. IBM's enormously successful small business computer, the 1401, shipped in 1960, also used the Stretch semiconductor circuits and packaging.[35]

Clearly, SAGE and Stretch played a vital role as government-funded development for IBM's computer technologies of the 1950s and early 1960s.[36] IBM records show that well over half of IBM R&D during this period was paid for by federal contracts. As late as 1963, the government was still paying for 35 percent of IBM's R&D.[37]

During the 1970s and 1980s, government-sponsored R&D resulting in serious impacts on IBM's commercial product line seems to have become much less common. For one thing, a big decline occurred in the relative importance of the government market, as the business computing market exploded with unprecedented growth. There also seems to have been an important shift in the nature of IBM's government projects—procurement of special purpose military systems came to dominate its business with the Defense Department, and the National Aeronautics and Space Administration (NASA) space program began to edge out defense procurement in the early 1960s.[38] By the 1970s, defense users were

35. Pugh, *Memories,* pp. 172–73, 188; and interview with Charles J. Bashe, IBM, June 8, 1984.

36. Ironically, because Stretch had gone well over its original budget and fell short of its original performance target by half, Stephen Dunwell, the leader of the Stretch project, was banished to a backwater of the IBM organization. In the mid-1960s, when IBM recognized that Stretch had played a crucial role in the genesis of IBM's most successful systems, Dunwell was rehabilitated and named a prestigious IBM Fellow. See Pugh, *Memories,* pp. 184–86; and Bashe and others, *IBM's Early Computers,* pp. 456–68.

37. Kenneth Flamm, *Targeting the Computer: Government Support and International Competition* (Brookings, 1987), pp. 96–97.

38. In 1966 space business accounted for 70 percent of IBM's federal systems division (FSD) revenues. By 1969, as the space program wound down, space-related activities were expected to drop to 30 percent of the division's revenues. See the IBM management committee's minutes of a November 8, 1968, meeting, contained in exhibit 384B-096 of *Telex* v. *IBM,* in the Baker library, Harvard Business School.

Two-thirds of FSD's total revenues from 1951 to 1970 were derived from just three

lagging behind commercial industry in the use of data processing technology. As informed IBM observers have noted, "The sheer volume of commercial applications made it far more practical to 'hitch a ride' by hardening commercially available technology rather than trying to amortize high development and tooling costs over much smaller DOD procurement quantities."[39]

Nonetheless, one can still identify cases of important benefits to IBM's mainline commercial products stemming from its later government work. Work on the NASA space program included large-scale software development. Thousands of programmers were needed to build complex control systems. From this effort came sophisticated software tools, program and test techniques, and software management concepts that greatly influenced IBM's software engineering systems.[40] Some of the advanced component technology used in IBM's highest-performance computer circuitry was developed with NSA support. IBM's first commercially available array processor, attached to a mainframe computer and used to speed up scientific calculations, was introduced in the 1970s. It was a derivative of work on advanced signal processors for military applications. Work on military communications systems has kept IBM on the leading edge of fiber optics technology.[41] Today, IBM's work on new, parallel computer designs builds directly on government-sponsored research in the academic world.[42]

---

principal activities (almost certainly the Bomb-Nav computer, SAGE, and (probably) the NASA space program). See the minutes from the meeting of September 2, 1970, exhibit 386-052 in *Telex* v. *IBM,* in the Baker library, Harvard business school.

IBM'S most important military system in recent years has been the System 4 Pi family of avionics computers, first delivered in 1966.

39. Olsen and Orrange, "Real-Time Systems," p. 408. These remarks are clearly referring to DOD procurement and should not be interpreted as minimizing the important advances in computer technology developed through research funded through the Defense Advanced Research Projects Agency (DARPA) and other federal programs.

40. See S. E. James, "Evolution of Real-Time Computer Systems for Manned Spaceflight," *IBM Journal of Research and Development,* vol. 25 (September 1981), pp. 424–25; H. D. Mills and others, "The Management of Software Engineering," Parts I-V, *IBM Systems Journal,* vol. 19, no. 4 (1980), pp. 414–77; Saul Rosen, "Programming Systems and Languages 1965–1975," *Communications of the Association for Computing Machinery,* vol. 15 (July 1972), p. 596; and interview with Bob Evans, June 12, 1984. Some standard commercial software products, including automatic output spooling systems and applications software used in oil refineries and electrical utilities, also stemmed from IBM's work for NASA.

41. See Flamm, *Targeting,* p. 50, note 11; and Olsen and Orrange, "Real-Time Systems," p. 408.

42. See Tobias Naegele, "Parallel Design Gets IBM Seal of Approval," *Electronics,*

The Economics of System 360

At the close of the 1950s IBM's continued dominance of the global computer market was far from assured. Rivals were announcing new technology (transistorized computers by Philco, supercomputers by Control Data), and poor management could easily have led IBM down the same path to decline that was followed by Sperry Rand, maker of the UNIVAC line. By the early 1960s, IBM was producing six different, and incompatible, computer product lines, and successful competitors for several IBM machines had begun to appear. The RCA 501 transistorized computers were offering cost-effective performance in the large-scale business market; Burroughs was working on its high-end 5000; the Control Data 1604 was very competitive in scientific applications; and the Honeywell 200, a low-cost and more powerful replacement for the IBM 1401, with software compatibility, was about to be announced.

By the late 1950s, computer producers, and IBM management, were beginning to see software emerge as the centerpiece of a data processing system. They realized that the complexity and cost of producing software was obstructing rapid progress in information processing. Software development costs had risen from less than 8 percent of computer manufacturers' total development expense, in the mid-1950s, to about 40 percent of costs in 1965. Hardware costs dropped from well over half to less than 40 percent of computer users' operating costs during the same period.[43]

Because software written for one machine was usually not usable on another, moving an application from one model of computer to another was a large and expensive programming task. A customer's investment in developing and using software "locked" the user into a particular manufacturer's system. Moving to another model, not to mention another manufacturer, meant a large fixed cost, requiring a large increment in performance or price competitiveness to make such a switch economically worthwhile.

Furthermore, to complicate a customer's choice among computer manufacturers and models, an average computer installation often ran a

---

vol. 58 (August 26, 1985), p. 16. IBM has also sought DARPA funding for some of its high-risk parallel computer work.

43. See Phister, Jr., *Data Processing*, p. 27, fig. 1.25.4, and p. 151, fig. 3.25.11. Many industrial and academic computer researchers began turning their attention to software problems. See R. W. Bemer, "Computing Prior to FORTRAN," *Proceedings of the National Computer Conference 1982* (Reston, Va.: AFIPS Press, 1982), p. 813.

mix of "business" and "scientific" applications. As a user's applications evolved, the mix of jobs, as well as the computers that optimized the performance of these tasks, was likely to change. Choosing a computer began to resemble a lifetime commitment: one's current choice could have long-term effects on one's later options.

IBM's management saw these problems developing. Its fragmented and incompatible product line was under attack at several points by a spectrum of competitors, and in response, IBM devised a strategy that would have far-reaching consequences for the future development of technology and industrial structure in computers. In 1961 an internal task force decided on the strategy, and in 1964, its fruit, a product line known as System 360, was announced. The essence of System 360 was the creation of a broad line of compatible computers spanning a large range of performances. The most powerful model was almost one thousand times more powerful than the least capable machine. Models specializing in both business and scientific features were available, with a high degree of software compatibility. Applications running on one machine were to be capable of running on any other machine in the line, with little or no change.

This was not the first time such a concept had been proposed. In the late 1950s, the U.S. Army had attempted to create a compatible group of machines, the so-called FIELDATA family.[44] Major manufacturers, including IBM, Sylvania, Philco, and Autonetics, had developed computers with some compatibility with this standard.[45] But the program was limited, and the military market for these machines was relatively small.

The System 360 family of computers, on the other hand, broke new ground in lowering the costs of computation. While running essentially the same software, a user could start on a small, entry-level machine, develop software, and move up to large-scale machines or onto a more

44. See Jean Sammet, "Self-Study Questions," *Annals of the History of Computing*, vol. 6 (January 1984), pp. 69, 72.

45. For a description, see W. F. Luebbert, "Data Transmission Equipment Concepts for FIELDATA," in *1959 Proceedings of the Western Joint Computer Conference* (New York: Institute of Radio Engineers, 1959), pp. 189–96. Computers with some FIELDATA compatibility listed in Weik, "A Third Survey," include Philco's AN/TYK 4V COMPAC and AN/TYK 6V BASICPAC models, IBM's AN/TYK 7V INFORMER, the Autonetics FADAC computer, and Sylvania's AN/TYK 1V and 2V MOBIDIC systems. FIELDATA compatibility was limited to common data and control codes, hardware interfaces for input-output and storage devices, voltage and impedance levels, and other interconnection characteristics.

specialized processor as workload and computing requirements changed. This capability made the 360 machines enormously attractive to business.

Cross-computer compatibility also created a valuable economic advantage for IBM. It was already by far the largest producer of computers and enjoyed significant economies of scale in marketing and service.[46] Since design costs, like research expenses, were relatively independent of the scale of production, IBM had already managed to further lower its unit hardware costs by standardizing circuit and component types and packages across a range of computers. Similar standardization had been applied to the interface of input-output equipment to IBM processors. A standard IBM peripheral device could be attached to many different computer models with little modification. By arranging for software to be shared among this same broad spectrum of machines, the unit costs for software development were also reduced to the minimum possible. The internal IBM standard, invented for System 360, had created the largest unified market in the world for software.

Economically, software and hardware are highly complementary inputs for a business—a decline in software costs probably increases demand for the hardware on which it runs. Hardware purchases are made with software cost and availability in mind; conversely, the market for a new software package depends in large measure on the present and future stock of installed machines on which it can be run. Thus the enormous reduction in software cost fed back into an expanding demand for IBM hardware, and vice versa. IBM had found the formula for linking a user's information processing costs in the most direct possible way to the size of IBM's market. Success reinforced success.

The design of the IBM System 360 architecture survives to this day, with some modifications, as the main internal IBM standard.[47] System 360 was expanded into the IBM 370 series architecture in the late 1960s. The principal deficiency of System 360, the lack of hardware needed to support time-sharing, was belatedly remedied when time-sharing systems developed with government support became increasingly popular. IBM's first successful time-sharing offering, TSO, in fact, drew heavily

---

46. See Brock, *U.S. Computer Industry*, pp. 27–68.

47. The 360 architecture made use of variable-length words, which permitted both long-word (scientific) and short-word (business) applications to run on the same machine, though the width of the internal data path varied from machine to machine and therefore optimized each machine for particular types of applications. The principal deficiency of the 360 design, remedied in the 370, was the omission of hardware for dynamic address

on research for DARPA's Project MAC at IBM.[48] In later years new features were added to create the architecture of the current line of large processors. The key in preserving the advantages of a standard architecture, while permitting evolutionary extensions of the design over time, has been to retain upward compatibility (figure 4-2). That is, as new extensions have been added, care has been taken to ensure that older software will generally run successfully on newer hardware (though the converse does not necessarily hold).

Much of the initial success of the System 360, in fact, was probably because of the great efforts put into giving machines in the 360 family some compatibility with software running on earlier IBM machines. IBM made the first extensive use of microprogramming in certain processors of its 360 line: various 360 models could be reprogrammed to emulate the instruction sets of the older IBM machines they replaced.[49]

The concept of a compatible family of computers created a unified market that greatly stimulated the commercial use of computers. By drawing the boundaries of this large, unified market (IBM had roughly 70 percent of the world market at the time) with a proprietary, internally controlled standard, however, IBM created serious obstacles for current and potential competitors.

The development of System 360 marked other important changes in the nature of competition in computers. For the first time, IBM drew heavily on the resources of its foreign R&D facilities in developing the product line. The 360/40, oriented toward scientific applications, was based on a design developed in IBM's Hursley facility in Britain, and the 360/20, the smallest machine in the line, was developed in IBM's

---

translation required to handle memory efficiently in time-sharing applications. The omission of this hardware led to problems when IBM belatedly developed a time-sharing system. Eventually, IBM introduced a special model (the 360/67) with this hardware. See Padegs, "System/360 and Beyond," pp. 377–81, 384–85. IBM uses other architectures in small minicomputers, personal computers, and industrial control computers.

48. See Karen A. Frenkel, "Alan L. Scherr, Big Blue's Time-Sharing Pioneer," *Communications of the ACM*, vol. 30 (October 1987), pp. 825–26; and Flamm, *Targeting*, pp. 55–58.

49. Microprogramming, first suggested by Maurice V. Wilkes of Cambridge University in 1951, involves fixing the instructions executed by a computer's central processing unit with data held in a fast read-only memory store, rather than through permanent electrical connections made physically in the hardware. To emulate another computer's instruction set, only a change of the read-only memory is then required. Different machines in the 360 line could emulate IBM's 1401, 7070, 7090, and 7080 computers.

Figure 4-2. *The IBM System 360 and 370 Architecture*

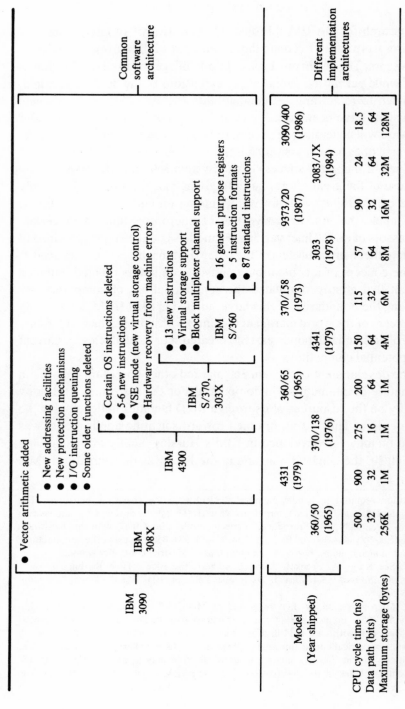

Model (Year shipped)	360/50 (1965)	4331 (1979)	370/138 (1976)	360/65 (1965)	4341 (1979)	370/158 (1973)	3033 (1978)	9373/20 (1987)	3083/JX (1984)	3090/400 (1986)
CPU cycle time (ns)	500	900	275	200	150	115	57	90	24	18.5
Data path (bits)	32	32	16	64	64	32	64	32	64	64
Maximum storage (bytes)	256K	1M	1M	1M	4M	6M	8M	16M	32M	128M

Sources: Based on D. J. Frailey, "Computer Architecture," in Anthony Ralston and Edwin D. Reilly, Jr., eds., *Encyclopedia of Computer Science and Engineering*, 2d ed. (Van Nostrand Reinhold, 1983), p. 276; and A. Padegs, "System 360 and Beyond," *IBM Journal of Research and Development*, vol. 25 (September 1981), p. 387; Andris Padegs, "Evolution of System/360-370 Architecture," *Communications of the ACM*, vol. 30 (April 1987), pp. 300–01; and "Hardware Roundup," *Computerworld*, August 20, 1984, p. 24; October 6, 1986, p. 65; and September 21, 1987, p. S14.

Table 4-2. *Importance of Foreign Markets to American Computer Firms*

	Foreign revenues as percentage of total revenues						
Firm	1960	1964	1969	1974	1979	1983	1985
IBM	20	29	35	47	54	42	43
Sperry	20	28	31	43	40	30	30
NCR	41	n.a.	41	51	54	46	46
Control Data	n.a.	n.a.	26	31	32	24	29
Digital	n.a.	n.a.	24	39	36	35	39
Honeywell	n.a.	18	33[a]	41	27	26	25
Burroughs	n.a.	n.a.	30	37	44	41	44
Hewlett-Packard	n.a.	n.a.	n.a.	n.a.	49	37	37
Wang	n.a.	n.a.	n.a.	n.a.	33	28	31
Data General	n.a.	n.a.	n.a.	n.a.	27	31	32
Unweighted average	27	25	31[b]	41	40	34	36

Sources: Phister, Jr., *Data Processing*, pp. 307, 309, 312, 314, 623; Robert Batt, "U.S. Vendors Eyeing Opportunities in Overseas Mart," *Computerworld*, May 14, 1984, p. 142; and Standard & Poor's Compustat data base.
n.a. Not available.
a. Data for Honeywell are for 1970.
b. The average for 1969 excludes Honeywell.

German labs.[50] IBM had already moved toward an integrated, worldwide operation when it established its World Trade Corporation in 1949 to manage international business. To reduce costs in manufacturing core memories, IBM had begun to shift the labor-intensive assembly of these components to low-cost "offshore" locations in Asia.[51]

By the mid-1960s, all aspects of IBM's operations were geared toward a single international market, with research and development, component production, and systems assembly allocated among different units around the globe, based on relative costs and the availability of specialized resources in different geographical locations. This shift outward into international operations by IBM was followed by its competitors and typified a more general shift toward foreign markets for U.S. computer producers. As table 4-2 shows, foreign revenues had roughly

50. See Evans, "IBM System/360," no. 9, *Computer Museum Report* (Summer 1984), pp. 14–16; Organization for Economic Cooperation and Development, *Electronic Computers: Gaps in Technology*, report presented to the Third Ministerial Meeting on Science, March 11–12, 1968 (Paris: OECD, 1969), p. 87; Pugh, *Memories*, pp. 197–98; and Alvin J. Harman, *The International Computer Industry: Innovation and Comparative Advantage* (Harvard University Press, 1971), p. 21.

51. Pugh, *Memories*, pp. 250–51. Manual assembly in Southeast Asia costs less than assembly in a fully automated plant in Kingston, New York. IBM shifted much of its core memory production for computers manufactured all over the world to these offshore facilities.

Table 4-3. *Data Processing Revenues, U.S. Computer Firms*[a]
Millions of U.S. dollars

Firm	1963	1973	1982	1986
IBM	1,244	8,695	31,500	49,591
Burroughs	42	1,091	3,848	} 9,431
Sperry	145	958	2,801	
Digital	10	265	4,019	8,414
Hewlett-Packard	n.a.	165	2,165	4,500
NCR	31	726	3,173	4,378
Control Data	85	929	3,301	3,347
Wang	n.a.	31	1,322	2,669
SDS/Xerox	8	60	n.a.	2,100
Honeywell	27	1,147	1,685	1,890
Data General	n.a.	53	804	1,288
Amdahl	n.a.	n.a.	462	967
General Electric	39	174	862	900
Cray Research	n.a.	n.a.	141	597
Philco	74	n.a.	n.a.	n.a.

Sources: Franklin M. Fisher, James W. McKie, and Richard B. Mancke, *IBM and the U.S. Data Processing Industry: An Economic History* (Praeger, 1983), p. 65; Phister, Jr., *Data Processing*, pp. 293, 622; and *Datamation*, vol. 33 (June 15, 1987), p. 46, and vol. 29 (June 1983), pp. 96–98.

n.a. Not available.

a. Data processing revenues include income from hardware, software, and service sales and rentals.

b. Burroughs and Sperry merged their computer operations into UNISYS in 1986.

doubled to a 40 percent to 50 percent share of total income for many U.S. computer firms by the mid-1970s.

IBM's U.S. Competitors

Although IBM has dominated the computer industry since the mid-1950s, the principal U.S. competitors of IBM have changed considerably since then (table 4-3). In the early 1960s, IBM's principal challengers were Sperry Rand, Control Data, and Philco, trailed by Burroughs (BGH), GE, Honeywell, and NCR (figures on the computer revenues of RCA are unavailable). Two producers of minicomputers, DEC and Scientific Data Systems (SDS), had also entered the business.

By the early 1970s, the cast was pretty much the same. The major competitors, all roughly similar in size, were Honeywell, Burroughs, Sperry Rand, Control Data, and NCR. DEC, while smaller, had grown dramatically; SDS, after explosive growth, had been bought out by Xerox, which presided over stagnation and decline in its new business; GE had dropped out of hardware manufacture, and RCA and Philco had dropped out of the computer business altogether. Three more recent entrants, Data General, Hewlett-Packard (H-P), and Wang Laboratories, had made a promising start in sales of smaller minicomputer systems geared toward specialized markets.

By the end of the seventies, the relative positions of IBM's competitors had changed considerably. DEC had climbed to the number two spot, trailed by Burroughs, Control Data, and NCR; the declining fortunes of Sperry Rand and Honeywell had pushed them to the rear. Hewlett-Packard, Wang Laboratories, and Data General had grown considerably at the lower end of the product line, and several new and specialized producers, including Amdahl (IBM-compatible mainframes) and Cray Research (large-scale supercomputers) had made important inroads into certain market niches.

However, using total revenues as a measure of the importance of competition presents some difficulty. By citing income from a variety of activities and markets, firms that have grown by specializing in particular markets and succeeding in those activities are mixed with companies that have had only fair success across a broad product line. An alternative measure would be the major U.S. computer models, defined in terms of either sales, performance, or workload in use. Figure 4-3 enumerates these machines over the 1952–75 period.

IBM initially dominated the computer market in the 1950s and early 1960s in part by producing the most powerful computers of the day. This situation has not, however, been true since the late 1950s—Philco and then Control Data produced the machines with the greatest computing capacity in the sixties and early seventies. IBM gradually focused less on the top end of the market for very large, high-powered processors and more on the bread-and-butter commercial mainframe markets, which it came to dominate.[52]

The importance of Sperry Rand's UNIVAC line of business computers, a leader in the 1950s and 1960s, has diminished considerably since the late 1960s. Aside from the pathbreaking UNIVAC I and the low-cost 1004 business machine, its most significant computers have

---

52. That is not to say that IBM abruptly abandoned high-powered processors. IBM made some efforts to develop large-scale supercomputers and produced the 360 model 90 series computers and the 360 and 370 model 195. These machines did not fare well against the competition from Control Data, however. Since the early 1970s, and until 1985, IBM had not introduced any model rated as a supercomputer. In 1985 it announced a vector version of the IBM 3090 with supercomputer-class performance. See Fisher and others, *IBM,* pp. 154–58; and Padegs, "System/360 and Beyond," tables 1 and 2, pp. 386–89.

Figure 4-3. *Important Computers according to Performance-Oriented Criteria, 1950–75*[a]

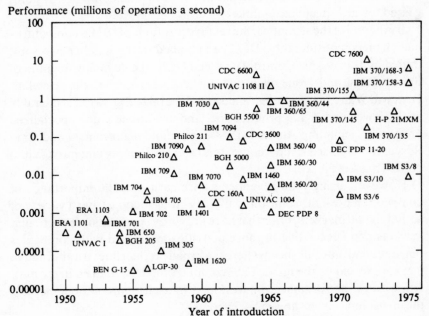

Performance (millions of operations a second)

Sources: Kenneth E. Knight, "Application of Technological Forecasting to the Computer Industry," in James R. Bright and Milton E. F. Schoemar, eds., *A Guide to Practical Technological Forecasting* (Prentice-Hall, 1973), pp. 383–87, 396–98; Phister, Jr., *Data Processing*, pp. 344, 346, 348, 350, 630, 633; and Padegs, "System/360 and Beyond," p. 387.
  a. Included in this figure are the best-performing machines according to value of installations, number of installations, and millions of operations (MOPs) a second. MOPs for each dollar spent and total MOPs for each machine are also criteria.

been in the high-end 1100 series scientific computing line, which can be traced to technological roots planted in the first ERA computers.

Other producers have also been strongest in specialized markets. Both Philco and Control Data made their impact by producing large, high-performance designs that often turned out to offer the best price performance for computationally demanding applications. Burroughs became a significant producer in the 1950s with the medium-sized model 205 and carved out its own special niche in the 1960s with a unique architecture, implemented in the 5000 line, that was the foundation for the company's later growth. The strongest products from Honeywell or NCR have addressed special needs (large time-sharing systems and communications, for Honeywell) or specialized market segments (retailing and banking, for NCR).

Finally, many firms were able to enter the industry by introducing low-end computers characterized by artful, no-frills implementations of existing technology, aimed at cost-conscious users. The pioneers of this path were the Bendix G-15 and Librascope LGP-30 in the 1950s and the CDC 160 and DEC PDP-5 in the 1960s.

Specialization and Competition

The technical differentiation of computers into application-oriented categories was apparent at the birth of the industry. Four distinct approaches to computer design on the scene in 1950, all of which were supported by military patrons, can be discerned. Eckert and Mauchly, with their explicit interest in commercial applications, produced a machine—the UNIVAC I—tailored to business use. Professor John von Neumann and his Princeton colleagues at the Institute for Advanced Studies (IAS) designed a machine focusing on the needs of scientific users. The MIT Whirlwind was oriented to real-time command and control applications, which were to spin off into process control and transactions processing designs used by industry. Finally, smaller companies focused on building small but affordable computers, using lower-performance components that made serious computing available to users on a budget; the NBS and the West Coast aerospace spin-offs set the pace on this front.

The UNIVAC I was a so-called EDVAC-type machine, built along the lines suggested in the 1946 EDVAC report. This class of machines was characterized by a "bit-serial" architecture—the internal data path within the computer handled one bit of data at a time—six or more bits, later called a "byte," were needed to represent an alphabetic character. Many multiples of this number, called a "word," were needed to represent a number with the high precision required for scientific calculations. Consequently, numerical calculations requiring a great deal of processor effort tended to run fairly slowly, since only one bit of data was being processed at any moment in time. Eckert and Mauchly put a great deal of effort into developing fast input-output devices for the UNIVAC I, particularly a rapid magnetic tape system that could read in 12,800 characters each second. By concentrating on fast input-output of data rather then computational speed on arithmetic calculations, Eckert and Mauchly produced a system ideal for business applications.

The second major architectural model for early U.S. computers was von Neumann's computer, built at the IAS in Princeton. The IAS design stressed performance on numerical calculations, using a so-called bit-parallel design—the internal data path within the IAS computer's central processing unit was many bits wide, wide enough, in fact, to transfer and process an entire word (forty bits of data on the original IAS computer) at once. The price paid for processing many bits of data concurrently was an increase in the complexity and cost of the central processing unit of the computer. For "number-crunching" applications, limited by the internal processing speed of the computer, sophisticated parallel circuitry made sense; for business applications in which processing tended to be limited by input-output of data from external storage devices, serial designs, inherently cheaper, often tended to be more cost-effective.

The third specialized niche, real-time control, required further development effort applied to the foundation established by Whirlwind. The SAGE project was the next step on this path.

The small, cheap computer, the fourth category of design, was the logical entry point for the company with good design talent but limited financial resources.

These distinctions were soon reflected in the activities of the infant commercial industry. One important case was that of IBM, which launched its computer line with a "scientific" machine, the 701, that drew heavily on the IAS design. But the differing needs of its customers soon became evident.

IBM quickly made a distinction between business and scientific computers. The business machine had an internal data path just wide enough to handle a character of data, with a fast, well-developed line of peripheral equipment to handle input and output. The scientific machines had a much wider data path to handle the large number of digits used in high-precision scientific calculations. They also had faster processor speeds and minimal peripherals. The 704 was the source of IBM's scientific line; IBM's large business machines came from the 705, and the popular and numerous small business systems were descendants of the 650.

The drive toward specialization and competition permeated IBM in the 1950s. The Poughkeepsie laboratory's personnel were the designers of the large scientific and business systems, while the Endicott facility developed expertise in small- and medium-scale business systems. Starting in the mid-1950s, regular design competitions between these labs, and later, IBM labs in San Jose, California, and Europe, determined which systems were to go to commercial production.

Sperry Rand, Control Data, and Cray Research

In the early 1950s, Remington Rand unquestionably led American computer firms in the development of technology. Eckert and Mauchly, lacking capital and troubled by huge cost overruns on fixed-cost contracts to build the UNIVAC, sold their company to Remington Rand in 1950. Even before this period, Remington Rand had been assembling a computer development group in Norwalk, Connecticut, under the direction of General Leslie R. Groves (who had directed the Manhattan project), by hiring a group of senior engineers away from Engineering Research Associates.[53] By the spring of 1952, ERA too was overextended financially and had been purchased by Remington Rand.[54] Thus Remington Rand had no less than three different computer development groups, together accounting for a good part of the stock of knowledge and experience with computers in the world at the time. It also had a three-year head start over any other firm in shipping a commercial computer product.

By many accounts, however, the three research groups, rather than cooperating, had a fragmented, rivalrous, squabbling relationship with one another. Most important, Rand was reluctant to invest resources in research and development, and successor machines to the UNIVAC I, aimed at commercial markets, were slow to be developed. By the time the competitive threat from IBM became clear in 1954, it was too late to respond quickly to the emerging competition. By the mid-1950s, Remington Rand had neither the resources nor the managerial vision to cope with the rapidly changing market, and in 1955, Remington Rand merged with a large defense contractor, the Sperry Corporation, to become the

53. Six to eight engineers from ERA left for Norwalk. See the unpublished interview with Emmett Quady by Robina Mapstone, May 15, 1973, available in the Smithsonian Institution, Washington, D.C.

54. See Tomash and Cohen, "Birth of an ERA," pp. 93–96. This description also draws on my interview with Arnold Cohen and Sidney Rubens at the Charles Babbage Institute, University of Minnesota, February 7, 1984.

Sperry Rand Corporation. The three research labs were grouped into a single division for the first time, and William Norris, one of the founders of ERA, became the director.

The conflict among the labs continued after the reorganization, however, and in 1957, Norris and a group of Sperry's engineers left to form the Control Data Corporation. The group that had formed ERA in the late 1940s was now largely split among two groups near St. Paul, Minnesota—the infant Control Data and the Sperry Rand St. Paul research lab. The Eckert and Mauchly Philadelphia group continued to work on the UNIVAC line, while the Norwalk lab developed smaller business machines for Sperry Rand. Eliminating wasteful duplication while preserving invigorating competition in research among these groups continued to be a serious problem for Sperry.

Until the mid-1960s, government support greatly helped in the development of Sperry Rand's computers. At Sperry's St. Paul research labs (formerly ERA), all of the commercial computers produced through the early 1960s had been direct spin-offs from computers designed for military customers. The successive models of the 1100 series scientific computers delivered in the 1950s had all been derived from designs for military computers. The UNIVAC 1107, delivered in 1963, although a company-sponsored design, used many pieces of technology developed for defense users, and the government funded much of its development cost.[55]

Other types of Sperry Rand computers also drew heavily on military work done at Sperry's three computer design groups in the 1950s. Their major military computers included special purpose computers like the Logistics computer, delivered by ERA in 1953. The Air Force Cambridge Research Center Computer, installed in 1956 after five years of government-funded development, pioneered the use of magnetic amplifiers as components in its logic circuitry.[56] Bogart was a character-oriented computer design, using diode and magnetic core logic, developed at Sperry's St. Paul labs. Five early solid state Bogart computers were built for NSA and first delivered in 1957.[57] Design automation techniques,

55. Fisher and others, *IBM*, p. 63, citing court testimony by J. Presper Eckert.

56. See Barbara Goody Katz and Almarin Phillips, "The Computer Industry," in Richard R. Nelson, ed., *Government and Technical Progress: A Cross-Industry Analysis* (Pergamon Press, 1982), pp. 186, 194.

57. Much of its logic design was used in the CDC 1604 and 160 computers when its

that is, using a computer to lay out the circuit design for a computer, were probably used for the first time in the United States with Bogart. The Athena ICBM guidance computer, built at Sperry's ERA shop and delivered to the Air Force in 1957, was one of the first transistor computers built.[58]

Central features of the design of the Bogart machines were also incorporated into the transistorized UNIVAC AN/USQ 20 military computer, the heart of the highly successful Navy Tactical Data System (NTDS), of which hundreds were built. Another member of the NTDS family of military computers, the UNIVAC 1206, in turn, developed into the commerical UNIVAC 490 real-time control computer. A military cousin of the 1206, the 1218 led to the commercial UNIVAC 418. Other special purpose military machines included the Target Intercept Computer and four special X308 computers delivered to a classified customer.[59]

With military support, certain advanced and experimental component technologies were being developed at Sperry in the 1950s, including magnetic amplifiers and magnetic thin films for use in computer circuitry. These technologies also found their way into Sperry Rand's commercial product line: magnetic amplifiers in the UNIVAC Solid State computer, magnetic thin film memories in the UNIVAC 1107.[60]

Architectural advances also resulted from government computer

---

designers left to join Control Data. See Snyder, "Influence of the U.S. Cryptologic Organizations," pp. 17–18.

58. ERA produced two experimental prototype models of the machine, one using magnetic amplifier logic, and code-named Magnetic Switch Test Computer (MAGTEC), the other using transistor logic called Transistor Test Computer (TRANSTEC). The transistor design won. By the late 1950s it had become clear that semiconductor technology offered clear advantages in cost and performance over the other alternatives being explored. Katz and Phillips, "Computer Industry," pp. 197, 202; and interview with James Thornton, Network Systems Corporation, February 7, 1984.

59. Snyder, "Influence of the U.S. Cryptologic Organizations," pp. 17–18; interview with James Thornton; interview with Arnold Cohen and Sidney Rubens; Fisher and others, *IBM*, pp. 63–64, 230; Weik, "A Third Survey," p. 866; and Katz and Phillips, "Computer Industry," p. 197. The X308 used magnetic amplifier logic and was built by the ERA group in St. Paul.

60. Katz and Phillips, "Computer Industry," pp. 194–98; and Fisher and others, *IBM*, p. 63. The UNIVAC STEP computer, announced in 1960, was an enhanced modification of the Solid State computer. The UNIVAC 1107, whose initial date of operation was 1962, was the first fully transistorized member of the UNIVAC 1100 line, again demonstrating Sperry's slow incorporation of new technologies into its successful products of the mid-1950s. Weik, "A Third Survey," p. 1084.

contracts in the late 1950s. When IBM dropped out of the competition, Sperry Rand was awarded the contract for the Atomic Energy Commission's Livermore Automatic Research Computer (LARC) in 1955.[61] The design for the LARC was highly innovative—two specialized processors, one dedicated to computation, the other to input-output, shared memory, and other system resources. Provision was also made to link two central processors.[62] The LARC was one of the first multiprocessor computer systems. Unfortunately, the component technologies it used were obsolete by the time it was completed in 1960. Nonetheless, the improved components, circuitry, and manufacturing techniques developed for LARC were later incorporated into the commercial UNIVAC III system, delivered in 1962.[63]

Research management continued to be a problem for Sperry. Some Sperry engineers complained that, aside from some aspects of the LARC and work on magnetic thin films, Sperry was conducting little research of an exploratory nature.[64] Even this research suffered from the fragmented and disorganized direction given to computer development at Sperry, though technically excellent products continued to be produced.

One strong point at Sperry during this period was its offerings in the area of remote access to computing systems—a 1968 IBM assessment concluded that UNIVAC had a commanding lead in systems with the capability of entering jobs from physically distant locations at high speed

61. As was also true for IBM and Stretch, Sperry vastly underestimated the cost of developing LARC. Sperry agreed to sell it to Livermore for $2.85 million, but total development costs were estimated at close to $19 million. When Sperry later tried to sell the machine to other customers, it quoted a price of $7 million. Only one other machine was sold, to the Navy's David Taylor Model Basin project. The Sperry engineers had supported the proposal, however, as a vehicle for developing technology for the next generation of commercial computers. See Katz and Phillips, "Computer Industry," pp. 186–88; and Fisher and others, *IBM*, pp. 57–59.

62. See R. Moreau, *The Computer Comes of Age: The People, the Hardware, and the Software* (MIT Press, 1984), pp. 95–98; and Rosen, "Electronic Computers," p. 26. Although LARC was designed as a dual-processor machine, the second processor was never built. Interview with Sidney Fernbach, May 9, 1984.

63. Fisher and others, *IBM*, p. 59, quoting court testimony by J. Presper Eckert. The UNIVAC III was the first descendant of the original UNIVAC I business computer line to employ transistor circuitry.

64. This was J. Presper Eckert's evaluation, quoted ibid., p. 62. There were, for example, five different groups at ERA working on thin film memory, and two in Philadelphia, all using different design and test equipment. Fisher and others, *IBM*, p. 62. The UNIVAC 1108 was judged a top-notch piece of equipment, offering superior price performance to competitive IBM products in IBM's internal product assessments of the late 1960s.

(so-called remote job entry).[65] This strength was almost certainly built on Sperry Rand's experience in developing such systems for NSA some years earlier.[66]

As with IBM, the direct role of government funding in Sperry's computer operations seems to have declined in the 1960s. Few commercial products developed after the early years of that decade can be directly connected to government research or procurement programs.[67]

In 1971, when RCA decided to get out of the computer business, Sperry Rand took over its computer operations. Despite the added revenues from RCA's customer base, however, Sperry continued its decline to fourth place (in revenues) in the U.S. data processing industry by 1973. Sperry had been number two in the industry, after IBM, throughout the early 1960s. The problem, perhaps, was that its product line, covering a broad range of general purpose scientific and business machines, was competing in a fairly direct way with IBM's main products. In more recent years Sperry's share of the computer market has continued to decline. In 1986 its computer business was merged with Burroughs to form UNISYS. The new company jumped to second place in sales among American computer producers.

Control Data's initial strategy, much like that of ERA a decade earlier, was to do government contract work and spin off commercial versions of this technology when possible and profitable.[68] Work done on government contract led to its first commercial offering, the CDC 1604.[69] The

---

65. See, for example, IBM, "Quarterly Assessment of the Product Line," November 27, 1968, Exhibit 123, *Telex* v. *IBM*, Baker library, the Harvard business school.

66. A system code-named Project Rye tied UNIVAC equipment together into a simple in-house time-sharing system, with a remote job entry emphasis, at NSA. Interview with Arnold Cohen and Sidney Rubens on February 7, 1984. Judging by its code name, it may have been part of the program to build the Farmer computer complex at NSA in the late 1950s that resulted in Projects Silo and Harvest at IBM. Snyder, "Influence of U.S. Cryptologic Organizations," p. 17, describes a remote-operated computer system with five outstations called ROB ROY, using a Sperry-built Bogart computer as its central computer, installed at NSA in late 1959. In any event, Sperry was deeply involved with developing high-speed remote job entry technology for NSA in the late 1950s and early 1960s; Sperry led the industry in this technology in the late 1960s.

67. Interview with Arnold Cohen and Sidney Rubens.

68. See the court testimony of William Norris, cited in Fisher and others, *IBM*, p. 90; and William Norris, "Entrepreneurism: The Past, Present, and Future of Computing in the U.S.A.," *Computer Museum Report*, vol. 1 (Spring 1987), p. 12.

69. The development of the CDC 1604 was funded by government users. The first machines went to U.S. and British intelligence agencies and the Navy. Rosen, "Electronic

small model 160 soon followed. Both 160 and 1604 were oriented toward scientific and engineering markets. The Control Data 160 was an early minicomputer, a market that was just beginning to blossom. In the early and mid-1960s, Control Data acquired the computer operations of Bendix and General Precision's Librascope group and successfully marketed their small computers as well.[70]

In 1962 Control Data announced its model 6600, a large and powerful "supercomputer" geared to scientific applications. Since delivery of the first 6600 in 1966 to the AEC's Lawrence Livermore National Laboratory, Control Data has focused on supplying large-scale scientific computers, and the most powerful computers available since then have often been CDC products. The 6600 was followed by the 7600 in 1969, the Star 100 in 1974, and the Cyber 205 in 1981, as Control Data continued to develop machines ranking among the most powerful computers of the day. The first models have always been delivered to government customers.[71] Control Data later diversified into the supply of computer peripherals and services, but its computer hardware has remained targeted at the high end of the scientific market.

The most serious competition for Control Data in the supercomputer market has been Cray Research, a firm started in 1972 by Seymour Cray. Cray, usually acknowledged as one of the top computer designers in the United States, had begun work with ERA in 1950 and rapidly assumed responsibilities for design at ERA, then at Sperry Rand, and still later, at Control Data, where he stayed until the 1970s. Cray did much of the design on the 6600, and its successor, the 7600. In 1976 Cray Research shipped the first Cray 1, a powerful supercomputer.[72] Improved versions

Computers," p. 23; Fisher and others, *IBM*, pp. 90–91; interview with James Thornton; and James L. Worthy, *William C. Norris: Portrait of a Maverick* (Ballinger, 1987), pp. 40, 223.

70. The Bendix G-15 and Librascope General Purpose Computer LGP-30, mentioned earlier, are usually considered the earliest commercial machines with some of the characteristics of a minicomputer.

71. The 6600, 7600, and Star 100 were first delivered to the Lawrence Livermore Laboratory, the Cyber 205 to the U.K. Meteorological Laboratories. See *Computers and Their Role in Energy Research: Current Status and Future Needs,* Hearings before the House Committee on Science and Technology, 98 Cong. 1 sess. (GPO, 1983), p. 258; and Hockney and Jesshope, *Parallel Computers,* p. 95.

72. The design team on the 6600 included James Thornton, who along with Cray, had joined ERA in late 1950. Interview with James Thornton, February 7, 1984. See also James Thornton, "The CDC 6600 Project," *Annals of the History of Computing,* vol. 2 (October 1980), pp. 338–48; and *Supercomputers,* Hearings Before the House Committee on Science and Technology, 98 Cong. 1 sess. (GPO, 1984), p. 366.

of this machine, along with the CDC Cyber 205, were the two highest-performance U.S. computers commercially available through the early 1980s.

Thus the most powerful scientific computers, including the products of both Cray Research and Control Data, and the scientific computer line of Sperry Rand, can be traced in fairly direct fashion to ERA, and indirectly, the wartime operations of the U.S. Navy's OP-20-G.[73]

Honeywell

Honeywell's computer operations, historically, had been salvaged from the failures of other would-be competitors. Its computer business traces its roots to the first projects initiated by the Raytheon Corporation in the late 1940s. (Raytheon's key personnel had come from Howard Aiken's laboratories at Harvard.) With sponsorship from NBS and ONR, it had produced the Raytheon Digital Automatic Computer (RAYDAC) in 1951. Unfortunately, the machine was technically obsolete by the time it was operational, and a second planned version was canceled. Raytheon also helped build other computers for classified defense applications in the late 1940s and early 1950s; the government funded all of these computer activities.[74]

In 1953 Raytheon's computer group began to work on a commercial spin-off from the RAYDAC, to be known as the RAYCOM. However, Raytheon, primarily a defense contractor, had little inclination to fund internally the R&D required. It had even less experience in commercial markets. Consequently, Raytheon formed a joint venture with the Minneapolis Honeywell Regulator Company in 1955, named the new venture the Datamatic Corporation, and transferred its computer group to the new operation.[75] This venture produced its first fruit in 1957, the Datamatic 1000, a large-scale business computer with vacuum tube logic

73. Engineers with ERA experience also played important roles in the Perkin-Elmer, Ampex, and Atlantic Research firms. See the interview with Emmett Quady.

74. Fisher and others, *IBM*, p. 68. One secret project, which has since been discussed in the open literature, was Nomad, a large-scale super-speed sorting machine. The project was undertaken for NSA. Considerable engineering work was done on high-speed tape drive systems. After delays, cost overruns, and the loss of key people, the project was terminated in 1954. See Snyder, "Influence of U.S. Cryptologic Organizations," pp. 13–14.

75. See W. David Gardner, "Chip Off the Old Bloch," *Datamation*, vol. 28 (June 1982), p. 241; Rosen, "Electronic Computers," pp. 15–16; and Fisher and others, *IBM*, pp. 69–70, on the history of Datamatic Corporation.

and core memory. But this machine did not offer good price performance. It sold poorly, and in that same year, Raytheon sold its interest in Datamatic to Honeywell.

Honeywell ultimately withdrew the Datamatic 1000, but its computer team began to work on the design of a new generation of transistorized computers, including the 800, 400, and 200 series. The 800 series had an innovative architecture and achieved moderate commercial success. The Series 200 was very successful competition in IBM's small business computer market. When IBM introduced the System 360, Honeywell responded by announcing a compatible family of computers based on the well-received model 200's architecture. In the early 1960s, however, Honeywell was still a small producer relative to the industry, with only 5 percent of corporate revenues coming from computers (see table 4-3).[76] Much of its growth was derived from further acquisitions.

The first of these came in 1966, when Honeywell purchased the Computer Control Corporation (CCC), a manufacturer of small computers for control and instrumentation applications.[77] Then, in 1970, when General Electric decided to quit manufacturing computer hardware, it sold these operations to Honeywell. GE's extensive computer business more than doubled Honeywell's computer revenues.[78] Finally, in 1975, when Xerox quit the mainframe computer business, Honeywell took over the maintenance and support services for the Xerox customer base.

These acquisitions propelled Honeywell to the number two spot in the U.S. computer industry by the early 1970s. However, Honeywell also had put together several different, highly fragmented, and incompatible lines of machines, limiting the possibilities of achieving any sort of scale economies in supporting this hardware and developing newer models. Many of the products Honeywell had inherited were competing

76. Rosen, "Electronic Computers," p. 22; and Fisher and others, *IBM,* pp. 236–37. Richard Bloch's product development team created the 200 system. See Gardner, "Chip Off the Old Bloch," pp. 71, 242.

77. Gardner, "Chip Off the Old Bloch," pp. 240–41. This was a homecoming of sorts, since Computer Control, known in the industry as 3-C, had been started in 1954 by Raytheon engineers who had left the NSA Nomad project to go into business for themselves. Their first product was a line of modular circuit cards, based on the Nomad designs, that could be configured into computer systems. These products were an early entry into the market for small computers, and 3-C was a competitor of DEC and SDS in the early 1960s. See Snyder, "Influence of the U.S. Cryptologic Organizations," p. 14.

78. See Phister, Jr., *Data Processing,* table II.1.310, p. 307.

in the same broad, general purpose business markets controlled by IBM.[79] Honeywell did not fare well during the remainder of the decade, and by the early 1980s, its position in the market had slipped badly.

Though Honeywell's computer operations can trace their roots to government computer projects of the early 1950s, only limited government support affected its efforts in technology development in recent decades. In the 1960s virtually none of its computer research benefited from federal monies.[80] When Honeywell took over GE's computer operations in the 1970s, however, it did absorb GE's longstanding participation (with the Massachusetts Institute of Technology) in the government-funded Project MAC time-sharing research and computer hardware and software descended from that effort. Extra secure versions of the Multics operating system, probably the most secure commercially available operating system, were produced with support from the Defense Department. Honeywell continues to lead in the important area of secure operating systems and related computing systems.[81] Other scattered examples of fallout from recent defense research benefiting Honeywell's commercial product line can also be found.[82]

79. Two notable exceptions were its line of control computers, and the time-sharing operating systems it offered, which included systems based on the GE-MIT Multics system. The time-sharing systems developed for SDS computers live on as Honeywell's CP40 operating system. In the 1970s Honeywell emphasized systems for distributed data processing, that is, linking machines and users to various computer resources through a network.

80. See Flamm, *Targeting*, p. 97, fig. 4-2, for the funding of its research in the early 1960s. In 1971 Honeywell submitted a statement to a British parliamentary committee stating that "U.S. Government funding of Honeywell Information Systems R&D was less than 1 percent of the company's 1970 R&D expenditure of $100 million. Even this small percentage was limited to special sub-system contracts for electronics or special-purpose devices that had little or no relationship to mainstream commercial EDP business." See *Fourth Report—The Prospects for the United Kingdom Computer Industry in the 1970's*, vol. III, House of Commons, Select Committee on Science and Technology (London: Her Majesty's Stationery Office, 1971), p. 93.

81. Interview with Professor Fernando Corbato, MIT, February 16, 1984. The Air Force sponsored Project Guardian, an effort to produce a secure operating system, at Project MAC in the early 1970s. See Massachusetts Institute of Technology, *Report of the President, 1974* (MIT Press, 1974). Honeywell produced the first computer system ever awarded the top A1 security rating by the Pentagon—see the advertisement in *Scientific American*, vol. 252 (April 1985), pp. 12, 13.

82. For example, Honeywell's DPS-88 mainframe computer uses packaging technology for electronic circuitry similar to that it had developed for the Defense Department's Very High Speed Integrated Circuit (VHSIC) program, and some of its new high-speed logic circuits are direct outgrowths of the VHSIC contracts. See

Honeywell retreated into its military markets in the late 1970s.[83] Finally, in 1986, Honeywell gave up on computers and its commercial computer operations were sold, though it retained a minority stake in a joint venture with Japan's Nippon Electric Company and France's Bull. Today Honeywell only markets commercial computer products made by others.

Burroughs

Burroughs was among the earliest U.S. firms to work on computers. In 1947 Irwin Travis, formerly director of research at the Moore School, left the EDVAC project to establish a computer research group at Burroughs. This group, drawn from participants in many of the big computer projects of the day, built several experimental computers, but did not produce its first commercial product, a small programmable electronic calculator, until 1956. Instead, Burroughs' entry into the large, general purpose computer field resulted from its 1956 acquisition of the Electrodata Corporation (formerly a division of the Consolidated Engineering Corporation), a small West Coast manufacturer. As noted, Electrodata built a computer, the Datatron, in collaboration with researchers at the Jet Propulsion Laboratory of the California Institute of Technology, with government funding. This machine had highly innovative features and sold well.[84] A more advanced model of the Datatron became the Burroughs 205 and put Burroughs on the map as a major computer producer.

During the late 1950s and early 1960s Burroughs helped to produce several important military computers that had a significant impact on its technology base. These machines included a computer to process data for the Air Force's SAGE air defense system and the guidance computer for the Atlas intercontinental ballistic missile (ICBM). One of these computers may have been the first transistorized computer to go into

---

Electronics, November 3, 1982, pp. 93–95, September 22, 1981, pp. 89–93, and February 10, 1983, p. 175.

83. Flamm, *Targeting,* p. 98, fig. 4-1.

84. The Datatron was the first mass-produced computer to feature index registers; it also had floating-point arithmetic. See Rosen, *Electronic Computers,* pp. 18–19; and Moreau, *Computer Comes of Age,* pp. 62, 66. IBM considered the Datatron serious competition for its model 650 when it was introduced; see Hurd, pp. 407–08.

mass production.[85] Many other military computers were also produced during this period.[86]

In 1961 Burroughs publicly announced a computer, the D-825, which it had built for a military command and control system. This machine had advanced and innovative architectural features, including the use of multiple processors, a hardware "stack" memory, and fast "scratchpad" memory in its central processing units. These ideas were absorbed into its subsequent commercial offerings—the Burroughs B5000 computer, and its successor, the B5500.[87] At the time, new high-level computer languages incorporating the idea of stack memory were being introduced, and the architecture lent itself to the use of this software.

The Burroughs commercial computer lines of the late 1960s and 1970s built on these architectural innovations.[88] This specialized approach to hardware and systems paid off in steady growth for Burroughs during the following two decades, and by the early 1980s, it closely trailed DEC as the top competition for IBM computers. Its absorption of Sperry's computer line, in the newly formed UNISYS, pushed a restructured Burroughs into a solid second place in 1986.

Burroughs became heavily involved in government-sponsored efforts to build advanced supercomputers in the late 1960s and 1970s. After 1965, the Defense Department's Advanced Research Projects Agency supported the development of the experimental ILLIAC IV supercomputer, a design that pushed the limits of available technology.[89] Burroughs was selected as the systems contractor to build the machine to specifications set by a University of Illinois design team. In 1976 Burroughs began delivering another large system, the Parallel Element Processing Ensemble (PEPE), based on a design originally produced by

85. The Smithsonian Institution makes this claim for the Atlas. The transistorized computer built by Burroughs for SAGE, however, seems to have been delivered earlier. See Smithsonian Institution Factsheet, "Atlas ICBM Guidance Computer (Mod I)," Air and Space Museum.

86. See Weik, "A Third Survey."

87. C. Gordon Bell and Allen Newell, eds., *Computer Structures: Readings and Examples* (McGraw-Hill, 1971), pp. 257–61; David J. Kuck, *The Structures of Computers and Computation*, vol. 1 (John Wiley and Sons, 1978), pp. 35, 257, 284–85, 343, 424; and Fisher and others, *IBM*, pp. 244–47.

88. Kuck, *Structures*, p. 343.

89. See Howard Falk, "Reaching for a Gigaflop," vol. 13, *IEEE Spectrum* (October 1976), pp. 65–69; and Hockney and Jesshope, *Parallel Computers*, pp. 17–18. ILLIAC IV pioneered the use of integrated circuits for computer memory, integrated circuit ECL logic, complex multilayered printed circuit boards, and computer-assisted design automation, as well as the radical ILLIAC IV parallel processor computer architecture.

the Bell Telephone Laboratories, for the U.S. Army's ballistic missile defense program. The experience with producing computer systems made up of large arrays of processing units led Burroughs to announce its Burroughs Scientific Processor (BSP) for commercial sale in 1977, but poor sales prospects led Burroughs to withdraw the product in 1980 before any had been sold. Nonetheless, the increasingly sophisticated computer systems that Burroughs shipped in the 1970s reflected its experience with state-of-the-art components and packaging technology, and advanced computer architectures.[90]

National Cash Register

National Cash Register (NCR), after passing up the unique opportunity to plunge into the computer business offered it by the Navy at the close of World War II, reconsidered when the commercial computer market began to grow in the mid-1950s. In 1953 the company purchased the Computer Research Corporation (CRC), one of the West Coast producers of smaller, magnetic drum-based computers that had spun off from Northrop. CRC had developed small computers under government contract for use in military applications. Further development of these products gave NCR a line of small business computers that it marketed successfully. In the late 1950s NCR produced a larger-scale system, the NCR 304, on which it had done work in design and development, but which was manufactured by General Electric and used GE's transistorized circuitry.

In the early 1960s NCR had some success in marketing a version of the Control Data 160 minicomputer under its own label, and in 1962, shipped its first transistorized computer, the NCR 315. Targeted at small businesses looking for a low-cost solution to data processing requirements, the NCR 315 was well received. Improvements made to the 315 sustained its computer operations through the mid-1960s, when a new line aimed at the same smaller business markets was introduced. NCR again continued a program of improvements to its products in the early

90. On the technology developed for ILLIAC IV and PEPE, see Hockney and Jesshope, *Parallel Computers,* and Baum, *System Builders.* Burroughs' main production computers (as well as the BSP), for example, used ECL logic chips, as pioneered in these machines. See Hockney and Jesshope, *Parallel Computers* p. 193. IBM, in contrast, did not use ECL logic chips in its mainframe computers until 1985. See "Hitachi CPU Challenges IBM," *Electronics,* March 18 1985, p. 17.

1970s and successfully expanded its share of these computer markets. The key to NCR's success has been its determined pursuit of a specific market segment, notably, banking and retailing applications of small- and moderate-sized business systems.

Bell Telephone Laboratories

Although not commonly thought of as a computer producer, American Telephone and Telegraph's Bell laboratories had a significant impact on computer technology during the past forty years. Bell labs' continuing advancement of semiconductor technology was directly related to its early work in computers. In the early 1950s, just after the transistor had been invented, Bell agreed to apply the infant technology to the construction of compact, ruggedized military computers for defense use. In 1951 the Transistor Digital Computer (TRADIC) project was begun, under contract to the U.S. Air Force. Bell wanted to produce a laboratory demonstration model of a solid state computer that could be used for airborne control applications. A second project, undertaken for the Navy at about the same time, was aimed at producing a special purpose radar tracking computer system using transistor technology.[91]

The laboratory prototype of TRADIC was delivered in 1954; a flyable field model was successfully installed in a C-131 airplane in 1957. The TRADIC was arguably the first large transistorized digital computer produced.[92] The success and reliability of the TRADIC system prompted Bell to begin a formal research program in transistor computers in 1954, aimed at exploiting new types of transistors with better switching and power consumption characteristics, and new magnetic materials and components for high-speed memories.

Concurrently, the Philco Radio Corporation had developed new alloy-junction transistors and disclosed new types of circuitry, known as direct-coupled transistor logic (DCTL), for use in computers. With Air Force support, Bell began work on a project to use the new DCTL

---

91. For descriptions of the early transistor computer projects at Bell labs, see C. A. Warren, B. McMillan, and B. D. Holbrook, "Military Systems Engineering and Research," in M. D. Fagen, ed., *A History of Engineering and Science in the Bell System*, vol. 2: *National Service in War and Peace (1925–1975)* (Murray Hill, N.J.: Bell Telephone Laboratories, 1978), pp. 625–36.

92. TRADIC did not, however, store programs internally. Instead, plugboards were used to simplify construction of the experimental machine. TRADIC used an electronic delay line for its memory.

circuits, as well as core memory, in an advanced computer to be called Leprechaun.[93] Bell finished Leprechaun in 1957 and delivered it to the Air Force in 1959.

However, AT&T was barred from commercial computer business unrelated to its primary communications activities by the terms of a consent agreement with the U.S. Department of Justice, drafted as part of the 1956 settlement of an antitrust case initiated by the U.S. government. The agreement permitted AT&T to supply such systems to the government and to keep working on designing computer systems as part of its contracts for military systems. These included the computing systems for the Nike-Zeus antiballistic missile system and the guidance systems for the TITAN and THOR-Agena ICBMs.[94] Sperry Rand's UNIVAC division produced both systems under the technical direction of Bell labs. They were early examples of Bell's collaboration with major computer systems producers on military contracts.

Military communications requirements also provided a stimulus to development of techniques for transmitting digital data to computers. The first military equipment to make significant use of transistors were modems (modulators-demodulators) built for the Army Signal Corps and used to transmit digital data from radar sites. Bell had also joined MIT, IBM, and Burroughs in developing the SAGE air defense system in the mid-1950s. One by-product of this program was the development of the first high-speed communications systems to transmit digital data to a computer over commercial telephone lines.[95] The equipment developed for these systems evolved into the modems sold on commercial markets, and AT&T rapidly grew into the most prominent producer of data communications equipment in U.S. markets.[96]

Throughout the 1960s, Bell's computer development work on the data processing requirements of antiballistic missile (ABM) systems continued. These systems provided some of the first experience with computer architectures linking multiple computer processors in parallel to speed

93. Leprechaun used both delay lines and magnetic core memory.
94. The Nike-Zeus computer system, first demonstrated in the field around 1961, was one of the first computers to use a multiple-processor architecture.
95. See S. E. Watters and others, "Communications," in Fagen, ed., *A History of Engineering and Science*, pp. 549–50, 579–80.
96. A modem converts digital data to an analog electrical signal at one end of a telephone line, and back to digital data at the other end. Phister, Jr., *Data Processing*, pp. 22, 76, 271, describes the dominance of the data communications market by Bell products.

computation. The very high data processing rates required for an effective missile defense led to development of the experimental PEPE, in the mid-1960s, as part of the NIKE-X ABM system. The later Safeguard ABM system used a Bell-designed central logic and control (CLC) computer, configured with up to ten processors to control its operation.[97] Both machines were steps forward in the development of parallel computer architectures.[98]

Although the 1956 consent decree effectively removed Bell from the market for general purpose computers, Bell continued to design and build special purpose telephone switching computers for use within the Bell system. They were designed with high reliability in mind, but more important, was the growth of software research in Bell labs.

Computer software research expanded in the early 1960s when Bell joined with MIT and GE in the Multics project, an important effort to develop a sophisticated time-sharing operating system, undertaken as part of Project MAC. Although Bell participated in the program from 1964 to 1969, it dropped out after realizing that the large, complex system would not be completed in a reasonable time.[99] Bell researchers who had worked on the Multics project persisted in developing a simplified time-sharing system for a small DEC PDP-7 computer, and this simplified operating system, UNIX, soon spread beyond Bell's boundaries, into computers for the academic research community.[100] Bell labs also

---

97. Bell Telephone Laboratories, "ABM Research and Development at Bell Laboratories," prepared for U.S. Army Ballistic Missile Defense Systems Command (Whippany, N.J.: Bell Telephone Laboratories, 1975), pp. 2-13, 2-15.

98. See, for example, Neil R. Lincoln, "Supercomputers = Colossal Computations and Enormous Expectations + Renowned Risks," *IEEE Computer,* vol. 16 (May 1983), pp. 41–44. All these developments meant substantial collaboration with the chief computer producers—UNIVAC on the CLC computer, and Honeywell (and later the Systems Development Corporation and Burroughs) on Parallel Element Processing Ensemble (PEPE). See also Baum, *System Builders,* pp. 146–47.

99. Interview with Victor A. Vysottsky, Murray Hill, New Jersey, April 30, 1984.

100. See Dennis Ritchie, "Evolution of the UNIX Timesharing System," *Microsystems,* vol. 5 (October 1984). Academic development of UNIX, particularly virtual memory versions of the system, and networking and communications extensions, implemented at the University of California, Berkeley, was financed by DARPA. See Phil Margolis, "The History of UNIX," *The DEC Professional,* vol. 5 (February 1986), pp. 18–19; and Donald W. Cragun, "Convergence Effort Combines 4.2 with UNIX System V," *Computer Technology Review,* vol. 6 (February 13, 1987), pp. 14–23. The development of an important new language, C, also took place at Bell labs as part of this effort. C was designed with ease of writing a compiler in mind, and rewriting UNIX in C permitted the UNIX system to be shipped to many different kinds of hardware

expanded software research into programming languages, computer network concepts, applications programs to increase the productivity of the Bell system, and theoretical computer science.[101]

By 1980 computer-related expenditure had risen to half of Bell labs resources.[102] When the Bell system was deregulated in the early 1980s, the restructured AT&T had the technology base needed to immediately become a serious competitor in the international computer industry.

Discretion over Valor: Philco, GE, and RCA

Competing directly with IBM, three companies tried hard to produce large mainframe computers during these decades, but after bloody battles, they had to retreat finally from the field of battle. Two of those firms—GE and RCA—are large firms with ample financial resources and technological expertise in electronics and electrical machinery.

The third firm, Philco, was also a large and diversified manufacturer of electrical equipment.[103] It had developed a fast and relatively reliable type of transistor in the early days of semiconductor technology in 1954, under government contract. In 1955, because Philco was the only firm making reliable surface barrier transistors, NSA awarded it a contract to build a transistor computer using the logical design of the ERA 1103, the first computer with core memory.[104] The National Security Agency wanted an even better machine that would use transistors instead of vacuum tube logic. In 1958 Philco delivered it—the SOLO, which NSA engineers finally debugged in 1959.

Other large contracts soon followed SOLO. For $1.6 million the Navy purchased a larger, improved computer, the CXPQ, for its David Taylor Model Basin research facility. Three airborne, transistorized computers were built for the Air Force. Philco later marketed a commercial version of SOLO as the TRANSAC S-1000, and an improved commercial S-2000 based on the CXPQ soon followed. When improved transistors were incorporated into the design, the original 2000 was dubbed the 210,

---

with relative ease. Portability of software written for UNIX among different types of hardware is an important feature of the UNIX operating system.

101. W. S. Brown, B. D. Holbrook, and M. D. McIlroy, "Computer Science," in S. Millman, ed., *A History of Engineering and Science in the Bell System*, vol. 5: *Communications Sciences (1925–1980)* (Murray Hill, N.J.: American Telephone and Teletype Bell Laboratories, 1984), pp. 371–85.

102. Ibid., pp. 369–70.

103. Fisher and others, *IBM*, p. 88.

104. Snyder, "Influence of the U.S. Cryptologic Organizations," pp. 61, 63–64.

and the new model sold as the 211.[105] Philco later introduced a smaller model 212. The Philco 210 and 211 were among the largest and most powerful computers of their day, true supercomputers.

Ford purchased Philco in 1961, however, in a bid to increase its defense business. At the time, the federal government was stepping up space and defense programs, and in response, Ford management decided to phase out Philco's other activities and focus on these new markets. By 1963 Philco had left the commercial computer business.

RCA's involvement with computers was lengthier and more intense than that of Philco. RCA had been doing research in analog computers for fire control during the Second World War and, after the war, continued this research, focusing on the development of novel electronic components. It had participated in von Newmann's IAS computer project, and its research in technology for core memory eventually embroiled it in the patent litigation surrounding MIT's claims for the memories developed by the Whirlwind project. One of the earliest electronic firms to jump into semiconductor research after Bell Telephone's 1947 announcement of the transistor, RCA worked on classified government computer projects in the early 1950s.

RCA invested a great deal of resources in its first commercial digital computer, the BIZMAC, which it developed under contract to the Army for logistics applications. This large system, designed for business use from the start, featured advanced concepts: up to two hundred tape drives could be connected to it and handled under program control with no human intervention, clearly a valuable feature for a machine designed to deal with large data bases. The BIZMAC took considerable time to develop, and, unfortunately, by the time it was first shipped in 1956, its component technology was outdated. It was slow and had a limited high-speed core memory: to quote Herbert Grosch, "the size of a house but with dog-kennel performance."[106]

In the late 1950s RCA was the main contractor for the Air Force BMEWS project. Though the central processing facility was subcontracted to IBM, RCA built some of the system's computers and later used the electronic circuitry and packaging developed for this project in its commercial computers.[107]

Though definitely more interested in other areas of its diverse portfolio

105. Fisher and others, *IBM*, pp. 88–89; Snyder, "Influence of the U.S. Cryptologic Organizations," p. 65; and Katz and Phillips, "Computer Industry," p. 203.
106. Grosch, "The Way It Was," p. 77.
107. Fisher and others, *IBM*, pp. 73–75.

of electronics investments, RCA plunged back into the commercial fray in late 1959 when it delivered the transistorized model 501. The 501, though slow, ran one of the earliest compilers for the standard business language Cobol and was a commercial success. In the early 1960s the company shipped two other transistor computers, the smaller 301 and the large-scale 601. According to RCA insiders, the 601 was a technical and financial disaster that seriously damaged its reputation; the 301, however, was a modest success.[108]

RCA was not in a particularly secure position when IBM announced the System 360 line in 1964. Faced with a new challenge, RCA opted for a novel solution—it decided to build a system that would be compatible with software written for the 360. RCA's plan, which led to its Spectra 70 series of computers, was one of the first attempts to compete with IBM by building a family of machines with some IBM compatibility. RCA's engineers took early IBM customer manuals and designed a system that would behave in functionally identical ways with the details disclosed in the IBM manuals. Unfortunately, RCA chose to use its own unique input-output structure, rather than IBM's blueprint, for its systems, which meant that all IBM software had to be rewritten. This move turned out to be a costly mistake.

RCA also competed by offering IBM-style function at lower prices. Two tactics were used. First, RCA created its machines to perform at levels midway between the levels attained by IBM models. Second, RCA employed modern integrated circuit (IC) technology. These circuits had dropped in price substantially after IBM froze its System 360 circuit design. RCA invested fairly little in research for the system—the Spectra 70 was developed in two years at a cost of $15 million, compared with about four years and one-half billion dollars invested by IBM in the System 360.[109] Consequently, RCA could deliver somewhat compatible computers two years after IBM's first announcement.

The strategy seemed moderately successful, and although some problems occurred, RCA's computer operations were generally financially solvent. Its big problems arose in 1970 when IBM announced its next important series of enhancements to System 360, the System 370. Although its stock of Spectra 70 machines (largely leased out to customers) was of far more recent vintage than IBM's 360, RCA faced the

108. Ibid.

109. Katherine Davis Fishman, *The Computer Establishment* (Harper and Row, 1981), pp. 182–83.

prospect of replacing them with new machines at lower prices. Furthermore, RCA could choose strict compatibility with the newer IBM systems and write off its previous user base, or it could go its own way with the incompatible Spectra architecture. Because of a possible, heavy financial drain well into the foreseeable future, RCA decided to quit the business. In 1971 RCA sold its existing computer operations to Sperry Rand.

General Electric's experience in computer manufacture was similar to RCA's in some respects. It began producing military computers in the late 1940s and continued these activities throughout the 1950s.[110] Its first commercial computer products were the Electronic Method of Accounting (ERMA) system, a specialized computer for check processing developed jointly with the Bank of America and the Stanford Research Institute, and its manufacture of the NCR 304 from NCR's design. Both were shipped around 1956.

General Electric did not enter the commercial market in a serious way, however, until 1961, when it delivered the first of its 200 series of small, general purpose computers. This was a very limited product line, however, even when supplemented by the DATANET-30, an innovative special purpose communications computer that was shipped in the early 1960s.[111]

Until 1963, GE had committed few resources to computer development and therefore had little to show. At the end of that year, GE took the plunge and announced two new computer lines: the 400 series of small business machines, and the 600 series, a pair of machines targeted at the large-scale general purpose mainframe market, particularly the

110. Its military computers included the OMIBAC, a scientific calculating machine used internally in ballistics studies; the Office of Air Research Automatic Computer (OARAC), built for and installed at the U.S. Air Force Office of Air Research in 1953; the HERMES, a missile guidance computer developed in the early 1950s; a lab model of a fire control computer developed in the mid 1950s; and the GEVIC, a solid state magnetic drum computer for fire control and guidance applications, developed in the late 1950s. See Wells, "Origins of the Computer Industry," p. 269; Weik, "A Third Survey," pp. 726–27, General Electric, *GEVIC Manual* (Johnson City, N.Y.: General Electric Light Military Electronics Department, circa 1958), p. 1.

111. This machine put General Electric into the lead in specialized communications, but was not followed with announcements of other products until the end of the 1960s. Other manufacturers had begun to ship similar communications processors by the mid-1960s—including the Control Data 8050/8090, the IBM 7740, and the Collins Data Central. See Moreau, *Computer,* p. 131; and Jarema and Sussenguth, "IBM Data Communications," p. 398.

IBM 7090/7094.[112] The year 1964 was marked by GE's acquisition of Machines Bull, the French business and computing machine producer, and Olivetti's electronics division in Italy. General Electric also announced another group of small computers, the 100 series, to fill out the product line.

A commitment to the newly born area of time-sharing accompanied GE's expansion into computers in the 1960s. In the early 1960s the company had worked with a group of researchers on the Dartmouth Basic system, one of the early forerunners of time-sharing, which allowed multiple users to use the Basic programming language interactively, simultaneously, on a single computer. In 1964 GE joined MIT's Project MAC, which the Defense Department had funded in an effort to produce an advanced time-sharing system. Special modifications were to be made to a GE 635 computer to allow it to carry out the specialized memory management tasks required for time-sharing. General Electric, along with the Bell Telephone Laboratories, had agreed to invest significant resources in developing the Multics time-sharing system in collaboration with MIT. GE thus became an early leader in time-sharing systems—by the end of 1968, it had fifty time-sharing installations in place around the world.[113]

Nonetheless, GE faced serious problems in the late 1960s. The technology of many products was aging—it had cut prices to bring price performance into line with IBM's System 360 but had made little progress in introducing newer products. And it had a highly incompatible mix of machines in different price and performance ranges. In 1970 just as GE was deciding whether to undertake a large, expensive new program of R&D investment, IBM announced the System 370. A big investment program would have been required, and GE had competing claims on these resources from its nuclear power and jet engine operations. Like RCA, GE decided to toss in the towel, and in 1970, announced the transfer of its computer hardware business to Honeywell.

Although GE had never entirely committed itself to computers, it never entirely left the field either. GE retained its financially prosperous computer services business. And in the early 1980s, as industrial automation appeared on the verge of remarkable growth, GE made serious new commitments to developing industrial automation equipment. Thus

---

112. General Electric even developed software to convert IBM 7090 programs to run on its 600 line. There were also conversion aids to transfer IBM 1401 software to the 400 series. Unfortunately, the 400 and 600 series were not compatible.

113. Fisher and others, *IBM*, p. 193.

GE continues to have big investments in a specialized and expanding area of computer systems manufacture.

The Minicomputer Invasion: DEC, SDS, and Their Kin

As described earlier, ancestors of the modern minicomputer had appeared in the middle of the 1950s in the form of the Bendix G-15 and Librascope LGP-30. These computers offered relatively low cost and performance but attracted new classes of users who could not have afforded the costs of a large mainframe computer. These computers usually used magnetic drum main memories, however, and were relatively slow.

In the late 1950s the first steps toward combining more advanced performance with lower costs were taken when researcher Kenneth Olsen left MIT to found the Digital Equipment Corporation (DEC). Olsen had done important work on the core memory for the Whirlwind project and had then been posted at IBM's Poughkeepsie plant for two and a half years to supervise MIT's joint work with IBM on developing the SAGE computers. After returning to MIT, Olsen had designed MIT's TX-0 computer, whose function was to test new core memories and driver circuitry. In 1957 Olsen and fellow MIT researchers found local venture capital to back their newly organized enterprise, DEC. Their initial product was a line of computer modules similar to those built for the TX-0 and its successor, the TX-2.

By 1961 they had decided to substitute a brand-new high-performance transistor just introduced by Philco for the older components of the TX-0 and market it as the Programmed Data Processor (PDP-1). The product offered reasonably high performance at a low cost ($120,000 for a complete system).[114] An immediate success with the local academic research community in Cambridge, the computer was soon being used in research on time-sharing systems being carried out at MIT and Bolt, Beranek, and Newman, a local consulting firm staffed with many MIT and Harvard academics. A total of fifty PDP-1s were manufactured, and even cheaper computers, like the PDP-4 and the PDP-5, based on technology developed at MIT, soon followed.[115] By virtue of its low price and reasonable performance, the PDP-5 in particular carved out a

114. W. A. Atherton, *From Compass to Computer: A History of Electrical and Electronics Engineering* (San Francisco Press, 1984), p. 295.
115. Ibid. Half of the sales were to one customer, International Telephone and Telegraph (ITT). See also Bell and others, *Computer Engineering*, pp. 123–208.

whole new market. In 1965 DEC introduced the PDP-8, using new components and manufacturing techniques that cut the cost to $18,000 for a complete system.[116] Demand for this system was enormous, especially among sophisticated scientific and industrial customers who used it for data reduction and analysis and process control. DEC reimplemented the same basic system using new components and packaging many times during the following decade.

Digital had by that time focused on new markets beyond very small, very low-cost machines. In 1964 the corporation delivered its first PDP-6, a larger-sized machine and the first commercial computer designed to support time-sharing, with a system price in the $350,000 to $750,000 range.[117] The PDP-6 later benefited from the intensive development of time-sharing systems in Cambridge, where the use of DEC hardware on projects supported by DARPA was common.

When appropriate software was marketed in early 1965, the PDP-6 became the first commercially available general purpose time-sharing system. This computer, large enough to compete with some of the smaller mainframe systems in IBM's line, was sold without the extensive software and support services bundled with IBM's products. It was targeted at a different set of users—the sophisticated academic and industrial users willing and able to develop their own applications to run on the hardware. In 1970 the PDP-6 was replaced by the PDP-10, which became the basis for various DEC systems targeted at many of the same markets as the middle and lower ends of IBM's 360 and 370 line—general purpose business data processing, as well as scientific and time-sharing applications. By the end of the decade, however, DEC had decided to end this foray into IBM's traditional markets and announced that it would not produce follow-up products for this series of large machines.

Instead, much of DEC's effort in the 1970s focused on the PDP-11 series of computers, introduced at roughly the same time as the PDP-6. The PDP-11 line became an entire family of compatible computers, aimed at the same sophisticated industrial and scientific market that had made its smaller computers a success. Systems configured around PDP-11s ran up to $250,000 in cost, offered very high performance, and sold well (more than fifty thousand were sold from 1970 to 1977).[118] In 1977 DEC announced the first model of a new line, with virtual memory, that

116. Ibid., p. 296; and Weik, "A Third Survey," p. 229.
117. Fisher and others, *IBM*, p. 274.
118. Ibid., p. 277.

continued the PDP-11 architecture, the VAX 11/780. The VAX computers offered performance approaching that of a mainframe at a fraction of the cost and were an immediate hit in the scientific marketplace. Ultimately, a new category, the superminicomputer, was coined to describe machines of the VAX class. The PDP-11/VAX architecture has since been elevated to the architectural standard for all DEC computers, small and large, and large VAX-based computer installations are currently being positioned by DEC as competition for even large IBM mainframes.

In retrospect, the academic and scientific markets chosen by DEC were a natural target for a new entrant to the industry. Because computers used in research often involve new applications or are dedicated to a single application, the advantages of access to a large software base for established applications are greatly reduced. New applications require new software. With computers mainly dedicated to just a few applications, the performance of the computer is more important than the availability of software. In both cases, high performance, or cost-effectiveness, is more important in the selection of a computer than compatibility with older software.

Scientific Data Systems (SDS) enjoyed an even more meteoric rise to success. Max Palevsky and Bob Beck, who had started in the computer business by working at Bendix in the early 1950s and had left to organize a computer division at Packard-Bell in 1957, founded SDS in 1961.[119] Once there, they interested Werner von Braun's missile development group, then part of the Army Ballistic Missile Agency, in purchasing a computer they were developing. The Packard-Bell computers built on a technology base developed on government contracts—designs produced for Packard-Bell's transistorized missile guidance computer, the Transistorized Real-Time Incremental Computer Expandable (TRICE), had been the basis for the circuitry used in Packard-Bell's successful, small 250 transistor computer. When Palevsky found Packard-Bell uninterested in producing a low-cost scientific machine based on the 250's design, he left with Beck and founded SDS.[120]

119. Fishman, *The Computer Establishment*, pp. 217–25, summarizes the brief history of SDS.

120. See the descriptions of the TRICE (Transistorized Real-Time Incremental Computer Expandable) and Packard-Bell 250 in Weik, "A Third Survey." Note that the PB 250 was architecturally similar to the British NPL Pilot Ace computer, a fact that Bell and Newell, *Computer Structures*, p. 191, attribute to Harry Huskey's having worked on the design.

The machine they then built, the SDS 910, was a small, high-powered scientific computer, well suited to real-time data processing and reduction tasks. It was the first nonmilitary computer to use high-performance silicon transistors. At $80,000 to $90,000 a system, it was one of the first modern minicomputers, selling well in the same instrumentation and control applications that DEC was going after with its early machines. SDS quickly followed with its models 920 and 930, improved versions targeted at the same markets.

One reason for the rapid success of SDS was patronage by NASA, which had absorbed von Braun's space program. The first SDS 910 was installed in NASA's Goddard Space Flight Center in 1962. NASA was to purchase many SDS machines for control, telemetry, and simulation applications during the 1960s—perhaps 40 percent of Scientific Data's production.[121]

Like DEC, SDS benefited from the government-funded effort to develop time-sharing. DARPA supported Project Genie at the University of California, Berkeley, which developed an advanced time-sharing system on a specially modified SDS 930. The modified 930 became the SDS 940, and along with the Berkeley software, was being marketed commercially by 1966, the second time-sharing product to become available.[122] Under this stimulus, SDS became a principal supplier of small time-sharing systems—Tymshare, one of the first computer service vendors, used an SDS 940 time-sharing system.

SDS enjoyed remarkable growth. Though it had been founded after DEC, its revenues surpassed those of DEC in 1964, and it continued to retain that lead through the rest of the decade.[123] Like DEC, it too had begun to produce some larger systems, and by the middle of the decade was competing with some segments of the bottom and middle of IBM's product line. After IBM announced the System 360, SDS launched the SDS 92, the first commercial machine to use integrated circuits.

In early 1969, the Xerox Corporation, eager to enter the computer industry, approached the SDS management. By the end of the year, SDS had been merged into the Xerox organization, and shortly after that, SDS began a steady decline. Some observers attributed the decline to Xerox's attempts to guide SDS away from its traditional scientific marketplace into the general purpose commercial market, toe-to-toe

121. Fishman, *The Computer Establishment,* p. 222.
122. See Bell and Newell, *Computer Structures,* p. 275.
123. Interview with Robert Spinrad, Palo Alto, California, February 1984.

with IBM. Others blamed the tapering off in NASA's capital expenditures. In any event, revenues and profits fell, and in 1975, Xerox announced its exit from the mainframe computer business, though it still maintains important activities in office automation equipment, computer peripherals, and research. Xerox's customer base in computers was absorbed into the Honeywell computer business.

Several other firms became important forces in the minicomputer business in the 1970s. One of these was Data General, founded by three former DEC engineers in 1968. Another was Prime Computer, which had been set up originally to build minicomputers using the Computer Controls Corporation (CCC) architecture after Honeywell lost interest in the CCC products it had absorbed in its takeover.[124] Hewlett-Packard moved from its traditional scientific instrumentation and calculator lines in the late 1960s into computers. Wang Laboratories Incorporated specialized in small systems oriented toward office automation. Wang, of course, was founded by the same An Wang who had worked in Howard Aiken's computer laboratory in the late 1940s and who had done seminal work on the magnetic core memory. And after 1974, Tandem Computers moved fault-tolerant computing techniques out of the military and aerospace markets and into commercial markets with its innovative computer systems.[125]

Amdahl and the Rise of the Plug-Compatible Manufacturers

In 1970 Gene M. Amdahl, one of IBM's most well-known computer architects, credited with the design of the IBM 704 and many important elements of System 360, left IBM to found a competing firm. Amdahl, thoroughly knowledgeable about the 360 and 370 architecture, decided that he could design and build a plug-compatible central processing unit and attach to it the peripherals manufactured by other plug-compatible manufacturers (PCMs), which in the 1960s had begun manufacturing so-called plug-compatible peripherals for the IBM System 360. In that way, without having to make the heavy investments required to build all parts

124. Gardner Hendrie, "From the First 16-bit Mini to Fault Tolerant Computers," *Computer Museum Report*, vol. 15 (Spring 1986), p. 7.

125. Ibid., pp. 8–9. Fault-tolerant techniques use redundant processors and other components to allow information processing to continue despite the failure of some part of the computer system. Another start-up with CCC roots, Stratus Computer, joined Tandem in the fault-tolerant commercial market in 1980.

of the system, it was now possible to become a competitive producer of the processor unit at the heart of a computer, purchase the needed peripherals, and package a complete system. Amdahl would then build a more powerful, IBM-compatible processor. The Amdahl strategy improved on RCA's failed attempt at IBM compatibility by sticking exactly to the IBM design while following RCA's path in using leading-edge components to offer superior price performance.

The recession of 1970 was under way, however, and Amdahl found it difficult to secure the necessary capital. He first approached Hitachi (a Japanese manufacturer, which turned his proposal down), then opened discussions with its rival Fujitsu.[126] At the end of 1972, Fujitsu reached an agreement with Amdahl to supply the new firm with funding in exchange for 24 percent of the equity in the new venture. The research and development were largely done in Amdahl's Silicon Valley facilities, while Fujitsu in Japan undertook the actual manufacturing. The first system, an immediate success, was installed in 1975; use of superior components made it possible to deliver IBM performance at less than IBM prices. Amdahl retired as chief executive of the company bearing his name in 1980, after differences over corporate policy with Fujitsu had emerged. In 1984 Fujitsu increased its stake in Amdahl to just under 50 percent, effectively taking control of the firm.[127]

Other PCMs soon followed Amdahl into the market, and they continue to constrain IBM's pricing. The most important was Itel, which marketed processors manufactured in Japan by Hitachi. Itel was sold to National Advanced Systems, a subsidiary of U.S. producer National Semiconductor. Through this subsidiary, National Semiconductor continues to market an ample number of IBM-compatible mainframe computers manufactured in Japan by Hitachi.

Reactions Abroad

The breadth and scope of the U.S. computer industry's activities had posed little competitive threat to foreign firms until the late 1950s. As

126. This account of negotiations with Japanese firms is based on George E. Lindamood, "The Rise of the Japanese Computer Industry," *Office of Naval Research Far East Scientific Bulletin*, vol. 7 (October–December 1982), pp. 57–58.

127. John W. Ventry, "The Global Industry . . . the Datamation 100," *Datamation*, vol. 31 (June 1, 1985), p. 96.

late as 1958, the annual production of digital computer systems in all U.S. firms amounted to a little more than 3,000 units, worth about $289 million.[128] Within just five years, however, that figure had increased to $822 million, and if attachments and peripherals were included, computers had probably become a billion dollar industry in the United States by 1963.[129]

In the face of rapidly growing shipments of U.S. computers into their markets, foreign governments began taking a decided interest in the competitive position of their national computer industries in the early 1960s. A contemporaneous boom in U.S. foreign investment, directed mainly into industrialized country markets, raised the issue of "the American challenge" to their industrial base.[130] Besides being a rapidly growing sector, important in its own right, computers became a symbol of a perceived lag in national firms' ability to produce the technology-intensive goods at the leading edge of economic growth. IBM's announcement of the System 360 in 1964 was the symbolic act that roused governments to act, and in the middle years of the 1960s all foreign countries with significant computer industries promoted programs to stimulate their competitiveness.

128. The 1958 Census of Manufactures counted 3,180 complete digital computer systems shipped in the United States in that year. U.S. Department of Commerce, Bureau of the Census, 1963 *Census of Manufactures*, vol. 2 (GPO, 1966), p. 35F-12.

129. Ibid. Besides shipments of complete digital systems, the Census counted about $434 million in shipments of parts and attachments to computing and accounting machines, a large share of which were probably computer peripherals.

130. The phrase was coined in 1967 by Jean Jacques Servan Schreiber in *The American Challenge*, translated by Ronald Steel (Atheneum, 1968).

CHAPTER FIVE

Competition in Europe

IN ALL the industrialized countries, research groups formed after the war to explore the new computer technology. In the 1950s, England, with one of the most sophisticated computer technology bases in the world, rivaled the United States as world leader in research. In the 1960s, Japan, France, and Germany launched large-scale efforts to develop a national computer industry.

The economic history of the European computer industries presents striking contrasts with the experience of the American industry. For one thing, European governments provided only limited funds to support the development of both electronic component and computer technology in the 1950s and were reluctant to purchase new and untried technology for use in their military and other systems. European governments also concentrated their limited support on defense-oriented engineering and electronics firms. The American practice was to support military technology projects undertaken by industrial and business equipment firms that were mainly interested in commercial markets. These firms viewed their military business as a development vehicle for technology that eventually would be adapted and sold in the open marketplace. In the United States trained personnel could move easily among firms in both the industrial and academic worlds, and entrepreneurs readily found venture capital to establish small start-ups interested in commercializing new technical developments. Undoubtedly, the resulting quick and easy diffusion of new technology helped propel the United States into its leading position in the fifties, sixties, and seventies.

Statistics on the installed base of computers in the United States, Europe, and Japan offer a useful introduction to the development of computer industries. Estimates of the stock of digital computers, including minicomputers and excluding specialized processors, installed in the

Table 5-1. *International Use of Computers*

	Total number of electronic digital computers in use[a]				
Year	United States	United Kingdom	France	West Germany	Japan
1950	2	3	0	0	0
1955	240	13	5	5	0
1960	5,400	217	165	300	85
1965	24,700	1,582	1,500	2,300	1,870
1970	74,060	6,269	5,460	7,000	8,800
1974	165,040	14,400	16,100	18,800	26,100

Sources: Author's count for 1950; and Montgomery Phister, Jr., ed., *Data Processing Technology and Economics* (Digital Press and Santa Monica Publishing, 1979), pp. 287, 289.
a. General purpose and minicomputers.

largest Western producing countries during the years 1950 and 1974, are shown in table 5-1. The United States widened its lead relative to other countries in the use of computers during these years, while Britain slipped from an initially strong position. Japan probably had the greatest growth in computer use.

Since U.S. computer manufacturers have substantial operations in foreign markets, however, these figures offer little clue to the relative strength of national computer industries. Table 5-2 provides some information on this score, tabulating the percentage of systems installed by national and U.S. computer firms. By the mid-1970s, U.S. firms controlled the U.S. market, shipped most of the computers sold in Germany, produced more than half the processors sold in Britain, and sold 30 percent to forty percent of the computers purchased in Japan. The weakest foreign computer industries at that time were those of

Table 5-2. *Importance of National Firms in International Markets*[a]

Year	United States	United Kingdom	France	West Germany	Japan
	Percentage of computers installed by U.S. firms				
1961	100	17	49	70	56
1966	100	51	51	72	35
1971	n.a.	50	50	78	32
	Percentage of computers installed by foreign firms				
1974	5	70–75	92–95	80–85	45

Sources: 1961–1971 from Phister, Jr., *Data Processing*, p. 289; 1974 from U.S. Department of Commerce, *The American Computer Industry and its International Competitive Environment* (Government Printing Office, 1976), pp. 9, 26, 33, 38, 42.
n.a. Not available.
a. Differences in classification by nationality seem to be responsible for large discrepancies between the two series.

France and Germany, the strongest those of Britain and Japan. British competitiveness has since slipped further, while the Japanese position has strengthened.

Britain

At the end of World War II, British scientists and engineers were competing with the United States in the race to build electronic computers. On the face of it, the British had important assets. First, Britain's Alan Turing had published a fundamental paper in theoretical computer science, which had attracted von Neumann's interest just before the outbreak of hostilities. Second, the Colossus, the first machine resembling a modern electronic digital computer, minus the internally stored program of later designs, had already been constructed by the British cryptologists at Bletchley Park in 1943. At the same time, the large U.S. Navy program at National Cash Register's (NCR's) secret Dayton laboratory was just starting. Third, the British military laboratories, especially the Telecommunications Research Establishment (TRE), and the British Post Office laboratories had acquired an expertise in high-speed electronic circuitry, used mainly in radar, that matched the know-how developed in the United States in similar programs.

The British labored under handicaps, however. The economic hardships of postwar recovery dominated British life in the late 1940s, and a program of technological development as broad and as costly as that undertaken in the United States was unthinkable. The British were striving to repair the massive damage inflicted by the war. Restoring stability to a war-battered economy and empire was the first priority. Less visibly, and more important, the readiness of the armed services to support highly speculative and risky ventures by high-tech start-ups in the United States was not matched in the more tradition-bound British culture. To some extent, these difficulties lingered beyond the immediate postwar years.

Even before the war ended, Alan Turing was discussing the possibility of using the new high-speed electronics technology to construct the abstract logical machine he had devised in his 1936 paper.[1] In late 1945, at the request of the National Physical Laboratory—roughly the British

1. Andrew Hodges, *Alan Turing: The Enigma* (Simon and Schuster, 1983), p. 295.

equivalent of the U.S. National Bureau of Standards—Turing prepared a report outlining the design of a stored-program electronic digital computer. This proposal, though referring to the Moore School EDVAC report that had preceded it by some months, differed considerably in its conception of an electronic computer and contained some ideas more advanced than the Moore School-von Neumann concept.[2]

At the end of the war, as the ENIAC was being completed, British visitors were permitted to visit the project at the Moore School.[3] As in the United States, interest in applying the new electronics technology to computational problems had developed, and British scientists were quick to seek support for similar projects in British research establishments. The free interchange between American and British scientists that had been encouraged during the war continued. British visitors to American computer projects in 1945 and 1946 included Turing, individuals from TRE and the British Post Office, and Maurice V. Wilkes of Cambridge University, who attended a six-week Moore School lecture series on the EDVAC design in 1946.[4] In 1945 the organizing committee of the Archibald conference on computing, at MIT, was composed of three Britons and four Americans, illustrating the rough parity between British and American computing technology at the time.

Although key British scientists had attempted to channel efforts into a single national computer project to be sponsored by the National Physical Laboratory, scientific and institutional rivalries led to the establishment of at least three principal electronic computer projects by 1947. One, at Manchester University, enjoying support from the British

2. See B. E. Carpenter and R. W. Doran, "The Other Turing Machine," *Computer Journal*, vol. 20 (August 1977), pp. 269–70; Hodges, *Alan Turing*, pp. 321–29. Advanced concepts not found in the Moore School EDVAC report included those of subroutines and a stack (a sequence of sequentially accessible memory locations used for subroutine linkage), and a separate register for the address of the next instruction to be executed.

3. The first non-American visitor to view ENIAC was J. R. Womersly, superintendent of the Mathematics Division in the National Physical Laboratory. He immediately arranged to have Turing start a computer project in his division after his U.S. visit in the spring of 1945. Hodges, *Alan Turing*, pp. 306–07.

4. Ibid., pp. 306, 317, 342; Simon Lavington, *Early British Computers: The Story of Vintage Computers and the People Who Built Them* (Digital Press, 1980), p. 26; Kent C. Redmond and Thomas M. Smith, *Project Whirlwind: The History of a Pioneer Computer* (Digital Press, 1980), p. 26; and Herman H. Goldstine, *The Computer from Pascal to von Neumann* (Princeton University Press, 1972), pp. 217–20. Also making the pilgrimage to the ENIAC in 1946 were Douglas Hartree, who with Wilkes organized the Cambridge project, and F. C. Williams, who was to help organize the Manchester Mark I project.

Ministry of Defence and TRE, was started under the direction of mathematician Max Newman. Newman directed the Colossus team at Bletchley Park during the war. Its efforts had focused on the use of a novel memory technology using standard cathode ray tubes, devised by F. C. Williams at TRE. Williams and Tom Kilburn, a colleague at TRE, joined Newman at Manchester to build a simple computer to test the "Williams tube" memory concept. TRE provided technical support, and the Royal Society and Ministry of Defence offered financial support for this effort.[5]

Wilkes, an applied mathematician who had also labored in TRE during the war, directed a second project established at Cambridge University. The Cambridge group received support from the eminent mathematician Douglas N. Hartree, who had been prominent in prewar numerical computing in Britain. Wilkes explicitly based his machine, the EDSAC, on the American EDVAC design.

The third machine was to be a small-scale prototype of Turing's proposed machine, the Automatic Computing Engine (Ace). This Pilot Ace would be designed and built at the National Physical Laboratory, using the componentry built under contract by the British Post Office. The Pilot Ace, regarded as the British "national" computer project, was the most original and ambitious of the three English computer projects and, in 1946, got off to the earliest start. The Manchester computer team did not assemble until the end of that year, while the construction of EDSAC began only a little earlier that fall.

Manchester

The original Manchester computer, a test bed for the Williams tube memory concept, was a small (1,024 binary bits of data could be stored in its memory) prototype in operation by the summer of 1948, the first functioning stored-program electronic digital computer ever built anywhere. The Manchester computer group then expanded the original design to include greater amounts of Williams tube memory, as well as a secondary, slower memory on a magnetic drum they designed and built. By the summer of 1949, this augmented machine, christened the Manchester Mark I, was operating reliably.

5. Lavington, *Early British Computers*, pp. 36–37; and Hodges, *Alan Turing*, pp. 390–91.

Turing had by this time left the Ace project and joined the Manchester group, which wanted primarily to put together advanced hardware for mathematical calculations. The group devoted much early effort to devising architectural innovations. In particular, the Mark I was also the first computer to use a magnetic drum and introduced the concept of the index register, which allowed rapid access to sequences of memory storage locations.[6] Computers designed at Manchester in the following decades were to maintain this reputation for architectural advance.

In the fall of 1948, scientists from the British defense program visited the Manchester prototype and were given a demonstration of its capabilities. Britain had just begun its own nuclear weapons development effort and showed great interest in using an advanced computational capability. In October 1948, the Ministry of Supply asked Ferranti Limited, a British defense contractor with headquarters in Manchester, to build a computer to the specifications of the Manchester University scientists. This machine, the so-called Ferranti Mark I, was installed at Manchester in early 1951. The British government paid roughly 175,000 pounds over a five-year period to build this computer.[7]

The Ferranti Mark I was arguably one of the first computers ever delivered commercially (Eckert and Mauchly had been exploring the commercial market for the UNIVAC I in the United States well before this period and delivered their first machine at roughly the same time). Between 1951 and 1957, Ferranti built and sold nine of these machines: two went to universities (Manchester and Toronto), one to an Italian research institute, three to the British defense establishment, and three to industrial customers in Britain.[8] The combination of government research support and a defense market quickly propelled Ferranti into the number one spot in the British computer industry. As one historian notes, "When they started selling computers in 1951 there was no real competition; the only impediment was the inertia of the customers."[9]

---

6. An index register, when incremented, points to the next location in memory and is useful in accessing tables and matrices. Rather than calculating the address of a desired memory location from scratch, use of an index register permits access to the next word of storage after one simple operation. See Lavington, *Early British Computers*, pp. 37, 111.

7. Lavington, *Early British Computers*, pp. 39–40.

8. Simon H. Lavington, "Computer Development at Manchester University," in N. Metropolis, J. Howlett, and Gian-Carlo Rota, eds., *A History of Computing in the Twentieth Century: A Collection of Essays* (Academic Press, 1980), pp. 440–42.

9. Lavington, *Early British Computers*, p. 78.

These numbers pose a striking contrast to the situation in the United States—forty-six UNIVAC Is were sold during roughly the same period.

Cambridge

The Cambridge EDSAC computer ran its first program in May 1949, becoming the second functioning stored-program electronic digital computer in the world. Its designers wanted a reliable and functional computer in operation as quickly as possible, and the hardware choices that went into the project were fairly conservative and modest in scale. The EDSAC processed data serially, bit by bit, used mercury delay lines as its memory, and was faithful to the published EDVAC design. University funds and a contribution of 2,500 pounds from the J. Lyons catering company financed the project. Lyons was interested in a version of the machine to be applied to its business needs.[10]

The Cambridge computer builders wanted primarily to run applications on their machine. They constructed the required stable hardware environment and soon focused on the development of computer software. They developed what may have been the first functioning symbolic assembly language, an extensive library of mathematical subroutines that could be used in the writing of scientific programs, and, in 1951, the first textbook on programming. Wilkes introduced the concept of microprogramming in 1951 as well.[11]

The Cambridge EDSAC also became the prototype for a commercial computer. The Lyons catering firm, interested in automating operations, financed an effort to develop a business data processing system based on the EDSAC. This new version of the EDSAC, the Leo (Lyons Electronic Office) computer, ran a test problem in the spring of 1951, and after the development and construction of a magnetic tape input-output system, first functioned as a full-fledged business computer

10. Ibid., chap. 6.

11. The registers and logical control circuits that define how the numerical codes that are instructions are interpreted by the computer can be wired together in a fixed fashion, or they can be organized as functional units whose relation to one another is determined by a pattern held in the computer's own memory. In the latter case, the functionality and definitions of operations that the computer is able to execute can be altered by changing the pattern held in this special memory, and the computer is said to be microprogrammable. This greater flexibility may be traded for some degradation in performance, compared with a machine in which the execution of instructions does not require that they be looked up in a control store and decoded.

system in late 1953. By late 1954, Lyons had decided to build a commercial system for sale to other customers, and, in 1957, delivered an improved model, the Leo II. Thus, in 1957, the year in which the last of the Ferranti Mark I computers was shipped, the first commercial computer descended from the 1949 EDSAC design was finally sold.

The National Physical Laboratory

The first British computer project to be started, the National Physical Laboratory (NPL) version of Turing's Ace design, was the last finished.[12] It went through a difficult development, marked by frequent personnel changes and poor organization.[13] Dependence on the British Post Office for the construction of required hardware added to the delay. The British Post Office (whose engineers had worked on Colossus during the war), unfortunately devoted few resources to the project because of preoccupation with the repair of the great damage done during the war to the telecommunications infrastructure.

The NPL project did have the advantage of the experience of Harry Huskey, one of the American engineers who had worked on the ENIAC. He had arrived at NPL for a sabbatical year in early 1947. When Huskey went back to the United States a year later, frustrated by the same problems that had led Turing and others to leave, however, he took with him some of the ideas introduced in the Ace, which were to show up in the American computers that Huskey later designed.[14]

The NPL computer group ultimately did manage to win the bureaucratic battles required to build their own electronics, and a radically simplified version of the Ace, the Pilot Ace, went into somewhat unreliable operation in 1950 and was in full use in 1952. The English Electric Company worked on the NPL project in its final stages, and a reengineered commercial version of the machine, the Deuce, was first

12. Contrast the record of the National Physical Laboratory with that of the U.S. National Bureau of Standards, which had been one of the last major organizations to begin an experimental computer project, and the first to finish.

13. See J. H. Wilkinson, "Turing's Work at the National Physical Laboratory and the Construction of Pilot Ace, Deuce, and Ace," in Metropolis and others, *A History of Computing*, pp. 101–14.

14. These included the Bendix G-15 and the Packard-Bell PB-250. See C. Gordon Bell and Allen Newell, eds., *Computer Structures: Readings and Examples* (McGraw-Hill, 1971), p. 191.

delivered (to its first customer, NPL) in 1955. About thirty-one versions of the Deuce were sold between 1955 and 1964.[15]

The National Physical Laboratory went on to build a full-scale version of Turing's Ace design. By the time the project was completed in 1957, however, the component technology used was obsolete, and that was the last of NPL's efforts in computer design.

Other Efforts

Besides these three principal British computer projects, there were other important early efforts. The Ministry of Defence built two large computers in its research laboratories. One, the Ministry of Supply Automatic Integrator and Calculator (Mosaic), was built between 1947 and 1954 by the British Post Office engineers. The largest of the early British machines, Mosaic was apparently used for an air defense application similar to that for which Whirlwind was designed. Housed on the premises of TRE, access to the machine was restricted. It had little impact on British computer design.

The Telecommunications Research Establishment computer (TREAC), built internally at TRE, was the other early military computer project. It was a parallel design, and like the Manchester Mark I, used the Williams tube as its primary memory technology. Design work for other small military computers for fire control was funded at Elliott Brothers, a small British scientific instrument maker, and this work led to further government contracts and a commercial machine, the Elliott 401, delivered in 1953.[16]

British Computers in the 1950s

In the United States, as noted earlier, the large defense market created fertile ground for expansion and experimentation in computer research.

15. Lavington, *Early British Computers*, pp. 74–75.
16. For details on TREAC and the Elliott 401, see Lavington, *Early British Computers*, pp. 56–60. Other important early computer work was done at the University of London by Andrew D. Booth, who built a series of programmable relay calculators in the late 1940s. A vacuum tube version of this machine was demonstrated in 1952, generated some interest in the British Tabulating Machine Company, and became the basis for BTM's Hollerith Electronic Computer (HEC) series computers. The prototype HEC was exhibited in 1953, and the commercial version, the BTM 1200, delivered in 1954. See Andrew D. Booth, "Computers in the University of London, 1945–1962," in Metropolis and others, *A History of Computing*, pp. 551–61.

During the 1950s the market widened from the military establishment to the business establishment as the technology improved and diversified. The U.S. government poured funds into commercially oriented firms like Sperry Rand and IBM, whose business products quickly capitalized on spin-offs of government-sponsored defense projects. In contrast, the British government concentrated limited defense research and military procurement funds in a handful of British engineering firms catering to a very specialized scientific and technical marketplace. These firms relied heavily on the advanced academic research conducted at British universities, research that remained remote from commercial industry.

Government Support for Military Computers

In 1949, after the Manchester computer project was under way, the British government set up the National Research Development Corporation (NRDC) to encourage the development of advanced technology. The corporation actively supported computer technology in Britain, but limited its help to only three British computer producers with significant defense contracts—Ferranti, Elliott Brothers, and later, Electrical and Musical Industries, Limited (EMI). At the earliest stage, the corporation administered patents for technology developed on government-supported projects; but soon it began to initiate research projects, the first one being an improved version of the Ferranti Mark I, a computer based on Manchester University research.[17]

Manchester University's star continued to rise. In 1953 its designers built a small machine that was probably the first operational transistor computer in the world.[18]

That same year, the Manchester University group was developing the successor to the Mark I, the MEG (Megacycle Engine) computer. Characterized by an architecture similar to the Mark I, improved components, and built-in floating-point arithmetic, the experimental MEG became the basis for the design of the commercial Ferranti Mercury computer, first sold to a customer in 1957.

Manchester's most significant computer project was probably the

17. C. Freeman and others, "Research and Development in Electronic Capital Goods," *National Institute Economic Review*, no. 34 (November 1965), p. 61.

18. It became the prototype for a transistor computer produced by the Metropolitan-Vickers Company in 1956 and manufactured in limited numbers, mainly for internal use.

Muse, begun in 1956 and later renamed the Atlas. The Muse/Atlas computer resulted from a conscious attempt to build a supercomputer, an extremely powerful, large-scale, scientific machine. At the time, IBM was developing the Stretch supercomputer for the U.S. Atomic Energy Commission and the National Security Agency, and Sperry Rand's UNIVAC division was building the LARC supercomputer for the Atomic Energy Commission. In response to this perceived technological competition from America, the head of the NRDC mounted a campaign to fund the Muse/Atlas on a similar scale. The drive met with little success and was hampered by continual internal bickering over technical and financial issues.[19] University funds, and some NRDC funding, paid for the first work on Atlas. Later development became a joint effort with Ferranti.

When completed in 1962, Atlas was among the most powerful scientific computers in the world. Designed with one of the first true operating systems, software for job scheduling and control, Atlas also implemented "virtual memory" concepts unavailable on other commercial machines until the late 1960s.[20] The design of this machine greatly influenced computer specialists around the world.[21] Unfortunately, it cost a great deal to develop, and sales for a machine of that size, power, and cost, in a narrow and specialized market, were rather slow. Although a technical success, the new computer did little for the Ferranti computer division's business prospects.

19. See John Hendry, "Prolonged Negotiations: The British Fast Computer Project and the Early History of the British Computer Industries," *Business History*, vol. 26 (November 1984), pp. 286–300.

20. Virtual memory allows the computer user to write programs using memory space that exceeds the physical main memory installed in a computer. It does so by "swapping" chunks of a much larger secondary memory in and out of the limited main memory. Special hardware was used on Atlas to translate user requests for memory not currently available into an automatic sequence of actions to retrieve the requested data from secondary memory. Similar mechanisms are used to implement time-sharing systems, and the Atlas concepts greatly affected the design of such systems. See for example A. Padegs, "System/360 and Beyond," *IBM Journal of Research and Development*, vol. 25 (September 1981), p. 380, discussing the origin of dynamic address translation facilities introduced in the IBM System 370.

21. Typical appreciations of the Atlas may be found in Bell and Newell, *Computer Structures*, pp. 274–275; and David J. Kuck, *The Structure of Computers and Computations*, vol. 1 (John Wiley and Sons, 1978), pp. 314, 315, 424. Emerson W. Pugh, *Memories That Shaped an Industry: Decisions Leading to IBM System/360* (MIT Press, 1984), p. 184, credits Atlas as the first computer able to match the performance of the IBM Stretch.

Several of Ferranti's other commercial machines of the early 1960s were based on spin-offs from a series of military computers built for defense applications.[22] But despite NRDC support and military procurement contracts Ferranti found itself competing precariously in the small British market with many other firms. In 1963 the rival International Computers and Tabulators (whose computer line was later absorbed into International Computers Limited [ICL]), bought Ferranti's computer division, and by the late 1970s, ICL was the sole surviving British manufacturer of mainframe computers. It based its chief computer line, the 2900 series, on the MU-5 computer designed at Manchester University. The 2900 architecture survives today in ICL's computer products.

The National Research Development Corporation also supported Elliott Brothers, the first British company to become involved with computers. In 1947 Elliott began developing a special purpose digital computer for a military fire control system, and this contract led to other orders for special purpose military computers. Logic circuits and electronic technology developed on these projects were essential ingredients in its first experimental general purpose computer, Nicholas, and in the subsequent 400 series of commercial computers. A group of the Elliott Brothers researchers left for Ferranti in 1953, and many of the same technologies were used in the Ferranti Pegasus, shipped in 1956.[23] Descendants of the Elliott 400 series, the 800 series computers, were the first commercial British transistor computers, shipped in 1958. Both the Elliott Brothers 400 series computers and Pegasus received research support from NRDC.

The Pegasus was especially important. Besides providing the foundation for the most significant computers produced by Ferranti, and later, ICL, it had a great international impact on computer design.[24] In

---

22. The Ferranti Argus process control computer, for example, was based on a military guidance computer. Other military computers built by Ferranti in the early 1960s included the Poseidon, Hermes, and the F1600 (also sold as a commercial product). See Freeman, "Research and Development," p. 72; and Lavington, *Early British Computers*, pp. 82–83.

23. The National Research Development Corporation also supported the Pegasus with a contract procuring nine of the machines (of the thirty eventually produced). Hendry, "Prolonged Negotiations," p. 284.

24. Bell and Newell, in their classic text on computer architecture, name Pegasus as the first computer to use an array of general registers, rather than specialized registers, to manipulate data. They also nominate it as having the best instruction processing design of all the computers discussed in their book. Bell and Newell, *Computer*

the sixties, Elliot concentrated on military and process control markets; it tackled commercial markets by manufacturing the NCR 315 under license from the American firm, for sale outside North America.[25]

English Electric, the third engineering firm to manufacture an important computer series, entered the computer field by helping NPL build the Pilot Ace, the eventual product of Alan Turing's first attempts to build a British computer after the war. Interest expressed by the Royal Aircraft Establishment in purchasing a variation on this machine led to the production of the Deuce, a commercial cousin of the original Ace, and English Electric's first computer.[26]

The technical experience of the firm was limited to this scientific machine. When the business market began to blossom in the late 1950s, English Electric was forced to license a commercially oriented design from RCA and sold a version of the RCA 501 in England as its KDP-10. It continued to design scientific computers, however, and its KDF-9 was a highly original machine that captured a large share of the university market.[27]

Computers for Business

The British business machine companies, which might have been expected to be in closer contact with the development of the commercial business market in the late 1950s, were sadly out of touch with the emerging electronics technology. The J. Lyons catering company, showed early interest in the business applications of digital computers by commissioning Cambridge University to build an improved version of the Cambridge EDSAC (the Leo) for its internal accounting and clerical tasks. But the company squandered its early lead in business computing. By the time the first improved Leo II was delivered to a

---

Structures, p. 170. Ferranti's defense computers and the design for the ICT/ICL 1900 series machines can be traced back to Pegasus.

25. Charles White, "European EDP," Datamation, vol. 12 (September 1966), p. 24.

26. According to Freeman, "Research and Development," p. 61, a Deuce ordered by the National Physical Laboratory (NPL) and the Royal Aircraft Establishment was the only order from British government departments for large computers in the late 1950s. The NPL built a version of Turing's original Ace design, but it was hopelessly obsolete by the time it was completed in 1957.

27. The English Electric KDF-9 was one of the first computers with a "stack" memory and was announced slightly before the first such machines in the United States, the Burroughs B5000 and its military cousin, the D-825. See White, "European EDP," p. 24, on its success in universities.

customer in 1957, its vacuum tube logic and delay line memory technologies were sadly out of date. A more advanced machine, the Leo III, was not ready until 1962.

The traditional British punched card equipment producers, British Tabulating Machine (BTM) and Powers-Samas Accounting Machines Limited, had no electronics technology and little independent research capability. Until 1949, BTM had been a licensor of IBM technology.[28] When IBM terminated arrangements with BTM, in that year, BTM was unable to compete on its own. Instead, it sought the assistance of Professor Andrew Booth, of London University, who had been building experimental relay computers on a shoestring budget. Booth had finished a small, experimental, magnetic drum-based digital computer in 1952, and this machine became the basis for BTM's first business computer, the BTM 1201, delivered in 1956.

When BTM needed to develop a new model, however, it was again forced to seek technology from outside its ranks, and its 1300 series was developed for it by engineers from the (British) General Electric Company (GEC).[29] When transistor computers came on the scene in the early 1960s, BTM, by then merged into ICT, once again had to turn outside, to EMI.

The other British punched card machine firm, Powers-Samas, had similar problems. Powers had developed close contacts with IBM's American competitor, Remington Rand. After the Second World War, Powers had been sold to the Vickers armaments firm, as part of an effort by Vickers to diversify into civilian engineering goods.[30] But Powers-Samas suffered from the same lack of technology as BTM did and was forced to seek cooperative research projects with Ferranti. These efforts bore little fruit, and in 1959 Powers-Samas merged with BTM to form

28. British Tabulating Machine Company (BTM) had the exclusive rights to sell IBM products in the British Empire, except in Canada. In exchange for that right, it had agreed to pay 25 percent of revenues from these products to IBM and could acquire any product for 10 percent over cost. After the end of this arrangement, BTM, like many American business equipment firms, continued to believe in punched card equipment and did not worry about the emergence of competition from digital computers until forced to. See the interview with Arthur Humphreys conducted by Erwin Tomash on February 28, 1981, available in the Charles Babbage Institute at the University of Minnesota, Minneapolis.

29. See the interview with Arthur Humphreys.

30. See the interview with A. T. Maxwell conducted by A. L. C. Humphreys, January, 9, 1980, available in the Charles Babbage Institute at the University of Minnesota, Minneapolis.

International Computers and Tabulators (ICT). A continuing struggle to acquire computer technology led newly formed ICT to arrange for the engineers at GEC working on the ICT 1301 to join ICT in 1961, and later, the EMI computer development team was acquired. ICT also obtained the technology for the RCA 301 computer under license.[31]

Decades of Decline

Thus, in the late 1950s, two groups of producers were present in Britain. The electrical equipment producers, like Ferranti, Elliott, and English Electric, were building computers oriented toward scientific calculations and military applications, had a solid technology base, and enjoyed important ties to academic research groups at Manchester and the National Physical Laboratory. What government support there was went to this group, as did most military computer procurement. The second group, the office machine manufacturers, were in a weak technological position, and except for Leo Computers, slow to realize how important the technological change taking place was. The business-oriented firms received no support from the British government.

Given this situation, the explosive growth in business computing in the early 1960s caught British industry unprepared. The military electronics producers continued to focus on the small market for high-powered scientific machines and military computers, as American computer firms took over the growing business market. As table 5-3 shows, English firms had delivered all the computer installations in Britain as of the end of 1959. In just three years, though, one-third of the British stock of computers was American product, and in another three years that fraction grew to more than half. The change in market shares is largely attributable to installations in new business markets and the lack of competitive British products. By March of 1965, the British computer industry had sold less than 600 machines worldwide (900 counting designs licensed from NCR) compared with perhaps 20,000 machines installed by American manufacturers.[32] The announcement of System 360 by IBM in 1964 merely accelerated a process of decline that had begun in the late 1950s.

The many, small British firms fighting over a limited British market

31. See interviews with Arthur Humphreys and A. T. Maxwell.
32. Hendry, "Prolonged Negotiations," p. 302.

Table 5-3. *Percentage of U.S. Computers in the British Market*[a]

End of year	Machines manufactured by, or under license from, U.S. firms	End of year	Computers produced by U.S. firms
1958	0	1966	51
1959	0	1967	52
1960	4	1968	52
1961	15	1969	51
1962	37	1970	49
1963	45	1971	50
1964	48	1972	50
1965	51		
1966	52		

Sources: Phister, Jr., *Data Processing*, p. 289; and Organization for Economic Cooperation and Development, *Electronic Computers: Gaps in Technology*, report presented at the Third Ministerial Meeting on Science, March 11–12, 1968 (Paris: OECD, 1969), p. 41.

a. Percentage of installed stock in the United Kingdom.

underwent wrenching upheavals in the early 1960s. The problems were most serious in the business equipment firms. Power-Samas and BTM merged to form ICT in 1959. The computer facilities of GEC and EMI were then acquired by ICT, in 1961 and 1962, and the technical links to RCA established. In 1964 English Electric acquired Marconi's computer activities. In 1963 Ferranti's computer division, with a technical success and financial failure on its hands after the introduction of the Atlas, was also sold to ICT. In that same year, Leo Computers merged with English Electric-Marconi's computer operations to become English Electric-Leo-Marconi Computers.

The deterioration in the share of the British market held by English firms continued, however, and when Harold Wilson became the prime minister in 1964, he explicitly favored active government support for a British computer industry.[33] In 1967 Elliott Automation was merged with the English Electric group to form English Electric Computers, and a licensing arrangement for RCA's Spectra series computers established. The British government played an important role in the merger, and a loan of fifteen million pounds from the Industrial Reorganization Corporation spurred English Electric to move forward on the deal.[34]

In 1968, under the leadership of Anthony Wedgewood-Benn, minister

33. See the interview with Arthur Humphreys.

34. See Alvin J. Harman, *The International Computer Industry: Innovation and Comparative Advantage* (Brookings, 1971), p. 34; and Nicolas Jecquier, "Computers," in Raymond Vernon, ed., *Big Business and the State: Changing Relations in Western Europe* (Harvard University Press, 1974), p. 210.

of technology for the Labor government, the two surviving British computer firms, along with the computer interests of defense electronics producer Plessey, were merged into International Computers Limited (ICL), the sole British manufacturer of large general purpose computers from that year until the present.[35] The British state actively participated in arranging and financing the formation of ICL, and government policies have since favored ICL with subsidies, loans, and preferential access to procurement.[36] In 1984 ICL was sold to Standard Telephones and Cables (STC), a British telecommunications company.

This rash of mergers left ICL with a highly incompatible product line, unfortunately, and agglomerated into one firm the problems of many elements. By 1974, only 25 percent to 30 percent of the installations in Britain were from British producers.[37] For all intents and purposes, the wave of important technical innovations that had marked British entries into the computer marketplace in the 1950s had entirely receded by the middle of the 1960s.

France

Computer design in France can be traced to the work of Louis Couffignal, who in the late 1930s wrote several papers describing the design of an electromechanical calculator based on binary arithmetic.[38] After the war, Couffignal and a group of researchers at the Institute Blaise Pascal worked on the construction of experimental hardware to be used in a parallel computer design. Couffignal had visited the Institute for Advanced Studies (IAS) project at Princeton, and the ENIAC in

35. Interviews with A. T. Maxwell and Arthur Humphreys. Note that several small British microcomputer manufacturers (including Sinclair Research and ACT Computers), scored some success in the late 1970s and early 1980s. Kenneth Flamm, *Targeting the Computer: Government Support and International Competition* (Brookings, 1987), pp. 159–68.

36. Ibid. For details on government support, see the next chapters. The British government initially took a 10 percent share in ICL at its formation; these shares were then passed to the National Enterprise Board, and later, they were sold.

37. See table 5-2, p. 135.

38. See Brian Randell, "An Annotated Bibliography on the Origins of Computers," *Annals of the History of Computing*, vol. 1 (October 1979) pp. 121–22; and R. Moreau, *The Computer Comes of Age* (MIT Press, 1984), p. 27.

1946.[39] This work apparently had little impact on the evolution of computers in France and remains largely unknown outside of France.

France, like Britain, lacked strong ties between university research and industry. Machines Bull, the most important force in French computers, was a French office equipment manufacturer with a strong prewar position in the European punched card business machine market and a reputation for high-quality equipment. After the war, Bull became aware of the rapid progress abroad in the new computing technology and hired a group of engineers to work on the new technology.[40]

In 1950 two of Bull's engineers traveled to the United States and England to observe the foreign developments in electronic computers. With the help of a third engineer, they designed an experimental electronic digital calculator, the Gamma 2, delivered in 1951. Bull followed up on this research by marketing the highly successful Gamma 3 electronic calculator in the 1950s. In the mid- to late 1950s, Bull developed machines linking these calculators to magnetic drums, and in 1958, introduced its first electronic digital computer, the Gamma Extension (ET), which used delay lines for primary memory, as well as the magnetic drum storage that had been developed. This rather late entry into the computer market used technologies that, even in the 1950s, were already obsolete.

The first French computer was produced by a much smaller computer firm, Société d'Electronique et d'Automatisme (SEA), headed by engineer Francois Raymond, and a part of the large Schneider conglomerate.[41] This company had started by designing and manufacturing analog computers for the military. Gradually, it branched out into the production of flight simulators, controllers for machine tools, and in the late 1950s, digital computers.[42] The first French computer, the CUBA (calculateur

39. Herman H. Goldstine, *The Computer: From Pascal to von Neumann* (Princeton University Press, 1972), p. 250.

40. Interestingly, Bull's punched card technology was not based on French research but on patents of the Norwegian inventor Fredrick Rosing Bull, purchased from Norwegian interests after Bull's death. See James Connolly, "History of Computing in Europe," internal IBM document (New York, IBM World Trade, ca. 1967), p. 22; Moreau, *Computer Comes of Age*, p. 25; and see "Bull's Rule in Europe," *Datamation*, vol. 7 (September 1961), p. 32.

41. The best references I found on the early (and poorly documented) history of the French computer industry are Moreau, *Computer Comes of Age*; and Jacques Jublin and Jean-Michel Quatrepoint, *French Ordinateurs—de l'affaire Bull a l'assassinat du Plan Calcul* (Paris: Editions Alain Moreau, 1976).

42. See Isaac L. Auerbach, "European Electronic Data Processing—A Report on

universel binaire de l'armament), was commissioned by a French military
laboratory; SEA then developed other models that were installed in
defense plants or sold commercially.[43] This computer used mercury
delay lines for main memory, and design and circuitry concepts based
on the published specifications of the U.S. IAS and SEAC computers.
The commercial models that followed added magnetic drums and replaced the delay lines with ferrite core storage; this hardware, as well as
how this memory was managed, was borrowed from concepts developed
in the United States and in the British Manchester Mark I. With little
government support for these later developments, only five of these
commercial models were sold by 1960.

Thus despite the fact that other, smaller French firms had taken the
lead in innovation, the larger, established Bull operation had captured
market leadership among French firms by the early 1960s. This was to
influence the evolution of France's policy toward computers.

The 1960s

By the late 1950s, three companies, IBM's wholly owned French
affiliate, Machines Bull, and SEA were producing general purpose
computers in France.

Bull's first small electronic computer, the Gamma ET, was reasonably
successful despite dated technologies. By 1962, 112 computers had been
installed, with two-thirds of them in France, the rest in other parts of
continental Europe.[44] During this period, Bull managed to claim more
than 45 percent of the French computer market.[45]

In the later 1950s, as highly visible scientific supercomputer projects
were started in the United States (the IBM Stretch, the UNIVAC LARC)
and Britain (the Manchester Atlas project), a similar project was begun
in France. In the United States, these expensive flagship projects were

the Industry and the State-of-the Art," *Proceedings of the IRE,* vol. 49 (January 1961),
p. 338.

43. See Arthur L. Samuel, "Computers with European Accents," *1957 Proceedings
of the Western Joint Computer Conference* (New York: Institute of Radio Engineers,
1957), pp. 14–17; Moreau, *Computer Comes of Age,* pp. 71–72; and Goldstine, *Computer
from Pascal to von Neumann,* p. 353.

44. "Datamation's International Computer Census," *Datamation,* vol. 8 (August
1962), p. 46.

45. Organization for Economic Cooperation and Development, *Electronic Computers: Gaps in Technology,* report presented to the Third Ministerial Meeting on
Science, March 11–12, 1968 (Paris: OECD, 1969), p. 41.

often paid for by demanding military customers. Britain offered little funding at first, but the government finally gave substantial support to the British Atlas. In France, Machines Bull apparently made the decision to build a competitive computer entirely on its own. Whether for prestige and technological credibility, or because it believed a large, untapped market existed for an advanced machine, undertaking this project was to prove a serious financial disaster for Bull.

Bull shipped its first Gamma 60 supercomputer in 1960. The machine was innovative—it had multiple processors sharing common memory and input-output resources. It was also a model for an advanced computer architecture, studied by computer designers of the time.[46] The design, in fact, was too advanced for the epoch—for example, there was no high-level programming language available to use all its features, and software had to be written in a primitive assembly language. Ideas for organizing the decomposition of a job into small tasks that could be executed concurrently in parallel were in their infancy, and problems run on the machine used only a fraction of the hardware's envisioned capabilities.

The Gamma 60 was also one of the first of these supercomputers to be completed.[47] New developments in transistor technology were then being incorporated into large computers with improved price performance, and the expensive Gamma 60 suffered in comparisons.[48] The other very large-scale computers finished during the early 1960s were not particularly profitable either. However, those machines benefited from heavy government subsidies, or, more important, created a technology base for the development of other computers that had the potential for big commercial sales.

Bull had neither the subsidy nor the product line. By 1964 it was

---

46. James Thornton, who with Seymour Cray began work on the design of the Control Data 6600 at about this time, recalls that a short course for practicing computer engineers on the design of giant computers, offered at UCLA in 1960, reviewed the Gamma 60 along with the Stretch, LARC, Atlas, and the University of Illinois ILLIAC II. See James Thornton, "The CDC 6600 Project," *Annals of the History of Computing*, vol. 2 (October 1980), p. 338.

47. The LARC was also delivered in 1960, Stretch in 1961, and Atlas and ILLIAC II in 1962.

48. Jublin and Quatrepoint, *French Ordinateurs*, p. 20, quote a price of a billion old French francs, more than $2 million. The Gamma 60 was designed to outperform the IBM 704 and 705, but it was soundly trounced when the newer IBM transistorized 7000-series machines were introduced. See OECD, *Electronic Computers*, p. 103; and Y. S. Hu, *The Impact of U. S. Investment in Europe: A Case Study of the Automotive and Computer Industries* (Praeger, 1973), pp. 119–48.

teetering on the brink of financial collapse. About a dozen of the Gamma 60 machines were sold over four years, and Bull was making little profit on an enormous research investment.[49] Nonetheless, the company was forced into a continuing development program by the unceasing pace of technological competition. Desperate for resources to invest, Bull repeatedly issued stock and sought new financing from lenders. Like its British competitors, Bull had not foreseen the rapid growth in machines optimized for business applications, and out of need, obtained a manufacturing license for RCA's 301 medium-scale business processor. There was little profit in that arrangement, and with European banks reluctant to lend, Bull began to seek capital abroad.[50]

Though the public sector played an important role in electronics research, the French government did not seem too concerned with computers. In 1963, for example, the French state directly and indirectly financed about 60 percent of electronics R&D.[51] Certainly, the government had not extended support by making large purchases. At the time of "L'affaire Bull," Raymond Aron complained in the pages of *Le Figaro* that more than three-fourths of the public sector's computer installations had chosen IBM over Bull. The French Atomic Energy Commission had paid $8 million for a high-performance IBM Stretch, rather than buy a cheaper Gamma 60.[52] There were some efforts to get two chief French industrial electronics firms (rivals of Bull as well as of each other), Compagnie Générale de Télégraphe sans fil (CSF) and Compagnie Générale d'Electricité (CGE), to make some arrangement with Bull. But after the dust from complex political and financial maneuvering had cleared, a controlling interest in Bull was sold to the American General Electric, just then in the midst of a big expansion of its computer business.[53]

The matter seemed to rest for a couple of years. There were some complaints within the new GE-Bull about decisions to kill off internal research projects started in Bull before the takeover, but they were

49. Moreau, *Computer Comes of Age*, p. 101. Of that dozen, eleven had been installed by mid-1962. See "Datamation's International Computer Census," p. 46.

50. Jublin and Quatrepoint, *French Ordinateurs*, pp. 20–23.

51. European Economic Community, *"L'industrie électronique des pays de la communauté et les investissements Américains"* (Collection Études), Serie Industrié, no. 1 (Brussels, 1969), p. 67.

52. Raymond Aron in *Le Figaro* of November 21, 1964, cited in Jublin and Quatrepoint, *French Ordinateurs*, p. 20; and Moreau, *Computer Comes of Age*, p. 101.

53. See Jublin and Quatrepoint, *French Ordinateurs*, pp. 17–27, on the maneuvers.

scarcely important to public policy.[54] More important, government authorities were concerned about the lack of a significant computer firm controlled by French financial interests. Two small French producers did exist in the mid-1960s—SEA continued to produce a few small machines oriented toward scientific applications, and a joint venture, CAE, was formed between CSF and CGE, to produce minicomputers under license from the American firm Scientific Data Systems (SDS). But these tiny French companies accounted for only 7 percent of the small French market in 1966.[55]

The year 1966 brought momentous changes in the French computer industry. The French government had continued to maintain a great interest in the health of the remaining small national computer producers and had favored a proposed 1964 agreement between the CSF/CGE joint venture and Britain's ICT to jointly develop and market a large computer. A minor crisis erupted in 1966, however, when it became publicly known that the U.S. government had turned down the proposed export of an American Control Data 6600 supercomputer in order to slow France's development of nuclear weapons.[56]

The ensuing debate in France led the government to propose the fusion of the CSF/CGE and SEA computer operations into a single "national champion" firm, the Compagnie International pour l'Informatique (CII). The government also created a jointly owned peripherals manufacturer known as Système et Peripheriques Associé aux Calcula-

54. The American General Electric had also purchased a controlling interest in Olivetti's computer division in 1964. Four computers—two at Olivetti and two at Bull—were under development at the time of the buyout. Development of two of these machines, one at Olivetti and one at Bull, was to be continued. The Olivetti machine was to become GE's model 115 small computer, and the Bull machine, designated as the Gamma 140 series, was ultimately killed off, leaving the French with some legacy of ill feeling. See J. H. Lorenzi and E. Le Boucher, *Memoires Volées* (Paris: Editions Ramsay, 1979), p. 108, citing a study by M. Delapierre and Ch. A. Michalet.

55. CSF merged with another French firm, Thomson, to become Thomson-CSF in 1967. Jublin and Quatrepoint, *French Ordinateurs*, pp. 33, 39, 46, 202. See also Jecquier, "Computers," p. 216.

56. Both Nicholas Jecquier and John Zysman argue that this incident was only one in a series of pressures that led to the Plan Calcul. Furthermore, none of the computers to be designed by CII had capacities comparable to the capacities of the CDC 6600. See Jecquier, "Computers," p. 202; and John Zysman, *Political Strategies for Industrial Order* (University of California Press at Berkeley, 1977), pp. 74–75. Ironically, the American export ban did not prevent the French *nuclearistes* from designing their bomb. According to Jublin and Quatrepoint, a CDC 6600 installed in a French software firm was secretly used by the weapons design group, and the required calculations were performed. See Jublin and Quatrepoint, *French Ordinateurs*, pp. 28–29.

teurs (SPERAC), established a government-funded computer leasing company to finance the purchase of CII's products, and formed a national computer research institute, the Institut de Recherche d'Informatique et d'Automatisme (IRIA).[57] Under this framework, dubbed the Plan Calcul, the government would subsidize CII during the 1967–71 period, and CII would develop and manufacture a broad line of four computers.

The plan was not a great success. Great resources were invested in CII, and in 1968 a companion program, the Plan des Composants, was begun to strengthen France's capabilities in semiconductors, a key input to computers. Most of that assistance went to organizations affiliated with CSF, and thus indirectly supported CII.[58] Yet little emerged from the effort. In late 1968, CII came out with its first computer, the medium-sized IRIS 50, largely based on technology transferred through its inherited licensing arrangements with SDS. Later computers designed by CII also relied heavily on SDS technology. Though some machines used internally produced designs, the net result was an incompatible product line.

The 1970s

By the early 1970s, despite massive government subsidies and the "rationalization" of the French electronics industry into three national champion firms dominating computers, semiconductors, and peripherals, respectively, little improvement in the performance of French industry occurred.[59] CII controlled roughly the same share of French computer production that its constituent elements had commanded in 1966, and prospects for growth seemed gloomy.[60]

57. See U.S. Department of Commerce, *Global Market Survey* (GPO, 1973), p. 44. At its formation, roughly 56 percent of CII was held by the CSF/CGE venture, 33 percent by the Schneider group, parent of SEA, and the remainder by the Ribaud group, another French conglomerate with electronics interests. The latter interests were largely sold by the end of the first Plan Calcul. Jublin and Quatrepoint, *French Ordinateurs*, pp. 34–35. The joint development agreement with the British firm ICT was abruptly canceled by the CSF/CGE venture after the formation of CII.

58. Zysman, *Political Strategies*, p. 79; and John E. Tilton, *International Diffusion of Technology: The Case of Semiconductors* (Brookings, 1971), pp. 129, 131. French government funding accounted for 45 percent of semiconductor research in 1968.

59. The three champions were CII in computers, Sescosem (controlled by Thomson-CSF) in semiconductors, and SPERAC (owned by Thomson-Brandt and CGE) in peripherals. See Jublin and Quatrepoint, *French Ordinateurs*, pp. 58–59.

60. Jecquier, "Computers," p. 217.

In 1970 when GE announced it intended to quit the computer business and sell these operations to Honeywell, the stage was set for another crisis and reorganization in the French computer industry. After further debate, the French government decided to permit Honeywell to purchase GE's French operations, but the correct strategy to pursue with CII remained an open issue.

Policymakers wanted to restructure the French computer industry to create the largest possible market for the national champion. The government hoped to reap the economies of scale inherent in a research-intensive product. The French market, however, was by nature limited in size, even discounting the formidable competition offered by IBM and Honeywell-Bull. The next logical step in this quest for market size was to cooperate with other European firms in a similar predicament and create a pan-European computer firm. The scheme was pursued, and in 1973, the formation of Unidata, a "European" computer company, was announced.

CII's partners in Unidata were Philips, the Dutch electronics giant, and Siemens, the largest German electronics producer. Philips had been trying to build up its small computer business for some time. But Siemens had avoided the costly competitive bloodletting in the European computer industry of the 1960s by licensing computer technology from RCA and marketing their computers with little commitment to costly R&D. This strategy abruptly ceased in 1971, when RCA quit the computer business. Siemens then pondered other alternatives.

The Unidata plan required each of the three participants to build part of a complementary, IBM-compatible line of computers. The relatively inexperienced Philips team was to produce the smallest model; Siemens would design two medium-sized machines; and CII would produce three medium and larger models. By 1974 the smaller models in this series had been developed, but development of the larger machines by CII lagged.

Even worse, the traditional rivalries among the three competitors were difficult to erase. Discord over control and marketing responsibilities, and overlapping and duplication in development, soon emerged. CII's corporate owners and important elements in the French government developed serious misgivings about the plan. The French participants began exploring other alternatives even before the ink had dried on the Unidata agreement. In 1974 the government changed in France, and the new team began a serious review of the arrangement. By 1975 the French politicians and industrialists had decided that buying into

Honeywell-Bull, with its access to the American market, looked like a better deal, and they withdrew from Unidata.[61]

In that same year an agreement with Honeywell was concluded instead, and the new firm, CII-Honeywell-Bull, began operations. The new firm was 53 percent owned by French interests, with the remaining 47 percent owned by Honeywell. Things changed again in 1981 as part of the restructuring carried out by the newly elected Mitterand government. The French government purchased a controlling interest in CII-Honeywell-Bull, and the now renamed CII-Bull was one of twelve nationalized sectors of French industry.[62] Finally, in 1986, Honeywell sold its computer business to its former joint venture foreign partners, CII-Bull and Japan's NEC. Bull will ultimately own the largest share (65.1 percent) of the new company, which took over the old Honeywell customer base.[63]

The French government actively participated in the zigs and zags of the French computer industry during this time by continuing to pump funding into computer development. The first Plan Calcul was followed by a second Plan Calcul during the 1971–75 period, and a third Plan Calcul during the years 1976–80. An informal policy of procurement preferences for CII products since the first Plan Calcul was followed by guaranteed procurement by the French government as a major element of the third Plan Calcul.[64]

Financial assistance to the electronics components industry, essential to advanced computers, also continued. The first Plan des Composants was followed with large infusions of aid to national semiconductor champion SESCOSEM in the 1970s. In 1977, after a national project to develop very large-scale integrated circuits (VLSI) had been kicked off

61. See Jublin and Quatrepoint, *French Ordinateurs*, pp. 181–91; and Angeline Pantages, Nancy Foy, and Andrew Lloyd, "Western Europe's Computer Industry," *Datamation*, vol. 22 (September 1976), p. 68. Philips then withdrew from the general purpose computer market; Siemens, after withdrawing from much of its computer activities, eventually replaced the missing part of its IBM-compatible line that was to have been manufactured by CII with large-scale mainframes supplied by Japanese PCM manufacturer Fujitsu.

62. See United States International Trade Commission, *Foreign Industrial Targeting and Its Effect on U.S. Industries, Phase II: The European Community and Member States*, USITC Publication 1517, Report to the Subcommittee on Ways and Means (Washington, D.C.: United States International Trade Commission, 1984), pp. 49, 52.

63. See Groupe Bull, *Annual Report, 1986* (Paris, 1987), p. 18.

64. See Jecquier, "Computers," p. 222, on the informal preferences, and Lorenzi and Le Boucher, *Memoires Volées*, p. 109, on the guaranteed procurement included in the third Plan Calcul.

in Japan, France implemented a similar four-year program, the Plan Circuits Intègres.[65]

It is less clear how useful these strenuous and costly efforts were. In 1972 CII and its Unidata partners, Siemens and Philips, accounted for about 12 percent of French computer installations. IBM claimed about 58 percent of this stock; Honeywell-Bull had another 18 percent. In 1980 a combined CII-Honeywell-Bull counted its products in 31 percent of French computer installations, while IBM accounted for 52 percent of the total.[66] Despite massive subsidies and noncompetitive government procurement, the national champion had maintained a roughly constant share of the market, repeating the experience of the first Plan Calcul.

Germany

Other than the United States and Great Britain, Germany had the strongest indigenous technology base on which to build a computer industry. German experiments with computers stem from the work of Konrad Zuse, who in the 1930s built a series of electromechanical calculators, the Z-1, Z-2, and Z-3. The Z-3, completed in 1941, was the first to be fully operational. This work was comparable in sophistication, though not in scale, to the independent efforts of George R. Stibitz and Howard Aiken in the United States.

In 1942 Zuse began work on a more ambitious design, the Z-4, finished in 1945, and installed in a German V-2 rocket plant. Like its predecessors, this machine used electromechanical technology; it survived the war and was leased to the Swiss Federal Polytechnic Institute in 1950, where it became the main computing facility for an important Swiss research group in computers.

Before the war, a colleague of Zuse at the Technical University of Berlin had begun to experiment with the use of vacuum tubes instead of relays in Zuse's logical design. The researcher, Helmut Schreyer, built a demonstration model in 1938.[67] During the war Schreyer built an

65. United States International Trade Commission, *Foreign Industrial Targeting*, pp. 138–39; and Giovanni Dosi, *Technical Change and Survival: Europe's Semiconductor Industry* (Sussex, U.K.: University of Sussex, 1981), p. 38.

66. Bertrand Bellan and others, *L'industrie en France* (France: Flammarion for the Centre de Recherche en Économie Industrielle, 1983), p. 228.

67. Friedrich L. Bauer, "Between Zuse and Rutishauser," in Metropolis and others, *A History of Computing*, p. 513.

electronic binary calculator, tested in 1944, and with Zuse, submitted a proposal to the German government for a two-thousand-tube electronic computer. The proposal was rejected as impractical.[68]

An important technology used in computers was developed for the German military during the war. The Germans built magnetic amplifiers for use in fire control systems on their naval vessels, and they also undertook a great deal of wartime research in magnetic materials. They developed the first successful magnetic tape recorder, the German Army "Magnetophone," as well as new types of ferrite materials. As described earlier, the captured German magnetics technology was used in building the first drum storage devices at Engineering Research Associates after the war, and the captured ferrite materials technology was used to produce the first core memories in the United States in the early 1950s. Soon after the war, in the late 1940s, the Max Planck Institute in Germany developed a magnetic drum for use in a computer.[69]

The turbulence of postwar Germany precluded any sustained attempt to follow up on these technological developments, but by the mid-1950s, several experimental machines had been built at various German universities and research institutions.[70] The work built on the prewar and wartime experience with electronics and computing technology. Many researchers at these German academic computing projects had also studied, or at least visited, the chief computer projects in the United States and England.

None of these academic machines led to German firms building commercial models, however, apparently because the Allies forbade the construction of certain electronic devices. In 1955 that ban was lifted, and Zuse (with Siemens and Standard Elektrik Lorenz, an affiliate of the

68. Goldstine, *Computer from Pascal to von Neumann*, p. 354; and Konrad Zuse, "Some Remarks on the History of Computing in Germany," in Metropolis and others, *A History of Computing*, p. 619.

69. Emerson W. Pugh, *Memories That Shaped an Industry: Decisions Leading to IBM System/360* (MIT Press, 1984), pp. 20, 39–40; Hodges, *Enigma*, p. 314; Zuse, "Some Remarks on the History," p. 620; Bauer, "Between Zuse and Rutishauser," p. 516; and Connolly, "History of Computing in Europe," p. E-16.

70. The most important efforts were at the University of Göttingen (location of the Max Planck Institute), the Munich Institute of Technology, the Institute for Practical Mathematics at Darmstadt, and the *Technische Hochschule* in Berlin. See Samuel, "Computers with European Accents," pp. 16–17; Everett S. Calhoun, "New Computer Developments Around the World," in *1956 Proceedings of the Eastern Joint Computer Conference* (New York: American Institute of Electrical Engineers, 1957), p. 6; Bauer, "Between Zuse and Rutishauser," pp. 516–17; and Goldstine, *Computer*, pp. 354–56.

American firm ITT) started development work on commercial electronic computers. Standard Elektrik delivered the first commercial installation in 1959. Siemens shipped its first computer, the transistorized 2002, in 1960, and Telefunken A. G. followed with the TR-4 computer in 1961. In developing their first generation of commercial products, all these firms recruited from the design groups assembled and trained in the university computing projects.[71]

Well before this time, IBM had established itself as the premier computer producer in Germany. By 1956 it had set up a production line for the IBM 650 in Stuttgart and had recruited some of the computer designers from the universities into its local organization.[72]

Zuse's firm remained a relatively small producer (maximum employment was 1,000 in the early 1960s) of specialized machines for scientific applications; its first electronic machine, the Z-22, was delivered in 1958. In 1964, Zuse, strapped for research funds, sold out to the Swiss firm Brown Bovieri Mannheim, which resold the business to Siemens several months later.[73]

Zuse and his colleagues in Germany, though having a small impact on the burgeoning market for commercial computing machines, had a significant impact on the academic computing research community. With research groups in German-speaking Switzerland and Austria, they formed a closely knit group from which many valuable software ideas associated with this "Central European" community grew. Important ideas about structured programming (which imposes discipline on programmers to simplify debugging and maintenance of programs), algorithmic languages (which simplify the programming of mathematical computations), and the semantic theory of programming languages (which simplifies the linguistic design of new programming languages) can be traced to Zuse and these German-speaking researchers.[74]

71. Bauer, "Between Zuse and Rutishauser," p. 517; OECD, *Electronic Computers*, p. 34; Connolly, "History of Computing in Europé," pp. E-27, E-28; and Calhoun, "New Computer Developments," pp. 6–7.

72. Calhoun, "New Computer Developments," pp. 6–7.

73. See Alwin Walther, "German Computing," *Datamation*, vol. 6 (September 1960), p. 27; OECD, *Electronic Computers*, p. 102; and Connolly, "History of Computing in Europe," pp. E-24, E-34. By 1960 the American Royal McBee Company's German subsidiary was also producing locally.

74. Zuse worked on a theoretical (in the sense that there was no machine on which it actually ran at the time) programming language, the *Plankalkül*, during the years 1945–1948. Lectures given by Zuse in 1947 and 1948 inspired German and Swiss

162   CREATING THE COMPUTER

Despite an early start, a highly developed technology base, and a strong academic research program, German firms did not begin to ship large volumes of commercial computer products until the early 1960s. The German government did little to guide computer development in the 1950s, other than to support computer construction in German educational and research institutions.[75] This ten-year lag behind the foreign competition presented German equipment manufacturers with some difficult decisions in the 1960s.

Entering the 1960s

Thus German engineers and scientists had an early research lead in the technology of ferrous magnetic materials and prewar experience in leading-edge computing machines. Yet, ironically, at the start of the 1960s German computer manufacturers were lagging well behind other European and Japanese producers.

Four German firms were marketing electronic computers by the early 1960s—Standard Elektrik Lorenz, Telefunken, Zuse, and Siemens. Given their late entry into the market, the large R&D costs required to produce small numbers of mainframe computers drained the resources of the German computer makers, and casualties began dropping out of the industry in the mid-1960s. Standard Elektrik discontinued its computer line in 1964, Telefunken was bought out by Allgemein Elektrizitäts Geselschaft (AEG), to become AEG-Telefunken in 1966, and Zuse, which had only made small scientific and industrial computers, became part of Siemens in 1967.[76]

The large electrical equipment producer Siemens had emerged as the leading German manufacturer of mainframe computers in the early 1960s.[77] After introducing its second internally designed computer, in 1963, however, it too decided to avoid the costly and draining research investments it had been making in computers. In 1964 Siemens negotiated

researchers to begin research in these areas. See Bauer, "Between Zuse and Rutishauser," pp. 515–22.

75. The *Deutsche Forschungs Gemeinschaft* (DFG) sponsored many of the university projects. See Calhoun, "New Computer Developments," p. 6.

76. Jecquier, "Computers," pp. 206–07, 216.

77. In mid-1962, Siemens had 20 of its model 2002 mainframes in European installations (17 in Germany), compared with 10 SEL machines (7 in Germany) and 2 Telefunken installations (both in Germany). See "Datamation's International Computer Census," p. 48.

a licensing arrangement with RCA and in 1965 began shipping RCA's Spectra 70 line as the Siemens 4004. Although Siemens was the largest German computer producer, its share of the German market in the mid-1960s hovered at about 5 percent.[78]

In the late 1960s, important changes occurred in German computing.[79] As the French Plan Calcul got under way in 1967, and British statesmen were arranging the consolidation of English computer firms, the German government pushed through its first Data Processing Program. A second Data Processing Program followed in 1969–70, lasting through 1975. The first program largely consisted of financial support for R&D efforts in computer hardware, while the second expanded to cover software, applications, electronic components, and peripherals. Unlike the French programs, the German funding agenda included considerable resources for research and education in the technology of information processing within the German university system.[80]

Most of the assistance went to Siemens, and to a lesser extent, the troubled AEG-Telefunken. The German government made some attempt to solidify the status of Siemens as the de facto national champion, including encouraging merger talks between AEG-Telefunken and Siemens in 1970. After the talks collapsed, the government encouraged the formation of a joint venture between AEG-Telefunken and a new firm on the German computing scene, Nixdorf Computer, to produce Telefunken's designs for large mainframe computers.[81]

The most important event of the period was the entry of Nixdorf Computer in 1968. By specializing in small minicomputers, Nixdorf expanded into a largely uncontested European market (the American minicomputer makers, although successful in the U.S. market, had not made large European investments by that early date). By the early 1970s,

78. Connolly, "History of Computing in Europe," pp. E-32, E-34, E-37; Robert B. Forest, "Close Cooperation: Europe's Best Hope," *Datamation*, vol. 17 (December 15, 1971), pp. 32–33; and Harman, *International Computer Industry*, p. 31.

79. The increased government support for computer R&D was preceded by increased government funding for electronics research. From 1962 to 1964, public funds for Germany's electronics R&D went from a 35 percent to a 45 percent share. EEC, *L'industrie électronique*, p. 65.

80. See Dosi, *Industrial Adjustment and Policy*, pp. 27–28, 82; and Jecquier, "Computers," p. 221.

81. House of Commons, *Fourth Report from the Select Committee on Science and Technology*, vol. 3: *The Prospects for the United Kingdom Computer Industry in the 1970s*, Session 1970–71 (London: Her Majesty's Stationery Office, 1971), app. 29; and Jecquier, "Computers," p. 206.

Nixdorf had become the only clear-cut success story in the European computer industry and had even set up an American affiliate in the U.S. market. After only slightly more than three years of operation, little Nixdorf's sales of small computers amounted to slightly less than half of giant Siemens' production of large mainframes.[82]

Although no formal procurement preferences were written into law during these years, in practice the government preferred German computers.[83] Whether because of these preferences or because of the accelerated development of the German industry, the position of German firms had improved considerably by the early 1970s. By 1969 Siemens had claimed 13 percent of the German market; by 1972 Siemens accounted for 16 percent of Germany's computer base; by 1975, 18 percent.[84] In the mid-1970s, Siemens was, along with the British ICL operation, one of the two chief indigenous forces in European computing.

Changes in the 1970s

The mid-1970s marked a period of restructuring for the German computer firms. Siemens, left stranded by RCA's withdrawal from the business, had entered the ill-fated Unidata tie-up with CII and Philips. When that arrangement collapsed, Siemens turned to the Japanese for IBM-compatible large mainframes to fill out the line of smaller IBM-compatible machines that it had developed for the aborted Unidata venture. This relationship endures to the present day: Siemens is a major vendor of Fujitsu's large mainframes, sold under the Siemens label in Europe. In 1974 AEG-Telefunken's computer operations, in recurrent crisis, were finally sold to Siemens.[85]

82. Jecquier, "Computers" p. 216; and OECD, *Electronic Computers*, p. 37. Nixdorf Computer was number 17 on *Datamation*'s list of the top one hundred computer firms in the world in 1986. See "The Datamation 100," *Datamation*, vol. 33 (June 15, 1987), p. 42. See also U.S. Department of Commerce, *Global Market Survey*, p. 51.

83. Jecquier, "Computers," p. 222. It was also alleged that the German government had issued an order requiring that by 1975, the IBM share of central government procurement of computers be reduced from 80 percent to 60 percent. See *Fourth Report from the Select Committee on Science and Technology*, vol. 3, app. 29.

84. *Fourth Report from the Select Committee on Science and Technology*, vol. 3, app. 19; U.S. Department of Commerce, *Global Market Survey*, p. 51; and Pantages and others, "Western Europe's Computer Industry," p. 75.

85. Another German firm, Bandische Anilin und Soda-Fabriken (BASF), competes with Siemens in the European computer market by marketing the large-scale computers made by Fujitsu's Japanese rival, Hitachi. See Fujitsu Limited, *Fujitsu and the Computer*

The great success of Nixdorf in pioneering the minicomputer industry in Europe led the German government to reevaluate its policies for supporting the computer industry. By the mid-1970s, when the third Data Processing Program (1976-79) was announced, a dramatic change had occurred in funding priorities. The government, rather than pushing Siemens alone as a national champion, adopted a policy favoring "dual championship." Nixdorf occupied the favored position in the smaller systems market. The third support program shifted resources away from supporting hardware development in large mainframe computers and toward small computers, terminals, peripherals, software, and university research and training.[86] Strategy shifted from confronting IBM in the established large-business systems markets to seeking competitive advantage in the newly emerging markets for small systems and office and factory automation.

The one unqualified success among the European hardware producers, Nixdorf, moved at an early stage to organize itself as an "American" computer company, with significant facilities and sales in the U.S. market. Rather than relying on the patronage of the state, Nixdorf expanded into newer applications and markets, establishing subsidiaries in the big world markets for computers, including the United States and Japan. As early as 1972, just a few years after its founding, Nixdorf was exporting 30 percent of its German production.[87]

Other European Developments

Many other European countries pursued computer projects in the 1950s. Some efforts resulted in commercial computer products, but none had a significant impact on world or national computer markets, with the possible exception of computers built in the Netherlands. There, in 1958, the Dutch firm N.V. Electrologica began production of a commercial computer line, and the Philips electrical equipment conglomerate

Industry in Japan (Tokyo: Fujitsu Limited, 1983), p. 8; and Pantages and others, "Western Europe's Computer Industry," p. 66. In 1986 Siemens scaled back its ties with Fujitsu (in the face of continued legal attacks by IBM against Fujitsu operating systems software) and formed a joint venture with BASF to sell Hitachi mainframes in Europe.

86. See Jecquier, "Computers," pp. 217–18; Pantages and others, "Western Europe's Computer Industry," p. 75; and Dosi, *Industrial Adjustment and Policy*, p. 82.

87. U.S. Department of Commerce, *Global Market Survey*, p. 51.

built several experimental computers. Philips acquired Electrologica in 1965 when the latter company faced problems in financing its research program.[88] To this day, Philips remains a significant presence in the European computer market.

Two important research programs exerted a significant influence on computer development, even though they did not strengthen the fortunes of national firms. One important group of Swiss researchers at the Swiss Federal Polytechnic Institute in Zurich, which had received Zuse's Z-4 in 1950, affected the evolution of software and programming concepts in Europe. The Swiss had close affiliations with Zuse and the German computer research community, and together, they worked on ideas that shaped the definition of the algebraic programming language ALGOL, to this day one of the principal languages for computer research. Many of these Swiss computer specialists became the core of IBM's Zurich Research Laboratory.[89]

Another country in which significant computer research, but no home-grown computers, appeared was Austria. There, a resourceful group led by H. Zemanek built an early transistorized computer with donations of components, equipment, and funds from a wide variety of industry and government sources. These researchers helped establish IBM's Vienna Laboratory—Zemanek's group physically moved their machine from Vienna's University of Technology to the IBM laboratory in 1961.[90] The Vienna computer researchers were active, with the Swiss and the Germans, in the ALGOL movement of the late 1950s. Later, at IBM this group produced seminal work on the semantics of computer programming languages. In the mid-1960s the Vienna lab formally defined IBM's main proprietary high-level programming language, PL/I.[91]

Summary

In the early 1950s, Britain alone among the industrialized countries enjoyed a computer technology base comparable with that of the United

88. Connolly, "History of Computing in Europe," p. E-25.

89. OECD, *Electronic Computers*, p. 35.

90. See H. Zemanek, "Central European Prehistory of Computing," in Metropolis and others, *A History of Computing*, pp. 601–05.

91. Ibid., pp. 605–07; and see P. Lucas, "Formal Semantics of Programming Languages: VDL," *IBM Journal of Research and Development*, vol. 25 (September 1981), pp. 549–61.

States. It has maintained a great capacity in advanced computer technology, but its strength has been derived from research conducted in universities. Britain's commercial computer industry has steadily declined.

In France, the quest for a national computer champion, after years of effort and early, aggressive financial support, foundered on the lack of a clear strategy. Neither IBM compatibility, nor the pursuit of new applications in new markets, emerged as a focal point for the French. Instead, French planners encouraged CII to develop and market products in direct competition with the heart of the IBM business systems line. This strategy was buried in 1975, when CII was merged with Honeywell-Bull. The fortunes of this reworked champion sank further with the decline of Honeywell in world computer markets. The nationalizations of the early 1980s, which left CII-Bull a truly French, though somewhat tattered, national champion, have done nothing yet to set a clear direction for the computer effort. Little was done over the years to create an academic core of computer expertise, and France to this day lacks a strong university research base.

Germany, after years of letting market forces set the pace for the development of German computer hardware, reconsidered in the late 1960s. France's policy model seems to have inspired the early selection of Siemens as a national champion, but Germany reevaluated this step in the mid-1970s. Policy shifted toward the fairly successful idea of funding a more diverse portfolio of firms and research institutions. Germany, despite its late start, now ranks with Britain in the strength of its computer industry and technology.

Figure 5-1 depicts the shares that major players in the European computer market staked out in 1986. Among the European firms, German companies clearly lead, trailed by the British and the French. Table 5-4 shows that the Europeans largely survive in sheltered domestic markets. With a few notable exceptions, European computer companies sell 80 percent, and even 90 percent, of their product in their regional, European market (the Common Market makes it a single market), and 60 percent or more of their output in their home country.[92]

Themes that crop up in the development of American computer companies are equally evident in Europe. The lack of an accelerated

92. The exceptions are Olivetti (70 percent of data processing revenues in Europe, 37 percent in Italy), which supplies products marketed in the United States by AT&T, and Compagnie Générale d'Electricité (92 percent in Europe, 48 percent in France), which acquired ITT.

Figure 5-1. *Relative Shares of the Top Computer Companies in the European Market*

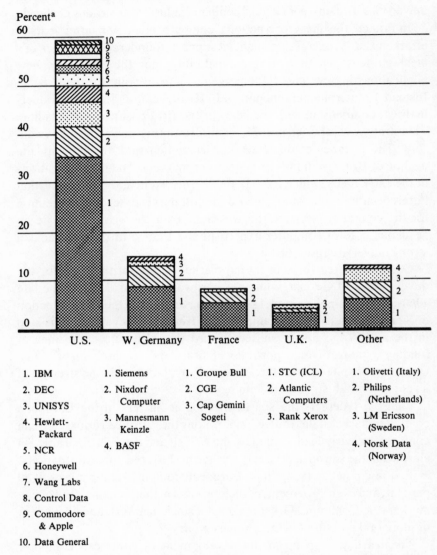

Percent[a]

U.S.   W. Germany   France   U.K.   Other

1. IBM	1. Siemens	1. Groupe Bull	1. STC (ICL)	1. Olivetti (Italy)
2. DEC	2. Nixdorf	2. CGE	2. Atlantic	2. Philips
3. UNISYS	Computer	3. Cap Gemini	Computers	(Netherlands)
4. Hewlett-	3. Mannesmann	Sogeti	3. Rank Xerox	3. LM Ericsson
Packard	Keinzle			(Sweden)
5. NCR	4. BASF			4. Norsk Data
6. Honeywell				(Norway)
7. Wang Labs				
8. Control Data				
9. Commodore				
& Apple				
10. Data General				

Sources: Sarah Underwood and Paul Tate, "The European 25," *Datamation,* vol. 33 (August 1, 1987), pp. 53–59; and author's calculations.

a. Percentage of data processing sales (hardware, software, services) in European markets by the twenty-five largest vendors. The top twenty-five accounted for $44.5 billion of a total European data processing market estimated at more than $70 billion.

Table 5-4. *The Top European Computer Producers, 1986*

Producer	Worldwide data processing revenues[a] (millions of dollars)	Share in European market (percent)	Share in home country market (percent)
Germany			
Siemens	4,387	88	65
Nixdorf Computer	2,075	92	52
BASF	521	79	n.a.
Mannesmann Keinzle	489	91	65
France			
Groupe Bull	2,568	94	66
Compagnie Générale d'Electricité	1,025	92	48
Cap Gemini Sogeti	420	70	37
United Kingdom			
STC (ICL)	1,756	81	63
Rank Xerox	459	81	n.a.
Atlantic Computers	431	92	62
Other countries			
Olivetti (Italy)	3,865	70	37
Philips (Netherlands)	1,763	87	n.a.
LM Ericsson (Sweden)	1,344	89	n.a.
Norsk Data (Norway)	349	91	55

Source: Sarah Underwood and Paul Tate, "The European 25," *Datamation,* vol. 33 (August 1, 1987), pp. 58–59.
n.a. Not available.
a. Hardware, software, and services.

development program for electronic component technology in Europe clearly hurt the competitiveness of the European industry. Nickel delay lines, plated wires, twistors, and other little-known memory and logic technologies were commonly found in European machines in the late 1950s and early 1960s. They were cheaper, not superior to, the transistors and ferrite core memories commonly used in America.[93] European computer makers did not have the benefit of the military development programs that lowered the costs of transistors, ferrite cores, and integrated circuits found in American machines. By the early 1960s, when the economic significance of computers was becoming evident to all, and a transatlantic lag in the technology a matter of historical fact, most

93. See, for example, Isaac L. Auerbach, "European Electronic Data Processing—A Report on the Industry and the State-of-the-Art," *Proceedings of the Institute of Radio Engineers*, vol. 49 (January 1961), pp. 330–33; and the discussion accompanying Calhoun, "New Computer Developments," pp. 7–8.

European firms were forced to seek access to American computer and electronics technology.

The competitive strategies that were tried by American firms also emerged in Europe in the 1960s. In a misguided quest for scale economies, European governments often favored the placing of all bets on an anointed national champion. The favored company often had strategic and technological ties to the giant American firms contesting IBM's markets in the United States. For the most part, large European computer makers attempted to compete head to head with IBM in their national markets, offering a similar line of products aimed at the same range of business markets. With a few notable exceptions, European industry ignored other strategies that were successful when tried in the United States, like targeting specialized niches and new applications and going after the high and low ends beyond the IBM product range.[94] A scarcity of venture capital may also partly explain the vacuum in the European industry.

In Europe, as in the United States, trained personnel were the vehicle of technology transfer. In Britain, the universities and the national research labs fed people and ideas to industry. The German computer companies drew their first design groups from the university computing projects. In France—which lacked a university or national laboratory technology base—companies sent trained engineers abroad to absorb new developments. France had to create a national laboratory to sponsor work on information technology because it lacked institutions to foster investment in basic research, training people, and commercial applications of new technology. Much the same story was repeated elsewhere in Europe.[95]

Commercial mainframe computer makers are still weak in Europe. Currently, the large computers sold by European computer companies are foreign products packaged with European labels. Siemens and ICL

94. Nixdorf was, of course, the most successful exception. Norsk Data, the only other clear success in the European industry, broke similar ground in the manufacture and sale of superminicomputers in European markets in the 1970s.

95. Sweden, for example, established a National Board for Computing to finance the development of digital computers and to sponsor the construction of the BARK relay computer and the BESK electronic computer—one of the many machines based on the IAS design—in that country. When budgetary problems led to the dissolution of the group building those machines in the mid-1950s, several designers left to build computers for industry (in the Atridaberg and at SAAB). See Calhoun, "New Computer Developments," p. 7; and Samuels, "Computers with European Accents," p. 15.

sell large-scale computers made by Fujitsu, while Olivetti and BASF place their labels on large machines made by Hitachi. Bull's largest computers are made by NEC. The market for large business machines in Europe is now mainly a competition between IBM and other American firms, and Japanese producers.

CHAPTER SIX

Computers in Japan

How did Japan succeed in the computer industry as Europe lost ground? The economic constraints on Japan in the early postwar years were at least as stringent as those felt in Europe. Yet by the mid-1960s, Japan—with Britain—was one of the few countries besides the United States that had developed a significant, indigenous commercial computer industry. By the late 1970s, the Japanese industry was second only to American producers.

In some respects, the spread of computer technology in Japan resembled the early years of computing in Europe. No large program of defense investment supported computing technology, and national research laboratories and universities carried out most of the early research. As was true in Europe, growing awareness of the commercial and strategic importance of the technology led to crash government programs to accelerate computer development in the mid-1960s. Finally, commercial links between Japanese and foreign firms were essential to Japan's acquisition of needed technology.

There were also many differences between Europe and Japan. After the early 1960s, Japan emphasized technological development of leading-edge components for computer systems. Marketing a less advanced, but completely homegrown computer, received less priority. And the firms that entered the field in Japan were neither defense contractors nor business equipment firms. Instead, they were the producers of communications equipment and electrical machinery.

Government policy also took a much different turn from that in Europe. Japan never handed over the entire domestic market to a favored company—a "national champion." Instead, support was given to a small group of highly competitive firms, and the virtues of competition were preserved even as limits on entry by outsiders were established. At an

172

early date the government tested cooperative research projects as a vehicle for extending financial support for technological development. They proved successful and became the organizational model for subsidies to research and development. Besides leveraging the return to investment in more generic and basic research (where individual companies often found the payoff difficult to capture), the cooperative research projects transferred technology and ideas among firms and between national laboratories and industry. This function was unusually important in Japan because the limited mobility of workers among large Japanese firms prevented the incessant migration of engineers among firms and laboratories that was crucial to the spread of technology in Europe and the United States.

First Steps

Two Japanese organizations, the Electrotechnical Laboratory (ETL) and the University of Tokyo, had developed computing and calculating machinery before the outbreak of World War II. In 1920 ETL researchers constructed punched card machines for use in the first census of Japan, but an earthquake destroyed the ten units built by 1921, and the census bureau had to import American tabulators.[1] Until 1954, when IBM Japan first shipped a locally produced product, there was no Japanese industry in punched card business equipment.

Work at the University of Tokyo began in the late 1930s on the design of a statistical tabulator with binary arithmetic. After the war ended, the Nippon Electric Company (NEC) and Fujitsu built two versions of this

1. The government's Electrotechnical Laboratory (ETL), founded in 1891 as a part of Japan's Communication Ministry, was rooted in the public policies to promote industrialization begun in Meiji Japan. After World War II, in 1948, the Electrical Communications Department of ETL was detached and became the Electrical Communication Laboratories of newly formed Nippon Telephone and Telegraph (NTT), Japan's state-owned communications monopoly. In 1952 ETL became a part of Japan's Ministry of International Trade and Industry (MITI). See Electrotechnical Laboratory, *Guide to ETL, 1983–1984* (Tokyo: ETL, 1983).

Unless otherwise noted, this discussion is based on Hidetosi Takahasi, "Some Important Computers of Japanese Design," *Annals of the History of Computing,* vol. 2 (October 1980); and Ryota Suekane, "Early History of Computing in Japan," in N. Metropolis, J. Howlett, and Gian-Carlo Rota, eds., *A History of Computing in the Twentieth Century: A Collection of Essays* (Academic Press, 1980), pp. 575–78.

machine.[2] In 1951, Dr. Hideo Yamashita, who had designed this statistical machine, attended a United Nations Educational, Scientific, and Cultural Organization conference on establishing an international computing facility, visited several U.S. computer projects, and returned to Japan enthused about the speed of vacuum tube digital computers. In 1952 Yamashita started the Tokyo Automatic Computer (TAC) project at the University of Tokyo, with the support of the Ministry of Education and the Toshiba company.[3] The TAC design was based on the Cambridge EDSAC, modified to use a cathode ray tube memory. The builders of this machine ran into serious technical problems, and TAC was not completed until early 1959.

Another technical influence on early Japanese computers stems from the late 1930s, when engineers at NEC published papers on the application of Boolean algebra to the design of electrical relay networks. This work was extended by researchers at ETL during the war, and in the late 1940s and early 1950s, ETL researchers began the construction of Japan's first relay computer using design techniques based on these principles. In 1952, a small pilot machine, the ETL Mark I was completed; in 1955 the full-sized ETL Mark II was finished. Fujitsu, at the time a small firm, had collaborated with ETL in building these machines and introduced its own machine using relay technology, the FACOM 100, in 1954. This machine was the first commercial relay computer marketed

2. The Nippon Electric Company (NEC) was established in 1899 as a joint venture between Western Electric (the U.S. firm) and a Japanese trading company. Since 1932, NEC has been associated with the Sumitomo business group. Fujitsu was originally the telephone division of Fuji Electric (which had begun as a joint venture of Furukawa Electric and the German Siemens company), and has strong ties to the Dai-Ichi Kangyo Bank (DKB) business group. Until 1960, Fujitsu was a small communications equipment producer supplying most of its product to the state-owned communications monopoly, NTT. See Julian Gresser, *Partners in Prosperity: Strategic Industries for the U.S. and Japan* (McGraw-Hill, 1984), pp. 113–15. NTT greatly resembled the U.S. AT&T monopoly, with one important qualification—it did not have a captive equipment producer (like AT&T's Western Electric subsidiary) to produce communications gear for it. Instead NTT had to rely on contracting with private Japanese equipment manufacturers.

3. See George E. Lindamood, "The Rise of the Japanese Computer Industry," *Office of Naval Research Far East Scientific Bulletin,* vol. 7 (October–December 1982), p. 63.

Toshiba (the Tokyo Shibaura Electric Company), established in 1879 as Japan's first producer of telegraph equipment, has been associated with the Mitsui business group since 1893.

by a Japanese firm. Starting in 1956, Fujitsu shipped improved designs as the FACOM models 128A and 128B.

An Evolving Industry

In 1956 researchers at ETL built the first transistorized computer operational in Japan, the Mark III. This small computer, with a 128-word delay line memory, used 130 transistors and 1,700 diodes for logic.[4] The point-contact transistors used were an early and unreliable implementation of semiconductor technology. In 1957 ETL built a somewhat larger and more practical machine, using a magnetic drum memory, 470 transistors, and 4,400 diodes. The newer junction-type transistors used in this machine, the ETL Mark IV, worked much better, and this computer served as the prototype for the first commercial transistor computers shipped in Japan by Hitachi and the Nippon Electric Company.[5] Other transistor computers based on ETL designs were produced by Fujitsu, Toshiba, and Oki.[6] The transistors used in these computers lagged behind those used in the United States, where new surface barrier transistors manufactured by Philco were setting new standards of speed and reliability in electronic computing machines. In 1959 ETL finished the Mark V, a much larger magnetic drum machine. It too became the prototype of commercial machines.[7]

However, ETL's earliest research on computers remained largely independent of the commercial objectives of Japanese business and

4. See Osamu Ishii, "Research and Development on Information Processing Technology at Electrotechnical Laboratory—A Historical Review," *Bulletin of the Electrotechnical Laboratory,* vol. 45 (1981), p. 21 (in Japanese).

5. Models based on the ETL Mark IV included the Hitachi HITAC 301, the NEC 2201, and the NEC 2203. The first NEC 2201 was completed in 1958. See H. Hatta, "A History and Future Trends of Computer Architecture at Nippon Electric Company (NEC)," *Japan Information Processing Society, Computer Architecture SIG Newsletter,* no. 52 (March 7, 1984), p. 2 (in Japanese). Toshiba and Fujitsu also introduced transistor computers based on the Mark IV over the 1958–59 period, while Oki, Matsushita, and Mitsubishi announced similar machines in 1961.

6. Tosaku Kimura, "Birth and Development of Computers," *Natural Sciences and Museums,* vol. 46, no. 3 (1979) Special Issue on Computers (in Japanese).

7. Hitachi's HITAC 102 was based on the Mark V. The Mark V was the first medium-scale Japanese computer to go into practical use at a computer center. See Ishii, "Research and Development in Information Processing Technology," p. 21.

government. Japan's Ministry of International Trade and Industry (MITI) did not take over ETL until 1952 and only emphasized computer development in the very late 1950s, when the commercial market began to blossom. In the early and mid-1950s, the giants of Japanese industry were equally indifferent to developing new technology with a few exceptions.[8] The transistorized ETL Mark III was actually the second electronic computer built in Japan; the first, finished earlier in 1956, was a small vacuum tube machine built at the Fuji Film Company to assist in lens design. This computer, the FUJIC, was apparently the only computer built in Japan in the 1950s that had not benefited from research carried out by a government lab or from direct financial assistance from a government agency. The first-generation technology used in the FUJIC was somewhat less advanced than that used in the ETL Mark III, completed later in 1956, and Fuji never did enter the computer business.

Another major government laboratory tried to lead Japanese firms into the computer business in the late 1950s. The Electrical Communication Laboratory of Nippon Telephone and Telegraph (NTT), and its international affiliate, KDD, in cooperation with the University of Tokyo, supported development of parametron-based circuits, which promised greater stability and reliability than vacuum tubes and were much cheaper in Japan than contemporary diodes and transistors. Much as the Ministry of International Trade and Industry's ETL had taken transistor computer technology under its wing, the NTT's laboratory in Musashino undertook the development of computers using the parametron.[9] The first of these machines, the M-1, was completed in 1958, and

8. A few exceptions proved the rule: the production of point-contact transistors by Sony for the Mark III, the joint development of the magnetic drum for the Mark IV by Sony and Hokushin, and the 50 percent discount on junction transistors given by Hitachi to ETL. Personal communication from Shigeru Takahashi, December 1985; Shigeru Takahashi, "Early Transistor Computers in Japan," *Annals of the History of Computing,* vol. 8 (April 1986), pp. 146, 149, 151.

9. In 1954 Eiichi Goto, a graduate student at Tokyo University, invented the parametron. By the end of 1956 the first parametron-based computer was in operation at Tokyo University. For a discussion of the principles of operation of the parametron, see Saburo Muroga, "Elementary Principle of Parametron," *Datamation,* vol. 4 (October 1958), pp. 31–34. See also Kimura, "Birth and Development of Computers."

MITI and NTT have sometimes continued to back different approaches to technology development. For example, recent artificial intelligence work sponsored by MITI (the Fifth Generation Project) has focused on the use of the Prolog programming language, while NTT work mainly uses the Lisp language. See, for example, M. Berger, "NTT Builds a Lisp Machine for Japan," *Electronics,* October 30, 1986, pp. 44–47.

an improved model, the M-1B, was ready in 1960.[10] The Japanese copied the architecture of the M-1 from the ILLIAC I, constructed by the University of Illinois. The M-1 pioneered technology that commercial companies, including Hitachi, NEC, and Fujitsu, would use in parametron computers. Apparently, the M-1 was also the first computer with ferrite core memory built in Japan.[11] However, advances in semiconductor technology rendered the parametron obsolete, and these commercial developments based on indigenous Japanese components were a dead end.

Other important university research projects followed the lead of ETL and NTT in the late 1950s and early 1960s. Toshiba and Hitachi developed transistor computers in cooperation with Kyoto University; Tokyo University and Fujitsu constructed a parametron computer; and Nippon Electric and Tohoku University built yet another parametron computer.[12]

Early Japanese computers were built in limited numbers in the late 1950s and were small, relatively low-cost machines whose technology lagged behind developments abroad. Fujitsu, for example, built only eight of the large, commercial relay computers it had developed in the 1950s.[13] When the technology developed at ETL and NTT began to be

10. See Y. Muraoka, "A History and Future Trends of Computer Architecture at Nippon Telephone and Telegraph Corporation," *Japan Information Processing Society, Computer Architecture SIG Newsletter,* no. 52 (March 1984), p. 1 (in Japanese).

11. Commercial machines related to the M-1 included the Fujitsu FACOM 200 and 201, the experimental Hitachi Parametron Computer HIPAC-1, and the NEC NEAC 1101 and 1102 series machines. Hitachi's HIPAC 101, based on the HIPAC-1, was the first commercial model, finished in 1958.

Japanese public universities (and therefore the Ministry of Education) collaborated with the commercial computer companies as well in developing parametron technology. The University of Tokyo built an experimental parametron machine, the PC-1, finished in 1958. A successor, the PC-2, involved collaboration with Fujitsu, which produced the design as the FACOM 202. See Kimura, "Birth and Development of Computers." The NEAC 1102 was designed and built jointly by NEC and Tohoku University.

12. The Toshiba-Kyoto machine became the Toshiba 3400 in 1964; Hitachi installed its 5020 at Kyoto in 1965; the Tokyo-Fujitsu collaboration led to the PC-2 parametron research computer, completed in 1961; and the NEC-Tohoku University project, known as the SENAC I, became the NEAC 1102 of 1959. See Hatta, "History and Future Trends"; F. Sato, H. Nahajo, and T. Mutanda, "A History and Future Trends of Computer Architecture at Toshiba," *Japan Information Processing Society, Computer Architecture SIG Newsletter,* no. 52 (March 7, 1984) (in Japanese); Lindamood, "The Rise of the Japanese Computer Industry," p. 62; Takahasi, "Some Important Computers," p. 336; and Kimura, "Birth and Development of Computers," pp. 5–6.

13. Takahasi, "Some Important Computers," p. 333.

Table 6-1. *The Growth of National Computer Production in Japan*

Fiscal year beginning	Number of systems installed						Foreign computers as percent of value
	Large		Medium		Small		
	Japanese	Foreign	Japanese	Foreign	Japanese	Foreign	
1957	0	0	1	0	1	1	n.a.
1958	0	2	0	1	3	2	93
1959	0	2	5	11	4	4	79
1960	0	5	13	28	18	2	73
1961	0	8	25	52	20	12	82
1962	2	10	63	72	40	9	67
1963	3	34	97	60	50	107	70

Sources: G. B. Levine, "Computers in Japan," *Datamation*, vol. 13 (December 1967), p. 23.
n.a. Not available.

used in small- and medium-sized electronic computers, limited numbers of machines were shipped at first. As the estimates in table 6-1 indicate, perhaps two medium and small computer systems were installed by Japanese computer producers in 1957, three in 1958, and nine in 1959. In 1960 the numbers increased greatly. Accompanied by a surge in imports of large- and medium-sized computers from abroad, an even greater increase in the number of medium- and small-sized Japanese machines swelled the count of computers installed in Japan. It was not until 1965 that the first truly large-scale computer built in Japan, by Hitachi, went into operation.

MITI organized a research committee in 1955 to study how best to accelerate the development of the domestic computer industry. The committee was made up of MITI (which included ETL) officials, NTT personnel, university research scientists, and representatives of industry. The committee's report urged more support for computer development, limits on foreign imports, and acceleration of the introduction of foreign technology through technical assistance and patent licenses.[14]

In 1957 the Electronics Industry Development Provisional Act was passed by the Diet, targeting electronics as a priority investment for Japan. Besides setting up an elaborate institutional framework for accomplishing these ends, the act authorized financial assistance to manufacturers, including direct subsidies to research and development, loans for commercial product development, and various types of loans and depreciation benefits for capital investments deemed consistent with

14. Eugene J. Kaplan, *Japan, The Government-Business Relationship: A Guide for the American Businessman* (Washington, D.C.: Department of Commerce, 1972), p. 80.

the MITI program. The government also permitted selective exemption from the antimonopoly law, allowing MITI to establish research and production cartels.

Fujitsu, Nippon Electric, and Hitachi successfully sought the eligibility of computer projects for the direct R&D support program right at the start, and MITI added computers to the list of industries eligible for the other benefits in subsequent years. Nonetheless, until the early 1960s, MITI did little to push computer technology through the menu of assistance programs set up in the 1957 act—the total subsidy to R&D awarded during the 1957–61 period was under $1 million.[15] Direct technical assistance from government labs or joint development efforts with universities continued to be the chief instrument of support for computer development in private firms until the early 1960s.

Enter IBM and Other Foreign Manufacturers

In 1957 and 1958, imports of computers increased significantly to meet demand in Japanese industry and government (figure 6-1). They accounted for roughly 70 percent to 90 percent of new computer installations in Japan through the early 1960s (table 6-1). MITI responded in 1958 by encouraging Japanese firms to establish the Japan Electronic Industry Development Association (JEIDA) to promote the marketing and support of Japanese computers and the electronics industry.[16]

By the late 1950s, as it became clear that computers would have a dramatic impact in the business marketplace, interest in developing a competitive line of computers began to stir among Japanese firms. In Fujitsu, which had been a small producer of communications equipment sold primarily to NTT, a separate department to handle electronics products and a computer factory were first established in 1961.[17] Fujitsu,

---

15. Ibid., p. 82.

16. James Connolly, "Chronology of Computing in Africa, Asia, Europe, and Latin America," internal IBM document (New York, IBM World Trade, ca. 1967), pp. A.P.5-6. The first foreign computer shipped to a commercial customer in Japan was a Bendix G-15 installed by Japan National Railways in 1957. Kimura, "Birth and Development of Computers."

See also Japan Electronics Industry Development Association, *Guide to JEIDA* (Tokyo: JEIDA, 1984), p. 1. MITI initiated the formation of JEIDA. Personal communication from Shigeru Takahashi, December 1985.

17. Takuma Yamamoto and Naotoshi Inoue, "History of the Development of FACOM," in *The Collection of Ikeda Memorial Articles: Centered on the Development of FACOMs* (Tokyo: Fujitsu, 1978) (translated from Japanese).

Figure 6-1. *Japan's Imports of Computing Machinery*

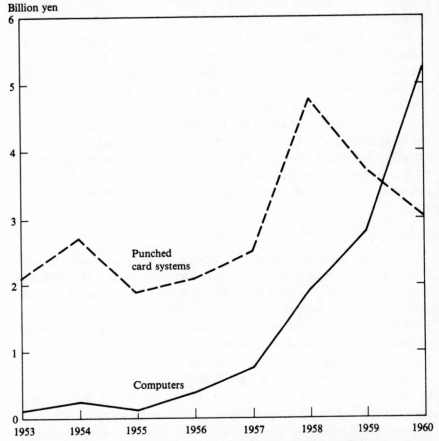

Billion yen

Source: *Jōhō Shori Gakkai Rekishi Tokubetsu Iinkai* (Special Committee on the History of Information Management), ed., *Nihon no konpūta no Rekishi* (The history of computers in Japan) (Tokyo: Ohm Publishing Co., 1985), p. 176.

even then, was unique in its commitment to computers. In the other important Japanese firms, all much larger industrial conglomerates, computers were usually only a small part of their business.[18] But by 1960 the dramatic surge in computer installations coincided with important changes in Japanese government policies affecting the production of

18. To this day, Fujitsu remains the only Japanese firm that is arguably a pure computer producer. In the mid-1970s, for example, about 72 percent of Fujitsu's sales were computer related, compared with 6 percent for Hitachi, 25 percent for Nippon

computers. In that same year, after protracted negotiations, IBM secured the right of its wholly owned Japanese affiliate to manufacture computers in Japan. IBM received guarantees for foreign exchange remittances in return for making its computer patents available under license to any Japanese firm.[19] By 1961 IBM was starting to import many of its models into the Japanese market for sale to private customers, and by 1963, had opened a manufacturing plant in Japan for its 1440 computer system.[20]

The arrangement worked out with IBM was special. Through the end of the 1960s, Japanese controls on foreign investment were tight, and with rare exceptions, forbade foreign investments in majority-owned subsidiaries. IBM's privileged position was the consequence of its prewar activities in Japan, and more important, its position as the market leader in computers.

The benefits to Japan from acquiring the right to license IBM's patent stock probably had little to do with technology transfer. As shall be argued later, in the computer industry, patents have generally been of little significance in competition between national firms in their home markets. And the IBM deal apparently included no arrangement to actively transfer technology to Japanese firms, other than through IBM's normal activities in purchasing inputs from Japanese suppliers. Japanese

---

Electric, 6 to 7 percent of Toshiba's business, 40 percent of Oki Electric's revenues, and 5 percent of Mitsubishi's revenues. By the early 1980s, the figures were Fujitsu, 65 percent, Hitachi, 13 percent, Nippon Electric, 21 percent, Toshiba, 4 percent, Oki, 38 percent, and Mitsubishi, 5 percent. See Edward K. Yasaki and Angeline Pantages, "Japan's Computer Industry," *Datamation*, vol. 22 (September 1976), pp. 97–102; Edward K. Yasaki, "Computer Industry—Japan," in Anthony Ralston and Edwin D. Reilly, Jr., eds., *Encyclopedia of Computer Science and Engineering* (Van Nostrand Reinhold, 1983), p. 354.

19. Firms involved in the initial licensing agreements included Oki, Hitachi, Nippon Electric, Fujitsu, Toshiba, Mitsubishi, Hokushin Electric, Matsushita, Shiba Electric, and TEAC. IBM was established in Japan before World War II but was confiscated as an enemy alien during the war. In 1949 its Japanese affiliate was reinstated by order of the Occupation authorities, and in 1953 the affiliate had built a new plant in Tokyo. The Tokyo plant began to ship punched card machines in 1957, and by 1959, had built a second plant. Connolly, "Chronology of Computing," internal IBM document, n.d., pp. A.P.3–8.

20. IBM computers were imported into Japan and installed in government installations well before 1960. Kazuhiro Fuchi, then a student, and now director of Japan's Fifth Generation Project, recalls that three IBM 650s located in a U.S. Army camp were among the first few machines in Japan. (Interview with Kazuhiro Fuchi, Tokyo, April 1984.) In 1958 the Atomic Research Institute installed the first IBM 650 in Japan. In 1959 the first 704 was placed with the Government Meteorological Agency. Connolly, "Chronology of Computing," p. A.P.6.

producers had simply gained the right to use any information gleaned from reading patent applications or disassembling IBM products, without legal challenge. IBM also reportedly agreed to limit the royalty on these patents to 5 percent and to yield to MITI's administrative guidance in setting Japanese production levels.[21]

Given that the rights to use these patents probably had negligible impact on the technological capabilities of Japanese producers, insisting on these licenses as a price for IBM's entry into the Japanese market probably reflected MITI's inexperience with the realities of technology transfer, particularly in the infant electronics industry.[22] After 1960, foreign tie-ups to the Japanese computer industry have almost always included active transfer of technology, either through a joint venture or through a manufacturing license that involves technical assistance from the foreign firm.[23]

This is not to say that the IBM agreement brought the Japanese computer makers no substantive benefits. First, it smoothed the way for Japanese computers to be sold one day in U.S. markets, the home turf of a powerful IBM. Second, having IBM produce and market its most sophisticated products in Japan meant gaining the benefits of informal technology transfer, personnel turnover, exposure of users to state-of-the-art equipment and systems, and procurement from Japanese suppliers.[24]

21. See Chalmers Johnson, *MITI and the Japanese Miracle: The Growth of Industrial Policy, 1925–1975* (Stanford University Press, 1982), pp. 246–47.

22. Legal considerations may also have played some role. Shigeru Takahashi has pointed out to me that IBM held a considerable number of Japanese patents at the time. Other U.S. firms with significant patent positions did not enter the Japanese market until well after IBM.

In fairness to MITI, though, it should be mentioned that the lawsuits, countersuits, delays, settlements, patent interferences, and the tangled web of cross-licensing agreements that ultimately were to establish the ineffectuality of patents in protecting evolutionary advances in electronics and computer technology were in progress at the time MITI cut its deal.

23. Unlike a patent license, which only grants the licensee the right to use the patented concept, a manufacturing license allows the recipient to produce a product, usually is accompanied by a transfer of know-how, and often means the purchase of components, subassemblies, and technical assistance from the licensor. See Organization for Economic Cooperation and Development, *Electronic Computers: Gaps in Technology*, report presented to the Third Ministerial Meeting on Science, March 11–12, 1968 (Paris: OECD, 1969), p. 44.

24. In Japan, most of IBM's staff is drawn from the national labor force. Though turnover is relatively low, it is not unknown for a Japanese IBM employee to be recruited into a domestic computer firm. In 1967, for example, a key executive of IBM Asia was

Japan cut a much less favorable deal with Sperry Rand in 1963. Sperry was able to enter only after accepting a minority interest in a joint venture with Oki Electric (49 percent). Consequently, however, the products of its affiliate, Oki-UNIVAC, were classified as "domestic," which led to favorable treatment of requests for import permits and access in competition for government procurement later in the decade.[25] Interestingly, no mandatory licensing of Sperry patents to other Japanese producers seems to have been incorporated into the arrangement.[26]

The negotiated entry of other foreign manufacturers and their technology into the Japanese market occurred during this same period. By that time it was apparent that despite five to ten years of experience with an active program of computer research and development pursued in government laboratories and universities, Japanese computers lagged far behind the technology available abroad. Accordingly, Japanese industry sought the transfer of technology from foreign companies, and the government sanctioned these arrangements. Tight MITI controls over licensing and technical assistance agreements with foreign firms made government approval essential.

Mitsubishi began to install the American Librascope LGP-30 computer in Japan in 1959, and in 1961, Hitachi signed with RCA. The Japanese trade ministry reportedly did not approve the Hitachi deal until its arch-rival, Nippon Electric, concluded an agreement with Honeywell in 1962. Mitsubishi arranged to manufacture a TRW computer in that same year. Toshiba was the last big company to arrange a foreign tie, when it reached an agreement with General Electric in 1964. Fujitsu was the only Japanese computer manufacturer that chose to develop its own

---

hired to become president of Fujitsu's FACOM computer division. See G. B. Levine, "Computers in Japan," *Datamation,* vol. 13 (December 1967), p. 24.

By the early 1980s, parts and subsystems purchased from Japanese subcontractors accounted for 60 percent to 70 percent of the value of IBM computer hardware manufactured in Japan. It was also claimed that IBM accounted for 70 percent to 80 percent of Japanese computer exports, so that IBM essentially provides great access to foreign markets for the products of the Japanese computer industry, as well as considerable foreign exchange. Interview with Tsuneo Saito, Japan Electronics Industry Development Association, Tokyo, April 1984.

25. See Kaplan, *Japan, the Government-Business Relationship,* pp. 84-85.

26. This is interesting because Sperry, at the time, probably had a patent position (which included the Eckert-Mauchly ENIAC patent claims and the magnetic drum and other patents produced by Engineering Research Associates) that was probably as significant as that of IBM. Perhaps by then experience showed that access to patents had little relation to a firm's competitive position in the market.

computer architecture, a commitment that guaranteed it a special position in the Japanese industry.

Thus, in the early 1960s, the Japanese computer industry depended almost wholly on foreign connections for its products. Many of the so-called domestic computers were Japanese nameplates slapped on equipment assembled from imported components and subassemblies. The amount of computer R&D undertaken by the domestic computer industry was limited. In early 1964, total employees in the computer divisions of all Japanese computer producers numbered 5,840, of which 1,240 were in sales departments.[27] Only Fujitsu devoted significant resources to building a research department.

Closing the Market

The shift to foreign technology was only one of the new policies implemented in the early 1960s. Other policies increased the protection for the Japanese computer market. The sharp rise in computer installations of 1960 was closely linked to increasing foreign imports (figure 6-1). In 1961, tariff rates were raised from 15 percent to 25 percent. Tight limits on foreign exchange allocated to the purchase of foreign computers, and permission to draw on those allocations, were controlled by MITI.

A complementary measure taken was the establishment of the Japan Electronic Computer Corporation (JECC), in 1961. With support from the Japan Development Bank, a state-controlled institution, and private computer manufacturers, JECC's charter was to purchase Japanese computers and lease them to domestic users.[28] That reduced the financial burden on manufacturers in a market in which the customer often rented the product. Formally, JECC was a joint venture by Japan's computer manufacturers into the computer leasing business, with strong support from the government.[29] For all practical purposes, though, JECC was a

27. Joseph C. Berston and Ken Imada, "Computing in Japan," *Datamation,* vol. 10 (September 1964), p. 28.

28. See Kaplan, *Japan, the Government-Business Relationship,* pp. 85–86. IBM computers manufactured in Japan were treated as foreign computers, while Oki-UNIVAC machines were considered domestic products.

29. The firms included in the Japan Electronic Computer Corporation (JECC) were Fujitsu, Hitachi, Mitsubishi, Oki, Toshiba, and Nippon Electric. Matsushita left in 1964 and rejoined JECC in 1979. U.S. International Trade Commission, *Foreign Industrial Targeting and Its Effects on U.S. Industries, Phase I: Japan,* Publication 1437 (October 1983), p. 133.

Table 6-2. *Market Share in Japan, General Purpose Computers*
Percent of value shipped by major vendors

Firm	Fiscal 1966	Fiscal 1975	Fiscal 1982
Japanese firms			
Hitachi	16	14	16
NEC	15	11	16
Fujitsu	10	24	24
Other Japanese	13	15	17
Total Japanese	54	64	73
U.S. firms			
IBM	n.a.	28	22
UNIVAC	n.a.	8	5

Sources: Fujitsu Limited, *Fujitsu and the Computer Industry in Japan* (Tokyo: Fujitsu Limited, 1983), p. 11; and Levine, "Computers in Japan," pp. 23–24. Figures do not include personal computers.
n.a. Not available.

quasi-governmental body under the indirect control of MITI, which supervised its establishment and appointed key officials. Roughly a third of the $2 billion in loans received by JECC over the 1961 to 1979 period came from the Japan Development Bank at below-market rates.[30]

JECC's computer leasing operations were structured to raise gradually the domestic content of Japanese computers. Manufacturers had to have a significant (20 percent in the mid-1960s) share of their content produced in Japan in order for their machines to be eligible for purchase by JECC. This percentage was ratcheted up, to 50 percent and then 75 percent, over time.[31]

These policies provided both foreign computer technology and a sheltered market to the Japanese computer firms. In 1961 Japanese firms had roughly 25 percent of the domestic market. By 1966 Japanese computer manufacturers were accounting for 52 percent of domestic sales, a percentage that was to climb steadily over the next fifteen years (table 6-2).

The National Technology Projects

Besides negotiated access to foreign technology and a protected market, a third set of programs shaped the evolution of the Japanese

30. Johnson, *MITI and the Japanese Miracle,* p. 247. United States International Trade Commission, *Foreign Industrial Targeting,* p. 133.

31. Alvin J. Harman, *The International Computer Industry: Innovation and Comparative Advantage* (Harvard University Press, 1971), p. 30; Kenneth Flamm, *Targeting the Computer: Government Support and International Competition* (Brookings, 1987), p. 252, table D-2; and Gresser, *Partners in Prosperity,* p. 120.

industry. In late 1960, after IBM had been given access to the Japanese market, MITI announced a "Five Year Program for National Production of Electronic Computers."[32] In 1961 the government passed legislation permitting ad hoc research associations to receive public funding, and in 1962 MITI urged computer makers to form an "Electronic Computer Research Association" and develop technology jointly. By 1963 a three-year program known as the FONTAC project, teaming Fujitsu, the NEC, and Oki under Fujitsu's leadership, was under way. The task of building a large transistor computer was given to Fujitsu. The large computer was to be tied to smaller satellite computers similar to the IBM 1401, to be developed by Nippon Electric and Oki.[33] The MITI financial contribution was small—$1.16 million during the years 1962–66.[34]

But the project was important to Fujitsu, the only important Japanese computer maker not to establish technological ties to a foreign company. Perhaps because of this, MITI gave Fujitsu the leadership of the FONTAC project. The computer produced by Fujitsu for this project in 1964, the FACOM 250, became the commercial FACOM 230-50, the first large model in Fujitsu's 230 family of compatible computers. The computer architecture developed on the FONTAC project, which formed the basis for the 230 series, served as Fujitsu's main product line into the late 1970s.[35] More important, the Electronic Computer Research Association was apparently the first cooperative research program established among competing Japanese computer firms.[36]

Subsequently, joint research projects became an important element in MITI's support for the Japanese computer industry. These projects often meant partial support from MITI, with the balance of funding supplied by the firms involved. The joint nature of the research, with participating firms sharing in the results, attracted firms, as did the matching government funding. The programs greatly leveraged the return to research expenditure by any single firm.

32. Kimura, "Birth and Development of Computers," p. 8.
33. Kaplan, *Japan, the Government-Business Relationship,* pp. 88–89; Kimura, "Birth and Development of Computers," p. 104; interview with Katsuya Hakozaki, Tokyo, April 1984.
34. This figure is given in Japan Electronic Computer Corporation (JECC), *EDP in Japan* (Tokyo: JECC, 1975), p. 9.
35. Yamamoto and Inoue, "History of the Development of FACOM," p. 4, chart 2, p. 6; and Shoichi Ninomiya, "Development of Technology—Survey of Technology Development in Circuits," in *Collection of Ikeda Memorial Articles,* chart 9, p. 19 (in Japanese).
36. See Kimura, "Birth and Development of Computers," p. 8.

MITI's Electrotechnical lab continued work on computer architecture during this period and apparently did not participate directly in the FONTAC project. Its efforts in the early 1960s focused on the ETL Mark VI computer, a large-scale machine inspired by the supercomputer projects under way in America and Europe in the late 1950s—the IBM Stretch, the UNIVAC LARC, and the Manchester University Atlas.[37] The Mark VI was completed in 1965 and incorporated most of the advanced hardware concepts of the time—two central processors linked together; a hierarchy of memory technologies that included magnetic cores, very high-speed magnetic thin film, tunnel diodes, and a large magnetic drum; and many circuit elements—50,000 transistors and 250,000 diodes.[38] This experimental machine was ETL's last wholly internal, serious venture into experimenting with computer architectures. Every firm in the Japanese industry had by this time already selected a proprietary architecture, and industry's needs had changed. ETL next shifted attention to guiding and directing collaborative projects with the big computer manufacturers and focused its internal efforts on components and leading-edge software.[39]

The catalyst for transforming the FONTAC experiment into a blueprint for technology development was IBM's announcement of the System 360 in 1964. The System 360 used hybrid integrated circuits. In fact these circuits were less advanced than the monolithic ICs that were becoming more widely available in the United States. Nonetheless, the 360 highlighted weaknesses in Japanese technology. (Japan's Nippon Electric Company did not build the first experimental Japanese IC until 1962.)

When IC development on a broader front first began among Japanese firms in 1964, digital computer applications were selected to lead the effort. In that year MITI awarded $80,000 in research money to the six Japanese companies then producing computers, to fund the development of specialized integrated circuits for computers. By late 1965, the three largest producers, Nippon Electric, Hitachi, and Fujitsu, had announced models containing some ICs, although Nippon Electric did not deliver its machine until 1966 and Fujitsu and Hitachi did not deliver until 1968.[40]

37. Ishii, "Research and Development on Information Processing Technology," pp. 21–22.
38. Ibid., pp. 21–24.
39. Ibid., pp. 5–6.
40. See Yasuo Tarui, "Japan Seeks Its Own Route to Improved IC Techniques,"

IBM's introduction of a comprehensive new line of compatible computers further highlighted Japan's technological vulnerability. In Fujitsu (the only technologically independent Japanese computer producer), existing models under development were hurriedly reorganized into the 230 "family" of machines with varying degrees of software compatibility.

But dependence on foreign technology constrained the response of the other Japanese computer firms. Not until RCA, General Electric, and Honeywell later announced their new lines of compatible computers were their Japanese licensees able to follow suit with machines adopting the architectures developed by their American collaborators. It had now become clear that despite an aggressive program to develop computers in Japan, reliance on technology licensed from abroad had not narrowed the technology gap, and in fact, the gap might even have been widening. The Japanese trade ministry responded by commissioning a new study of industry strategy.

The final report, released by MITI in 1966, set out a new framework for the industry.[41] It identified the computer industry, for the first time, as the single most important element in the future economic growth of Japan and set three objectives for government policy: an indigenous computer technology base, an increased share of the domestic market for Japanese computers, and greater profitability for Japanese computer makers. The latter two goals were addressed by maintaining the formal and informal trade barriers around the Japanese market and by having the national leasing company, the Japan Electronic Computer Corporation, fix prices for computer equipment and limit price competition.[42]

Electronics, December 13, 1965, pp. 90–93. Although the MITI grants were supposed to cover half of the research costs of the companies involved, Tarui notes that rarely were more than one-third of the costs covered by the funds. The completed research was to be made available to all participating companies.

See Japan Electronic Computer Corporation (JECC), *Konputa Noto* (Computer notes) (Tokyo: JECC, 1983), pp. 539–41, for the delivery dates for these machines. The first Japanese computer containing ICs seems to have been NEC's 2200 series model 500. During the 1960s, Nippon Electric was the technological leader in the commercial Japanese semiconductor industry.

41. For an extensive discussion of this report, see Kaplan, *Japan, the Government-Business Relationship,* pp. 91–92.

42. Until the early 1970s, restrictive quotas and tariffs continued to limit foreign imports, while restrictions on direct investment sealed off other means of entering the Japanese market. In 1972, some quotas on peripheral equipment were eliminated. In the mid-1970s, further liberalization of the terms of entry for imports and foreign

The first objective stimulated the development of a national R&D program to build on the successful FONTAC experience of the early 1960s. The first national computer project was the five-year "Very High Speed Computer System" (VHSCS) program, begun in 1966, which brought together the five chief manufacturers and ETL. This project teamed Fujitsu, Hitachi, and Nippon Electric in building the hardware for a large time-sharing computer aimed at the IBM System 360 Model 67, which had been announced in 1965. Toshiba and Oki were united in building peripheral equipment for the system. In practice, true cooperation among these business rivals proved difficult to create. The three main contractors for the central processor were also teamed in an unsuccessful joint venture, Nippon Software, to develop an operating system and applications for the machine.

But by the time this project had ended in 1972, important results—especially in ICs for use in computers—had been achieved. Hitachi, which, along with its U.S. partner RCA, had switched to an IBM-like design similar to that pursued in the project, brought out its large-scale 8700-8800 computer systems in 1973, based on the machine produced by this effort. Although Hitachi made the greatest use of the VHSCS technology, the other major manufacturers also benefited. Nippon Electric used the component technology developed for the project in its own line of high-performance Honeywell-compatible machines. Fujitsu's first use of high-performance logic circuitry in its product line came after similar work had been pursued on this project.[43] Other important

---

investment was gradually phased in, though computers remained one of the last protected bastions of Japanese industry through the long period of liberalization. See, for example, U.S. Department of Commerce, *Global Market Survey—Computers and Related Equipment,* (GPO, 1973), pp. 72–73; Ira L. Magaziner and Thomas M. Hout, *Japanese Industrial Policy* (London: Policy Studies Institute, 1980), pp. 86–87; and Leslie Donald Helm, "The Japanese Computer Industry: A Case Study in Industrial Policy" (M.A. thesis, University of California, Berkeley, 1978), p. 102. There have also been more recent reports of MITI's using its powers to control computer prices. See Julian Gresser, "Japan's Industrial Policy and the Development of the Japanese Computer and Telecommunications Industry," in Subcommittee on Trade of the House Committee on Ways and Means, *High Technology and Japanese Industrial Policy: A Strategy for U.S. Policymakers,* 96 Cong. 2 sess. (GPO, 1980), p. 26.

43. See Ninomiya, *Development of Technology,* p. 19. I am referring to ECL (emitter-coupled logic), a high-speed circuit design usually used in high-performance computers. The variant developed in Japan as part of this effort was called CML (current-mode logic). Work on Fujitsu's first ECL machine, its model 230/75, began in 1970, near the end of the VHSCS program. Though a report of the National Research Council, Computer Technology Resources Panel of the Computer Science and Engi-

advances in electronic components, including Japan's first semiconductor memories, developed on this project, added substantially to the national technology base.[44]

The ETL focused internal efforts on the development of an experimental time-sharing system modeled after similar developments in the United States. The resulting system, ETSS (for Experimental Time-Sharing System) was the first serious version of such a system in Japan, and it influenced the commercial time-sharing system developed by Hitachi.[45]

Even before this first national computer R&D project ended, MITI and the Japanese computer manufacturers had begun work on a second program. The second project, known as PIPS (Pattern Information Processing System), focused on themes related to artificial intelligence (AI)—character recognition, image and speech recognition and understanding, and special hardware to support these functions.[46] Clearly, the broad research effort in artificial intelligence that had already been under way in the United States for ten years inspired the program. Other elements (a one-chip, sixteen-bit microprocessor, a special purpose parallel image processor, and a data base machine) seem to have been reactions to ongoing developments in U.S. computer technology.

The PIPS program extended over twice the time period and more than doubled the budget of the earlier VHSCS program. It brought together ETL and nine Japanese manufacturers—NEC, Hitachi, Fujitsu, Matsushita, Mitsubishi, Oki, Toshiba, Sanyo, and Hoya Glass. Although previous projects had been most useful to Fujitsu (FONTAC), and then

neering Board, "The Computer Industry in Japan and Its Meaning for the United States" (Washington D.C., National Research Council, 1973), p. 7, asserts that the 230/75 drew heavily on VHSCS technology, this was apparently not true. Fujitsu did purchase NMOS storage devices from Nippon Electric for use in the DIPS-1 computers it built for NTT, and Nippon Electric's NMOS chips used VHSCS technology. Personal communication from Shigeru Takahashi, December 1985.

44. Besides ECL, the chief component technologies developed for this project included large-scale integrated circuits, a high-speed semiconductor cache memory, and wire memories. All but the last item became part of the standard vocabulary of high-performance computer designs.

45. Interviews with Kazuhiro Fuchi and Akio Tojo, Tokyo, April 1984.

46. The rather vague term "artificial intelligence" is used here to refer to the use of computers to perform speech and image processing and understanding, expert systems, and other research on computer-assisted inference and decisionmaking applied to computerized knowledge bases. See Electrotechnical Laboratory, "Pattern Information Processing System: National Research and Development Program" (Tokyo, Electrotechnical Laboratory, 1978), pp. 1–5.

Hitachi (on VHSCS, teamed with Fujitsu by MITI at the time), PIPS apparently had the most immediate impact on Toshiba and NEC (also teamed at the time). The computer architecture supported by NEC and Toshiba, based on an operating system developed by GE and taken over by Honeywell when GE sold its computer business, was chosen for the project.[47] Probably the most important commercial fallout from the project was the development of the first Chinese-character (Kanji) word processing program for the Japanese language, created in Toshiba by a team participating in the PIPS program.[48] Other important spin-offs included a speech recognition system developed and sold by Nippon Electric, an image processor (Tospix) and Kanji optical character reader made by Toshiba, and a parallel image processor marketed by Hitachi.[49]

Although the initial objective of PIPS included a prototype "fourth generation" computer system, such a large-scale integrated system was apparently never completed.[50] In contrast to the earlier projects, PIPS was targeted on more theoretical and basic research themes, rather than on the development of commercial systems. This project invested in developing the state-of-the-art computer expertise needed to begin more advanced work. The so-called Fifth Generation Program and the flurry of other computer-related research projects announced by Japan in the late 1970s and early 1980s sit firmly on a knowledge base built up during the decade-long PIPS program.

MITI's activism in the 1960s was not confined to the national technology projects. It had also pushed through a proposal to form a cartel for the production of punched card, paper tape, line printer, and magnetic drum peripheral equipment in 1969 and 1970. Though the cartel did exist for a while, it had little impact on the industry in the long term. In 1967,

47. ETL reportedly wanted to use Digital Equipment Corporation (DEC) equipment for the project—a natural choice, since DEC hardware was widely used in artificial intelligence (AI) research in the United States, and the large stock of available software would have provided a ready starting point for more advanced work. Instead, a system manufactured in Japan was chosen. Given this constraint, the NEC/Toshiba architecture was the logical choice, since a General Electric system had been the vehicle for Project MAC time-sharing and AI-related research in the United States.

48. Personal communication from Akio Tojo, November 1985. See also Rodney Clark, *Aspects of Japanese Commercial Innovation* (London: Technical Change Centre, 1984), pp. 71–73.

49. Lindamood, "Rise of the Japanese Computer Industry," p. 64; and communication from Akio Tojo.

50. See Japan Electronic Computer Corporation, *EDP in Japan*, p. 9; National Research Council, "Computer Industry in Japan," pp. 81, 91–92; and Electrotechnical Laboratory, "Pattern Information Processing System," pp. 4–5.

with MITI support, the Japan Information Processing Development Center had been founded to train computer personnel, and in 1970 the Information Technology Promotion Agency was established to promote software research. MITI's mandate to supervise the development of the computer industry, set into law in 1957, and confirmed by its report of 1966, was established anew by laws passed in 1971, and again, in 1978.[51]

Turmoil in the 1970s

Large research projects with a more explicitly commercial, short-term objective were also undertaken with MITI's assistance in the 1970s. The announcement by IBM of the System 370 in 1970 initially stimulated these efforts. Shock waves were also sent through the U.S. computer industry. In short order, RCA and General Electric left the computer business, and their Japanese licensees, Hitachi and Toshiba, were left with serious problems. Hitachi, along with RCA, had been working on systems intended to be highly compatible with the IBM architecture, and the Japanese company was left high and dry when RCA sold its computer operations to Sperry Rand. Toshiba was in somewhat better shape, since Honeywell had made a decision to shift to the General Electric architecture after purchasing General Electric's business. Consequently, Toshiba sought a marriage with Honeywell. Unfortunately, Honeywell was already linked to Nippon Electric.

Honeywell's decision to shift to the General Electric operating systems created serious problems for Nippon Electric, which had been working jointly with Honeywell in developing a new architecture and now found itself with an orphaned technology base.[52] Mitsubishi's former source for computer technology, TRW, had sold its computer business in the late 1960s, and Mitsubishi was scrambling to conclude a new arrangement with Xerox Data Systems. Thus two of the big three Japanese computer makers—Hitachi and Nippon Electric—were cast adrift by the upheavals in the U.S. computer industry, and the smaller manufacturers were in similar or even worse straits. The third principal

51. Kaplan, *Japan, the Government-Business Relationship,* pp. 93–96. Lindamood, "Rise of the Japanese Computer Industry," pp. 62–63.

52. This loss caused NEC to lose confidence in its relationship with Honeywell, and NEC began to go in its own directions after that decision. Extensions and improvements to the basic General Electric architecture devised by NEC for its ACOS operating system were later adopted in part by Honeywell. By the late 1970s, a considerable flow from NEC to Honeywell characterized technological relations between the two firms.

force, an independent Fujitsu, was equally threatened by the new wave of commercial technology, emphasizing time-sharing and virtual memory, that had crested in the United States.

The confusion created by the convulsions in the U.S. computer industry was compounded by the imminent liberalization of the Japanese market. Under American pressure, the Japanese government had agreed to abolish most import quotas by the mid-1970s, precisely when domestic computer producers were faced with a new technological challenge from abroad. The simultaneity of disruptions to the flow of foreign technology and the shift to a more open market posed a difficult problem for the domestic industry.

MITI's response took two complementary paths. One, it poured new funds into research and development. Rather than favoring longer-term, more basic areas, as the PIPS program did, MITI concentrated on an immediate commercial response to the IBM System 370. Second, MITI rationalized the industry—three major firms and three smaller producers were dividing half of a market a fraction of the size of the U.S. market, with each firm attempting to produce a complete and competitive range of models. To make these firms more competitive in an open market, and to reap at least some of the economies of scale inherent in the use of research and development effort, MITI tried to get the six largest Japanese computer producers to form three development and production ventures from their fragmented computer divisions.

In 1971, at MITI insistence, Fujitsu and Hitachi agreed to develop jointly a line of IBM-compatible equipment. Nippon Electric and Toshiba agreed to work on models using an improved operating system based on the GE-Honeywell architecture, and Oki and Mitsubishi were to develop yet another line of data processing equipment. Within each of those product lines, cooperating firms were to specialize in particular models and applications complementary to those of their partner. This cartelization of the industry was to be supported by a substantial joint research effort, to which MITI would contribute generous funding. The program, explicitly targeting the development of commercial products during the 1972–76 period, was known as the "3.5 generation" program.[53] Ironi-

---

53. The "3.5" terminology derives from the view that IBM's System 370 was only a marginal half-generation advance over its so-called third-generation 360 system. The Japanese effort was intended as a marginal advance over the 3.5 generation System 370, and for that reason is sometimes called the 3.75 generation program. See Japan Electronic Computer Corporation, *EDP in Japan*, p. 9; and Lindamood, "Rise of the Japanese Computer Industry," p. 65.

cally, the program succeeded in meeting many of its objectives, but in ways different from those originally intended by the MITI planners.

Research and development investments in computer technology within Japanese equipment manufacturers doubled during the 1971–76 period.[54] Firms leaped into the MITI-sponsored effort. Internal company R&D was sacrificed in favor of funding of the joint research associations. In 1972 and 1974 internal R&D declined substantially in absolute terms as the cooperative effort expanded dramatically. When spending within the research associations is added to the companies' internal efforts, computer R&D tripled over the same five-year period.

When the dust cleared, only three Japanese computer firms remained in the mainframe computer business—the strongest and most committed producers,—Fujitsu, Hitachi, and Nippon Electric. Mitsubishi and Oki did produce a line of computers, the COSMOS series, under the auspices of the 3.5 effort, but eventually they withdrew from the manufacture of large computers, although both companies continue to make smaller systems and peripherals. Mitsubishi, a large and financially strong conglomerate, suffered a further blow when Xerox Data Systems, its second choice of a significant foreign partner, also withdrew from the business in the mid-1970s. The Toshiba-NEC team produced a line of computers using the ACOS operating system, based on the old General Electric system, but Toshiba too chose to drop out of large systems after the end of the project.[55]

Nippon Electric continued to develop a new operating system and architecture. After the mid-1970s, it began carving out a specialized niche in computer markets, emphasizing the integration of communications applications with specialized computers. This "communications and computers" strategy proved reasonably effective, and by the early 1980s, NEC trailed only Fujitsu and IBM in Japanese sales.[56] Honeywell, originally the source for NEC's technology, had gradually become heavily dependent on technology and hardware supplied by NEC.[57]

Fujitsu and Hitachi chose to try to build equipment compatible with the IBM 360-370 standard. Securing the technology was not a simple

54. Flamm, *Targeting*, p. 249, table D-1.

55. See Charles L. Cohen, "NEC's CPU Leapfrogs IBM," *Electronics Week*, vol. 58 (March 11, 1985), p. 17.

56. In 1981 Fujitsu had Japanese sales of 456 million yen, IBM, 429 million yen, NEC, 333 million yen, and Hitachi, 288 million yen. If NEC's small personal computers had been excluded, it would have trailed slightly behind Hitachi. See *Fujitsu and the Computer Industry in Japan* (Tokyo: Fujitsu Limited, 1983), p. 11.

57. Cohen, "NEC's CPU Leapfrogs IBM," p. 17.

task, and a fortuitous event greatly helped. In late 1970, Gene M. Amdahl, one of IBM's top designers, left IBM to start his own venture and build a high-end, large-scale computer compatible with the System 360-370 architecture. Amdahl wanted to build a large central processor and buy attachments for this processor from the large, plug-compatible industry that had developed in the United States to supply IBM customers with IBM-style peripherals at a lower price or with higher capacity or performance.[58] Amdahl ran into financial difficulties, and determined to get funding, he turned to the Japanese computer producers.

He struck a deal with Fujitsu. In 1972, for the purchase of 24 percent of Amdahl's equity, Fujitsu was given the right to exchange technical information with Amdahl. In 1974 the Japanese company announced that it would manufacture computers in Japan for Amdahl to sell in the U.S. market.[59] This was a turning point for the Japanese computer industry. At last it would acquire the ability to produce computers competitive with the latest IBM models.[60]

Now Fujitsu and Hitachi could together produce an "M-series" of IBM-compatible computers, with Fujitsu producing the largest and smallest models, and Hitachi making two intermediate-sized machines. The first machines in this series were announced jointly in 1974, but cooperation between the two companies did not last long. By 1975 both companies had developed new models competitive with those that were supposed to be the exclusive province of the other.[61] The one more lasting area of cooperation was in a joint venture to develop and market IBM-compatible peripherals and terminals (this, too, finally dissolved in 1986). Both companies continued to compete in producing IBM-compatible computers, with Fujitsu relying on information about new IBM developments gleaned through its Amdahl connection, and Hitachi relying on public information, and other less open methods to stay abreast of IBM's changing product line.[62]

58. Gene M. Amdahl, "The Early Chapters of the PCM Story," *Datamation*, vol. 25 (February 1979), pp. 113–14.

59. Lindamood, "Rise of the Japanese Computer Industry," p. 57.

60. In a candid interview in which he described how Fujitsu was able to respond so quickly to new products introduced by IBM, Fujitsu's chairman Taiyu Kobayashi was quoted as saying, "If you want me to come right out and say it, our method is the Amdahl company. Highly reliable information is funneled to us through Amdahl." See Soichiro Tahara, "IBM Is a Tiger Turned Loose in a Field," *Bungei Shunju*, vol. 60 (September 1982), pp. 94–105 (translated from the Japanese).

61. Gresser, *Partners in Prosperity*, p. 125.

62. See Tahara, "IBM Is a Tiger"; John D. Halamka, *Espionage in the Silicon Valley* (Berkeley, Calif.: Sybex, 1984), pp. 124–47.

Thus the technical links to the United States made possible the new Fujitsu and Hitachi strategy of building IBM-compatible computers. Survival in that market requires superior price performance, and equally important, rapid response to any changes in the IBM product or pricing strategies.[63] Amdahl gave Fujitsu much more than the secrets of the IBM architecture—Gene Amdahl's game plan had been to aggressively incorporate leading-edge technology into his products to give them superior price performance, and Amdahl technical innovations also influenced Fujitsu. The crucial "top-hat" packaging technology needed to cool the high-density circuitry used in its modern, large-scale main-frames was taken directly from Amdahl by Fujitsu.[64]

Superior performance requires a technological edge, which then meant advanced semiconductor technology. From 1976 to 1979 MITI sponsored another large research project to bring Japanese producers to a state-of-the-art technology in semiconductors. By all accounts, this government project succeeded in providing its participants, Fujitsu, Hitachi, Mitsubishi, Nippon Electric, and Toshiba, with the important basic production technology required for very large-scale integrated circuit (VLSI) chips. The VLSI program, including work on ultrafine lithography and electron beam etching, brought its participants to the frontiers of advanced semiconductor technology, making Japanese computer producers formidable competitors in the market for IBM-compatible computers.[65]

63. See also the 1982 interview with Fujitsu chairman Kobayashi for more details about Fujitsu's tie-up with Amdahl in "IBM Is a Tiger," pp. 94–105.

64. This is a distinctive "top-hat" cooling system developed by Amdahl, which uses a circular metal tower with a stack of plate-like fins to radiate heat from an IC, to which it is attached, into a circulating air flow. This system is not commonly found (outside of Amdahl) in the U.S. industry. The system seems to have been used in ICs developed for the PIPS program as well. See Electrotechnical Laboratory, "Pattern Information Processing System," p. 28. Fujitsu continues to use this system to cool ICs in its high-performance computer products. It was observed by the author in 1984, for example, on the chips found in Fujitsu's VP series supercomputers. Comparable circuitry found in American high-performance computers generally uses fluids pumped through the circuit packaging to remove built-up heat. See also Alan Cane, "State of the Art at ICL," *Financial Times,* April 25, 1985, p. 40.

65. About 1,000 patents are estimated to have been produced by the project. See U.S. General Accounting Office, *Industrial Policy: Case Studies in the Japanese Experience* (GPO, 1982), pp. 7–8. For a view of the program by a Japanese insider that stresses the major technical achievements of the program—in one micron device technology, submicron process technology, and 64K dynamic memory devices—see Yoshio Nishi, "VLSI Technology Perspective," presentation to the China Electronics

NTT and Computers

Though MITI and its technical arm, ETL, have been the most visible actors in shaping public policy toward computers in Japan, and certainly guided the development of key technologies, they have not been the only significant force. National Telephone and Telegraph (NTT) had taken the first steps toward a VLSI project in early 1975, when it organized a VLSI group composed of Hitachi, Fujitsu, and Nippon Electric.[66] The focus of NTT's project was semiconductors oriented toward telecommunications applications. Only after considerable effort on MITI's part did NTT agree to join part of its project to the program organized by MITI and directed by ETL.

In the late 1950s, before the computer industry had become an explicit national priority, and MITI had begun its large-scale programs to develop the industry, NTT had been at least as visible as MITI. The parametron technology developed in its labs had been used in the first machines produced by Nippon Electric and Hitachi. The experimental M-1 parametron computer produced by NTT's Musashino lab, for example, became the prototype for the Fujitsu 201 computer.

Rather than focusing on a vision of the broad needs of Japanese industry, however, NTT has pursued its own agenda, and telecommunications applications have always topped those priorities for the roughly 2 percent of revenues expended on R&D. In this respect it has resembled AT&T's Bell labs; unlike AT&T, however, NTT has no internal capability to produce equipment for its own use and has instead depended on outside suppliers. Traditionally, the main suppliers of equipment to NTT have been Nippon Electric, Fujitsu, Oki, and Hitachi, often referred to as the NTT "family." In 1977, 70 percent of NTT's purchases of communications equipment went to this family of suppliers. For the same firms, NTT's business accounted for about 20 percent to 30 percent of sales.[67] Thus NTT has transferred much of the fruit of its internal research efforts, as well as that conducted jointly with its outside

---

Seminar, World Bank, Washington, D.C., October 22, 1987. The capture of a big chunk of the U.S. semiconductor market (particularly in dynamic random access memory chips for computer applications) by Japanese semiconductor producers occurred during and after the final phases of the VLSI project.

66. See Gresser, *Partners in Prosperity,* pp. 126–27.

67. Gresser, "High Technology and Japanese Industrial Policy," p. 3; and *The Economist,* "Japan's Telecommunications Slogan Is Still: Japan First," May 17, 1980, p, 63.

associates, to this family of suppliers that, coincidentally, includes the principal forces in the Japanese computer industry.

In the early 1960s, as MITI's gaze turned to computers as the foundation for a transformation of Japanese industry, NTT was focusing on building computers for internal use. Its experience in building the experimental M-1 parametron computer led to the production model CM-1, and in 1963, the transistorized CM-100, which were used internally for billing and other applications.[68] In the mid-1960s, NTT became interested in data communications networks and time-sharing and began research on systems that evolved into its current Digital Data Exchange Network.

Several years after this work began, NTT started a program oriented toward producing computer hardware able to support the telecommunications networks and time-sharing applications it hoped to develop. Research on the so-called NTT (or Dendenkosha) Information Processing System (DIPS) was started in 1968.[69] There were strong links between DIPS and MITI's VHSCS project—the design of hardware and software for both systems was quite similar, and the first DIPS computer borrowed high-performance logic technology developed for the MITI machine. The memory IC developed for the VHSCS computer was also used in NTT's DIPS machine.[70] The three NTT contractors participating in DIPS—Nippon Electric, Fujitsu, and Hitachi—were also three of the five participants in the big MITI computer project.

After a DIPS-0 prototype was completed in 1971, each of the three companies built production models of these large, multiple-processor machines, intended for time-sharing applications. Using this technology, NTT inaugurated the first Japanese time-sharing service offered over the public telephone network in 1972.[71]

The DIPS-I computers were followed with a research and development program for a successor, the DIPS-II series, introduced in the late

68. See Muraoka, "History and Future Trends of Computer Architecture," pp. 1–2.

69. Gresser, "High Technology and Japanese Industrial Policy," p. 10.

70. See National Research Council, "Computer Industry in Japan," pp. 91–92; Lindamood, "Rise of the Japanese Computer Industry," p. 69; *Background Readings on Science, Technology, and Energy R&D in Japan and China,* Committee Print, Committee on Science and Technology, 97 Cong. 1 sess. (GPO, 1981), p. 34; and Ishii, "Research and Development on Information Processing Technology," p. 325.

71. National Research Council, "Computer Industry in Japan," pp. 7, 57–58, 82; Lindamood, "Rise of the Japanese Computer Industry," p. 69; and see Department of Commerce, *Global Market Survey—Computer Equipment,* p. 70.

1970s, and by the appearance of the DIPS-II computer architecture on VLSI chips in the early 1980s. The same three core Japanese computer companies—Fujitsu, Nippon Electric, and Hitachi—also produced models in the DIPS-II series.[72]

The DIPS series has been important in the very large-scale, high end of Japanese computer makers' product lines. At Fujitsu, for example, about 157 large-scale computer systems had been ordered before the development of the large machines in its current IBM-compatible M-Series line. Of these 157 earlier large-scale machines, about 56 were DIPS computers built for NTT.[73] The largest M-Series machine manufactured by Fujitsu in the early 1980s, the M-382, is reportedly almost identical in design to the DIPS-II Model 45 built for NTT earlier. And Fujitsu's most advanced current "Hawk" line of mainframe computers uses logic, memory, and architecture developed with NTT, including a new water-cooled packaging technology.[74]

But NTT's role has been preeminent in developing semiconductor technology. NTT's laboratories are considered by some analysts the most important resource in Japanese semiconductor R&D.[75] The absence of an internal production arm has meant that the continuous flow of new technology from NTT's labs is rapidly transferred to industry through the supplier-customer relation the large Japanese computer producers have traditionally enjoyed with NTT.[76] NTT has also been a

72. See Muraoka, "History and Future Trends of Computer Architecture," pp. 1–2; and National Academy of Sciences, *International Developments in Computer Science* (Washington, D.C.: National Academy Press, 1982), p. 5.

73. Fujitsu Limited, *Fujitsu and the Computer Industry in Japan*, p. 7.

74. By 1983 Fujitsu had also built the first versions of its VP series supercomputers, which married IBM software compatibility to Cray-like number-crunching potential. The relation between the M-382 and the DIPS 11/45 is noted in Gresser, *Partners in Prosperity*, p. 122, Cohen, "NEC's CPU Leapfrogs IBM," p. 17, and Lindamood, "Rise of the Japanese Computer Industry," p. 69. Other pieces of DIPS technology have shown up in NEC's newest high-performance mainframes, introduced in 1985; see Cohen, "NEC's CPU Leapfrogs IBM," p. 17; and see *Datamation*, vol. 31 (October 1, 1985), p. 9.

75. This is the conclusion of the Office of Technology Assessment. See Office of Technology Assessment, *International Competitiveness in Electronics* (GPO, 1983), p. 197.

76. Commercial products that have emerged from joint research by companies and Nippon Telephone and Telegraph include 16K, 64K, and 256K memory chips, fiber-optic cable technology, and data transmission systems. United States International Trade Commission, *Foreign Industrial Targeting* p. 153. Despite being cut out of the MITI VLSI project, Oki Electric managed to market a 64K RAM chip because of its

big customer for, and influence on, the development of very large-scale computers oriented toward time-sharing applications through the DIPS program. Because of a history of monopoly control over the national telecommunications grid, however, some within the Japanese industry argue that NTT has stunted the growth of telecommunications-based applications and computer network research in Japan.[77] In Japan network technology is by most accounts a glaring weak point on the current computer scene.

Although NTT has been less visible to the public than MITI, its support for Japanese technology is no less important. NTT spending on R&D has greatly exceeded the public support for computer R&D administered by MITI.[78]

Summary

In the mid-1960s Japan emerged as a potentially important force in the international computer industry, largely on the strength of hardware developed by using technology licensed from abroad. By the mid-1970s the technical capacity of Japanese computer manufacturers roughly equaled that of the American firms from which their technology had originally been licensed. However, by that time, the Japanese computer industry consisted of three chief players. Two—Fujitsu and Hitachi—opted to build IBM-compatible equipment, with its great risks and potential rewards, as their business strategy. The third, Nippon Electric, turned to communications (an application in which IBM has historically been its weakest in technology) and built up markets with specialized processors aimed at particular applications. Thus the two main strategies pursued in the U.S. industry over the years have been the same ones to emerge in the Japanese computer industry after liberalization exposed the national market to international competition.

links to NTT. Office of Technology Assessment, *International Competitiveness in Electronics,* p. 481. An early Nippon Electric 32-bit microprocessor grew from joint research that it had conducted with NTT. Gresser, *Partners in Prosperity,* p. 138. The NTT Data Communications Network Architecture was developed by NTT jointly with Hitachi and Oki. National Academy of Sciences, *International Developments in Computer Science,* p. 5.

77. NTT had excluded private suppliers (both Japanese and American) from selling time-sharing services over the public telephone net. See National Research Council, "Computer Industry in Japan," pp. 63–64, 83.

78. Flamm, *Targeting,* p. 139.

Figure 6-2. *Relative Shares of the Top Computer Companies in the Japanese Market, 1986*

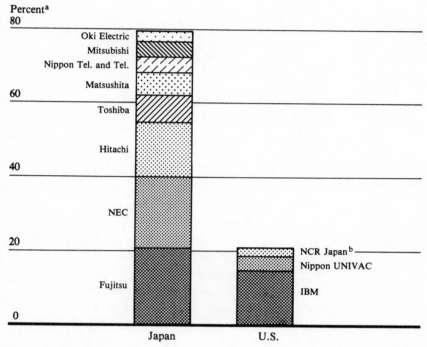

Percent[a]

Sources: Robert Poe, "Living with the High Yen," *Datamation*, vol. 33 (September 1, 1987), pp. 92–96; and author's calculations.

a. Percentage of data processing sales (hardware, software, and services) in the Japanese market by the eleven largest vendors. The top eleven accounted for $26.4 billion of a total Japanese data processing market estimated at $30.4 billion.

b. Estimate.

Today, the Japanese computer industry is second only to that of the United States. In the Japanese market, national producers account for 80 percent of sales (figure 6-2). The contrast with Europe is striking. But like European producers, Japanese companies have yet to transfrom themselves fully into world-scale businesses. The domestic market generally accounts for 80 percent of sales (table 6-3). Japanese firms, though progressing rapidly, follow a trail blazed by American counterparts.

Historically, the great diversity in attitudes toward competition by computer industries in the industrialized countries is striking. At one extreme, France and Britain sought consistently the maximum benefit

Table 6-3. *Top Japanese Computer Producers, 1986*

Producer	Worldwide data processing revenues[a] (millions of dollars)	Share in Japanese market (percent)
Fujitsu	6,576	83
NEC	6,325	81
Hitachi	4,729	81
Toshiba	2,605	76
Matsushita	1,944	84
Nippon Tel. and Tel.	1,161	100
Mitsubishi	1,345	82
Oki Electric	880	76

Sources: Robert Poe, "Living with the High Yen," *Datamation*, vol. 33 (September 1, 1987), pp. 94–95.
a. Hardware, software, and services.
b. Estimate.

from economies of scale and tried aggressively to restructure their industries into a single national firm. At the other extreme, despite the dominance by IBM of the industry since the mid-1950s, U.S. policies have often backed small new companies producing innovative, state-of-the-art machines outside of the commercial mainstream.

Japan has compromised, rationalizing more basic, precompetitive research through support of joint projects, yet preserving downstream competition in applications by highly competitive firms. Germany also lies somewhere in the middle. It started by emulating the Anglo-French model of favoring a particular company—the national champion—then reevaluated and adopted a more diversified program of support. To the extent that one can ascribe success to these different organizational models, history shows that a more diversified approach to support for technology development has worked best.

CHAPTER SEVEN

How Computer Firms Compete

CONVENTIONAL economic descriptions of competitive markets are inadequate for analyzing a high-technology industry. The traditional, standard analysis of an industry composed of very many producers of a stable, homogeneous product falls wide of the mark in computers. In the computer industry competition is based on successful R&D investments that create a temporary technological monopoly. Indeed, the ever-changing product market in a high-technology industry is largely a reflection of competitive struggles played out in the laboratories where new technology is developed.

Though the theoretical literature on the dynamics of competition in industries dependent on heavy research and development investment is growing, the first results of these explorations are inconclusive.[1] Contributions within the literature have often focused on one or another single element of the interaction among firms, with highly simplified assumptions made about all other aspects of economic competition. Even with

---

1. Two recent articles that contain extensive bibliographies of this literature are M. L. Katz and C. Shapiro, "R&D Rivalry with Licensing or Imitation," *American Economic Review*, vol. 77 (June 1987), pp. 402–20; and Partha Dasgupta and E. Maskin, "The Simple Economics of Research Portfolios," *Economic Journal*, vol. 97 (September 1987), pp. 581–95. Typically, the predictions of these models require assumptions about firms' behavior and entry, empirical parameters that reflect the distributions of outcomes of research projects, and the extent to which new knowledge can be captured for private use by its creator. Some important questions have no clear answer, including whether or not an incumbent "dominant" firm is likely to introduce a particular innovation, and whether competition encourages too much or too little, too similar or dissimilar, research effort relative to a social optimum. About the only conclusion on which virtually all models agree is that market mechanisms are unlikely to generate the socially optimal portfolio of research investments.

203

these heroic assumptions, the resulting theoretical models have been complex, and behavioral predictions vague.

In this chapter, instead of a theoretical analysis, I focus on an empirically plausible description of industrial competition in computers. I present an interpretation of how competition in computers has developed, grounding it in the industry's historical record.

In this view the principal focus for competition among computer producers has been entry into new markets, either for new products or in new types of applications. A process of technological differentiation, with new competitors defining new market niches, has been central to the way in which competition has evolved. In contrast, in established computer markets economic forces seem to have led to increasing dominance by a few firms.

Three driving forces have shaped the economics of competition in computers. First, innovation in computer technology has continued at an extraordinarily rapid pace. Second, significant economies of scale and scope exist in the use of technology, especially in the development of new products. The importance of these economies has been reinforced by the product design strategies of individual firms. Third, an innovating firm faces inherent difficulty in capturing the benefits of investment in innovation, an oft-noted problem intrinsic to research and development.

The Pace of Technological Progress

The exceedingly quick rate of technical advance in computers has always guided the development of the computer industry. An annual decline of perhaps 25 percent in the real costs of the hardware that supplies information processing capacity is almost a full order of magnitude greater than the steepest sustained price declines observed at the time of the Industrial Revolution.[2] Even if one looks only at modern industrial history, the speed at which computers have improved remains impressive. In telecommunications, another high-technology industry known for extraordinary cost declines, the cost of transmitting data over

2. See Kenneth Flamm, *Targeting the Computer: Government Support and International Competition* (Brookings, 1987), p. 9.

telephone lines dropped roughly two orders of magnitude over twenty years, about a full power of ten less than the improvement in computer price performance during the same period.[3]

Two major consequences emerge from this remarkable history. First, the potential demand for new and greatly improved hardware has always been highly uncertain, adding another layer of risk to the technological uncertainty already associated with an R&D project. Second, the unceasingly rapid declines in the costs of information processing have constantly pushed computers into new applications.

Since its start, the industry has persistently underestimated the demand for computing power. When the first mammoth computers were built, the belief prevailed that no commercial market existed for the services that such behemoths could provide. Howard Aiken, fighting for support for the Mark I at prewar Harvard, hotly contested the assertion that his machine would wind up as an unused museum piece. Yet even he argued against efforts by J. Presper Eckert and John W. Mauchly to build a stored-program computer after the war, claiming that existing machines had more than enough capacity to do any problem that the equipment might conceivably be called upon to solve.

Most established firms saw only a highly uncertain demand for the new technology. National Cash Register, despite the enormous advantage it would have had in pursuing the technologies developed on its premises by OP-20-G during the war, and an open invitation from the Navy to accept subsidies for further work in the area, committed what must be called one of the greatest errors in the history of high technology. It eschewed computer development and returned to its solid, profitable, and relatively low-risk business equipment sales. Even IBM, at the time certainly one of the most technologically progressive businesses in the United States, with an ongoing program of support for pro bono demonstration computing projects, did fairly little to investigate electronic computers until Eckert and Mauchly's struggle to build a business computer had borne some fruit. And IBM did not move decisively until the government had removed most risk and guaranteed a market.

Even after the early computers were developed, businesses continued

3. The line and termination costs for a 3,000-mile private line used to transmit digital data, during the period 1955–75, are used to arrive at this conclusion. See Montgomery Phister, Jr., *Data Processing Technology and Economics* (Digital Press and Santa Monica Publishing, 1979), pp. 547–48.

to underestimate the demand for the new machines.[4] Predicting demand when enormous cost declines have deposited a producer on a distant and entirely unfamiliar region of a demand curve is an uncertain proposition. The lesson, perhaps, is that with a sufficiently new and advanced concept, demand is created by a learning process. Users begin to understand how a radically new piece of technology can fit their needs only through experience with it. Certainly, this theme appears early and prevails throughout the history of information processing technology.

Furthermore, because much of the uncertainty connected with a radical technological advance involves gathering information about demand, firms have tended to go slowly in pursuing ambitious leaps forward. To test the waters, a product must be developed, usually at great cost, then marketed. Much of the information about demand then generated ends up in the public domain, available to any observer tracking the development of the new market. If the product is successful, other firms can follow with much less risk; if unsuccessful, the pioneer alone bears the cost. Thus much of the informational return from embarking on a radically new project cannot be captured by the pioneer. Given the large investments needed to develop a new machine, a tendency toward conservatism has often limited the risk to individual companies.[5]

The reluctance of big firms to gamble big sums on large and risky development projects prevailed outside of the United States as well. British firms hesitated to invest large sums in such research and generally moved into computers only when the British government supplied them with the resources and markets to do so. To this day Britain remains

4. For example, IBM sold roughly twice as many of the large System 360 processors as had been forecast. Bob O. Evans, "IBM System/360," *Computer Museum Report*, vol. 16 (Summer 1984), p. 17; and Bob O. Evans, "System/360: A Retrospective View," *Annals of the History of Computing*, vol. 8 (April 1986), pp. 17, 176. The forecast was made despite a history of chronic underestimation of the demand for the new IBM computers in the 1950s. See Cuthbert C. Hurd, "Computer Development at IBM," in N. Metropolis, J. Howlett, and Gian-Carlo Rota, eds., *A History of Computing in the Twentieth Century: A Collection of Essays* (Academic Press, 1980), pp. 408–09, 411–13.

5. Even for a large company, the development costs for a large project can raise the specter of insolvency and failure. IBM's big investment in the System 360 (well over 700 million dollars in development costs, probably close to a billion (1964) dollars, during a period in which annual profits ran in the range of 200 million dollars to 300 million dollars) was regarded by the organization as a critical "you bet your company" project. See Emerson W. Pugh, *Memories That Shaped an Industry: Decisions Leading to the IBM System/360* (MIT Press, 1984), pp. 205–07; 264.

dependent on university researchers—rather than corporate laboratories—for most of the innovation in its products. In France and Germany, the large firms did not produce their first computers until the late 1950s, and small start-up firms pushed them into doing so. In Japan, firms relied on the government to furnish most of the research for the machines they built in the 1950s and early 1960s, and it was not until the mid-1960s that significant corporate research labs were set up.

Throughout the history of computer development, dramatic cost reductions have spawned the substitution of information processing for more traditional inputs to production. With every decline in the cost of using computers, new applications for computers sprang up. Machines of all sizes became less expensive, cost-effective for the first time, and use of computers fanned out into new applications and industries. As prices continued to decline, and new applications grew into large markets, intense specialization in computer design began to occur.

Specialization dates back to the earliest days of computing. In the first computer projects researchers could choose simpler designs that used less complex componentry, or they could opt for more sophisticated designs that sought to achieve higher performance with much more complicated hardware and demanding engineering. A good example of this distinction was the difference between so-called serial designs, with central processors that handled one bit of data at a time, and parallel designs that had circuitry that allowed processors to deal with an entire "word" at once (consisting of many bits grouped into a larger parcel of data). The first computers to be produced were, for good reason, usually of the inherently simpler serial type of circuitry.[6] The more complex and expensive parallel machines arrived later, but they achieved much better computational performance (see table 2-1). The MIT Whirlwind, by far the most costly of the first parallel designs, engineered for the real-time speeds needed for command and control applications, represented an

6. The delay line memories used in the first computers were inherently serial and therefore lent themselves naturally to serial designs. However, even after computers generally switched to bit-parallel (by word) processor architectures, serial designs were sometimes used in lower-performance machines because of cost. A classic example is the first computer produced by Scientific Data Systems, which adapted a parallel design similar to a Packard-Bell (its engineers came from Packard-Bell) computer to use a bit-serial data path and transistorized logic. By incorporating new, higher-speed transistors, this machine achieved the performance levels of contemporary parallel designs at a fraction of their cost because of the reduced circuit complexity, component count, and assembly cost. Interview with Robert Spinrad, February 13, 1983, Palo Alto, California.

extreme case of how cost, complexity, and careful engineering could be traded off to achieve high performance.

Finally, the cost of circuitry came down to the point at which most general purpose computers used bit-parallel designs. The complexity and cost of a processor then became a question of how large the size of a "word" ought to be.

By the mid-1950s, two different markets had developed. Business machines traded smaller word sizes for lower costs and greater reliability (with less failure-prone components and interconnections). These machines had fast input-output devices to speed the flow of large volumes of characters from archives of business records. Scientific machines had large word sizes, high-performance processors, and specialized hardware for doing arithmetic quickly.

If there were no cost constraint, and performance were the only objective, one could design a machine with specialized hardware to perform any kind of task. In practice, machines tended to lie between these extremes, with hardware and design choices determining advantages in particular types of applications. Although one might assume that military customers would tend to require high-performance scientific machines, this was not always true. Cryptological applications, for example, had some features of business applications in that they needed to process large volumes of textual data. Military customers also bought many of the early "business" machines for logistics, supply, and recordkeeping applications.

The other key dimension in which computers began to diverge was in size and cost. The technology of remote computer use had not yet been developed, and to computerize, a user had to acquire a rather large and lumpy capital good. It soon became apparent that smaller business and scientific users could not justify large investments or rental rates, but could, in fact, profitably employ smaller, less powerful, and less costly equipment. Less than state-of-the-art memory speed and size permitted other cost-cutting economies. Firms sprang up to service this market, and machines such as the IBM 650, Bendix G-15, and Librascope LGP-30, discussed earlier, established a low-end business and scientific market. The minicomputers of the 1960s represented the next stage in the evolution of the low end of the computer market.

Continued cost declines made even greater specialization economic. By the early 1970s, computers optimized for such applications as industrial and laboratory control, communications, file control, time-sharing, and terminals had appeared, adding new complexity to the old dichotomy between business and science.[7]

Depending on constantly changing criteria for cost and size, computers are labeled supercomputers, mainframes, minicomputers, superminis, microcomputers, and in the early 1980s, "supermicros" and "minisupers" (also known as crayettes, which fell between a supercomputer and a supermini in size and performance). Mainframes and supercomputers were often grouped together as "general purpose" computers, though the increasing power of minis and micros in the late 1970s left even these fuzzy categories under assault by the force of technological advance.

Finally, the continuing pace of technological advance in computers effectively barred less technically progressive firms from entering the computer business. In the mid-1960s, economists and industrial analysts popularized the concept of the product-cycle.[8] It was argued that investment in R&D created a technological advantage initially, but that as the technology diffused (or the product matured), imitators entered the business, and manufacturing cost, rather than technological advantage, began to determine competitiveness.

The product cycle was thought to work as follows. In the initial stages, as a product is developed and refined, keeping production close to research laboratories and markets offers economic benefits. In the latter stages of the product cycle, manufacturing cost becomes the central fact of economic life. Production migrates to cheaper locations, often abroad, and even into foreign companies that made little or no R&D investment. Finally, a mature product with a widely understood technology is manufactured as a commodity in extremely competitive markets. Little or no technological rent is collected by the manufacturer.

If technology had moved at a slower pace, this cycle might well have held true in computers. Only a modest improvement in performance might not have prevented a foreign or domestic producer with lower manufacturing costs from introducing a cheaper version of an older product that competed effectively with the most advanced technology. But the cycle did not apply in computers. Very rapid technological

7. See C. Gordon Bell, J. Craig Mudge, and John E. McNamara, *Computer Engineering: A DEC View of Hardware Systems Design* (Digital Press, 1978), pp. 15–18.

8. See Raymond Vernon, "International Investment and International Trade in the Product Cycle," *Quarterly Journal of Economics*, col. 80 (May 1966), pp. 190–207.

advance effectively truncates the later stages of the product cycle. Very large improvements in price performance more than offset international differentials in the manufacturing costs. Rapid and sustained technological advance may foreclose competition based on marginal differences in manufacturing cost.[9]

Economies of Scale and Scope

The economies of scale inherent in the use of the results of research and development have shaped competition among computer producers. The cost of developing a new product is approximately independent of the volume in which that product is finally manufactured.[10] The unit cost of designing a product therefore declines with the number of units sold. All other things being equal, the firm with the largest share of the market will then have the lowest unit costs.

Because research and development is a big part of the cost of producing a product as research intensive as computers, economies of scale in the use of research tend to be a driving force in the economics of the industry. In recent years, research and development costs in computers have, in the aggregate, hovered at about 12 percent of sales by the U.S. industry.[11]

9. The exception that proves the rule is at the low end. Here, commodity-like, low-performance products that use off-the-shelf components and designs can be built with little or no R&D investment. Effectively, however, these products are not high-tech goods. They have always been the entry point for new producers, who are looking for an advantage based on manufacturing cost.

10. The costs of development are not totally independent of manufacturing volume, of course. For a high-volume product, making additional fixed investments in product design and manufacturing processes to lower the costs of mass production may be worthwhile. As a first approximation, however, it seems reasonable to argue that the development cost is independent of market size. Historically, at IBM, the decision to undertake production of a new model computer seems to have meant coming up with an estimate of development costs, establishing the limits on price based on current models of IBM's own line, as well as those of competitors, forecasting the minimum number of units required to earn a normal rate of return, and then determining whether that number of units could be sold at the appropriate price. See Hurd, "Computer Development at IBM," pp. 407–09; Gene M. Amdahl, "The Early Chapters of the PCM Story," *Datamation*, vol. 25 (February 1979), pp. 113–15; Evans, "IBM System/360," pp. 12–18; and Gerald W. Brock, *The U.S. Computer Industry: A Study of Market Power* (Ballinger, 1975), pp. 27–41. Significantly, IBM's pricing of a new computer model is constrained by competition with its current product line. A new entrant lacking an existing product line would not face those constraints.

11. See Flamm, *Targeting*, p. 5, table 1-2.

Since value added is about 55 percent of sales in computers, about 22 percent of value added in the industry has gone into research and development.[12] Typically, then, about one-fifth to one-quarter of computer industry value added has been R&D cost.

Economies of scale in product development are not the only possible source of competitive advantage connected with a larger share of the market. Some evidence points to economies of scale in the marketing and maintenance of computer systems, but these seem much smaller than those affecting the development costs for an integrated computer system.[13] More important, companies have focused on economies of scope in product development in order to use the results of a fixed investment in R&D in the widest array of products. Firms have sought to translate their presence in a variety of markets into a source of lower product costs.[14]

By setting internal company standards for computer components and peripherals, larger producers, especially IBM, have spread the costs of research and development across a broad line of computer systems. By requiring that all systems draw on a common library of circuitry and components, calling on the connections to disk and tape storage units to follow common companywide technical specifications, and establishing other standardized features for computer hardware, firms have translated sales across a broad range of markets into a potent source of lower costs for product development. One standardized attachment might as well be

12. The R&D figure is the NSF's 1980 estimate for the office, computing, and accounting machinery industry, the value-added ratio for computing equipment, from the U.S. Bureau of the Census, *1982 Census of Manufactures* (GPO, 1985), p. 35F-5. The R&D figure refers only to current expenses—the cost of capital equipment used in R&D has not been accounted for in these numbers.

13. See Brock, *U.S. Computer Industry*, pp. 32–37; and Franklin M. Fisher, John J. McGowan, and Joen E. Greenwood, *Folded, Spindled, and Mutilated: Economic Analysis and U.S. vs. IBM* (MIT Press, 1983), pp. 176–218, for IBM's rebuttal to arguments for the existence of scale economies in most of these areas, though not in research and development. There it is argued that rapid diffusion of new technology permits "follower" firms to match the market leader's costs at small output levels. This argument does not deny the existence of cost advantages for an innovating market leader over the temporal "window" during which followers do not yet have free access to the new technology, but instead interprets them as a necessary condition for a firm to be able to earn the technological rents that justify investment in research and development. This is just the classical Schumpeterian argument that some degree of monopoly power is required to stimulate innovation.

14. The "economies of scope" terminology is described in J. C. Panzer and N. D. Willig, "Economies of Scope," *American Economic Review*, vol. 71 (May 1981), pp. 268–77.

plugged into a whole range of computer systems, rather than every new system requiring the development of a whole new line of peripherals.[15] In a sense, IBM has built its current command of the international computer market on deliberate policies adopted to squeeze the maximum possible economic advantage, in the form of lower costs, from its ability to impose technical standards across an array of products. An industry composed of smaller and more fragmented producers, with little cooperation among themselves, would be unable to duplicate this strategy.

Software, because it has come to dominate expenditures on information processing, emerged as a primary area in which to exploit economies of scope. By risking a large investment in developing a software standard spanning most of its computer line, IBM developed the System 360—and institutionalized its position as market leader.

Economies of Scope and Software Standards

The demand for particular computer systems has often depended on software, a highly specialized input to a specific hardware system. Software written for one system is usually a poor substitute (that is, requiring great expense for adaptation) for software run on other systems. Although the depreciation rate on hardware is relatively high, because of both physical wear and tear and rapid technical change, the depreciation rate on an investment in software seems rather small. Obsolescent hardware is scrapped, but old software of good quality is often maintained and improved and even adapted to run on new hardware if necessary.

The interrelation between software and the hardware for which it is designed has been a key technical link shaping the economic development of computers and the computer industry. Companies have derived a great deal of commercial benefit from constructing successively more standardized ways for software to utilize features of hardware. In the earliest days of computers, programs were written in codes specific to a particular manufacturer and model. High-level programming languages, invented to simplify programming, made it much easier to adapt code

15. For interesting discussions of the evolution of hardware standards in IBM, see Evans, "IBM System/360," p. 14; Pugh, "Memories," p. 25; and the following citations in *IBM Journal of Research and Development*, vol. 25 (September 1981): A. Padegs, "System/360 and Beyond," pp. 381–82; E. J. Rymaszewski, J. L. Walsh, and G. W. Leehan, "Semiconductor Logic Technology in IBM," pp. 606–13; D. P. Seraphim and I. Feinberg, "Electronic Packaging Evolution in IBM," pp. 619–26; and P. W. Case and others, "Design Automation in IBM," pp. 631–44.

written for one computer system to another. But the machine code generated from a high-level language is often less efficient than programs written in lower-level languages. High-level language is also less able to utilize the full performance and features of a particular computer system. Consequently, a less machine-specific program meant a price was being paid in the level of performance possible.

The introduction of the concept of a compatible family of computers on a large and commercial scale proved a turning point in the economic history of the industry. The announcement of System 360 in 1964 cemented IBM's dominance of the computer market during the following decades. The fixed cost of writing a complex program could now be spread over a much wider market, and the cost of implementing such an application for an individual user greatly reduced.

As long as new hardware was designed to run applications written for last year's computers, a company could further reduce the unit cost of software by recouping development costs over future generations of machines, as well as over a line of machines with varying ranges of performance at any moment in time. Users could further economize on the fixed costs they incurred in learning to utilize particular computer programs by using the same old software on larger and more sophisticated machines as their needs increased. IBM had, in fact, invested great resources in making System 360 software compatible with earlier models of IBM computers, pioneering the first extensive use of microprogramming in a commercial computer line. With the flick of a switch, many of the machines in the System 360 line could emulate the instruction sets of older IBM computers.

Now technical standards, by definition, are incompatible with perfect competition in the sense that economists use the phrase. Collusion or cooperation or imposition by higher authority is required to establish a common set of rules to which computer designs must conform. What could not be done in a perfectly competitive marketplace, however, could be accomplished easily within the boundaries of a single firm. IBM, by virtue of its overwhelming share of world computer markets in the early 1960s, was able to make an internal standard it had designed for System 360 into an industry standard.

Economists are just now beginning to explore the economics of product standards, a central fact of economic life in the computer industry for more than two decades. In general, these simplified models support common-sense propositions that might be easily accepted in the industry:

history significantly shapes current standards, and, from the social perspective, the interplay of market forces can lead to either insufficient or excessive standardization.[16]

Response by Competitors

Producers could choose from three basic strategies to offset the cost advantages that IBM enjoyed because of the enormous market for its products. First, a producer could make products that conformed to IBM standards, performed in a functionally identical way when plugged into an IBM computer system, but offered a better price or performance than the equivalent IBM unit. The first hesitant and imperfect steps on this path were taken by RCA. The so-called plug-compatible manufacturers (PCMs), who first began to offer IBM-compatible peripherals, then processor and memory units, in the late 1960s and early 1970s, chose this route. The strategy was and is difficult and risky since it requires the manufacturer to have a research and production technology base more advanced than IBM's in some respect.[17]

Even when it was possible to produce a big improvement in hardware incorporating the IBM standard, long-term success was not guaranteed. Because IBM controlled the standard, it also had the power to change it unilaterally. Not surprisingly, IBM has sometimes resisted the acceptance of standards other than internal ones.[18] When serious competition for its products developed, IBM could guarantee itself a one- or two-year lead in product markets by altering the standard. As competitors scrambled to decipher the latest round of technical changes necessary

16. See Stanley M. Besen and Garth Saloner, "Compatibility Standards and the Market for Telecommunication Services," in Robert M. Crandall and Kenneth Flamm, eds., *Changing the Rules: Technological Change, International Competition, and Regulation in Communications* (Brookings, forthcoming).

17. The emergence in the 1980s of commodity personal computer (PC) products, using a widely understood, open architecture and standard, off-the-shelf components might seem to require further analysis. However, even with these relatively "standardized" PC "clones," staying competitive with IBM on the basis of manufacturing cost alone has been difficult. Increasingly, even PC clones rely on specialized PC chip sets that perform the functions of an IBM PC but reduce the number of chips required (and cost) by using special integrated circuits packed with more electronic functions per chip. The high tech (and profit) in these products is in the specialized components; the manufacturer is merely an assembler and packager of purchased inputs.

18. IBM initially resisted some industry standards, for example, the ASCII character set and the Cobol business programming language.

to ensure compatibility with new software and hardware features, IBM would already be developing another round of improvements.[19] And, of course, seizing the lead in price performance was no easy trick, given the size and widely acknowledged excellence of IBM's research effort.

To IBM's competitors, constructing a common standard not controlled by IBM would create an alternative to forever chasing after a cunning IBM. This aspiration has been an increasingly persuasive argument for IBM's competitors in recent years. The current promotion of AT&T's UNIX operating system, designed with portability of software across hardware of diverse manufacture in mind, is an attempt to construct a standard not dominated by the actions of IBM. On the other hand, the issue of how the nascent UNIX standard is to be controlled, and by whom, raises difficulties that have yet to be resolved. Nonetheless, IBM's competitors around the world have begun to move toward establishing UNIX as an alternative on a cooperative basis.[20]

Standards do not, however, solve all problems. A widely adopted standard, almost by definition, incorporates features suited to a broad spectrum of applications. Particular features needed for specialized applications, or that allow special features of hardware to be used, may not fit into a general purpose standard. Furthermore, as new applications are developed, they may require significant changes to existing standards.[21] The inherent complementarity of computer software and hardware is a force arguing for a single standard to reduce costs to computer

19. The widely publicized 1983 industrial espionage case involving Japanese manufacturer Hitachi, which makes IBM-compatible mainframe computers and subsystems, developed from Hitachi's efforts to acquire information about the technical details of a new IBM product line. See John D. Halamka, *Espionage in the Silicon Valley* (Berkeley, Calif.: Sybex, 1984), pp. 124–45.

20. Japanese producers, with the support of the Ministry of International Trade and Industry (MITI), have been working with AT&T to adapt and license a version of UNIX with modifications suitable for Japanese language applications. The most important European computer producers announced in 1985 their adoption of UNIX as the standard operating system in their next generation of products. The principal American competitors of IBM have also announced the availability of UNIX on many of their newly introduced products. See *New York Times*, February 19, 1985; and *Wall Street Journal*, February 19, 1985, for the European initiatives. See also Robert J. Crutchfield, "The New Sperry Unixvac," *Datamation*, vol. 31 (January 15, 1985), pp. 44–48.

21. As an example, it might be argued that IBM's failure to incorporate the dynamic address translation hardware required for a high-performance time-sharing system into the System 360 design slowed the development of time-sharing applications among users of IBM equipment. The most important revision of the 360 standard incorporated into System 370, its successor, was the use of this specialized hardware.

users. At the same time fine tuning technology into specialized structures best suited for a particular application pushes against the economic impulse toward standardization.

An economic trade-off between specialization and product cost is then created.[22] This trade-off guarantees the viability of a second strategy to compete against the cost advantages gained through control of a widely used standard: technological differentiation and specialization.

In existing applications, where software has already been developed, the second strategy could be based on developing a product with a large improvement in performance. If a sufficient advance in price performance were achieved, a user might find it worthwhile to write off the existing stock of IBM-compatible software and undertake the costly investment required to write new software from scratch, maintain it, and run it. But for a marginal improvement in hardware performance, the cost savings would not compensate for the investment needed to produce new code or adapt programs to run on a different computer architecture.

More commonly, the second strategy has meant developing products in market niches that IBM has not yet covered with the umbrella of a unified product line. The most successful U.S. competitors have followed this route. IBM sometimes lagged in the introduction of smaller, low-end models, and in the production of very high-performance, very large-scale mainframe computers oriented toward scientific applications. Successful competitors have challenged IBM by pursuing these markets.

The smaller systems that IBM sold did not use the 360-370 architecture (with its high overhead, it was unsuitable for smaller machines), and because of IBM's lag in entering these specialized markets, it did not carve out the largest market share. Consequently, much of the software-based advantage that IBM had in its unified market for larger, general purpose mainframe computers did not extend to the specialized markets, where competition is far more oriented to price and performance characteristics of the hardware. Developing specialized high-performance operating systems, optimized for certain applications, and offering them on a compatible line of computers as an alternative to the IBM

22. In a stable environment with fixed technology economists study this problem as monopolistic competition. Given static technology, the conclusion emerging from this literature is that product differentiation is not great enough from society's point of view. See Avinash K. Dixit and Joseph E. Stiglitz, "Monopolistic Competition and Optimum Product Diversity," *American Economic Review*, vol. 67 (June 1977), pp. 297–308.

line is a variation on the second strategy. Burroughs' introduction of a unique, specialized computer architecture in the early 1960s is an example.

Doing sufficient R&D to keep one's product roughly competitive with IBM is a third possible strategy. This strategy presumes that a user's existing investment in applications software, operational experience, and personnel training provides a sufficient incentive for the customer not to defect to IBM. Historically, this choice has been the least effective strategy, since the much smaller market share of IBM's competitors has driven up the unit costs of both hardware and software. The long-run effectiveness of this tactic remains open to question. To date, many firms have failed, and no firm has clearly succeeded in challenging IBM in its bread-and-butter business mainframe markets by offering merely a comparable product line.

Reaping the Benefits of Research Investment

The most important feature of competition in a technology-intensive activity, like the manufacture of computers, is the fleeting nature of the competitive advantage that a successful research effort creates. The formal knowledge set down in technical papers and the collective experience of the human beings who have worked on a project are the tangible outcome of research and development. Of the two, the critical store of technology has clearly been people.

The Nature of Technology Transfer

Engineers trained on the first computer projects were largely responsible for the development of the industry. New products and firms can be traced directly to individual engineers who left the first projects, and using their accumulated experience, tried creating a commercial product. This phenomenon is by no means unique to the computer industry—the semiconductor industry has grown through much the same process.

Basic and applied research, the smallest part of the R&D cost, by virtue of their relatively concentrated and formalized nature, are probably the most easily transmissible and least appropriable forms of knowledge.[23] It is very difficult to control the flow of such a compact and cheaply transmitted form of information. Because it is so difficult to capture and reserve exclusively for the internal benefit of a private firm, legal institutions and sanctions are the only viable method of reserving the rights to its use for the exclusive benefit of its creators. Since, as shall be argued, in the electronics industry in general, and the computer industry in particular, the legal protections of the patent system have been ineffective, and often irrelevant, such efforts are likely to be greatly underfunded, relative to their social returns.[24]

But experience in development resides in the engineers who have worked on a project. As long as employee turnover remains reasonably low, much of a firm's investments in product development will remain sealed within the boundaries of the firm. The results of research and development expenditure will leak out only gradually to competitors, as employees leave and take with them partial, fragmentary pieces of the technology relevant to a firm's product line. By taking measures to reduce employee turnover, a company may even be able to limit further the diffusion of its stock of technical know-how to competitors.[25] Thus the leakage rate on information garnered from more applied and developmental expenditures may be slower and may be responsive to efforts to control it.

Typically, then, a firm's investment in research creates a technological advantage, which yields a return to the firm until its competitors have copied the technical advance. This extra return, or technological rent, dissipates over time with diffusion of the advance into the stock of knowledge widely available to those involved in the industry. Maintaining a technological advantage, and the technological rents derived from it, requires continuous investments in the development of new technology.

23. In 1979 only 1.5 percent of the costs of research and development performed in the U.S. computer industry was classified as basic research, another 11 percent as applied research. See National Science Foundation, *Research and Development in Industry 1979* (GPO, 1981). The statistics refer to "office, computing, and accounting machinery," which includes computers as its largest segment—about 80 percent of sales in the 1982 Census of Manufactures.

24. For an analysis of basic research see Richard R. Nelson, "The Simple Economics of Basic Scientific Research," *Journal of Political Economy*, vol. 67 (June 1959), pp. 297–306.

25. IBM comes to mind as a firm widely known for excellent employee compensation and employment security, as well as low turnover. Rather than reflecting an uncommon measure of benevolence, this may well be a highly rational strategy in a business dependent on preserving the security of internal technical know-how.

Basic research is essential to the general advance of technology, but difficulties in appropriating it for an individual firm's exclusive use lessen the incentive for private firms to undertake it. Technological advance in an entire industry rests on basic research, yet its rapid rate of diffusion to others makes it a relatively unimportant factor in the outcome of competitive struggles among individual firms within that industry.[26] Because development efforts can probably best be captured by an individual firm, they are the most important focus for a private firm's R&D expenditure.

As noted throughout this book, a veritable thicket of new firms and products stems directly from the first, few scattered projects in computer development. The medium of transmission for this expertise was the skilled manpower that had labored on the pioneering efforts. Some lines of development are especially direct and straightforward. In 1980, for example, Cray Research and Control Data were the two U.S. producers of so-called supercomputers, the largest-scale, fastest computers in existence. The roots of both of these firms can be traced back to the Second World War, to the engineers who were working on large cryptanalytical machines built for the U.S. Navy's Communications Security Group (OP-20-G).[27]

The Role of the Patent System

Contrary to some expectations, the protections offered by the patent system have not proved important in guaranteeing computer firms the exclusive use of the fruits of their expenditures on research and development.[28] This, in fact, is typical of the entire electronics industry.[29] The

26. Large firms, with large market shares (IBM, for example) seem to fund proportionately more basic research, perhaps because so much more of the overall benefit for the industry is captured within their market share.

27. Control Data has since spun off its supercomputer operations into a new subsidiary, Engineering Technology Associates (ETA). The head of ETA, Lloyd Thorndyke, like the top leadership of Control Data, was an alumnus of ERA.

28. This evaluation is shared by Brock, *U.S. Computer Industry*, pp. 63–65; and John Varick Wells, "The Origins of the Computer Industry: A Case Study in Radical Technological Change" (Ph.D. dissertation, Yale University, 1978), pp. 227–49. IBM's team of analysts, Fisher, McGowan, and Greenwood, note, "Technology is freely available, and personnel circulate among firms. . . . Many of IBM's competitors were founded by former IBM employees." See Fisher and others, *Folded, Spindled, and Mutilated*, p. 176.

29. See C. T. Taylor and Z. A. Silberston, *The Economic Impact of the Patent System: A Study of the British Experience* (Cambridge, U.K.: Cambridge University Press, 1973), pp. 280–312.

reasons are both technical and historical. The rapid rate of technological advance, coupled with the snail's pace at which patent disputes are resolved in the courts, has meant that conflicts over the rights to new technology are often economically moot by the time they are settled legally.[30] A complex computer system draws on many different technological elements, from many sources. The ownership rights to an advance produced by combining many disparate elements are often cloudy.[31] Coupled with the marginal, incremental nature of many of the technical advances, which build on work done by others, determining which of many parallel and similar efforts was the "first" to generate a successful innovation is often rather arbitrary.[32] Even defining the exact nature of

30. More than half the transistors introduced in the late 1950s were obsolete in about two years, as were semiconductors used in computer systems in the mid-1970s. Memory products at IBM have generally had about a one-year life span. See John E. Tilton, *International Diffusion of Technology: The Case of Semiconductors* (Brookings, 1971), p. 83; Douglas W. Webbink, *The Semiconductor Industry: A Survey of Structure, Conduct and Performance* (Washington, D.C.: Federal Trade Commission, 1977), p. 131; and William E. Harding, "Semiconductor Manufacturing in IBM, 1957 to the Present: A Perspective," *IBM Journal of Research and Development*, vol. 25 (September 1981), p. 653.

Wells, after reviewing patent cases affecting the top eight U.S. computer firms during the 1950–76 period, found only five computer-related cases settled in the courts. They were generally decided only after many years: for four of the cases, seventeen, fourteen, six, and twenty-three years after the original patents were issued (and patents are usually issued several years after applications are filed). The most famous case, involving the original ENIAC patent applications by Eckert and Mauchly, was finally resolved after twenty-six years. In none of these five cases were the patents upheld.

31. Taylor and Silberston, for example, note that up to 90 percent of the electronics patents they had considered were cited as of doubtful validity by the sources they consulted. See Taylor and Silberstone, *Economic Impact of the Patent System*, pp. 294–95.

32. As Pugh points out, early proposals for core memories included various independent developments: proposals by Eckert and Chu included in the 1946 EDVAC report; a patent application for an electronic relay circuit using a ferromagnetic core by F. W. Viehe in 1947; ideas explored by Jan Rajchman at RCA; schemes developed by Jay Forrester at MIT; the ideas of An Wang at Harvard; and research undertaken at the University of Illinois and IBM by Mike Haynes and others. All involved the principle of using electrical inductance to change the polarity of a ring of ferromagnetic material, though they used many different methods to access and alter the state of a particular bit of memory. Thus it is hard to say who first invented the concept. In the end, the method most commonly used in commercial computers was the scheme devised at MIT by Jay Forrester, who is usually honored as the developer of the core memory. Nonetheless, before MIT and RCA settled their conflicting claims out of court (and RCA accepted the validity of MIT's patents) in 1964, a Patent Office Board of Interferences had granted most of Forrester's patent claims to RCA. See Pugh, *Memories*, pp. 87–89, 210–12.

a particular innovation, when similar and closely linked concepts are being explored in many different places, is difficult.[33]

Instead of depending on protection offered by the patent system, a general pattern of extensive cross-licensing of patents among computer manufacturers has emerged. Competitors are granted the right to unchallenged use of a company's patented concepts in exchange for agreements not to contest the firm's products in patent courts. Agreements made between IBM and ERA, IBM and Sperry Rand, Bell and Sperry Rand, IBM and RCA, IBM and British producer ICL, and IBM and Cray Research were typical of the pattern.[34] The larger computer producers, however, do possess a reasonably broad portfolio of patents to create a credible threat of effective countersuit if a product is challenged on patent grounds. But the extensive patenting activity that occurred in computer technology has essentially been a defensive exercise, intended to deter competitors from mounting a legal challenge to a firm's technology.[35]

33. An important exception to the general lack of importance of patents in competition among firms was MIT's struggle to extract compensation from commercial computer producers for the Forrester magnetic core memory patents, a by-product of the Whirlwind and SAGE projects. After a determined legal fight, MIT forced RCA to accept the Forrester patent claims and extracted a $13 million settlement from IBM in 1964. Significantly, MIT was not in the computer business and therefore was not vulnerable to countersuits by the computer manufacturers who might threaten sales of a rival product line.

34. Erwin Tomash and Arnold A. Cohen, "The Birth of an ERA: Engineering Research Associates, Inc. 1946–1955," Annals of the History of Computing, vol. 1 (October 1979), p. 91; Brock, U.S. Computer Industry, pp. 166–68; Pugh, Memories, pp. 86–87; Paul Stoneman, Technological Diffusion and the Computer Revolution: The U.N. Experience (Cambridge University Press, 1976), p. 92; and see "Back Scratching," Datamation, July 1, 1984, p. 64.

35. At roughly the time IBM learned that MIT and others were planning to actively pursue patent concepts related to the core memory, IBM purchased patents filed by Wang and Viehe in the area and concluded a cross-licensing agreement with RCA, the other serious challenger in the field. Pugh, Memories, pp. 86–88. In general, IBM displayed a great propensity to purchase the rights to use computer-related patents in the 1950s, including the use of the British Manchester computer patents owned by NRDC (Simon Lavington, Early British Computers: The Story of Vintage Computers and the People Who Built Them (Digital Press, 1980), p. 104), and Technitrol's patent on magnetic disk memory systems (Brock, U.S. Computer Industry, pp. 64–65), both purchased for nominal sums. When General Ceramics tried to negotiate significant royalties for rights to ferrite core technology, IBM perfected an alternative process based on a manufacturing technology acquired from Philips, at much lower cost. (Pugh, Memories, pp. 119; 152–153). When more than nominal sums were requested by the inventor, alternative inventions with some legal claim to priority were sought and

The early history of the industry may also have shaped these attitudes toward patents. First, the heavy government involvement in funding computer research in the early years of development in the United States helped to throw many of the basic ideas about digital computers into the public domain. Certain crucial pieces of early work, but certainly not all, done on government contracts were effectively removed from any private company's portfolio. This event may well have undermined any later claims built on these early projects.[36] The government's right to use concepts developed on projects it had funded free of royalty also made it difficult to claim exclusive rights over such work, especially in the early days of the industry when the government was the single largest customer for computer systems.[37]

The other chief early government influence on the role patents were to play in the industry was a series of antitrust actions filed against some of the most important firms in the nascent industry, notably AT&T and IBM. In 1949, the year the transistor was invented, the Justice Department started an antitrust suit against AT&T. In the following years, as the suit was being litigated, and probably at least partially in response, AT&T adopted an extremely open and liberal attitude toward the use of its crucial semiconductor patents and even actively worked to transfer production know-how to other firms. The 1956 consent decree that

---

purchased and used as bargaining chips in subsequent negotiations for cross-licensing agreements.

IBM's attention to acquiring a portfolio of patents in important areas of computer systems in these early days may be explained by its late entry into the industry; furthermore, its dominance of the punched card industry in the 1930s depended on key patents that it had owned, particularly the rotary card printing machine known as the Carroll press, invented in 1922 by IBM engineers. See Thomas Graham Belden and Mona Robins Belden, *The Lengthening Shadow: The Life of Thomas J. Watson* (Little, Brown, 1962), p. 309.

36. The dispute between Eckert and Mauchly, the Moore School, and von Newmann, over credit for the 1945 draft EDVAC report, was resolved by the Army's legal experts when they ruled that because of the time elapsed since the release of the report, all ideas had been placed in the public domain. After bitter conflict, the parties also forged an agreement to refrain from filing patent claims on ideas *not* mentioned in the report, further muddying the waters for later claims related to the basic ideas for a digital computer system.

From that point on, it would be almost impossible for anyone to build patent walls around the right to manufacture computers with standard von Newmann-type architectures. See Nancy Stern, *From ENIAC to UNIVAC: An Appraisal of the Eckert-Mauchly Computers* (Digital Press, 1981), pp. 96–99.

37. One big computer patent case, *Technitrol* v. *Control Data Corp. et al.*, was apparently lost for these reasons. See Wells, "Origins of the Computer Industry," pp. 232–33.

settled the suit required AT&T to license, free of royalty, all its existing patents to any interested domestic firm, although AT&T could ask for cross-licensing benefits.[38] This action had pervasive effects on the restrictive use of patents in the semiconductor industry and, naturally, on the computer industry, its main commercial customer.

A similar episode affected IBM in the mid-1950s. In 1952 the Justice Department began an antitrust suit against IBM over its practices in the punched card equipment business. A consent decree was also negotiated in 1956. The decree required, among other provisions, that IBM license any applicant to use all of IBM's existing and future (through 1961) punched card and computer patents at reasonable rates.[39] Not until 1985, after more relaxed attitudes toward antitrust had become well established in government, were these decades-old consent decrees reported to be under review.[40]

Thus intrinsic difficulties in capturing the results of research and development expenditure have affected competition among computer firms. The varying degrees of appropriability of different sorts of R&D have greatly affected the mix of projects carried out within industry.[41] The diffusion of technology through employee mobility, and the general lack of protection afforded by patents, have resulted in competitive pressures to maintain research investments in even the most advanced firms in the industry. And there have been few legal obstacles to creative firms exploring the fringes of the technology in an effort to define new markets.

In recent years, there has been some movement toward increasing the importance of intellectual property rights in the computer industry, but the net effect is still difficult to assess. Since 1978, IBM has registered a copyright for its new systems software products, and in 1980, the U.S. Congress passed the Computer Software Act, which explicitly extended copyright protection to computer software. Other recent cases have

38. See Tilton, *International Diffusion of Technology*, pp. 76–77; and Taylor and Silberston, *Economic Impact of the Patent System*, p. 297.

39. See Brock, *U.S. Computer Industry*, pp. 155–57; Fisher and others, *IBM*, pp. 34–35; and Wells, *Origins of the Computer Industry*, p. 240.

40. See *Wall Street Journal*, March 5, 1985.

41. American firms involved in joint cooperative research in the Microelectronics and Computer Technology Corporation consortium in the early 1980s, for example, have noted that these projects have tended to be more basic and longer term in nature than their own internal efforts. Few firms funded any research into artificial intelligence until the early 1980s when the feasibility of certain types of applications had been demonstrated by university research projects capitalizing on decades of earlier research.

raised the issue of whether or not software's user interface, its "look and feel," is protected by copyright. And both IBM and Digital Equipment have moved aggressively in the courts against smaller competitors alleged to have improperly used the larger companies' proprietary information. Whether these actions represent a transitory phenomenon, a tactical move by the strong to pressure the much weaker, or a fundamental change in direction for the industry remains to be settled.

Security Restrictions

As already noted, the U.S. government funded the early development of computer technology. Given the military origins of most of this funding, the relaxed attitudes toward dissemination of research, leading to a relatively free flow of information about U.S. computer research, were especially interesting.

The structure of information flow was not utterly unrestricted, however. It can best be envisioned as a pyramid. The most privileged, sensitive design groups working on classified military applications formed the top of the information pyramid. These groups had access to information from all other government computer projects, and doors to industrial research facilities were often opened to them as well. The computer groups in Engineering Research Associates and, perhaps, internal design facilities at the National Security Agency, belonged to this most privileged class of researchers.[42]

Below the apex of the information pyramid stood other groups with some security restrictions placed on their work. But their internal research memoranda circulated widely among the U.S. community of computer designers. The MIT Whirlwind project, as well as the Moore School ENIAC and EDVAC groups, probably fits into this group. At the base of the pyramid was research disseminated openly, not only in the United States but also abroad. The Standard Eastern Automatic and Institute for Advanced Studies computers belonged in this group of projects.[43]

42. Tomash and Cohen, "Birth of an ERA," p. 89, describe the access ERA researchers were given. The Navy's Office of Naval Research (ONR) gave ERA the task of assembling a report on the engineering state of the art in 1947, and ONR's decision to publish this report put much of this knowledge in the public domain.

43. As noted earlier, French computer designers in SEA drew on the published details of the SEAC and IAS machines, while Japanese designers at Nippon Telephone and Telegraph adopted the IAS (and its clone, the ILLIAC I) architecture to take advantage of the availability of ILLIAC I software.

It seems clear that the very open position on information flow taken by the scientists running the military services' computer research programs helped bring about the rapid diffusion of computer technology within U.S. industry. Firms had few problems in applying the knowledge gained from their military contracts to the development of commercial products, and these spin-offs were the prevailing pattern of entry into the computer business in the 1950s. The Office of Naval Research was especially active in devising ways to encourage the use among industry and academics of the research it had supported. It sponsored numerous educational courses, open symposia, and conferences in the late 1940s and 1950s, commissioned surveys of computer technology and use at frequent intervals, and published a widely read newsletter on digital computing through the late 1960s.[44]

When security restrictions were imposed, the pace of technological advance slowed. An early algebraic programming language, and algorithms to be used in implementing it, were devised by a researcher at the Naval Ordnance Laboratory in 1948, but were not published in the open literature.[45] Consequently, some of these ideas were not developed openly until the early 1950s. In England, the first real compiler (a program to translate high-level programming statements into machine language) was apparently functioning in 1952 for use in nuclear weapons research, but was not made available for general use.[46] This particular wheel also had to be reinvented. And one of the largest of the early British computer projects, and the only one using a bit-parallel architecture, the TREAC, constructed at the elite Telecommunications Research Establishment military research labs, had virtually no influence on British industry because of its isolation from civilian research.[47]

The tradition of relatively open computer research continued to mark U.S. military support for computers through the late 1970s. In the early 1980s, as geopolitical competition between the superpowers was increasingly channeled into technological dimensions, some retreat from this historical tradition began. The effects of increasing security controls

44. See Mina Rees, "The Computing Program of the Office of Naval Research, 1946–1953," *Communications of the ACM*, vol. 30 (October 1987), pp. 830–47.
45. See Donald E. Knuth and Luis Trabb Pardo, "The Early Development of Programming Languages," in Metropolis and others, *A History of Computing*, pp. 211–12.
46. Ibid., pp. 227–33; and Lavington, *Early British Computers*, pp. 40–43.
47. Lavington, *Early British Computers*, pp. 54–56.

over technological information on the competitiveness of commercial industry have now become an important policy issue.

Technological Differentiation and Competition

These three elements—the unrelenting pace of technological advance, the economies of scale and scope to be reaped through the establishment of technical standards, and the difficulties of appropriating the returns on certain kinds of research investments—have channeled competition in the development of computer systems. Consequently, an ever-finer technological differentiation in markets for information processing services has occurred.

Historically, either the creation of new products targeting untapped markets or the achievement of levels of price and performance not matched by older machines has propelled new firms into the computer industry. Examples abound: Control Data with large-scale scientific supercomputers; Digital Equipment Corporation and Scientific Data Systems with small high-performance scientific machines; Burroughs with a unique special purpose architecture; and Apple Computer with microcomputers.

With few exceptions, strategies based on challenging established industry leaders on their home ground have failed. The reasons seem clear. Unless the established leader is slow to react, unprepared for the constant investment in research required to maintain a competitive edge in a technology-intensive business, or simply poorly managed, market leadership provides self-reinforcing advantages.

Adequate research investment, however, is clearly the key to success. Without sufficient investment in research, technological leaps by competitors can render all other advantages irrelevant. It is not always necessary, however, for a company to be first with a product. If a solid technology base is maintained, sufficient to react quickly to the actions of potential competitors, then a dominant firm can afford to let competitors take the risks of pioneering a new product or process. If the challenger succeeds, and the leader can respond quickly with a similar offering, nothing is risked. The advantages of incumbency continue to hold. Conversely, the innovative failures give the dominant firm considerable information about the nature of a highly uncertain market at no cost or risk to its own fortunes.

In fact, an unchallenged market leader may have a considerable incentive to slow the pace of innovation in an industry. This "Arrow effect" follows from the realities of dominance.[48] For the established leader, a new product may very well compete with its existing product lines in some markets. Profits on the new product are then partially offset by lost profits on other offerings. For a new entrant, there is no offsetting loss, and the perceived return to entry will be higher. A similar logic holds for other types of innovation, including cost-cutting improvements in manufacturing processes. An innovating entrant able to capture a market on the basis of new technology will always receive a greater return than an established, unchallenged monopolist who adopts the same plan.

The growth of the microcomputer market in the early 1980s exemplifies these economic realities. Microcomputers started to become an important product in the late 1970s, and for a while it seemed that Apple Computer, which had carved out a dominant position in the still-infant market, might well be establishing its Apple II product line as a standard in this booming market. IBM, initially slow to develop a micro, responded by announcing the IBM personal computer in late 1981 and mounting an effective challenge to the Apple product line. But IBM's exploding microcomputer sales in 1982 and 1983 were less lucrative than a first glance might indicate. Between 1982 and 1983, IBM's micro revenues were estimated to have grown by $2.1 billion. However, this remarkable growth was offset by an estimated $400 million decline in office systems revenues and a $200 million decline in minicomputer revenues, probably

---

48. This is the classic argument made by Kenneth J. Arrow in "Economic Welfare and the Allocation of Resources for Invention," in National Bureau of Economic Research, *The Rate and Direction of Inventive Activity: Economic and Social Factors*, Special Conference Series, no. 13 (Princeton University Press, 1962), pp. 609–26. Arrow formulated the argument by assuming that a single firm has a monopoly position in investing in a particular R&D project. He then compared the incentive to undertake the R&D investment in a monopolized industry with that of the same firm facing a competitive market. Allowing competition in R&D considerably complicates the analysis. Jennifer Reinganam, "Innovation and Industry Evolution," *Quarterly Journal of Economics*, vol. 100 (February 1985), pp. 81–99, extends Arrow's argument to an idealized industry with competition in R&D generating a sequence of innovations over time. John Vickers, "The Evolution of Market Structure When There Is a Sequence of Innovations," *Journal of Industrial Economics*, vol. 35 (September 1986), pp. 1–12, explores the implications of different assumptions about the behavior of a firm on the incentives of incumbent and challenger firms to innovate. Katz and Shapiro, "R&D Rivalry," have recently constructed a model in which industry leaders tend to pioneer minor innovations, while entrants tend to develop major innovations that are easily imitated.

because customers for those products were switching to the popular IBM personal computer. Apple, of course, did not have to take such declines into account when it made investments in developing micros.[49] It may behoove the established leader to hold off on the introduction of an innovation until a serious threat from a competitor exists.

The enemy of size and market dominance, of course, is the organizational sluggishness and bureaucratic costs that are inherent in large and complex organizations. Beyond a certain point, a large organization may have an institutional inertia that is immune to the actions of its individual parts. The timely flow of information from root to branch in an enormously large business may be much more costly than in a small, and therefore inherently more flexible, organization.

This hypothesis is certainly consistent with the frequent observation that small entrants seem disproportionately important in the history of technological innovation. Significant decentralization and seemingly constant internal reorganization seem necessary if a large organization is to succeed in technology-intensive enterprises. IBM, for example, has seemed to outside observers to be constantly tearing up organizational charts and restructuring itself, usually in the direction of further decentralization. This may well be the price that large firms pay to achieve the flexibility needed for success in fast-moving, technology-intensive industries.

In new applications, however, the field is open for competition. There is no significant existing software investment to lock new users into a family of compatible hardware products. Thus, in older established markets, the economics of the computer industry seem to argue for increasing concentration on the supply of technology-intensive products. This tendency to increasing concentration is counterbalanced by a constant probing of the fringes of the technology, in new and unexplored markets, by would-be entrants into the industry. These new markets, because of their possible overlap with older products at the margins of existing markets, are probably somewhat less attractive to an established leader until a serious challenge is discerned.

Differentiation in Computers

Before the mid-1950s, the few prototype computers were largely oriented toward so-called scientific applications (wide data paths, spe-

49. See Pamela Archibold, "Fathoming the Industry," *Datamation*, June 1, 1984, pp. 54–55, for the IBM sales figures.

cialized arithmetical hardware). In the early 1950s, however, the success of the UNIVAC pioneered a new, business-oriented market. By the mid-1950s, smaller computers were being introduced, and distinctions between large and small, business and scientific machines, arose. In the late 1950s, with the increasing power and lower costs created by continued technological advance, the commercial business market had finally begun to dominate growth.

The large computers of the day represented hefty fixed investments, and as it was realized that the information processing requirements of a major corporation often meant a mix of applications, some businesslike, some scientific, a general purpose center also began to emerge. The rising importance of software costs gave additional thrust to the development of standards in general purpose computer markets. In the early 1960s, a mainframe center had emerged in the market, with smaller- and larger-scale processors specializing in business and scientific tasks crowding its periphery.

By the mid-1960s, cheaper minicomputers specializing in real-time industrial and scientific control, time-sharing, and communications applications had invaded the market in droves, and by the 1970s, the business cousins of these computers had defined an emerging office systems market. The gap between large mainframes and the very largest-scale supercomputers had increased in the mid-1960s, and during the next decade the distance widened. Minicomputers had also reached upward in performance, to become superminis, brushing against the performance of small mainframes. The end of the 1970s saw the low end of the market dive still lower, as small, inexpensive computers took the form of the mass-produced microcomputers for home and office and the stand-alone workstation for science and industry. This growth represented the application of constantly cheapening computing power to new and different applications. As the market deepened and widened, new firms pioneered in these emerging product niches.

It is difficult to provide a more precise description of the intricate process of technological differentiation that characterized the development of the computer during these four decades. In large part this stems from the inherent fuzziness of the definitions of particular classes of products—these definitions have usually been made on the basis of cost and performance, and as costs dropped and performance increased in all types of hardware and markets, older definitions were replaced by newer but equally arbitrary categories.

Nonetheless, available statistics do support this general picture.

Figure 7-1. *Distribution of Value of Installed U.S. Computer Base, by Monthly Rental Class.*

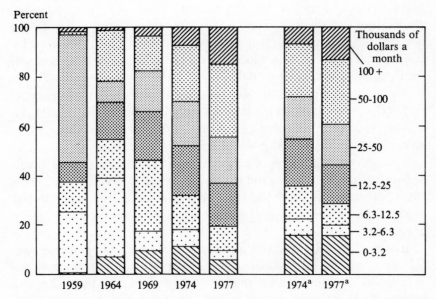

Source: Montgomery Phister, Jr., ed., *Data Processing Technology and Economics*, 2d ed. (Digital Press and Santa Monica Publishing Co., 1979), pp. 303, 618, 621.

a. General purpose machines include mini- and small business computers.

all types of hardware and markets, older definitions were replaced by newer but equally arbitrary categories.

Nonetheless, available statistics do support this general picture. Figure 7-1 charts the changing distribution of the installed stock of computers over time, in the United States. The distributions are made on the basis of monthly rental, which coincides with system size and performance. Clearly, a marked historical trend has shown increasing diversity in the distribution of computer installations by performance level.

IBM's place within this galaxy of markets has shifted over time. In the early 1950s, when IBM entered the computer business, government users still accounted for an overwhelming share of computer revenues, and IBM's efforts were necessarily oriented toward its federal business. Its first efforts in the business field were not an overwhelming success.[50]

50. Its scientific machines, on the other hand, were widely acknowledged for their

with the UNIVAC. It was withdrawn after a short time, replaced by the 705.

It may be argued that IBM's eventual success in business computers followed the classic recipe for success: pioneering a new market. One key factor in Sperry Rand's fall from market leadership was its failure to introduce a smaller, cheaper version of the large and costly UNIVAC I business computer. The IBM 650, announced in 1953 and first installed in late 1954, was such a machine and an instant success, paving the way for the IBM 704 and 705 in business markets a year later.[51] The 650 was probably the first real mass-produced computer, with more than one thousand built. UNIVAC's failure to respond with timely technological improvements to its large machine or with competitive products in the smaller business systems market began the company's long decline.

As the computer market of the late 1950s began to increasingly be dominated by business applications, so too did IBM shift its focus. IBM's 700, and later, transistorized 7000 series computers had been the largest, fastest computers of the day when introduced in the 1950s. The Stretch computer, shipped in 1961, was probably the last IBM machine to so stand out in the large-scale scientific, high end of the computer market. With the phenomenal growth of business computing in the late 1950s, IBM's product line shifted toward the center of gravity of the business market. From the mid-1960s on, IBM sat firmly astride the general purpose, mainframe computer market for business.

To this day, general purpose business computer systems remain IBM's core market—in 1984 IBM probably accounted for 76 percent of mainframe computer sales by U.S.-based firms, compared with an overall share of computer-related sales by U.S. firms under 50 percent.[52] From its impressive base in the center of the computer market, IBM has reached into the smaller, more specialized markets of the periphery.

51. Phister, Jr., *Data Processing Technology*, p. 333, estimates IBM's computer revenues in 1956, the year after it had probably passed UNIVAC in market share, as follows: rentals from the IBM 650: $259,000 a month; rentals from the IBM 704: $800,000 a month; rentals from the IBM 705: $840,000 a month. The 704 and 705 were not installed until late 1955, a year after the first 650s were delivered.

For an analysis of the 650 as IBM's critical point of entry into the business systems market, see George Schussel, "IBM vs. REMRAND," *Datamation*, vol. 11 (May 1965), pp. 63–64.

52. The mainframe estimate is cited in David E. Sanger, "Sierra Adds Power to I.B.M.," *New York Times*, February 13, 1985; IBM's 1983 data processing revenues of $40.2 billion compared with a total of $91.8 billion for the top one hundred U.S. firms, or about 44 percent, see Archibold, "Fathoming the Industry," pp. 53, 60.

The most successful of IBM's chief American competitors have followed the opposite tack in facing off with the market leader (figure 7-1). They have usually started in more specialized markets, at either the high or low end of the product spectrum and gradually shifted their product mix into the central, core business markets. Thus DEC moved from its minicomputer base into production of the larger-scale, general purpose PDP-6 (and its descendants, the DEC 10 and 20 systems) in the late 1960s and 1970s.[53] Similarly, Control Data moved downscale from its huge supercomputers of the mid-1960s to smaller machines targeting more general purpose, commercial markets over the same period.

Japan's Challenge

Only Japanese producers seem to have had any visible success in competing against IBM in its general purpose, mainframe, business computing market. Fujitsu and Hitachi, in the 1970s, entered the business market with IBM-compatible mainframes and continue to focus on these core IBM products. To some extent, this strategy may have been thrust upon them: as technological followers, attempting to catch up with foreign producers, they were ill-situated to attempt to carve out new markets based on innovative designs. Instead, they focused on manufacturing a cheaper, higher-performance version of a standard product.

The minimal requirement for survival with this strategy is superior price performance, which the Japanese producers have pursued by investing heavily in semiconductor technology. Viewed in this light, Japan's much-publicized, government-sponsored semiconductor development projects of the 1970s highlighted a vital ingredient in a strategy based on a direct competition for IBM's business mainframe market. Since certain types of semiconductor technology were a weak point in

---

53. See Bell and others, *Computer Engineering*, chap. 21, for further details. Even though the PDP-6 was an entry into the large general purpose systems market, it was designed with specialized Fortran scientific programming and time-sharing applications in mind. Thus it was aimed at a particular niche in the large systems market. In retrospect, DEC's entry into the market for larger systems was not a great economic success. See ibid., pp. 487–89, 518. In 1983 DEC decided to cancel this line of machines, scrapping a $50 million investment in a planned upgrade. See Archibold, "Fathoming the Industry," p. 66. DEC, second only to IBM in U.S. computer sales (before the Burroughs-Sperry merger), has been standardizing its products on the architecture used in its popular VAX series of superminicomputers.

IBM's technology base in the early 1970s, this move was an attempt to build strength where weakness in the market leader may have been perceived.[54]

The long-term prospects for this path remain uncertain, however: IBM has invested huge amounts in semiconductor technology and by the early 1980s was clearly on the leading edge of the technology.[55] IBM still controls its internal standard, and by making artful improvements at any moment it chooses, can force an imitator to struggle through another round of catching up. By the early 1980s, it seemed that the new option chosen by Fujitsu and Hitachi was to target a market abandoned by IBM in an earlier decade—that of large-scale supercomputers—and gamble that producing these machines, with the added fillip of some degree of compatibility with IBM, would provide a broad enough niche for a solid footing in the world market.

The other major Japanese producer, Nippon Electric, had chosen to center its strategy on specialized application with promising future growth: the integration of communications with computers. The historical scorecard clearly points to specialized applications as the more promising route to profitable competition with the leader, and it remains to be seen how successful either of these routes will prove as Japanese producers continue to emerge from the shelter of their national market on a large scale.

The key development in international competition in computers in recent years has been the steady and rapid advance of Japanese computer technology, to the point at which Japan has achieved parity with the United States in many commercial products. The announced intention of Japan to begin a quest for leadership in important frontier research areas in the 1980s, in the guise of the oft-mentioned Fifth Generation project, led to discussion and reactions around the world.

In some respects, even the bold technical goals in this ambitious program reflect a shrewd assessment of economic realities. After all, if advanced parallel computers or new types of software products render existing technology obsolete, so that whole new methods of programming

54. In the late 1960s IBM executives acknowledged their weakness in certain types of semiconductor technologies in internal management committee meetings. The minutes are reproduced as part of the testimony of A. G. W. Biddle, in *The Industrial Reorganization Act*, Hearings before the Senate Judiciary Committee, 93 Cong. 2 sess. (GPO, 1974), pt. 7, p. 5109; and Brock, *U.S. Computer Industry*, pp. 126–32.

55. In 1984 IBM was among the first semiconductor producers to announce the fabrication of a million-bit (megabit) random access memory chip.

are needed, then the existing stock of software—the basis for much of IBM's advantage in global markets—will gradually be replaced. A new generation of fundamentally different types of advanced products would open up a vast new market, in which past hegemony will offer minimal advantage.

CHAPTER EIGHT

The Changing Face of Competition

THE FIRST decades of the computer's history were a period of trial and error, as companies groped to understand how to deal with a new kind of competition centered on constant technological revolution. Even as the industry was absorbing the costly lessons, new realities were altering the parameters of competition. It is probably accurate to suggest that the computer industry "has never been close to long-run equilibrium in its entire existence."[1]

Can one even now discern the seeds of future change in the present, and if so, where are the dynamics of industrial competition in computers shifting? How has the role of government changed? What features of this industry are generic, important in any technology-intensive activity, and which ones are specific to computers?

The Computer Industry Today

It took almost twenty years for the economic fundamentals shaping competition in the computer industry to become established and at least another decade for these forces to work to full effect. The upheavals that shook the computer business in the late 1960s and early 1970s were the result. By the mid-1970s, things had settled into a fairly stable pattern, with IBM dominating the mainstream of business computing and several well-established but smaller firms nibbling at the margins in emerging markets not covered by the umbrella of IBM's general purpose architecture. Firms continued to enter the industry as advances in technology

1. Franklin M. Fisher, John J. McGowan, and Joen E. Greenwood, *Folded, Spindled, and Mutilated: Economic Analysis and U.S. Vs. IBM* (MIT Press, 1983), p. 149.

opened up new markets, but IBM could always be counted on to contest any new niche that grew to substantial dimensions. In the late 1970s those of IBM's traditional competitors who lacked a coherent strategy for differentiating their products saw their share of the commercial mainframe market steadily decline. Sperry and Honeywell, in particular, had to beat a retreat into the military market as their business users defected to the IBM camp. In the end these companies had to sell out to stronger firms.

Yet as had proven true in the past, the incessant, rapid advance of computer technology was to upset the apparent balance that had been struck. By the mid-1980s some of the scales of market power had been tipped, and a new restructuring could be discerned in the industry. Indeed by then an opinionated observer might have argued that two basic themes were driving change in the industry. First, the uncertainties of rapid technological change are formidable even for a company with great resources like IBM, and unanticipated shifts can still upset the established balance. Second, experienced competitors now understood the significance of economies of scale and scope, and some of those potential gains would be increasingly realized by them through new business strategies.

Technological Impulses

Improvements in electronic components dominated the technological changes reshaping the market in the 1970s, especially extraordinary declines in price and the vastly improved performance of semiconductors.[2] As the history related here has made clear, competitiveness in computer systems requires access to the best available component technology. IBM entered the 1970s with a relatively weak position in semiconductor technology, a vulnerability that was to be remedied gradually through huge R&D investments during that decade. Japanese firms, levering new-found strength in semiconductors into a strategy for entering the computer market, exploited that weakness by creating high-performance computer products compatible with the IBM architecture.

Dramatic technical advance in semiconductors has taken the form of

2. See Kenneth Flamm, "Economic Dimensions of Technological Advance in Communications: A Comparison with Computers," in Robert Crandall and Kenneth Flamm, eds., *Changing the Rules: Technological Change, International Competition, and Regulation in Communications* (Brookings, forthcoming).

increased numbers of electronic circuit elements being squeezed onto a single integrated circuit (IC) and improved speed and reduced-power requirements for ICs. Consequently, a rapid decline occurred in the size and cost of the hardware needed to supply a given amount of computing power.

In 1971 the Intel Corporation announced the first simple microprocessor, which integrated on a single chip all elements of a rudimentary central processing unit (CPU) for a computer. Computers designed around this primitive device were too simple for any but the most basic, low-performance applications (like a simple calculator), but by the mid-1970s, with steady progress in cramming more circuit elements on a single chip, moderately high-performance computers could be produced by connecting a relatively small number of chips. Minicomputers based on this new generation of denser LSI (large-scale integration) chip technology, by the mid-1970s, could handle reasonably serious business and office applications.

As was true in the past, improvements in price and performance based on the new components were also felt in large computers at the high end of the market. New and more demanding applications were soon developed to take advantage of the vastly cheapened cost of information processing at the top end of the spectrum of computer performance.

But the growth of applications at the lower end of the market far outstripped increased demand for larger and more capable computers. In 1974 machines defined as minicomputers accounted for 9 percent of sales in the United States; a decade later, that percentage had doubled to 19 percent, and a new product, the microcomputer, had ballooned to a 35 percent share of the computer market.[3] The rapid growth at the low end was even more striking because the first successful mass market microcomputer, the Apple II, fundamentally dependent on the same improvements in semiconductor technology, was not introduced until 1977. When microcomputer sales are added to minicomputer shipments, as shown in figure 8-1, the rapid shift in the structure of the computer marketplace in the late 1970s and early 1980s is even more dramatic. That staple of the computer marketplace, the mainframe computer, had been dethroned from its place at the cutting edge of growth in the

3. Computer and Business Equipment Manufacturers Association, *Computer and Business Equipment Marketing and Forecast Data Book* (Hasbrouck Heights, N.J.: Hayden Book Co., 1985), p. 87.

Figure 8-1. *U.S. Domestic Computer Consumption*

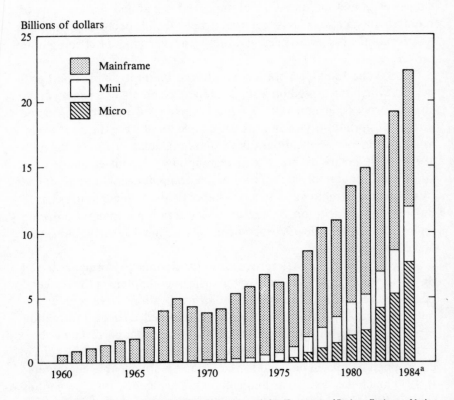

Billions of dollars

Source: Computer and Business Equipment Manufacturers Association, *Computer and Business Equipment Marketing and Forecast Data Book* (Hasbrouck Heights, N.J.: Hayden Book Co., 1985), p. 87.
   a. Estimate.

commercial marketplace and today—by any definition—accounts for well under half of computer sales.

   The other technological development to redefine the computer marketplace was a leap forward in communications technology. Again, new components were critical, as high-speed communications links based on new technologies, which included digital switches and optical fiber, were brought to the mass market. Reduced costs and increased speed for data transmission made it economic to link computer users with machines in physically distant locations and to spread computing demands among large numbers of machines. In a sense, it was a generalization of the idea of time-sharing, with individual users linked to many computers rather than to a single machine. It also became possible to share expensive,

Figure 8-2. *Values of Computers Shipped to the U.S. Market*

Billions of dollars [a]

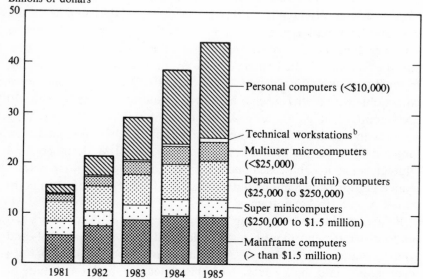

Source: Unpublished data from Dataquest Inc., San Jose, Calif., cited in U.S. Bureau of the Census, *Statistical Abstract of the United States, 1987* (Government Printing Office, 1986), p. 747.

a. Statistics depicted in figure 8-1 differ from those in figure 8-2 because of differences in categorizing computers, as well as differences in the extent to which peripheral equipment incorporated into a system is counted.

b. Excluding computer-aided design and manufacturing systems shipped by original equipment manufacturers.

special purpose computing resources among the many computers plugged into a communications network.

Figure 8-2 provides an alternative disaggregation of growth in American computer installations in the early 1980s. This more detailed accounting shows that, within the mini- and microcomputer classes, sales of the least expensive types of machines grew most rapidly. The 1980s marked the passage from an era of large, centralized computer installations to a world in which vast numbers of more inexpensive machines, distributed widely among users, are tied to one another and to a shrinking number of specialized, centralized computing resources.

Consequences for the Industry

The sudden shift of the commercial center of gravity toward the lower end of the computer market created certain difficulties for IBM. Its unified general purpose System 370 architecture—with a complex instruction set and sophisticated functions with a relatively high processing overhead—was oriented toward larger machines. IBM had entered the minicomputer market in the early 1970s, with a succession of low-end offerings: for general purpose applications, the System 3 and its successor, the System 38, the System 32, the System 34, and the System 36; for real-time use, the System 7 and Series 1. These machines were compatible with neither each other nor the general purpose System 370 architecture. The public rationale for creating this Babel of operating systems and instruction sets was a familiar one. Each product had been targeted at a particular market niche, and the IBM designers and strategists had in each case concluded that advantages in price performance in those applications outweighed the benefits of software compatibility with IBM mainframes.[4]

Related problems cropped up in communications. IBM planners had not foreseen the enormous growth in demand for remote terminals and communications applications.[5] Communications functions had not been incorporated into the System 360-370 architecture, and a multitude of incompatible communications programs were devised to link various IBM machines for specific applications. In 1972 IBM announced an integrated communications architecture, the Systems Network Architecture (SNA), but this was more a series of temporizing measures—constantly modified and extended—to permit minimal communications among various combinations of the proliferating varieties of IBM machines, than a broad vision of a smoothly integrated system for linking the far-flung reaches of IBM's product line.

Matters worsened when IBM shipped its first microcomputer, the IBM Personal Computer, in 1981. Yet another family of operating systems, software products, and communications needs joined the IBM lineup. The enormous success of this new family of products, and another software standard, would compound the snowballing difficulties in getting IBM's varied family of products to talk to one another. This issue of "connectivity" has now joined software compatibility as a

4. For the rationale for introducing these systems, see R. L. Taylor, "Low-End General Purpose Systems," and Thomas J. Harrison, Bruce W. Landeck, and Hal K. St. Clair, "Evolution of Small Real-Time Computer Systems," *IBM Journal of Research and Development*, vol. 25 (September 1981), pp. 429–35, 441–44.

5. A most useful discussion of these issues by a former IBM insider may be found in Bob O. Evans, "System/360: A Retrospective View," *Annals of the History of Computing*, vol. 8 (April 1986), pp. 171–74.

Figure 8-3. *Shifts in the Allocation of Development Resources at IBM, 1950–80*

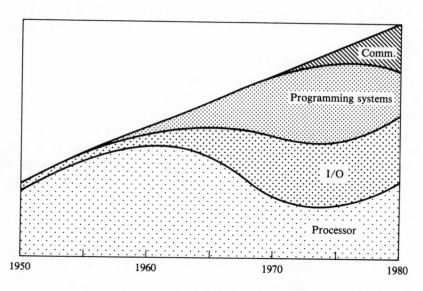

Source: Bob O. Evans, "System/360: A Retrospective View," *Annals of the History of Computing,* vol. 8 (April 1986), p. 176.

principal determinant of the costs faced by a user when selecting a computer system. In an era of cheap telecommunications, when every computer is easily linked to others over a multitude of networks, convenient use of data created and stored on other computers—like use of software written for other computers—is essential to reduce the unit cost of processing information.

The proliferation of incompatible systems and standards had a negative effect on the productivity of IBM's investments in product development. As programming became a greater and greater part of user costs for information processing, it became more important to invest in developing better software that ran on one's machines, in order to sell more computers. The compatibility of the System 360 line had allowed IBM to shift more resources into developing software and improved peripherals for its computers in the late 1960s (figure 8-3).

As IBM strayed from the path of compatibility and unification in the 1970s, however, it had to reduce the resources going into software and devote more effort to solving the communications problems that had developed. Hardware investments were also spread out across increasingly incompatible families of machines—different types of controllers and adapters, for example, had to be developed to attach peripherals to the low-end machines. The economies of scope introduced by developing a standardized hardware interface for the entire System 360 line were diluted.

By contrast, many of IBM's competitors, having learned the lesson of compatibility the hard way through the costly experience of competing against IBM, moved to integrate their product line into a single, unified standard. Digital Equipment Corporation, in particular, adopted the architecture of its highly successful VAX series of superminicomputers for all computers, large and small, in its product line, in the 1980s.[6] It also invested considerable resources in developing a single, unified communications architecture that allowed these machines to connect easily to one another, and in high-speed networking technology that permitted clusters of machines to divide and share workloads. In the midst of a general slump in computer sales in 1985 and 1986, as IBM's sales weakened, DEC confounded the industry by experiencing an unprecedented boom in demand for its products. The improved connectivity of DEC's machines, and its unified architecture, are usually credited with this feat. Other computer manufacturers moved in a similar direction.[7]

New Strategies: Standards

Thus, by the early 1980s, the economic advantages of software compatibility were well understood by the computer industry. With cheaper communications a new reality, connectivity had emerged as the new face of the same old issue, with sharing of data, rather than software, the crux of the matter.

But the hand of history weighs heavily on the options available to a computer producer. For one thing, old standards and products cannot be simply abandoned abruptly and written off, without providing a

6. The VAX architecture was an extension of the PDP-11 architecture introduced by Digital Equipment Corporation (DEC) in the 1960s. DEC discontinued other architectures, including those used in its PDP-6, PDP-10, and PDP-8 products.

7. For example, in the spring of 1986, Hewlett-Packard announced a single new architecture to replace its three incompatible lines of business, engineering, and real-time computers. The new products offer varying degrees of compatibility with the older machines. See "A Simple Design May Pay Off Big for Hewlett-Packard," *Electronics,* March 3, 1986, pp. 39–44.

horrible lesson guaranteed to scare off potential customers. Perhaps more important, with any competitor of IBM still facing a market that is a fraction of the size of the leader, it is hard to see how any new product line can offer economic advantages to software users and producers that are even remotely comparable to those enjoyed by IBM customers. If other computer firms were to hope to break out of the more specialized niches and new applications that had given them their initial entry into the broader, mainstream business computing market, a new strategy was needed.

That new strategy has now become clear. The key, as before, is standards. By banding together and setting industrywide standards for interfaces between processors and peripherals, and communications between computers, and by settling on a standard operating system permitting a software application to run on many different types of computers, other computer vendors would have access to a market with at least approximately the volume of IBM's sales.

Today, groups of companies have joined together on an unprecedented scale to develop hardware, software, and communications standards. In the United States, manufacturers are developing standards for hardware and communications under the sponsorship of the Electronics Industry Association, the Institute of Electrical and Electronic Engineers (IEEE), and several joint, cooperative industrial undertakings. The nonprofit Corporation for Open Systems and the firms (led by General Motors) jointly developing the Manufacturing Automation Protocol are especially important.[8] Other general purpose standards continue to be developed under military sponsorship, then voluntarily adopted in

---

8. Examples include the 802 network standards of the Institute of Electrical and Electronic Engineers; see J. Robert Lineback, "IBM Bridging Scheme Roils the Local Net Community," *Electronics,* November 27, 1986, pp. 29–30. The Manufacturing Automation Protocol (MAP) group recently joined the Corporation for Open Systems (COS). See Bob Wallace "COS, MAP/TOP Groups Establish Bridge Council," *Network World,* vol. 4 (February 9, 1987), pp. 2–52; Byron Belitsos, "'Challenge for COS: Do or Die by 1988," *Network World,* vol. 4 (April 20, 1987), pp. 1, 29–31; Michael Fahey, "Open Is As Open Does," *Network World,* vol. 4 (July 20, 1987), pp. 37–40; The American National Standards Institute's (ANSI) Small Computer System Interface (SCSI) is widely supported by many manufacturers. See Denise Caruso, "Finally, A SCSI Standard; But There Are Still Loose Ends," *Electronics,* May 26, 1986, pp. 46–47. The EIA devised the RS-232 serial interface standard known to millions of PC users. And the Society of Automotive Engineers is currently working on a standard networking scheme for automative electronics. "Electronics Newsletter," *Electronics,* February 19, 1987, p. 17.

commercial markets because of the historical momentum resulting from their use in advanced, leading-edge defense systems.[9]

Government-backed efforts to define new standards have energized this trend. In Europe, Japan, and the United States, government and industry have jointly set up new organizations to develop the so-called Open System Interconnection (OSI) standard, proposed by the International Standards Organization (ISO), which is aimed at allowing easy communications links between computers of diverse manufacture. An OSI development effort joined by all the major European computer producers has been given added clout by pressures from government authorities calling for the eventual adoption of OSI in all systems sold in European markets.[10] In the United States, the nonprofit Corporation for Open Systems—with both broad corporate and government participation—is spearheading the development of OSI and related standards.[11] Even IBM has announced its intent to make its proprietary communications scheme, the Systems Network Architecture, compatible with OSI, and recently set up another European research group to join in the necessary development effort.[12] OSI is also the focus of Japanese support for efforts at standardizing communications between computers.[13]

9. The most commonly used data communications network protocol, for example, is TCP/IP, taken from the Defense Advanced Research Projects Agency's ARPANET. See Kenneth Flamm, *Targeting the Computer: Government Support and International Competition* (Brookings, 1987), p. 61. In 1985 TCP/IP was used by 90 percent of users connected to computer networks. See "Local Networking," *Network World*, vol. 3 (December 1, 1986), p. 21.

10. See, for example, Robert T. Gallagher, "Europe Finally Gets Moving On Standards Making," *Electronics*, April 28, 1986, pp. 48–49; Robert T. Gallagher, "OSI Rains on IBM's Parade," *Electronics*, February 25, 1985, pp. 35–36; Robert Rosenberg, "Closing In On Open Systems," *Electronics*, May 31, 1984, pp. 78–83; and Geoffrey Charles and Louise Kehoe, "Why Rivals Are Clubbing Together," *Financial Times*, January 23, 1986, p. 19.

11. As of mid-1987, Data General, DEC, Hewlett-Packard, Wang, and IBM were shipping OSI-compatible products. "Vendor Support for Open Systems Interconnect Model," *Network World*, vol. 4 (July 20, 1987), p. 13.

12. A transaction-processing protocol developed by IBM (LU 6.2) was even incorporated into the draft OSI standard in early 1987. See Paul Korzeniouski and Amiel Kornel, "ISO Incorporated LU 6.2," *Network World*, vol. 4 (February 2, 1987), p. 5.

13. IBM's Japanese affiliate and Nippon Telephone and Telegraph (NTT) are currently involved in a joint network services venture using OSI protocols. NTT's proprietary network architecture is similar to OSI, with extra functions added to the standard international protocols. The same six firms that participated in MITI's grand design for restructuring the Japanese computer industry in the early 1970s (Fujitsu, Hitachi, NEC, Toshiba, Oki, Mitsubishi), along with NTT as an observer, formed a

In the all-important area of software compatibility, AT&T's UNIX operating system is the center of most effort outside of IBM. That system, explicitly designed to permit increased software portability, represents the latest, and for the first time, coordinated, effort by competitors to challenge IBM's enormous advantage in installed computer base.

In Europe, the principal European computer firms now offer at least some computer systems running UNIX and have announced their intention to offer UNIX as an option on their future machines.[14] In Japan, even the large computer vendors that went the IBM-compatible route in the mainframe market now make UNIX available on at least some of their systems, and development of a Japanese-language version of UNIX is a major objective of the new, government-sponsored Sigma Project.[15] This goal is given added urgency because IBM-compatible producers, Fujitsu and Hitachi, find it increasingly difficult to obtain up-to-date operating systems software to run on their hardware products. In the United States, most major computer vendors (and even IBM, on its scientific and engineering products) now offer UNIX as an option on their computers. In many cases, a user has a choice of running a single proprietary operating system, UNIX, or both systems simultaneously.[16] This preserves the user and software applications base that runs on the vendors' proprietary operating systems and that has been built up in their traditional markets. Yet new types of applications—and markets—

---

joint venture in 1987 to develop OSI standards in Japan. See "Six Computer Manufacturers Join Venture To Develop OSI Protocol," *Japan Economic Journal*, vol. 25 (April 18, 1987), p. 9. See D. Brandin and others, *(JTECH) Japanese Technology Education Program Panel Report on Computer Science in Japan* (La Jolla, Calif.: Science Applications International Corporation, 1984), pp. 3-35–3-54; G. Turin and others, *Japanese Technology Evaluation Program (JTECH) Panel Report on Telecommunications Technology in Japan* (La Jolla, Calif.: Science Applications International Corporation, 1986), p. 3-34.

14. See Flamm, *Targeting,* p. 166; and Robert T. Gallagher, "Europeans Are Counting on UNIX to Fight IBM," *Electronics,* July 10, 1986, pp. 121–22.

15. Jonathan Joseph, "Japanese Quit On IBM Software, Turn to UNIX," *Electronics Week,* vol. 58 (June 10, 1985), pp. 30–31; Charles L. Cohen, "International UNIX Standard Is Up and Running," *Electronics,* December 9, 1985, p. 16; Neil W. Davis, "Sigma Project Aims To Overcome Nation's Deficiency in Software," *Japan Economic Journal,* vol. 25 (May 2, 1987), p. 14; Robert Pre, "Government-Backed Sigma Project Eyes Standardization of Software," *Japan Economic Journal,* vol. 25 (July 19, 1986), p. 18.

16. DEC offers both its proprietary VMS and its version of UNIX as operating systems; Hewlett-Packard offers its Spectrum operating system and UNIX.

can be addressed, using the standard UNIX interface to move new software onto a vendor's hardware.

The federal government has also extended important support to UNIX through recent procurement actions and is actively supporting the development of POSIX, a nonproprietary (that is, not controlled by AT&T) UNIX-like standard currently being defined under the auspices of the IEEE.[17] If future government procurement requires POSIX, and the Europeans, Japanese, and a significant number of American computer firms continue the move toward a single UNIX-like system, a true worldwide software standard may yet emerge.

New Strategies: International Alliances

Support for the establishment of industrywide product standards has not been the only shift that is aimed at making significant economies of scale and scope available to firms besides IBM. Economies of scale in the use of the results of research and development have increasingly been the objective of new types of research alliances among firms. With sharply increasing frequency, industrywide joint ventures to develop new technologies have been announced in recent years. Examples in the United States of cooperative research ventures, which bring together a wide spectrum of firms interested in supporting more basic, generic technology development include organizations like the Microelectronics and Computer Technology Corporation, the Semiconductor Research Corporation, and the Software Productivity Consortium.[18]

These efforts have been more than matched by a surge in more limited arrangements among individual private firms to collaborate on particular applied, product development projects. A 1984 study of technology-oriented joint ventures involving European electronics firms counted eleven new agreements in 1980, twenty-eight in 1981, thirty-five in 1982, and forty in 1983.[19] Often these venture have had a distinctively multi-

---

17. See Rick Vizachero, "UNIX Users Work toward Standards Set," *Government Computer News,* vol. 6 (February 13, 1987), pp. 1, 5; Ron Schneiderman, "NBS Will Propose Validation Policy for UNIX," *Systems and Software,* vol. 5 (January 1986), p. 15; Rick Vizachero, "NBS Hurrying to Adopt POSIX as FIPS," *Government Computer News,* vol. 6 (November 6, 1987), pp. 1, 8; and Brian Boyle, "UNIX vs. POSIX," *Digital News,* November 2, 1987, pp. 30–31, 41.

18. See Flamm, *Targeting,* pp. 114–18.

19. See Paul Betts, "Olivetti's Case for AT&T Pact," *Financial Times.* May 31, 1984, p. 19. Another study found about the same breakdown for cooperative agreements

national complexion. Of the two hundred agreements concluded by the European electronics firms between 1979 and 1984, 51 percent involved American and European firms, 31 percent European and Japanese interests, and only 18 percent other European firms. A similar rise in the relative importance of joint ventures has been noted in direct investments by foreign firms in the United States.[20]

There are many good reasons why joint development projects often seem to involve international linkages. Most important, they are a way for firms to share some of the huge costs of the research and development necessary for the creation of new products. International tie-ups avoid some of the domestic antitrust complications that might otherwise arise. Also, firms of different nationalities often have marketing networks that emphasize different regions, and certain conflicts that might arise with domestic partners are avoided. Often, national capabilities in computer technology are a politically sensitive matter and a serious military and strategic interest. For these reasons—and political pressures from interested national firms—computer markets have often been surrounded by significant barriers—formal and informal—to foreign vendors. Joint ventures clearly have an easier time penetrating these markets, since the joint investment takes on a national character that enables it to receive preferential treatment in the markets of all participants.

Implications

What consequences may flow from these new industrial strategies in years to come? The increasingly important role of product standards, and the rise of joint R&D—often with an international twist—are already changing the rules of the game.

First, nonproprietary standards—whether of the official sort established through the actions of industry or government, or the realities set by market forces—are clearly becoming a potent force in the computer

---

signed by European firms between 1982 and 1983—50 percent with U.S. companies, 20 percent with Japanese, 18 percent with other Europeans. See "Crowning Europe's DP Royalty," *Datamation*, vol. 30 (September 1, 1984), pp. 160–62.

20. In 1982, 79 of 1,145 foreign direct investments in the United States were joint ventures, compared with 47 of 1,203 in 1981. Of the 79 such joint ventures counted by the Commerce Department in 1982, 40 were with Japanese partners, versus 10 of 47 in 1981. "Are Foreign Partners Good for U.S. Companies?" *Business Week*, no. 2844 (May 28, 1984), p. 59.

and communications industries.[21] Their long-term impact may be to reinforce a growing bifurcation in these industries. A high-technology segment, dominated by the economics of investment in research and development, and a distinctive "low-technology" sector, with much more modest requirements for technological resources, have emerged.

At the high-technology end of the industry, the spread of software and communications standards makes it possible for system builders to concentrate on developing a superior, technologically innovative piece of a larger system without mastering all the details needed to construct the entire system. A manufacturer can build modems, or memory boards, or communications software, or special hardware to accelerate scientific calculations without investing great effort in developing the innards of the systems to which these components are to be interfaced. Standard operating systems and communication architectures will mean that a computer user will be less locked in to a single manufacturer's products by the investments of the past. Integrating a competitor's products into existing installations without costly expenditures becomes possible.

The net effect of this accelerating spread of nonproprietary standards will be, in all likelihood, to make these markets more crowded. It will be easier to focus on developing a small piece of a large system well, easier to bring it to market, and easier to use it. As the traditional difficulties of integrating different suppliers' equipment and services diminish, smaller performance differentials will convince users to switch vendors. Competition and the pace of technological innovation may well increase.

At the lower end of the technology spectrum, increasing competition will also intensify. Standard interfaces between the parts of a system will mean that a system builder can plug components and subsystems, procured from outside, into an unsophisticated system with little or no mastery of the technologies required to produce the components. It is now possible to build a simple "commodity" computer using standardized components and a well-defined standard architecture, with little or no R&D investment. Access to components, and minimal engineering

21. Michael L. Katz and Carl Shapiro draw a useful distinction between proprietary standards (which they call sponsored standards) and nonsponsored standards. Sponsored standards cannot be used without the approval of the standard setter, and nonsponsored standards lie in the public domain. Clearly, only those aspects of a manufacturer's internal standard explicitly protected by legal property rights ought be considered as sponsored, and historically, there have been few such protected designs in the computer industry. See Michael L. Katz and Carl Shapiro, "Technology Adoption in the Presence of Network Externalities," *Journal of Political Economy*, vol. 94 (August 1986), pp. 822–46.

and manufacturing know-how, is sufficient to enter these markets. The proprietary technology in these machines is buried in the components and the manufacturing processes used to produce them cheaply, not in the design of the system in which they are embedded.

Clearly, these large new markets will be extremely competitive. The best example to date of a commodity computer—one that may set the pattern for the future—is the IBM Personal Computer (PC) family of microcomputers. In that case, IBM's crash program to enter that market in minimal time, with adequate software and peripherals, led IBM to publish most technical details of the machine's architecture, purchase an operating system from an outside vendor, and use standardized, nonproprietary components.

Though a great success, the IBM PC soon began to attract imitators.[22] Five years after its launch, numerous "clones," often assembled from imported parts in Southeast Asia, were steadily eating away at IBM's market share and profits. IBM has reacted by including more proprietary elements in the technology designed into the successors to the PC.[23] But these are only delaying actions. The existence of a low-end, commodity computer market is now guaranteed for years to come by the enormous stock of useful software available to run on fairly simple, inexpensive machines.

As noted throughout this book, competition in smaller, low-end machines, with the use of lower-performance, more mature technologies, has always been a point of entry into the industry. What is new and different now is that the spread of standards and easy availability of high-quality components for computer systems has drastically lowered the technological ante required to build the simplest systems. The firms competing in these "commodity" computer markets will face the conventional economic problems of a mature manufacturing industry, not those of high technology. Relative input prices, factor productivity, and manufacturing technology around the world will determine where and

22. However, IBM's successful late entry into the field was at least in part a consequence of the pioneer, Apple Computer, committing classic errors. Apple delayed following up on its successful 1977 vintage Apple II with newer technology and ignored software compatibility issues when a follow-up to the Apple II, the Macintosh, was finally introduced.

23. The Personal Computer Convertible introduced in 1986 and the new PS/2 family of personal computers introduced in 1987, for example, make extensive use of proprietary custom logic chips; the PS/2 also introduced a new proprietary interface standard. IBM also announced a proprietary operating system product (OS/2 Extended Edition) that will be required to run many applications on the new system.

how these products are manufactured. Thus, in all markets for computer systems, at both high and low ends, the widespread adoption of nonproprietary standards spells intensified competition.

A second big change in the computer industry results from closer ties among producers based in different national markets. This growing internationalization of computer producers has potentially important consequences for relations between the firm and the state. In the past, much technology policy has been guided by the assumption that the interest of the nation was synonymous with the well-being of the firm. But the assumption that technology is somehow "national," that the fruit of investments in technology can be kept within a country's boundaries, is increasingly unrealistic. High-technology firms, on their own initiative, have been crossing national frontiers to establish overseas research facilities or to participate in joint development projects.

In a sense, this is merely the commercial fruition of an international blurring of frontiers that has already occurred. People, after all, are the medium of technology—and since more than half of the doctoral graduates leaving American engineering schools for jobs in American industry these days are foreign nationals, these commercial ventures only formalize economically, at the commercial level, what has long been true in practice at the individual level. The development of technology-intensive products is today based on the efforts of an international community of scientists and engineers.

Aside from enforcing its imperatives, even defining a national interest is a confusing matter in a world of complex multinational alliances among industrial giants. For example, IBM's American competitors have sometimes been aligned with foreign partners in attempts to invade the traditional business computer markets historically dominated by IBM.[24] Is IBM's strong presence in these markets around the globe in the United States' national interest? Are other American firms' efforts to challenge IBM, which may well benefit allied foreign interests as well, likely to improve the national welfare if successful? And if these questions are to be left to markets to decide, what if the market continues to vote for increased internationalization of the principal teams of players competing in the computer market? One may only conclude that appeals to the national interest will be an increasingly contentious guide for policy,

24. For example, American firms participate in the European X/Open development group, which is working to establish the Open Systems Interconnection standard as an alternative to the IBM Systems Network Architecture, and American companies are backing UNIX in cooperation with Japanese and European groups.

as international tie-ups in technology-intensive industries continue to multiply.

Competition in computers has always involved more than mere price. In the 1950s a process of increasing technological differentiation marked the development of competition in computers. In the mid-1960s internal proprietary standards developed for the IBM System 360 redefined the rules of the game. Today the formulation of nonproprietary, industry standards and a new wave of international linkups are once again driving the industry in new directions.

The Role of Government

Clearly, the modern electronic computer would probably have been developed, with or without the assistance of government, military interest, or the pressures of a world war. In the 1930s Alan Turing's work clearly sketched out the basic concept of the computer as a generalized information processing machine, two-state electronic switches had been available since the 1920s, several large-scale programmable relay calculators had been built around the world, and proposals to build electronic calculators had been advanced by several researchers before the outbreak of war.

Nonetheless, the pace of advance would have been far slower without government interest. As it was, nearly five years passed between the original formulation of the idea of the stored-program electronic computer and the development of the first full-fledged implementations of the concept, despite a well-financed, diverse, and broad program of investment in the United States. Conceivably, it might well have been decades before that point would have been reached without that active and expensive government support. Commercial interests faced enormous obstacles to justifying an accelerated and expensive program of computer development.

First, the magnitude of the investment required meant great risk to the company. As it was, most of the original American computer projects suffered from huge cost overruns and long delays. The desperate need born of being locked in mortal combat on a global scale led political and military authorities to gamble on investing in a wholly untried, and in some respects, technically unlikely scheme.

Governments invested an extraordinary amount of resources in computing technology during the war: when Bletchley Park was developing the first Colossus machine, roughly half of the staff of the British Post Office laboratories was tied up in the project; the U.S. Naval Computing Machinery lab at National Cash Register's Dayton facility employed 1,100 people. The ENIAC, at the Moore School, ended up costing more than half a million (current) dollars to bring into operation. The only peacetime project that approached this scale of expenditure was IBM's effort with Howard Aiken to build the Harvard Mark I relay calculator; IBM probably spent several hundred thousand dollars on this project before the Navy took it over during the war. And while the design of the Mark I was a big advance in computation, the electromechanical components and machinery used were conservative and, though constructed on a vastly larger scale, were little advanced over standard practice in commercial business equipment.

The great leap into the unknown that both Colossus and ENIAC made meant the use of highly experimental electronic circuitry, using notoriously cranky and unreliable tubes. In Britain, the jump was a desperate gamble, a race against time, as the Bletchley Park cryptanalysts struggled against the lengthening times required to crack increasingly complex German codes. In the United States, an overloaded Army ballistics laboratory battled to keep up with an increasing backlog of demands for computations, and against the advice of the U.S. computing establishment, chose to gamble on an untested technology. Even then, it was only because its funding bypassed the established scientific community, and perhaps, because it had found the support of a powerful scientific figure (John von Neumann, who was concerned about the enormous computational demands of nuclear weapons design), that ENIAC was built despite the objections of the experts.

Under the pressure of wartime demands, ways were explored and found to make vacuum and gas-filled tubes perform well enough to do a useful job: in England, through the simple expedient of never turning the machine off, in Pennsylvania, by running the tubes at voltages far below their rated capacity. The 18,000 inherently unreliable tubes that J. Presper Eckert and John W. Mauchly used in their calculator seem, even today, a daring act of imagination and a stirring testimony to the skills of their engineering. More important, it was a project with little obvious commercial payoff, enormous costs, and a solid consensus of scientific opinion that it was likely to fail.

Second, it is unclear how, having proved the feasibility of a large and complex system using an inherently unreliable set of components and techniques, a private business could have prevented competitors from seizing on its success to build similar complex systems. As it was, Eckert and Mauchly devoted much of their time during the completion of ENIAC to working on patent applications. They ended up filing broad and sweeping patent claims in 1947, which, after years of legal battles, were granted in 1964. When these claims were tested in court, the Eckert and Mauchly patents were overthrown in 1973. Patents have never proved particularly important in shaping the computer industry.

Government and Computer Innovation

Government investment in research and development was critical to the initial development of the technology in the United States and abroad. Overseas, where computer development usually trails the lead set by American producers (though this lead has shrunk considerably in certain areas), government programs to support investments in computer technology grew rapidly in the 1960s and 1970s and continue to be significant and visible.

But in the United States, public investment in the technology underwent a great transformation in the sixties and seventies. After a large commercial market emerged in the early 1960s, the aggregate share of federal spending in both computer research and sales declined rapidly, as growth in business computer use exploded. The federal share of clearly identifiable, computer-related R&D expenditure declined from perhaps two-thirds, in the 1950s, to half, in 1965, to one-quarter, in 1975, to 15 percent in 1979 (however, it has since risen again to 20 percent).[25] The federal share of the general purpose computer stock fell even faster: from more than half of American computers in the mid-1950s, to one-fifth in 1960, to one-tenth in 1965, to one-twentieth by 1975.[26]

Has the government—so crucial in the technological developments that drove the first two decades of events described in this book—now become irrelevant? The answer to this question is not simple. Although the government still exerts a powerful influence on the development of technology, the nature of that influence has changed. In the 1950s, before a large commercial market existed, the government role was pervasive.

25. Flamm, *Targeting*, pp. 100–03.
26. Ibid., pp. 107–09.

However, as a commercial industry matured in the mid-1960s, the government role switched to one of sponsoring basic research and infrastructure and what might be called leading-edge technological projects in which R&D was divorced from shorter-term commercial benefit.

As noted, the fundamental concepts for the design of a bread-and-butter business computer in 1987 are not terribly different from the designs of 1965. Some marginal architectural improvements have been made, and enormous improvements in component cost and performance have been achieved. Nevertheless, the latest computers embody concepts that have been floating around for decades.

Innovation in the industry has tended to be incremental, focused on addressing the needs defined at the margins of existing markets and on improving established products by the use of faster, cheaper components. Since the mid-1970s, the market for smaller, cheaper computers has grown the most and in this area government users have been stragglers on a trail blazed by business users.

In the United States the government has mostly supported basic research, innovative and untried designs for large computer systems, and high-performance components. However, the expensive, high-performance experiment of today has often worked its way down into the everyday technology of tomorrow.

Even today, in the commodity computer market of the 1980s, it is not difficult to identify key pieces of technology that can be traced back to government-supported research projects. The computer networks that link today's mini- and microcomputers to other machines, the fancy graphics, the "mouse" and graphics tablet used to draw complex designs, the modems that bring computer users together over the public telecommunications network—all have at least some roots in expensive and exotic research projects funded by the taxpayer in past decades.

And products that are now at the leading edge of the commercial market—systems and languages using the concepts of "artificial intelligence," special computers designed to run this programming efficiently, new and different kinds of computers with "parallel" processing capabilities, ever more powerful supercomputers—are just emerging from research programs fueled by government spending.

In short, although the enormous industry that the computer has spawned now drowns in its vastness the relatively small sums that are expended on leading-edge technology by government agencies, public support still primes the pump of tomorrow's technology. Recent changes in the industry promise an ever more competitive, increasingly internationalized industry. Consequently, levering the fairly small but very important sums spent on leading-edge research and development into effective support for commercial competition has acquired renewed importance.

Implications for High-Technology Industries

This book has analyzed the complex web of events that led to the creation of the computer and the computer industry. This particular group of technologies, so economically and strategically significant, with its pervasive effects on society, creates an intrinsically important story, offering some broad insights into the present and future of the industry.

I have described the details of a shifting alliance between government and industry, a partnership that was reflected in the dramatic postwar expansion of industrial research activity in the United States and abroad. In the beginning, that relationship largely enlisted firms, distinterestedly rising above their narrow commercial interests for the sake of the national defense. As time wore on, the economic benefits of that alliance came to be appreciated by all, and eventually, coalesced into support for a new social function of government.

Other industries, also among the most technology-intensive economic sectors, paralleled the computer industry in their development. The semiconductor industry, the aerospace industry, producers of medical, scientific and engineering instrumentation, and advanced materials firms continue to share much beyond historical similarities. Together, they account for a large part of American high-technology industry. The common denominator of these industries—a requirement for atypically heavy investments in research and development in order to even enter the market—leads them to share common economic problems and common solutions to those problems. At the same time, very different characteristics of technologies and products may lead to distinct industrial structures. A serious analysis of technology-intensive industries should focus on the following issues.

APPROPRIABILITY. As noted earlier, in electronics and electrical equipment in general, and computers in particular, patents have rarely been crucial in determining the outcome of competition among firms. The limited ability of firms to build patent walls around innovations contrasts with the situation in certain other technology-intensive industries, particularly chemicals and pharmaceuticals, where patents have successfully protected a company's technology.

As international competition has intensified in the computer industry in recent years, an increasing emphasis has been placed on strengthening legal protections for new technology. Some firms have become more aggressive in taking legal action against infringements on their patent claims, while others have staked out new types of claims (the "look and feel" of software, for example). If these recent developments are to reverse the historical trend, their effects may work both for and against the national interest. Clearly, impeding the easy diffusion of technology to foreign firms may increase the technological rents collected by American firms in foreign markets. But making diffusion more difficult within the United States may slow down the freewheeling, fast-moving pace of technical advance that has brought demonstrably great benefits to the nation. Striking a considered and reasonable compromise ought to be an important objective of public policy in the next several years.

ECONOMICALLY STRATEGIC INDUSTRIES. Access to state-of-the-art components has been critical in producing a competitive computer system. The history of the computer industry abounds with examples of good systems designs that failed commercially because of obsolete components. This dependence is shared with all industries that rely on advanced electronics.

Because much of high-technology industry requires advanced electronic components, ensuring ready access to that componentry ought to be a central concern of contemporary technology policy. More generally, the outlines of an economically meaningful definition of a "strategic" industry may be suggested. When the technological quality of an industrial input is critical to its user industries, it can be economically important to ensure that the input not become the monopoly of a single supplier, be it a single company or a foreign country. Such a single supplier can usually maximize his profit by withholding the advanced input from the existing user industry, then enter that industry and monopolize production of the final good.[27] The resulting misallocation of resources might

---

27. See John M. Vernon and Daniel A. Graham, "Profitability of Monopolization by Vertical Integration," *Journal of Political Economy*, vol. 79 (July–August, 1971), pp. 924–25.

even justify a costly government effort to create technological competition where, otherwise, none might exist.

IMPORTANCE OF STANDARDS. Standards acquire economic significance when the cost or benefit of producing or using a product depends on the number of other users and products. In complex systems, like computers, development of pieces of a system typically means large and approximately fixed R&D costs, and the costs of adapting a given subsystem for use outside its original design parameters are high. Average cost for the product will vary in a direct way with the number of other customers and products drawing on the same technology base.

In any high-technology industry where the product is integrated into a large, complex system (for example, computers, communications, other electronic systems), the institutional incentives for, and constraints on, standard-setting activity will seriously affect market structure. The role of government in directly setting standards and overseeing the public interest in the collusive private pacts that establish technical ground rules for entire industries will become increasingly important.

RATE OF TECHNOLOGICAL CHANGE. The magnitude of the rate of technological advance directly affects the nature of industrial competition. Marginal differences in production cost, usually the key to commercial success in more mature, less rapidly evolving industries, can be dwarfed by the advantages of leading-edge technology in the most rapidly advancing products. Even large differences in manufacturing cost can be rendered irrelevant by huge declines in cost associated with improved technology—the sheer speed of technical progress can truncate normal product cycles.

Indeed sustained technological advance can indefinitely postpone the erosion of market share and profitability by foreign competitors with lower production costs as older products are rendered obsolete before low-cost imitations can move to market. And the kind of healthy, competitive market that has been created with successful entry by new challengers in computers—dependent on the pioneering of new markets and applications—is only possible when technological advance is rapid enough to create sizable new niches in which the new entrants can grow.

ECOLOGY OF A HIGH-TECHNOLOGY INDUSTRY. Competition in a product with large R&D costs—a high-tech good—appears to counterbalance two conflicting economic forces. On the one hand, the relatively fixed nature of R&D costs may tend to favor concentration in established product markets, as economies of scale and scope in the use of technology are exploited. On the other hand, the "Arrow" effect—the greater incentive that a new entrant may have to develop a new technology that at least partially displaces products of established producers in older markets—pushes outsiders to the fore as agents of technical change.

The net effect may be a dynamic balance. New firms become disproportionately important in driving new products and markets, only to grow or be absorbed into big firms as their market matures and becomes established. Or, if they are unable to make the transition, they fail. This balance between the new firm forcing its way into an industry on the strength of a leading-edge technology, and the large, established firms dominating older markets with advantages of scale and scope, seems fairly typical of a broad variety of high-technology activities.

PEOPLE AS THE MEDIUM OF TECHNOLOGY TRANSFER. The history of high-technology industry is largely the chronicle of the movement of its researchers and product developers from opportunity to opportunity. Any attempt to control or encourage the flow of technology must necessarily consider the free movement of the individuals who are ultimately the store of that technology. Even the divergence between private and social returns to investment in technology, to which public policy is addressed, is linked to the inability of a firm to capture and control the knowledge and experience absorbed by its personnel. A nation that looks to high technology for its economic future must, above all, invest in the skills of its labor force.

INTERNATIONAL ORIENTATION. High technology is inherently global in outlook. The same relative fixity of cost in technology investments, which creates economies of scale and scope in their use, also argues for the widest possible market. With a larger market, unit costs decline and returns on investments in technology increase. Marginal investments in R&D may even hinge on the extra returns that are collected in foreign markets. Any nation that stakes its economic future on living by its wits, and collecting the economic returns on investments in technology, ought to seek an open international trading system for technology-intensive goods and services.

In simpler times, America's greatest economic strengths were industrial brawn and natural resources. Today, growth and prosperity depend crucially on technology and on the capacity to cope with continuous, accelerated change. The development of the computer industry may be remembered as much for exemplifying a new pattern for economic growth, as for the world-shaking technology that it accidentally unleashed on us all.

Appendix

AN ATTEMPT to trace the impact of government-sponsored projects on an industry's technology base can be undertaken at two levels. Much of this book examines the details of how particular projects affected commercial firms with direct or indirect links to the efforts. This detailed, "micro" view, however, provides no overall, "macro" view of how representative, or significant, the outcomes of these government-sponsored activities were in relation to the technological development of the industry as a whole.

This appendix offers a macroevaluation of the overall importance of technologies derived from work enjoying significant government support. I informally canvassed the technical literature on computer design in order to locate lists of important or significant advances in computer systems. Choosing what appears on these lists, of course, is a subjective exercise, reflecting the viewpoint and biases of a particular author. But, in most cases, the lists were constructed by authors whose objectives were primarily technical, unrelated to any particular point of view on the efficacy or importance of government sponsorship of R&D in computer technology.

As noted in chapter 2, these compilations show a consistent, pervasive pattern: through the mid-1960s, by which time most elements of the standard design of the present generation of commercial computer systems had been developed, many important advances in computer design, and component technology, originated in projects receiving some form of government support.

Table A-1. *Principal Developments in Computer Technology*

Concept	Approxi-mate date	Early use of concept	Govern-ment funding for R&D	First sales to govern-ment	Comments
Components					
Rotating magnetic storage	Early 1950s	Developed by several organizations for use on first-generation computers.	Yes	Yes	ERA pioneered the technology for use by the National Security Agency
Magnetic core memory	Early 1950s	Whirlwind I at MIT	Yes	Yes	Memory Test Computer at MIT. ERA 1103 was the first production computer shipped with core memory.
Transistor	Late 1950s	TX-0 at MIT in 1956; IBM 7090 was first major commercial computer to use.	Yes	Yes	First transistors were used in military products. Other candidates are Manchester University MEG (1953); Bell labs TRADIC (1954).
Semiconductor integrated circuits	1964–65	Many computer manufacturers concurrently developed computers using ICs in the mid-1960s.	Yes	Yes	First such commercial machines shipped by SDS and RCA.
Design					
Stored program computer	1946	EDVAC report (University of Pennsylvania)	Yes	Yes	EDVAC report, joint product of Eckert-Mauchly, von Neumann. All three projects received government funding.
	1949	EDSAC (Cambridge University)	Yes	Yes	
	1952	IAS (Princeton University)	Yes	Yes	
Index register	1950	Manchester Mark I. Later other machines continued to advance effective address-calculating process.	Yes	Yes	Supported by British Ministry of Defence.

Feature	Year	Example			Comments
Error correcting code	1950	Hamming code, later used on Rice I computer.	Yes	Yes	Hamming worked at Bell labs. Rice computer supported by AEC.
Microprogramming	1951	EDSAC 2 (1958); the IBM 360 computers (1964); elements can be found in MIT Whirlwind (1951).	Yes	No	Concept introduced by M. Wilkes, Cambridge University. Whirlwind funded by government; System 360 a commercial project.
Interrupt mechanism	1953	ERA 1103	Yes	Yes	
Graphics display	1953	MIT Whirlwind	Yes	Yes	
Floating-point hardware	1955	IBM 704	No	Yes	Other possible claimants are Amdahl's WISC, at University of Wisconsin (1954), funded by university; CEC 205 (1954). First 704 shipped to AEC lab at Livermore in 1955.
I/O Processors:					
A. Data channel	1958	IBM 709	No	Yes	First 709 shipped to AEC Livermore lab.
B. Programmable I/O processor	1963	Control Data 6600	Yes	Yes	First 6600 shipped to AEC Livermore lab.
Redundancy	1957	SAGE air defense system	Yes	Yes	
Cache memories	1958	IBM 360/85 (1969)	No	n.a.	First commercial use.
Hardware pushdown stacks	1960	English Electric, KDF-9	No	No	Alternate U.S. candidate is Burroughs D-825 military computer.
Instruction pipelining	1961	IBM 7030 Stretch	Yes	Yes	
Multiple arithmetic units	1961	IBM 7030 Stretch	Yes	Yes	
Hardware protection	1962	BBN's PDP-1	No	No	
Virtual memory	1962	Atlas computer	Yes	Yes	Built by Ferranti from Manchester University design.
Multiterminal support	1962	BBN's PDP-1 system	No	No	
Tagged operands	1962	B5000?	No	No	Built by Burroughs.
Multiple central processors	1962	D-825	Yes	Yes	Military computer, built by Burroughs.

Sources: Harold S. Stone and others, "Hardware Systems," in Bruce W. Arden, ed., *What Can Be Automated? The Computer Science and Engineering Research Study* (MIT Press, 1980), pp. 319–20. Author added columns 4 through 6 and made corrections in columns 2 and 3.
n.a. Not available.

Table A-2. *Key Developments in Memory Technology*

Concept	Date	Government funding for R&D	First sales to government	Comments
Primary memory technology				
Williams tube	1948	Yes	Yes	Manchester Mark I
Mercury delay lines	1949	Yes	Yes	EDSAC
Core memory	1953	Yes	No	Memory test computer, MIT
Monolithic IC memory	1967	Yes	Yes	IBM 360/91. Special purpose memory, first commercial use of IC memory.
Secondary memory technology				
Magnetic tape				
Plastic magnetic tape	1949	Yes	Yes	First used in BINAC experimentally. Disclosed by Raytheon in 1949 and shipped in a functioning system in 1952.
Magnetic tape drive	1951	Yes	Yes	Uniservo, developed by Remington-Rand/ UNIVAC.
Vacuum column	1953	No	Yes	IBM 726 drive, shipped with IBM 701.
Two-gap head	1958	No	No	IBM 729 tape drive
Cylic redundancy error checking codes	1965	No	No	IBM 2401 tape drive
High-torque, low-inertia motor	1969	No	No	IBM 2420 tape drive
Magnetic disk files				
Magnetic drum storage	1948	Yes	Yes	Demon system, built for naval intelligence by ERA. First shipped in a commercial computer system in the ERA 1101, delivered in 1950 to NSA.
Hydrodynamic (self-acting) air bearing	1956	Yes	Yes	First used on magnetic disk drive in North American Aviation/Autonetics RE-COMP military computer in 1956; also developed for magnetic drum for SAGE computer by IBM in 1957.

Table A-2. *(continued)*

Concept	Date	Government funding for R&D	First sales to government	Comments
Moving-head disk drive	1957	No	No	IBM 350 unit. Had laminated metal head, hydrostatic (pressurized) air bearing. Prototype demonstrated in 1955; shipped with IBM RAMAC 305 system in 1957.
Moving-head disk drive with hydro-dynamic air bearing	1962	Yes	Yes	IBM 1301 drive, developed for Stretch.
Magnetic card	1962	No	No	NCR. Card Random Access Memory System
Removable moving-head disk	1963	No	No	IBM 1311
Ferrite head	1966	No	No	IBM 2314 drive
Composite ferrite-ceramic-glass head	1971	No	No	IBM 3330 drive
Winchester taper-flat slider	1973	No	No	IBM 3340 drive
Magnetic thin film head	1979	No	No	IBM 3370 drive

Sources: Martin H. Weik, "A Third Survey of Domestic Electronic Digital Computing Systems," Report 1115 (Aberdeen, Md.: Aberdeen Proving Grounds, 1961), pp. 237, 817, 978–79; John Varick Wells, "The Origins of the Computer Industry: A Case Study in Radical Technological Change" (Ph.d. dissertation, Yale University, 1978), p. 268; the following citations appear in *IBM Journal of Research and Development*, vol. 25 (September 1981): E. W. Pugh and others, "Solid State Memory Development in IBM," p. 591; A. Padegs, "System/360 and Beyond," p. 387; L. D. Stevens, "The Evolution of Magnetic Storage," pp. 666–67, 669–72; and J. M. Harkers and others, "A Quarter Century of Disk File Innovation," pp. 678, 681–82; Samuel S. Snyder, "Computer Advances Pioneered by Cryptologic Organizations," *Annals of the History of Computing*, vol. 2 (January 1980), p. 61; Charles J. Bashe and others, *IBM's Early Computers* (MIT Press, 1986), pp. 195, 287; Edward K. Yasaki, "Fragments of Computer History," *Datamation*, vol. 22 (September 1976), p. 135; and telephone interview with Louis D. Stevens, October 6, 1986.

Table A-3. *Important Technological Advances in Computer Hardware*

Concept	Date	Early use	Government funding for R&D	First sales to government	Comments
Memory organization					
Index register	1949	Manchester Mark I (U.K.)	Yes	Yes	Funded by British Ministry of Defence.
Indirect addressing	1955	IBM 704	No	Yes	First machine shipped to AEC lab at Livermore.
Programmed segments	1961	Rice University computer	Yes	Yes	Funded by AEC.
Boundary register set	1962	IBM 7094	No	Yes	First machine delivered to AEC Livermore lab.
Paging	1962	Ferranti/Manchester Atlas	Yes	Yes	Development supported by funding from NRDC.
Named segments	1964	Burroughs B5500	No	No	No direct channel known.
Protected pages	1965	IBM System 360	No	No	
Two-boundary register set	1965	UNIVAC 1108	No	No	No direct channel known.
Protected words	1966	IBM 1800	No	No	Machine was used for industrial process control.
Pages and segments	1966	GE 645	Yes	Yes	Development funded by DARPA as part of Project MAC.
	1966	IBM 360/67	No	No	Drew heavily on ideas from MIT CTSS system.
Named, shared segments	1968	Burroughs B6500	No	No	No direct channel known.
Processor parallelism					
Serial-by-bit organization	1946	EDVAC design	Yes	Yes	First machines built were EDSAC, BINAC and SEAC.
Parallel-by-bit organization	1950	ERA 1101	Yes	Yes	Designed for and delivered to NSA.
Interrupts	1953	ERA 1103	Yes	Yes	First delivered to AEC Livermore lab; used in ballistic missile early warning system.
One-instruction buffer	1960	IBM 7090	No	Yes	
Lookahead	1961	IBM 7030 Stretch	Yes	Yes	Funded by NSA and AEC.
Multiple instruction buffers, data operators in processor	1964	Control Data 6600	Yes	Yes	First delivered to AEC Livermore lab; advance payments.
Pipelining	1967	IBM 360/91	Yes	Yes	First delivered to NSA, R&D support given.

Processor functions

Microprogramming	1951		No	No	Proposed by Wilkes at Cambridge. First implemented in EDSAC 2, 1958.
I/O Channel	1958	First used on IBM 709	No	Yes	First delivered to AEC Livermore lab.
Microprogramming	1961	TRW AN/UYK military series	Yes	Yes	Also used in EDSAC 2, 1958.
Microprogramming	1965	IBM System 360	No	No	First commercial use.
Specialized algorithms	1968	IBM 2938	No	No	Hardware used to speed up specialized operations.
Array processor	1968	ILLIAC IV	Yes	Yes	Delivered in 1972. Special hardware for matrix arithmetic.

Processor structure

One processor	1949	EDSAC	Yes	Yes	
Two computers, duplexed	1957	SAGE	Yes	Yes	
One processor, multiple I/O channels	1958	IBM 709	No	Yes	
Multiple processors, Multiple I/O channels	1962	Burroughs D-825	Yes	Yes	Military computer.
Two computers, duplexed	1962	ComLogNet	Yes	Yes	Two types of duplexed processors incorporated into a node of a military store-and-forward network.
Local area network	1964	Octopus network	Yes	Yes	Built at AEC Livermore lab.
Wide area network	1966	ARPANET	Yes	Yes	Sponsored by DARPA; first network experiments in 1966. ARPANET became operational in 1973.

Sources: C. Gordon Bell and Allen Newell, *Computer Structures: Readings and Examples* (McGraw-Hill, 1971), fig. 2c, p. 45, p. 71; Maurice Wilkes, *Memoirs of a Computer Pioneer* (MIT Press, 1985), p. 188; Simon Lavington, *Early British Computers: The Story of Vintage Computers and the People Who Built Them*, p. 114; Bashe and others, *IBM's Early Computers*, p. 180; Kenneth Flamm, *Targeting the Computer: Government Support and International Competition* (Brookings, 1987), pp. 59–60; Daniel P. Siewiorek, C. Gordon Bell, and Allen Newell, *Computer Structures: Principles and Examples* (McGraw-Hill, 1982), p. 393; Martin H. Weik, "A Fourth Survey of Domestic Electronic Digital Computing Systems," Report 1227 (Aberdeen Proving Ground, Md.: Ballistic Research Laboratories, 1964), pp. 259, 375–78; and R. Moreau, *The Computer Comes of Age: The People, the Hardware and the Software* (MIT Press, 1984), p. 116. Author added final comments and minor adjustments to source material.

Table A-4. *Important Technological Advances in Computer Software*

Concept	Date	Early use	Government funding for R&D	First sales to government	Comments
Time-sharing operating systems					
Special purpose time-sharing systems					
	1957	SAGE	Yes	Yes	
First general purpose time-sharing systems					
	1962	BBN PDP-1 system	No	No	No direct channel known.
	1962	MIT CTSS system	Yes	Yes	First large-scale, practical system.
	1963	SDC Q-32 system	Yes	Yes	
	1965	PDP-6 time-sharing system	No	No	No direct channel known.
	1966	Project Genie system	Yes	Yes	Developed at Berkeley for SDS 940.
Remote job entry-oriented operating systems					
	unknown	Project Rye, NSA	Yes	Yes	Sperry Rand dominated commercial field in late 1960s.
	1963	Carnegie RJE system	Yes	No	
Dedicated application time-sharing systems					
	1963	JOSS	Yes	Yes	Algebraic interpretation system, developed at RAND.
	1964	Basic	Yes	No	Jointly developed by GE and Dartmouth, with NSF funding.
	1964	Culler-Fried system	Yes	Yes	Developed at TRW.
	1965	SABRE air reservation system	No	No	Drew on SAGE experience; developed by IBM for American Airlines; first large-scale real-time transaction-processing system.

Second-generation time-sharing systems

Year	System			Notes
1966	First version of IBM CP/CMS	No	No	None; run on IBM 360/40; later adapted to 360/67; built on CTSS.
1968	First experimental Multics	Yes	Yes	Developed at MIT, built on CTSS.
1968	TSS for IBM 360/67	No	No	Largely regarded as a failure.
1972	TENEX operating system	Yes	Yes	Developed for DARPA, at BBN; used as base for DEC TOPS-20 system.
1973	UNIX operating system in regular use	No	No	Developed at Bell labs; designed for software portability; later development enjoyed DARPA support.

Batch operating systems

Simple monitors

Year	System			Notes
1954	Whirlwind comprehensive operating system	Yes	Yes	Developed at MIT for Project Whirlwind.
1955	GM monitor for IBM 701	No	No	Developed by General Motors.
1959	SHARE operating system	No	No	For IBM 704; developed by General Motors and North American Aviation, distributed through the SHARE users group.

Multiprogramming, multiprocessor operating systems

Year	System			Notes
1960	First multiprogramming system	No	No	Experimental system built for Stretch.
1961	First use of virtual memory	Yes	Yes	Atlas Supervisor, built for Ferranti/Manchester Atlas.
1963	First multiprocessor system	Yes	Yes	Developed by Burroughs for D-825 military computer.

Advanced, third-generation operating systems

Year	System			Notes
1963	Master Control program	No	No	Developed by Burroughs for B5000.
1965	IBSYS, for IBM 7090	No	No	Developed by IBM.
1966	OS/360 (first versions)	No	No	Developed by IBM.

Table A-4. (continued)

Concept	Date	Early use	Government funding for R&D	First sales to government	Comments
Major programming languages					
APT	early 1950s	First for specialized application (numerical control)	Yes	Yes	Developed on MIT Whirlwind.
Fortran	1954	First widely used algebraic language	No	No	Developed at IBM.
Flowmatic	1955	First business language	No	No	Developed at Remington Rand.
IPL	1957	First list processing language	No	No	Developed at Carnegie-Mellon.
Comit	1957	First string processing language	No	No	Later replaced by Snobol, developed at Bell labs.
Cobol	1959	Most used business language	Yes	Yes	Sponsored by DOD, required in defense procurement.
Algol 60	1960	Theoretical algebraic language	No	No	Developed by international committee, heavy European influence.
Lisp	1960	Main list processing language	No	No	Developed by John McCarthy; main language of AI; later funded by DARPA.
Jovial	1959	First real-time control language	Yes	Yes	Developed at SDC for DOD; still used.
GPSS	1961	First widely used simulation language	No	No	
APL	1962	Interactive algebraic language	No	No	Developed at IBM.
Basic	1965	Widely used algebraic language	Yes	No	GE and NSF supported development at Dartmouth.

Name	Year	Description			Notes
PL/I	1965	Powerful algebraic language	No	No	Developed by IBM with SHARE.
Pascal	1970	First widely used language using structured programming concepts	No	No	Developed at University of Zurich.
C	1973	General purpose language	No	No	Developed at Bell labs; easy to write compilers (portability).

Assemblers, loaders, compilers

Name	Year	Description			Notes
First subroutine library	1950	EDSAC	Yes	No	Developed at Cambridge, U.K.
First compiler	1952	AUTOCODE, used on Manchester Mark I	Yes	Yes	Developed for nuclear weapons research, restricted use.
First commercial compiler	1952	A-0	No	No	Developed for Remington Rand by Grace Hopper.
First algebraic language compiler	1953	Laning and Zierler system	Yes	No	Developed for Whirlwind at MIT.
First assembler	1956	SHARE assembly program	Yes	No	Developed at United Aircraft; distributed by SHARE IBM users group.
First macro assembler	1960	Bell assembler	No	No	Written by McIlroy and Eastwood at Bell labs.
First widely used macro assembler	1961	Developed for PDP-1	No	No	Developed at MIT.
First linking loader	1963		No	No	Developed at MIT.

Sources: See table A-3; Flamm, *Targeting*, p. 56; M. A. Auslander, D. C. Larkin, and A. L. Scherr, "The Evolution of the MVS Operating System," and R. J. Creasy, "The Origin of the VM/370 Time-Sharing System," *IBM Journal of Research and Development*, vol. 27 (September 1981), pp. 472, 485, respectively; Norman Weizer, "A History of Operating Systems," *Datamation*, vol. 27 (January 1981), pp. 118–19; C. Gordon Bell, J. Craig Mudge, and John E. McNamara, *Computer Engineering: A DEC View of Hardware Systems Design* (Digital Press, 1978), pp. 490–91, 511; interview with Arnold Cohen and Sidney Rubens, February 7, 1984; and Jean E. Sammet, *Programming Languages: History and Fundamentals* (Prentice-Hall, 1969), pp. 4, 143–44, 176, 229, 316, 331, 406, 416, 524–25, 542, 605, 653.

Index

Advanced computer architecture: Burroughs' experience, 118; EDVAC, 105; federal funding role, 28, IBM Systems Network Architecture, 244; innovations in, 13, 18, 21–23; origins in Stretch computer, 92–93; von Neumann design, 106. *See also* Electronic digital computers; Mainframe computers

AEC. See Atomic Energy Commission

Aiken, Howard, 8, 41, 58, 61, 113. 131, 159

ALGOL computer language, 166

Alexander, S. N., 69n

Alrich, John 67n

Amdahl, Gene M., 84, 141, 195, 58n, 64n

Analog computer, 32n, 123; development by RCA, 36, 52, 57, 58, 83; IBM's "Bomb-Nav," 87

Apple: graphic display systems, 24; microcomputers, 227–28

Argonne National Laboratory, 52

Aron, Raymond, 154n

ARPA. *See* DARPA

Arrow, Kenneth J., 227n

Artificial intelligence: as leading-edge technology, 254; defined, 27, 46n: federal funding, 26, 27, 28; Japanese R&D investments, 190–91

Asher, Norman J., 17n

Atanasoff, John W., 31, 32

Atherton, W. A., 127n

AT&T: barred from commercial computer manufacturing, 120; development of digital data communications, 89; UNIX operating system, 121, 215, 245. *See also* Bell Telephone Laboratories

Atlas computer, 45

Atomic Energy Commission (AEC): Livermore Laboratory, 91, 109–10; Los Alamos National laboratory, 91; software development, 27, 90; supercomputer development, 20, 21

Auerbach, Isaac L., 169n

Ballistic Missile Early Warning System, 93–94

Bamford, James, 41n

Bashe, Charles S., 19n, 31n, 32n

Basic research: and technological advances, 219; federal funding, *1960s*, 253; organizations for, 246, percentage of U.S. computer industry R&D, 23n, 218n; nonproprietary, 217–18; on semiconductors, 246

Bauer, Friedrich L., 159n

Baum, Claude, 88n

Beck, Bob, 129

Belady, L. A. 93n

Bell, C. Gordon, 19n, 52n, 92n

Bell Telephone Laboratories, 117; 30–36, 48; impact on computer technology, 119–22; military contacts, 119–21; R&D expenditures as percentage of income, 122; semiconductor technology advancement, 119; software development, 121

Ballan, Betrand, 159

Bemer, R. W. 96n

Bendix Aviation, 66; development of G-15 computer, 66, 67, 75, 112

Berston, Joseph, 184n

Besen, Stanley M., 214n

Betts, Paul, 246n

Biddle, A. G. W., 233n

Bigelow, Julian, 52n

BINAC, 51, 66

Bloch, Erich, 63n

Bloch, Richard, M., 60, 114n

Blum, Joseph, 38n

Bombe, 61; origins, 37; technology employed in, 37n

Booth, Andrew, 142n, 147

Boyle, Brian, 246n

Brandin, D., 244n

Brock, Gerald W., 85n

Brooks, Frederick P., 60

271

Brown, W S. 16n
Buck, Dudley, 56n
Bull, Fredrick Rosing, 151n
Bull, France, 171; acquisition by GE, 126, 154; development of electronic calculator, 151; general purpose computer manufacturer, 152; supercomputer, 153
Burks, Arthur W., 57n
Burroughs Corporation, 67, 96, 104; advanced computer architecture, 118; development as computer manufacturer, 116–18; IBM competitor, 102, 103; market edge, 117; scientific processor, 118, 120
Bush, Vannevar, 31, 32, 32n, 36, 42, 47, 48
Business computers: IBM development 94, 231; modern design, 80–81n

CALDIC, 20, 43
Caldwell, Samuel, 31, 48
California Institute of Technology, 66; Jet Propulsion Laboratory, 116
Cambridge University, U.K., 138
Campaigne, Howard, 38n, 41n, 61n
Cane, Alan, 196n
Card programmed calculator (CPC), 68
Carpenter, B. E., 137n
Caruso, Denise, 243n
Case, P. W., 212n
Cass, James, 65n
Cathode ray tubes (CRTs), 14n, 56, 57, 74
Centralab: development of electronic circuit components, 17
Centralized computer installations: shift away from in 1980s, 239
Central processor: function explained, 11; technological innovations, 11, 21–23
Chao, S. K., 21n
CIL. See Compagnie International pour l'Informatique
Clark, Rodney, 191n
COBOL, language, 25, 26, 60, 124
Cochrane, Rexmond C., 69n
Cohen, Arnold A., 43n, 83n, 109n
Cohen, Charles L., 194n, 245n
Colossus, Mark II, U.K., 39, 136, 138, 251, 252
Columbia University, 31
Commercial competition: and compatible computer lines, 131–32; and technological advances, 257; and technological differentiation, 4, 226–32; dynamics, 203–34; European versus U.S. strategies, 170; Japanese versus European strategies, 172–73; Japan's challenge to IBM, 232–34; responses to IBM market domination, 217–27, 131–32; relation of tech-

nological change to competition, 257; role of economics of scale and scope, 210–12; role of industry standards, 243, 247–51; specialized markets, 105–07
Communications, computers: and commercial markets, 238; innovations, 84, 120; integration with communications equipment, 2; military applications, 90
Communications Supplementary Activities Washington (CSAW), 39
Compagnie International pour l'Informatique (CII), France, national champion firm, 155
Compatible computers, 124; as competitive strategy, 97; Honeywell line, 114; IBM market dominance, 98, 213; Japan, 189; manufacturers, 188; PDP-11 lines, 128–29; UNIX, 245
Compton, Karl T., 36n
Computation on computers: speeds, 8; related systems, 115
Computer components: improvements 8–9, 13, 19–21; military R&D expenditures, 109; technological advances in electronic components, 81n, 236
Computer Control Corporation, 114, 131
Computer manufacturers: as reshapers of industrial economy, 257–58; European firms, 134–71; IBM and chief U.S. competitors, 102–33; industrial competition, 203–34; Japanese firms, 172–258; origins in military projects, 29–77; post-WW II development of U.S. firms, 80–133; U.S. domestic and international market shares, 135
Computer projects, Australia: SILLIAC, CSIRAC, 52
Computer projects, France: CUBA, 151; Gamma ET, 152
Computer projects, Israel: WEIZAC, 52
Computer projects, Japan: Cosmos series, 194; FACOM *230–50*, 180; Librascope LPG-*30*, 183; M-*1*, 176; M-*113*, 177; M-*382*, 199; Parametron, 177; Tokyo Automatic (TAC), 174; *8700–8800* systems, 189, 3.5 generation program, 193, 53n. *See also* Pattern Information Processing System (PIPS)
Computer projects, Sweden: BESK, 52, 170n; SMIL, 52
Computer projects, U.K.: BTM *201*, 147; Deuce, 141. 146; Elliott *400* series, 142, 145; Heath Robinson, 36n; KDF-*9*, 146; KDP-*10*, 146; Mark I, 142, 143; Megacycle Engine (MEG), 143; MOSAIC, 142; Muse (Atlas), 144; Pegasus, 145; TREAC, 142; *400* series, 145; *800* series,

145; *1300* series, 147; *2900* series, 145. *See also* EDSAC; Colossus Mark II

Computer projects, U.S.: ABNER, U.S. Army, 70; ALWAC, Logistic Research Corporation, 106; Apple II, Apple, 237; Athena ICBM, U.S. Air Force, 109; AVIDAC, U.S. Army, 52; BIZMAC, RCA, 123; BMEWS, U.S. Air Force, 123; Bogart, U.S. National Security Agency, 108; Bomb-Nav, IBM, 87; B *5000* and *5500*, Burroughs, 117; Cyber *205*, Control Data Corp., 112; Datamatic *1000*, Datamatic Corp. 113, 114; DATA-NET-*30*, GE, 125; Datatron, Electrodata Corp., 116; D-825, Burroughs, 117; ERMA, GE, 125; FIELDATA, U.S. Army, 97; G-15, Bendix Aviation, 66, 75, 129; JOHN-NIAC, Rand, 52; LARC, Sperry Rand, 144; Leprechaun, U.S. Air Force, 119–20; LGP-*30*, Librascope, 67, Navy Tactical Data System, 109; Nike-Xeus antiballistic missile system, U.S. Air Force, 120; ORACLE, U.S. Atomic Energy Commission, 52; ORDVAC, U.S. Army, 52; Parallel Element Processing Ensemble (PEPE), Burroughs, 117; PDP series, DEC, 127, 128; POSIX, 246; SABRE, IBM, 89; Scientific Processor, Burroughs, 118; SDS *910* series, SDS, 130; SOLO, U.S. Air Force, 122; Spectra *70*, RCA, 149, 162; Star *100*, Control Data Corp., 112; SWAC, NBS, 71, 74; S-*2000* Philco, 122; U.S. Air Force, 119; TRANSAC S-*1000* and S-*2000*, Philco, 122; TX-0 and TX-2, DEC, 127; AT&T, 121, 245; VAX *11* and *780*, DEC, 129; *100*, *200*, *400*, *600* series, GE, 125–26; Control Data model *200*, Honeywell, 114; model *205*, Burroughs, 116; model *210*, *211*, Philco, 123; model *301*, RCA, 124, 148, 154; model *304* NCR, 118, 125; model *315*, NCR, 118; *400* and *600* series, GE, 125; *501* and *601* series, RCA, 96, 124; model *604*, IBM, 63n; Defense Calculator, IBM, 82, 87,; model *701–09* (*7090*), IBM, 64, 93, 96; *1100* series, Sperry Rand, 104, 108; model *1101* and *1103*, ERA, 46n, 122; model *1401*, IBM, 96; model *1600* and *1604*, Control Data Corp., 112; model *6600*, Control Data Corp., 112; *7000* series, IBM, 53, 93–96; model *7090* and *7094*, IBM, 126; model *7600*, CDC, 112. *See also* Analog computer; BINAC; CALDIC; EDSAC; ENIAC; IBM *360* computer series; ILLIAC; MANIAC; Mark IV series; Missile guidance systems; ORDVAC; SAGE; RAYCOM; SEAC; UNIVAC; von Neumann-design computer; Whirlwind computer

Computer projects, U.S.S.R.: BESM, 52

Computer Research Corporation (CRC), 118; development of magnetic drum computers, 66

Computers, France: acquisition of BULL, 126; as nationalized industry sector, 158; business applications, 151; CAE's minicomputers, 155; national champions, 156n; origins and development of computer industry, 150–54; semiconductor champion, 158

Computers, Japan: competitive strategies, 1980s, 232–34; cooperative projects, 185–87; FONTAC project, 186; foreign technology transfers, 179, 181, 184; growth of national production, 178; IBM's Japan operations, 181–82; national development policies, 172–73, 178; origin and development of computer industry, 172–202; top manufacturers, 202

Computers, Switzerland: major innovations in software and programming concepts, 166

Computers, U.K.: business applications, 146–48; decline of manufacturers, 148–50; government research labs, 136; intelligence applications, 136; mainframe computers, 145; mathematical applications, 138; military applications, 143–46; origins and development of computer industry, 136–50; punched card equipment, 147; technological innovations, 139; technology base, post-WW II, 134; university-based research, 143; U.S. share of U.K. computer markets, 149

Computers, U.S.: development and evolution of computer industry, post-WW II, 8–28, 80–133, 235–58; role of patents in computer development, 219–24. *See also* Computer projects: U.S.; Computer manufacturers; Research & Development, Computer-related, U.S.

Computers, West Germany: academic applications, 161; commercial applications, 160–66; electronic computers, 162; mainframe development, 162; military applications, 160–61; origins and development of computer industry, 159–65; software development; 161; technological innovations originating from, 169

Computer Software Act (1980), 223

Condon, Dr. Edward V., 71
Consolidated Electrodynamics Corporation (CEC), 67; development of Datatron, 205
Control Data Corporation, 219, 232; development as supercomputer manufacturer, 112–13; Librascope computer, 67; major IBM competitor, 102, 103, 104, 108; model *604* computer, 96
Connolly, James, 179n
Corbato, Fernando, 115n
Corning Glass, 71
Corporation for Open Systems, 243
Couffignal, Louis 150
Crandall, Robert, 236n
Crawford, David, 63n
Cray Research: U.S. supercomputer manufacturer, 112–13, 219
Cray, Seymour, 153n
Creasy, R. J., 26n
Cryptanalysis: computer innovations originating in, 37, 70n; role in U.S. computer development, 39, 40, 61, 70, 229
Curtiss, John, 69, 71, 73n

Danko, S. F., 17n
Dantzig, George, 70
DARPA. See Defense Advanced Research Projects Agency
Dartmouth College: development of Basic computer language, 26
Dasgupta, Partha, 203n
Data General Corporation, 131
Datamatic Corporation, 113
Davis, Neil W., 245n
DEC. See Digital Equipment Corporation
Defense Advanced Research Projects Agency (DARPA), 117; role in developing graphics display technology, 24; time-sharing, 26, 99, 121n; R&D expenditures for supercomputer, 117; UNIX, 121n
Defense, Department of 18, 27, 115; funding for computer R&D, 16, 26, 27n, 68; procurement of IBM systems, 94; removal of computer development program from NBS, 72. See also Military sector; Defense Advanced Research Projects Agency (DARPA)
Delay relay computers, Models 5 and 6, 61
Desch, Joseph, 31, 31n, 39, 47
Devere, Gerald., 24n
Differential analyzer, 32; development program at Northrop Aircraft, 66
Digital Data Exchange Network, Japan, 198
Digital Equipment Corporation (DEC),

127, 130; as IBM competitor, 102, 103; competitive strategies, 232, 242
Dumey Arnold I., 39n
Disk storage systems, 19
Dixit, Avinash K., 216n
Doran, R. W., 137n
Dosi, Giovanni, 159n
Dunwell, Stephen W., 62n

Eastman Kodak, 41
Economies of scale and scopes: in competitive strategy, 4, 210–17; defined, 4; impact of software development on, 212; securing IBM market domination, 80
Eckert, J. Presper, 29, 33n, 47, 48, 49, 50, 51, 57, 60, 62, 64, 66, 69, 70, 73, 82, 105, 107, 252
Edison, Thomas A., 35
EDSAC, U.K., 33n, 51, 138, 146, 174
EDVAC, 49, 50, 54, 57, 70, 74, 105, 116, 137, 224
Electrical and Musical Industries (EMI), U.K., 143
Electrodata Corporation, 116
Electronic calculator: prototype, 31
Electronic digital computer, 39; as joint public-private sector venture, 69; development, 31n, 36, 81, 113, 136, 147; federal R&D funding, 40, 51; technological innovations originating from, 8, 62. See also ENIAC
Electronic equipment, 32; and hi-tech industries, 256; and technological progress, 32–33; in radar development, 33, 36. See also Electronic digital computer.
Electronics Industry Association (EIA): role in developing computer industry standards, 243
Electronics Industry Development Provisional Act, Japan, 178
Electrotechnical Laboratory (ETL), Japan, 173
Elliott Brothers, U.K., 143, 145
El-Tronics, 66
Engineering Research Associates (ERA): development of intelligence applications, 44; general purpose computer, 45, 62, 73, 83, 90, 107, 108; magnetic storage development, 19; origins, 43n, 44n, 107n; scientific computer, 113, 166, 224
Engstrom, Harold, 43n
ENIAC, 8, 29, 31–32n, 33n, 39, 48, 54, 57n, 66, 137, 141, 150, 252, 253
European Community Competitive strategies, 171; economic history of European

versus U.S. computer industry, 134;
government R&D funding, Europe versus U.S., 167; joint ventures, 246; markets for European computer, 167
Evans, Bob O., 31n, 88n, 240n
Everett, Robert, R., 46n

Fagen, M. D., 16n, 30n, 41n, 119n
Fahey, Michael, 243n
Federal government: advanced technology funding, 254; basic research funding
3, 23; declining role in computer R&D,
18, 25–26, 111; federal versus private
sector role in computer R&D, 251; fiscal
assistance to computer firms, 2, 3, 6, 16,
17–20, 25–26; math and science com-
puter R&D, 2–3, 31; military computer
R&D, 5, 16, 17, 18, 20, 23–24, 26; na-
tional labs, 35, 39; technology policy, 2–
3. See also Military sector; Private sec-
tor
Fenberg, L., 212n
Femmer, Max, 63n
Ferranti, U.K., 143, 145
Fisher, Franklin M., 83n, 211n, 235n
Fishman, Katherine Davis, 124n
Flynn, Michael J., 11n
Foreign markets, computer: IBM's role,
101
Forest, Robert B., 163n
Forrestal, James V., 42n
Forrester, Jay, W. 41, 53, 58
Fox, Philip, 63n
Frankel, Stanley, 65n
Frenkel, Karen A., 99n
Friedman, William F., 35n
Fuchi, Kazuhiro, 181n, 190n
Fujitsu, Japan, 132, 173, 179, 186, 189,
232, 233, 245; computer R&D, 175, 177,
178; IBM-compatible mainframe manu-
facturer, 164, 170, 180n; joint venture
project, 187

Gallagher, Robert T., 244n
Gardner, W. David, 60n, 113n
General Electric Corporation, 27, 83; acquisition of Bull, France, 126; as IBM
competitor, 102, 103, 114, 115, 118; development as computer manufacturer,
122, 125–27; Japan operations, 183; military computers, 125n
General Electric Corporation (GEC)
U.K., 147
General Motors (GM): graphic display
computer terminals, 24
General Precision, 66; Librascope division, 66

General purpose computers: explained,
33; ERA's role in development, 45;
U.S. Navy development, 50n; in Japa-
nese markets, 185
Glauthier, T. James, 26n
Gödel, Kurt, 33
Goldstine, Herman H., 32n, 47, 151n
Government Code and Cypher School
(GC&CS), U.K., 34, 37
Graham, Daniel A., 256n
Graphics display technology: commercial
development, 24, 56; origins in Sage
system, 23–24
Greenwood, Joen E., 211n, 235n
Gresser, Julian, 174n
Grosch, H. R. J., 85n
Groves, General Leslie R., 107
Gruenberger, Fred J., 65n

Haanstra, John 20n
Halamka, John D., 195n, 215n
Harding, William E., 220n
Hardware, computer: component func-
tions defined, 10; technological innova-
tions, 11–12. See also Advanced com-
puter architecture
Hargreaves, Barrett, 24n
Harman, Alvin, J., 67n, 101n, 149n, 185n
Harrison, Thomas J., 240n
Hartree, Douglas N., 138
Harvard University, 41; development of
Mark I-IV series, 43, 58–59; Computa-
tion Laboratory, 60
Hakozaki, Katsuya, 186n
Hatta, H., 175n
Haynes, Mike, 220n
Helland, Joe, 20n
Hendrie, Gardner, 131n
Hendry, John, 144n
Hewlett-Packard Corporation, 66; as
IBM competitor, 103
Higgins, W. H. C., 30n
High-technology industries: and elec-
tronic componentry, 256; and patents,
219–24; dynamics of industrial compe-
tition, 235–58; IBM as industry leader,
80–133; international joint development
projects, 250; international scope, 258;
organizational restructuring, 228; role
of R&D investments, 1, 2, 23n, 34n,
218; WW II as catalyst, 2
Hitachi, 132, 171, 177, 189, as IBM-compatible mainframe manufacturer, 237;
joint R&D venture, 187; supercomputer manufacturer, 233
Ho, Charles P., 19n
Hoagland, Albert S., 20n

Hockney, R. W., 12n
Hodges, Andrew, 33n, 37n, 136n
Hoff, Marcian E. Jr., 25
Hogan, C. Lester, 18n
Holbrook, B. D., 119n
Holerith, Herman, 30
Honeywell Corporation, 96; acquisition
    of GE French operations, 156–57; as
    IBM competitor, 102, 103, 104; com-
    patible computer lines, 14; develop-
    ment as computer manufacturer,
    113–16
Hopper, Grace, 60
Houg, Roy, 20n
Howlett, J., 30n, 87n
Hughes Aircraft, 67
Humphreys, Arthur, 147n, 150n
Hurd, Cuthbert C., 53n, 87n
Huskey, Harry, 66, 74, 75, 129n, 141

IAS. See Institute for Advanced Study
IBM: as U.S. market leader, 80–133;
    business computer, 65, 231; commer-
    cial spinoffs from defense contracts,
    95; competitive role shift, 230–31; fac-
    tors in early success, 82; foreign oper-
    ations, 99, 101, 166, 173; joint project
    with Harvard University (Mark I), 58–
    59; microcomputer, 240; patent cross
    licensing, 221; punched card equip-
    ment, 183; proprietary standards, 251;
    R&D as percentage of net income, 86;
    role in technological innovations, 21,
    24, 31–2, 88, 89, 90, 92; scientific ap-
    plications, 99; Systems Network Ar-
    chitecture, 244; time-sharing system,
    26. See also Computer projects: U.S.;
    Computer manufacturers.
IBM 360 computer series: compatible
    line, 98; deficiency, 99; economies of,
    96–102; functions, 98n
ICL. See International Computers Lim-
    ited
ILLIAC, 52, 117, 177
Imada, Ken, 184n
Information processing: origins in cryp-
    tanalysis, 37; technological differentia-
    tion in computers, 226
Input-output peripheral equipment: ex-
    plained, 10; graphics display terminals,
    24; IBM 350, 20; impact on IBM
    growth, 83; NBS R&D, 69, 71
Institut de Recherche d'Informatique et
    d'Automatisme (IRIA), France, 156
Institute Blaise Pascal, France, 150
Institute of Electrical & Electronic Engi-
    neers (IEEE), 243, 246

Institute for Advanced Study (IAS), 34,
    49, 50; development of von Neumann-
    designed computer, 42; commercial
    spinoffs from research, 52–53, 64, 67,
    105, 123, 150
Integrated circuit development: Europe,
    Japan, U.S., 13, 17, 17n, 18, 25
Intel Corporation: development of micro-
    processor, 24, 25, 237
International Computers & Tabulators,
    U.K., 145, 148
International Computers Limited (ICL),
    U.K., 145, 150; status as major Euro-
    pean firm, 164
International Standards Organization
    (ISO), 244
Investment, computer-related R&D: and
    production economies, 210n; federal
    versus private sector role in, 23–25;
    national policy for, 2; role in high-tech-
    nology industries, 2, 218, 23n, 24n;
    technological rents on 218
Iowa State University, 31
Ishii, Osamu, 175n
Itel, 132
Iverson, Kenneth E., 60

James, S. E., 95n
Japan Electronic Computer Corporation
    (JECC), 184
Japan Information Processing Develop-
    ment Center, 192
Japan Development Bank, 184
Jarema, David R., 89n
Jecquier, Nicholas, 149n, 155n
Jesshope, C. R., 12n
Johnson, Chalmers, 182n
Joint development projects: European
    firms, 246; impact on industrial devel-
    opment strategies, 247–51; and nonpro-
    prietary industry standards, 248; Japa-
    nese firms, 176n, 189; U.S. firms, 65n,
    121, 246
Joseph, Jonathan, 245n

Kahn, David, 35n
Kaplan, Eugene J., 178n
Katz, Barbara Goody, 67n, 108n
Katz, Michael L., 203n, 248n
Kilby, Jack S., 17n
Kilgore, Senator Harley, 68
Kimura, Tosaku, 175n
Kirby, Robert L., 38n
Knuth, Donald E., 225n
Kobayashi, Taiyu, 195n
Kuck, David J., 117n
Kyoto University, Japan, 177

Landeck, Bruce W., 240n
Languages, computer: private sector development, 25, 27. *See also* COBOL
Lavington, Simon, 137n, 139n
Le Boucher, E., 155n
Leehan, G. W., 92n, 212n
Leiner, A. L., 71n
Levin, Richard C., 16n
Lewin, Ronald, 37n
Lindamood, George E., 132n
Lindgren, Nilo A., 24n, 31n
Lineback, J. Robert, 243n
Linkups, computers: as 1980s market trend, 238–39; facilitated by ISO, 244; IBM Systems Network Architecture, 244; international, 251
Linvill, John G., 18n
Logistics Research Corporation, 66
Lorenzi, J. H., 155n
Los Alamos National Laboratory, 52
Luebbert, W. F. 97n
Lloyd, Andrew, 158n

McGee, W. C., 27n
McGowan, John J., 211n
McKie, James W., 83n
McLaughlin, Richard A., 84n
McMillan, B., 119n
McNamara, John E., 92n
Magnetic drum computers, 66; German development, 160; IBM development, 45n
Magnetic storage: innovations in, 6, 13, 14, 15, 19–21, 71n, 88, 92
Mainframe computers, 125; domestic consumption, 238; European manufacturers, 145, 162, 170–71; Japanese manufacturers, 232; loss of market dominance, 237–38
Manchester University, U.K., 57, 137, 143
Mancke, Richard B., 83n
MANIAC, 52
Manuel, Tom, 19n
Manufacturing Automation Protocol, U.S., 243
Mark I-VI series: Harvard/IBM project, 41, 43, 58–59, 61, 62, 187, 252
Market trends, computer-related, 235–58; shaped by technological advances, 4, 6, 15
Maskin, E., 203n
Massachusetts Institute of Technology (MIT): Center for Machine Computation, 55–56; development of time-sharing system, 26, 31, 32; Lincoln Laboratories, 56, 71, 72, 88, 105, 120, 123,

127; Servomechanisms Laboratory, 36 41, 43, 47, 48, 53; U.S. Navy-funded R&D, 36n
Mauchly, John W., 29, 31, 47, 48, 49, 50, 51, 57, 60, 62, 64, 66, 69, 70, 73, 82, 105, 107, 252
Maxwell, A. T., 147n, 150n
Meader, Ralph I., 44
Memory, computer internal: development in U.K., 138; function explained, 10; technological innovations, 11, 14, 58, 119–237
Mendelson, Jerry, 65n
Metropolis, N., 30n
Michigan State University, 52
Microalloy diffused transistors (MADTs): defined, 92n, 92
Microelectronics and Computer Technology Corporation, 246
Microprocessors: developed by Intel Corporation, 24, 237; domestic consumption, 238; IBM development, 240; technological origins, 19n; university-based research, 19n
Military sector: commercial spinoffs from military computers, 13–24, 17, 19–21, 24, 26–28, 29, 46, 89, 91, 111, 113, 120, 122, 123; IBM computer projects, 86–95; missile guidance systems R&D, 65–66, 87, 93, 109; R&D expenditures, Post-WW II, 78–79; technological innovations from military computers, 17–20, 22, 24, 29–77, 116; university-based research, 47
Millman, S., 16n, 122n
Mills, H. D., 95n
Minicomputers: and technological differentiation, 227; domestic consumption, 238; in West Germany, 163; manufacturers, 102, 103, 108, 131, 160; market dominance in 1980s, 239–40; origins and development, 127–31
Ministry of Defense, U.K., 138, 142
Ministry of International Trade & Industry (MITI), controls over foreign firm licensing agreements, 183, 184; policies for computer industry development, 178, 179, 182
Minker, Jack, 38n
Missile guidance systems, 65–66, 87, 109, 110n; technological origins from, 116, 120, 121
MIT. *See* Massachusetts Institute of Technology
MITI. *See* Ministry of International Trade and Industry
Mitsubishi, 183

Monopoly power: as strategic goal in hitech industries, 203; and scale and scope economies, 258; rents on technological advances, 226
Moreau, R., 62n, 110n
Mudge, J., Craig, 92n
Mumma, Robert, 31, 31n, 39, 47
Muraoka, Y., 177n
Mutanda, T., 177n

Nahajo, H., 177n
Naegele, Tobias, 95n
NASA. See National Aeronautics and Space Administration
National Advanced Systems (NAS), 132
National Aeronautics and Space Administration (NASA), 94, 95, 130; R&D expenditures for space program, 130; software development, 95
National Bureau of Standards (NBS): demise of computer R&D program, 71–72; electronic computer R&D, 51, 52, 64; magnetic disk storage R&D, 19, 43; peripherals R&D, 71; post-WW II manager of computer research, 69, 74–75, 113, 137; rebuilding computer R&D division, 73; SEAC R&D, 70
National Cash Register (NCR), 30, 31, 32, 39, 43, 47, 75; development as computer manufacturer, 118–19, 136, 252; IBM competitor, 102, 103, 104
National laboratories, 35, 39; R&D role in IAS/von Neumann-designed computer, 52. See also Atomic Energy Commission; National Applied Mathematics Laboratories (NAML); U.S. Army; U.S. Navy
National Physical Laboratory, U.K., 136
National Research Development Corporation (NRDC), U.K., 143
National science and technology policy for computer industry, post WW-II, 2–3, 69, 171
National Science Foundation (NSF), fiscal assistance for university-based research, 26, 42; role in basic research, 76, 90
National Security Agency (NSA), 91, 108, 122, 144, 224
National Semiconductor Corporation, 132
Naval Computing Machinery Laboratory (NCML), 39
NBS. See National Bureau of Standards
Nelson, Richard R., 16n, 67n, 108n, 218n
Newell, Allen, 52n, 117n
Newton, Arthur R., 18n

Newman, Max M. A., 38, 138
Niemann, Ralph A., 61n
NIH. See National Institutes of Health
Nippon Electric Corporation (NEC), Japan, 173, 175, 183, 187, 189, 233
Nippon Telephone and Telegraph (NTT): Electrical Communications laboratory, 176
Nisenoff, N., 14n
Nishi, Yoshio, 196n
Noble, David F., 42n
Norris, William, 44, 44n, 108, 111n
North American Aviation: Autonetics division, 67; development of RECOMP, 20
Northrop Aircraft, 65, 66, 68, 118
Noyce, Robert N., 25
NSA. See National Security Agency
NSF. See National Science Foundation
NTT. See Nippon Telephone and Telegraph

Oak Ridge National Laboratory, 52
Office of Naval Research (ONR), 225; CALDIC development, 20; establishment, 42; R&D expenditures, 43, 54, 59, 66, 69, 84, 113. See also U.S. Navy
Oldham, W. G., 19n
Olivetti, Italy, 126, 170
Olsen, Kenneth, 127
Operating systems: batch, 25; time-sharing, 26, 99; POSIX, 246; UNIX, 121n, 215, 245

Packard-Bell, 129
Padegs, A., 93n, 212n
Palevsky, Max, 129
Palmer, Ralph, L., 33n, 62, 63
Pantages, Angeline, 158n
Panzer, J. C., 211n
Pardo, Luis Trabb, 225n
Parmalee, R. P., 93n
Patents: cross licensing, 22, 45n; federal role, 222; granted by IBM to Japanese firms, 181; IBM portfolio, 222n; IBM proprietary rights in Stretch system, 91n; in EDVAC system, 50; role in U.S. computer industry development, 219–24; revoked on ENIAC, 31–32n; U.S. laws protecting, 223
Pattern Information Processing System (PIPS), Japan, 190–91, 198
Pearson, R. T., 21n
Pendergrass, James T., 50n
Pennick, James L., Jr., 41n

Personal computers: Apple graphics display system, 24. *See also* Minicomputers; Microprocessors
Pfefferman, Murray, 75n
Philco Corporation: as major IBM competitor, 96, 102, 103, 104, 117; development as computer manufacturer, 122–23, 127; military contracts, 16, 91
Phillips, Almarin, 67, 108n
Phister, Montgomery, Jr., 14n, 82n
Piore, Emanuel R., 84
Plan Calcul, France, 155, 158
Plan des Composants, France, 156, 158
Porter, V. J., 20n
Post Office Research Station, U.K., 38, 136, 137, 142, 252
Pre, Robert, 245n
Prices, computer: rapid decline through technological advances, 1, 13, 25. *See also* Economies of scale and scope
Prince, M. David, 24n
Prime Computer Corporation, 131
Private sector: development of major computer firms post-WW II, 80–133; federal versus private sector investments in computer R&D, 251; origins of U.S. commercial computer industry, 29, 46–51; role of industry standards, 5; technological origins from, 17, 21, 23, 25–26
Pugh, Emerson W., 40n, 84n, 87n, 160n
Punched card equipment: IBM market dominance, 30; in Japan, 173, 223; in U.K., 147; military intelligence applications, 37n, 41, 83

Quady, Emmett, 45n, 65n

Rabinow, Jacob, 19, 71n
Radar, 33; computer tracking system, 119; technological origins from, 33n
Rajchman, Jan, 32n
Ralston, Anthony, 24n, 27n
Rand Corporation: development of JOHNNIAC computer, 67; graphics display technology, 24; IOSS computer language, 26, 52
Randell, Brian, 31n, 150n
RAYCOM, 113
RAYDAC, 43, 60n, 113
Raymond, Francois, 151
Raytheon Corporation, 43, 65, 113, 114
RCA: analog computer development, 36, 52, 57, 58, 83; development as computer manufacturer, 122–25, 146, 149, 157, 188; *501* transistorized computer, 96, 111

Redmond, Kent C., 137n
Rees, Mina, 59n, 225n
Remington Rand Corporation, 30, 51, 82, 83; technological leadership, 147
Rents: on technology, defined, 218; temporary nature of, 226
Research and development (R&D), computer-related, France: national funding policy, 156, 167; national champions, 156n; national institute for, 155; absence of industry and university R&D, 151; on semiconductors, 156; Plan Calcul, 156
Research and development, computer-related, Japan: as response to IBM, 193; basic research, 173; cooperative government and private sector projects, 173, 196; government funding of research associations, 186; government labs, 176; joint domestic industry ventures, 189; law supporting, 178; national policies, 178, 184, 188; NTT's role, 197–200; semiconductor research, 189–90; software development, 192; through foreign technology transfers, 179, 182
Research and development, computer-related, U.K.: government funded, 141, 142; government R&D funding, U.K. versus U.S., 143; IBM funded, 99; intelligence applications, 37–39; military applications, 143–46; post-WW II policy for technology development, 166–67; university funded, 137–40
Research and development, computer-related, U.S.: as part of competitive strategy, 217; as percentage of IBM's net income, 86; corporate role, 89, 121; declining federal role, 111, 253; federal funding to industry, 3, 16, 18–20, 116, 123, 253, 254; federal versus private sector investments, 251; impact of IBM market dominance, 80; impact on price declines, 1; in government labs, 17, 19, 35; military applications, 5, 16–18, 20, 25–27, 41, 116, 119, 120, 123; NBS role, 74–75; private sector funding, 6, 17, 18, 20, 25, 26, 89, 121, 122, 236; scientific applications, 48, 94, 112, 128, 129, 130; university based, 18, 20, 24, 26, 53–58
Research and development, computer-related, West Germany: funding for mainframe computers, 162, IBM funded, 99, 101; state funding for hardware and software development, 163; state role parallel to U.S. government R&D role, 167

Rochester, Nathaniel, 63n
Rota, Gian-Carlo, 30n, 87n
Rubens, Sidney, 109n
Rymaszewski, E. J., 92n, 212n

SAGE air defense system, 21, 23, 27, 58, 87, 116, 120, 127, 156; development costs, 88; real-time control, 106; technological innovations originating from, 89
St. Clair, Hal K., 240n
Saloner, Garth, 214n
Sammett, J. E., 27n, 51n
Sanger, David E., 231n
Sangiovanni-Vincentelli, Alberto L., 19n
Scalzi, C. A., 93n
Scheaffer, Craig R., 73n
Schnockel, J. W., 21n
Schreyer, Helmut, 159
Scientific computers: IBM's R&D investments, 17, 99; origins in Electronic Research Associates and U.S. Navy computers, 113
SEAC, 14n, 15, 45n, 57n, 70, 71, 74
Seeber, Rex R., 62
Seifert, William E., 27n
Selective Sequence Electronic Calculator (SSEC), 61
Selmer, Ernst, 67n
Semiconductors: basic research, 246; French R&D, 156; IBM R&D, 119, 236; IBM's technological edge, 233; invention, 15; Japanese R&D, 189–90; price performance, 25; technological advances, 19n, 237; U.S. military R&D, 16
Semiconductor Research Corporation, 246
Seraphim, D. P., 212n
Serial design computer. See von Neumann design
Servan Schreiber, Jean Jacques, 133n
Shapiro, C., 203n, 247n
Shapiro, Carl, 248n
Sherry, Michael S., 42n
Shockley, William, 57n
Siemens, West Germany, 157, 159, 161, 170; electronic computer development, 160; Fujitsu vendor, 164; leading mainframe manufacture, 162
Schussel, George, 231n
Silbertson, Z. A., 219n
Silo project, 91
Slutz, Ralph J., 74n
Snyder, Samuel S., 41n, 44n, 83n
Software development: Bell Laboratories, 21; copyright protection, 223; evolution, IBM, 241; IBM/GE compatible software lines, 126n; industry standards, 245–46; Japanese R&D, 189, 192; linked with information processing innovations, 96; private sector leadership, 25–26; scientific and engineering applications, 68, 80; U.S. federal R&D, 26, 27, 95; West Germany, 161
Spinrad, Robert L., 130n, 207n
Sprague, Richard E., 65n
Software Productivity Consortium, 246
Sperry Rand Corporation: as major IBM competitor, 62, 103; components developed for AEC supercomputer, 20; development as computer manufacturer, 107–11, 120, 125, 144, 231; technological edge, 107
Standard Elektrik Lorentz, West Germany, 160
Standard Modular Systems (SDS), 92
Standards, computer industry-related: defined, 5; developers, 243, 244; economic impact of industrywide, 242–46, 257; for software, 246; IBM proprietary, 251; impact of international joint development projects on nonproprietary, 246–51
Stern, Nancy, 222n
Stevens, Louis D., 20n, 89n
Stibitz, George R., 30, 30n, 32, 48, 60, 159
Stiglitz, Joseph E., 216n
Stoneman, Paul, 221n
Stretch computer, 21; 62n, 90, 94, 144; technology originating from, 91, 92, 93n
Strom, Leland D., 17n
Suekane, Ryota, 173n
Supercomputers: AEC development program, 20, 21; Control Data Corporation R&D, 96, 112; Cray Research Corporation R&D, 112–13; ETL Mark VI, Japan, 187; Gamma 60, France, 153; IBM development program, 103n; UNIVAC LARC, 152; ILLIAC IV, 117, 123; Manchester Atlas, U.K., 152. See also Stretch computer
Sussenguth, Edward H., 89n
Swiss Federal Polytechnic Institute, Switzerland, 159, 166
Systems Network Architecture (SNA), 140
Systems Development Corporation: development of Jovial computer language, 26

Tahara, Soichiro, 195n

Takahasi, Hidetosi, 173n
Tandem computers, 131
Takahashi, Shigeru, 179n
Tape processing machine, IBM, 64
Taylor, C. T., 219n
Technical University of Berlin, West
  Germany, 159
Technological differentiation, computer-
  related: as market strategy, 4; in specialized markets, 105; role in computer
  competition, 226–32
Technological progress, computer-related: effect on copyright protection,
  219–24, 247–51; impact on economies
  of scale and scope, 14, 210–17; impact
  on restructuring post-WW II economy,
  1–2, 255–58; international orientation,
  258; major technological innovations,
  8–28; national policies for, 2–3; private
  sector versus federal funding role, 251–
  53; relations of change rate to competition, 6, 257; rents on progress, 218,
  226; role of personnel in technology
  transfer, 251–53; U.S. versus Europe,
  post-WW II, 167, 169, 170–71
Technology transfer, nature of, 217–18
Telecommunications Research Establish-
  ment (TRE), U.K., 37, 38, 136, 137,
  138
Telefunken, West Germany, 162
Texas Instruments, 18
Thomas, Richard B., 75n
Thornton, James, 109n, 153n
Tilton, John E., 156n, 220n
Time-sharing computer systems: DARPA
  R&D, 26, 28; general purpose system,
  128; IBM 360 series, 99; Japanese
  R&D, 189–90; Project MAC, 115;
  SDS's supplier role, 130; technological
  origins of, 99; UNIX system, 121, 126
Todd, John, 71n
Tohoku University, Japan, 177
Tokjo, Akio, 190n
Tomash, Erwin, 43n; 83n
Tomayko, James E., 49n
Toshiba Corporation, Japan, 174, 175,
  183, 189
Trade: Distribution of computer firms in
  international markets, 135; Japanese
  computer imports, 80; Japanese import
  policy, 188–89n; U.S. computer im-
  ports, 239. See also Patents: cross li-
  censing.
Transistorized computers, 114; Japanese,
  175, 177, 185; origins in missile guidance systems, 116, 122, 124, 129
Travis, Irwin, 116

TREAC, U.K., 142
Tropp, Henry, 31n, 66n
Truman, President Harry S., 42
TRW, 67
Turing, Alan, 33, 33n, 37, 49, 136, 137

Unidata, pan European computer com-
  pany, 157, 159
UNISYS, 17
United Aircraft, computer division, 67
UNIVAC, 14n, 20n, 51, 60, 64, 69, 70,
  73, 82, 96, 103, 105, 107, 109, 110, 120,
  144, 229, 231
University-based research, 18, 20, 24, 26,
  31, 121, 167
University of California, Berkeley:
  CALDIC development, 43; magnetic
  recording technology developed by
  San Jose laboratory, 20; semiconduc-
  tor innovation, 19n
University of California, Los Angeles,
  66, 70, 72; Institute of Numerical Anal-
  ysis, 70
University of California, Stanford: Stan-
  ford Research Institute, 24, 125
University of Illinois, 52, 117
University of Pennsylvania, 40; Moore
  School, 47, 49
University of Tokyo, 173, 174, 176, 177
U.S. Air Force, 59, 116, 119, 122, 123;
  Cambridge Research Center, 108; computer-related procurement projects, 18,
  69; R&D expenditures, 17, 23, 24, 55,
  66, 87, 108, 109. See also Missile guidance systems
U.S. Army: Aberdeen Proving Grounds,
  32; Ballistic Research Laboratory
  (BRL), 47, 48; Office of Scientific Research and Development, 48; semiconductor R&D expenditures, 17
U.S. Navy, 69, 109; Bureau of Aeronautics, 42; Naval Computing Machinery
  Laboratory (NCML), 44, 52, 252; Naval Research Laboratory, 35, 44n;
  Navy Tactical Data System, 109; R&D
  expenditures, 61, 87; technology development, 34–36, 41, 44, 113; U.S. Navy
  intelligence, 35; U.S. War Department,
  funding for differential analyzer, 32

Van Dam, A., 24n
Ventry, John W., 132n
Vernon, John M., 256n
Vernon, Raymond, 209n
VHSIC (Very High Speed Integrated Cir-
  cuit) program, Defense Department de-
  velopment, 115n

Viehe, F. W., 220n
VLSI (Very Large-Scale Integrated Circuits), France, 158; Japan, 196
von Braun, Werner, 129
von Neumann design computer, 12; application to scientific computers, 53, 57, 62, 65, 67, 105, 123, 136, 252; described, 11n, 13, 34, 45, 49, 52
Vysottsky, Victor, 92n

Walker, Dennis M., 24n
Wallace, Henry A., 68
Walsh, J. L., 92n
Walther, Alwin, 161n
Wang, An, 58, 59, 131
Wang Laboratories, Inc.: as minicomputer manufacturer, 103, 131; origins, 60
Warren, C. A., 16n, 119n
Watson, Thomas, J., Sr., 59, 61, 64, 84, 88
Watson, Thomas, J., Jr., 64, 76, 84, 85, 88
Watters, S. E., 120n
Webbink, Douglas W., 220n
Wedgewood-Benn, Anthony, 149
Weeks, Sinclair, 72, 73
Weik, Martin, H., 74n, 87n
Wiener, Norbert, 56n
Welchman, Gordon, W., 37, 38n
Wells, John Varick, 77n, 219n
Welsh, H. J., 20n
Wenger, Rear Admiral Joseph, 44n
Western Electric: government procurement projects, 16, 88

Wexelblat, R. L., 25n
Whirlwind computer, 56, 207, 224; commercial spinoffs, 56n, 105, 123, 127, 142; MIT project, 5, 23, 41, 43, 45, 50; origins and influence on computer industry, 53–58, 64, 87; technical specialization, 105; military R&D expenditures, 76
White, Charles, 146n
Wildes, Karl C., 24n 31n, 56n
Wilkes, Maurice, V., 50, 99n, 137, 138
Wilkinson, J. H. 141n
Williams, F. C., 57, 138
Williams, M. R., 59n
Williams, S. B., 60
Willig, R. D., 211n
Witt, R. P., 71n
World Trade Corporation, IBM, 101
Worthy, James L., 112n
Wynn-Williams, C. E., 31

Xerox Corporation as IBM competitor, 102, 114, 130; development of graphics display technology at Palo Alto Research Center, 24

Yamamoto, Takuma, 179
Yamashita, Hideo, 174

Zemanek, H., 166
Zuse, Konrad, 159, 161
Zysman, John, 155n

Flamm, Creating the computer

DATE	
MAY 1 —	
GAYLORD	